The Good News

And Its Proclamation

THE GOOD NEWS
AND ITS PROCLAMATION

Post-Vatican II Edition of
The Art of Teaching Christian Doctrine

JOHANNES HOFINGER, S.J.
in collaboration with
FRANCIS J. BUCKLEY, S.J.

UNIVERSITY OF NOTRE DAME PRESS
Notre Dame   London

IMPRIMI POTEST:
John F. X. Connolly, S.J.
Praep. Prov. Californiensis

NIHIL OBSTAT:
Joseph Hoffman, C.S.C.
Censor Deputatus

IMPRIMATUR:
✠ Leo A Pursley, D.D.
Bishop of Fort Wayne-South Bend
February 14, 1968

LIBRARY OF CONGRESS CATALOG CARD NUMBER: 68-17065
MANUFACTURED IN THE UNITED STATES OF AMERICA

To
Father Josef Jungmann, S.J.
Revered Teacher and Fatherly Friend
in Honor of His Eightieth Birthday

Preface

This book contains the substance of the many courses in catechetics I have been privileged to direct during the past twelve
years. In the summer of 1955 I lectured on "The Kerygmatic
Approach to Christian Doctrine" at the University of Notre
Dame at the invitation of the ever-memorable Father Michael
Mathis, C.S.C. In those days it required the courage of a Father
Mathis to invite a foreign missionary to conduct a course on
"kerygmatics." I must acknowledge also a great debt to the bold
pioneers of the University of Notre Dame for opening the doors
to the sweeping changes that have since transformed the catechetical scene in the United States and the world—especially in
the missions.

Special gratitude is due Father Bernard Schuerman, S.J., of
St. Louis University, because, besides translating my booklet
Nuntius Noster, he persuaded me to prepare this book. Sincere
thanks are also accorded Father Joseph Ramsauer, S.J., who
wrote the summary of "Our Message" at the beginning of Part
II. And last, but not least, I want to thank Mrs. Mary Perkins
Ryan for her work on the original edition, not only for polish-
ing my poor English, but also, I am happy to say, for improving
the ideas themselves in many sections.

Without doubt the most important single catechetical event
occurring between the first and second editions of this book was
the International Study Week on Mission Catechetics held at
Eichstätt, Germany, in July, 1960. Nearly all the world's leaders
in catechetical science attended, and substantial agreement on
the main elements of modern catechetics was reached. The
record of this accord is formulated in the Study Week's "Con-

clusion" and in its "Program of the Catechetical Apostolate," both of which have been included in the appendix of this edition. Comparison of the Study Week's findings with the text of this book will, we humbly submit, reflect the accord between the two.

This new, third edition clearly reflects the impact of Vatican II on catechetics. The Study Week in Eichstätt in 1960 had stated that the faith is presented through "liturgy, Bible, systematic teaching, and the testimony of Christian Living." Each of these four areas has been profoundly affected by the Council. The four great conciliar constitutions, On the Sacred Liturgy, On Divine Revelation, On the Church, and On the Church in the Modern World, have set down principles which will shape the life of the Church for decades, if not centuries. Not only did the Council ratify and approve what the leading catechists had been saying about the need to harmonize teaching and life, but it went far beyond their visions and opened up new horizons and perspectives. Because of this it was necessary to rethink, reorganize, and considerably expand Part Two of previous editions. The basic principles remained intact; their expression and amplification in the light of the Council I entrusted to my collaborator, Father Francis J. Buckley, S.J., of the University of San Francisco. He also helped introduce the teachings of the Council throughout the rest of the book.

Besides the major conciliar constitutions, the decrees On the Bishops' Pastoral Office, On the Apostolate of the Laity, On the Church's Missionary Activity, and to some extent the Declaration on Christian Education, were discussed and applied to catechetics by the International Study Weeks of Bangkok, Katigondo, and Manila in 1962, 1964, and 1967. Much of the thinking of these groups is reflected in a new chapter which has been added to Part One, "The Impact of the Missions on Catechetics," as well as in some selections from their conclusions, which have been added to the appendix.

The Decree on Priestly Formation made it possible for us to omit a chapter on the role of kerygmatic theology in priestly formation, which had appeared in previous editions. That battle has now been won.

The wealth of excellent, easily available texts for children and guides for teachers have rendered unnecessary any sample lessons in this edition.

The growing emphasis on adult education throughout the whole Church will, we trust, make this book even more helpful and timely than before. It was written for those who have the task of proclaiming the Good News of Jesus Christ. The Council has reminded us that each Christian has that task!

Johannes Hofinger, S.J.

Manila, Philippine Islands
Feast of St. Francis Xavier, 1967

Contents

I OUR TASK

  1. Toward a Better Understanding of
     Our Catechetical Task   3
  2. The Central Theme of Our Message   15
  3. The Proper Goal of Our Catechetical Apostolate   23
  4. The Impact of the Missions on Catechetics   29
  5. Initiation Into the Mystery of Christ
     Through Biblical Catechesis   43
  6. Progressive Initiation Through the Liturgy   53
  7. Progressive Initiation Through Systematic Catechesis   64
  8. The Right Ordering of Catechetical Material   73
  9. Catechetical Method As Handmaid of the Message   85

II THE CONTENTS OF OUR MESSAGE
  THE JOYFUL TIDINGS OF JESUS CHRIST

Introduction   103
Preliminary Instruction: The Riches of Our Vocation   105

THE ETERNAL LOVE OF GOD FOR US

GOD THE CREATOR
  1. God and His Creation   110
  2. The Elevation   114
  3. The Fall—Original Sin   117
  4. The Covenant   120
  5. Types of Christ   123

CHRIST THE SAVIOR
   6. The Incarnation   130

THE PUBLIC LIFE OF CHRIST
   7. The Baptism of Jesus   133
   8. The Temptations of Christ   136
   9. The Miracles of Jesus   139
  10. The Words of Jesus   141
  11. Christ and His Disciples   144
  12. The Titles of Jesus   145
  13. The Passion and Death of Christ   150
  14. The Resurrection and Ascension   153

THE HOLY SPIRIT
  15. The Holy Spirit   157
  16. The Most Holy Trinity   160

THE CHURCH
  17. The Church in Action   165
  18. The Church in Being   168

THE SACRAMENTS
  19. The Effect of Baptism   175
  20. The Obligation Contracted at Baptism   178
  21. The Institution of the Holy Eucharist   182
  22. The Sacrifice of the Mass   185
  23. The Institution of the Sacrament of Penance   190
  24. Christian Suffering and Death, and Our Sacramental
      Preparation for Definitive Union with Christ   193

THE RESPONSE OF OUR GRATEFUL LOVE
How We Are To Answer God's Love by Christian Living 199
Christian Life Made Up of Prayer and Action   202

OUR FILIAL RESPONSE BY CHRISTIAN PRAYER:
DIRECT WORSHIP
  25. The Excellence of Christian Prayer   205
  26. Filial Worship   208

OUR FILIAL ANSWER BY CHRISTIAN WORK:
INDIRECT WORSHIP
27. The Christianization of the Family   212
28. The Sacrament of Matrimony and the
    Sanctity of the Body   214
29. Fraternal Love and Assistance   219
30. The Right Attitude of the Christian to
    Material Goods   223
31. Love of Truth and Esteem of Good Reputation   225
Longing for Perfect Worship   229

THE LAST THINGS
32. Death and the Particular Judgment   231
33. The Resurrection and General Judgment   233

HELL AND HEAVEN
34. Hell   237
35. Heaven   240

III THE HERALDS OF CHRIST
     THEIR PERSONALITY AND FORMATION
1. "Kerygmatic Spirituality" for the Heralds of Christ   247
2. Lay Teachers and the Catechetical Apostolate   253
3. Religious and the Catechetical Apostolate   264
4. Training Sisters for the Catechetical Apostolate   274
5. Theological Training for Sisters and Brothers   281
6. The Priest and the Catechetical Apostolate   290
7. Kerygmatic Theology: Its Nature and Its
   Role in Priestly Formation   297

APPENDIX
EXTRACTS FROM THE
INTERNATIONAL CATECHETICAL STUDY WEEKS
  Eichstätt Study Week   319
  Bangkok Study Week   334
  Katigondo Study Week   338
  Asian Catechetical Study Week   341
BIBLIOGRAPHY   344
INDEX   347

Part I
Our Task

CHAPTER ONE

Toward a Better Understanding
Of Our Catechetical Task

A most promising catechetical movement has been in existence in the Catholic world for more than sixty years. And especially during the last thirty years its progress has been most successful, not only in its expansion to nearly every country in the world but even more in the deeper understanding and clarification of its program. For the great improvement in religious education which has been brought about by the catechetical movement has been due chiefly, in the final analysis, to a deeper and more accurate understanding of the work of catechetics.

ON THE TRACK OF A BETTER METHOD

During the first few decades of its existence the catechetical movement stressed methods above all. It sought to improve religious instruction by relating it more closely to daily life and by introducing more of what are now called "visual aids." That this should have been the first step is quite understandable in relation to the circumstances existing at that time in the countries in which the catechetical movement arose. In Germany, France, Austria, and Belgium especially, great advances had been made in the teaching of secular subjects by the application of the findings of applied psychology. But in the field of religion, before the beginning of the catechetical movement, teachers had for far too long held complacently to the timeworn, dry method of analyzing and thereby explaining the text of the catechism.

To realize what this meant in the concrete, let us recall the lengthy, difficult, and pictureless catechisms of those days, splendid models no doubt of precise formulation of the Church's doctrine, but equally splendid models of a completely unpsychological presentation of that doctrine. To make matters worse, children were generally required to learn these unchildlike catechisms by heart, word for word. We do not need to say that the result in many cases was mere mechanical memorizing of abstract texts, the meaning of which was often grasped in part or perhaps not at all; and that these memorized texts offered the well-meaning, but helpless, child next to no nourishment for his religious life.

But how was it possible for so many catechists to be content with such an unsuitable method for such a long time—and that in an era when secular subjects were already being taught by far more attractive methods? One of the most important reasons surely was that these teachers lacked an adequate comprehension of their cate-chetical task. How could a teacher who realizes that in giving reli-gious instruction he is the living instrument of the Divine Catechist ever acquiesce in the use of such an un-Christlike method?

The better catechists of the time, animated by a genuine apostolic spirit, recognized, it is true, the great danger of this situation. In earlier times the children of good Christian parents had grown up naturally, as it were, into good Christian living. Religious instruc-tion in the schools had only a supplementary role; it organized and deepened the religious knowledge already acquired by the children in their homes and in their parish community. But now, particu-larly in the great industrial centers where the great mass of the people were rapidly becoming more and more estranged from reli-gion, a Christian milieu for the children's formative years could no longer be presupposed. Cases multiplied in which children were found to have brought next to nothing from their homes in the way of religious instruction. The school, therefore, had to furnish every-thing which had formerly been supplied by the Christian home, both in the way of an example of Christian living and of direct instruction. Under such circumstances, abstract teaching, divorced from the realities of daily life, was foredoomed to failure, since it went over the heads of the children and past their hearts. In fact, such instruction not infrequently did more harm than good, for, far from overcoming the religious indifference brought by the chil-dren from their homes, it succeeded only in boring them to the point of rebellion against the catechism class and, ultimately, against religion itself. Obviously, only a method of instruction which was concrete, lively, and interesting could be expected to cope with this difficult problem.

This was the situation in central and western Europe at the beginning of the century when the catechetical movement began its work. And it is not difficult to show that the situation in other countries was not very different and that it soon became almost identical, owing to the ceaseless improvement in secular teaching methods together with the equally ceaseless spreading of the problems brought by expanding industrialism. The same was true in the United States, especially with regard to the situation of Catholic children attending public grade schools (according to reliable statistics, now more than 50 percent of the total number). These millions of children could be kept and formed for Catholic living only by additional religious instruction of a high level both from the didactic and from the religious point of view.

The principal postulates of the first period of the catechetical renewal in Europe may, then, be summarized as follows:

1. Religious instruction must adapt itself to the child's psychology: it must, therefore, begin with the visual and the concrete. Accordingly, during the first years of school the biblical-historical approach should take precedence over the systematic order of the catechism.

2. Religious instruction on the school level should not only communicate religious knowledge but also, and above all, should establish religious dispositions and convictions. It should, therefore, as a matter of principle, address itself to the whole human being: it is his heart and will, above all, that must be formed to the image of Christ. The question, then, is one not only of clear, intelligible instruction but primarily of effective education that forms the young person and equips him for Christian living. In this program the stressing of religious *education* rather than religious *instruction* alone was the result, not so much of a timely adaptation of modern teaching methods, but rather of a clearer and deeper insight into the nature of our catechetical task.

It may be that in this first period the importance of methods was sometimes overestimated and, in fact, considered to be the only thing needed for a good and effective kind of catechesis. Such a view is of course wrong and has fatal consequences. But we should not forget that these efforts toward finding better methods came, in the final analysis, from a renewed and deepened sense of the great responsibility of catechists and that the discovery of such methods was absolutely necessary in those days of old-fashioned, lifeless teaching.

Moreover, since the end of the thirties a deeply religious examination of the nature of our catechetical apostolate has been undertaken, and this has done away with the exaggerations of the first phase of the movement. Such has been the case, at least, in central and western Europe, where in the last years before World War II a second phase of the catechetical renewal was inaugurated.

RECOVERING THE CHRISTIAN MESSAGE

Beginning with this second period of the catechetical movement, however, the realization became evermore widespread that a true catechetical renewal must also concern itself with the *content of religious instruction*. This does not mean, of course, that traditional Catholic doctrine be changed in order to conform with modern fashions of thought, nor that it be watered down to suit the secularized outlook of modern society. Far from it. But quite apart from anything like this, legitimate problems do exist concerning the content of religious instruction.

For teaching to be successful it is of the utmost importance that the teacher know how to select the most significant points in the abundance of material at hand. He must be able to present the subject matter to his students from the angles which have the greatest formative value, from the angles which will cause the students to welcome this teaching. He must arrange the topics so that dominant ideas stand out unmistakeably, so that the most important things are recognized as such by the children, while less important matters are used to serve as illustrations or to bring to life the basic themes.

A catechetical movement sincerely intent on more than a superficial success had to ask itself sooner or later whether these things were being done, and an honest facing of facts led to a clear realization that religious teaching was not being carried out in this way. Nor was it a question merely of the qualifications of individual teachers; it was recognized that there were widespread and significant deficiencies in the customary religious instruction, deficiencies which urgently demanded that the catechetical renewal give its attention also to the question of the content of religious instruction.

This change of outlook on the part of catechetical leaders was occasioned particularly by a work of the famous liturgist Rev. Joseph A. Jungmann, S.J., of Innsbruck: *Die Frohbotschaft und unsere Glaubensverkündigung* (Regensburg: Pustet, 1936).[1] This

---

[1] It is rather significant that no English version of this fundamental book was made available until 1962, when, due to the initiative of the East Asian Pastoral Institute in Manila, Fr. William Huesman, S.J., presented *Good News Yesterday and Today, With Essays in Appraisal of Its Contribution* (New York: Sadlier, 1962).

book demonstrated convincingly the fact that our teaching of the truths of the faith, in spite of all the advances of theology during the centuries, and in spite of the improvements that had taken place in the previous decades in catechetical methods, as a whole sadly lacked the inspirational power and the perspective of value which characterized the ancient manner of teaching found in the classical Roman liturgy and in the religious writings of the patristic era. Our teaching of the faith, both in catechetics and in sermons, does not sufficiently stress what is essential and central in Christian doctrine. Above all, it does not adequately communicate the truths of the faith from that point of view which is intrinsically proper to the proclamation of the Christian message. Christian doctrine, after all, claims to be a "gospel," a glad tidings. It must therefore succeed primarily in presenting the Christian religion as something desirable and valuable, as something to be received with joy and to be experienced as joyful.

One may not, of course, minimize the hard demands of Christian morality. Nor did the early Church do so. On the contrary, she insisted on them boldly, without compromise or sugarcoating. But the difficult demands were not in the forefront of Christians' consciousness. "Gospel" means "good news." The ideal teaching of Christian truth must, therefore, result above all in grateful recognition of those incomparable gifts that we have received from our loving Father through Christ: the divine life to which we were reborn in baptism, which increases and grows strong in us by means of the sacraments; membership in the family of God which we enjoy by grace in the community of the Church; and the pledge of eternal happiness to which we look forward in hope. Viewed against such a background, the rigorous demands of Christian morality themselves share in the beauty and glory of the new order of things given to us in Christ.

Father Jungmann further pointed out in this same book that in earlier centuries when Christian doctrine and Christian life were still a dominating force in the West it was not so imperative as it is now to emphasize clearly and forcefully what is central and most valuable in Christianity. But today we must not shut our eyes to the fact that even in so-called Catholic countries the Christian religion itself is in danger among the masses of the people; it must fight for its very existence against extraordinarily vital and powerful foes. No longer is one or other doctrine questioned—as was the case in former times—but Christianity as a whole is challenged. For this reason it is all the more necessary today to bring out, as powerfully and attractively as possible, its essential content and worth.

The improvement of religious instruction as to its content, called for by Father Jungmann, accordingly entails the right selection of matter, its right ordering, and the right emphasis or "spotlight" put on the individual truths of the faith. And this selection, ordering, and emphasis must be clearly oriented to the goal of Christian instruction, which is nothing other than the building up and fostering of Christian life. And while it is true, of course, that the entire Christian revelation must without exception be at least implicitly believed, this does not mean that all the data of revelation must be "proclaimed" in the same way.

Since the appearance of Father Jungmann's book the name *kerygma* (a publicly announced message) has come to be more and more generally given to those aspects of revelation which were meant to be explicitly and emphatically proclaimed. The Greek word is used seven times in the New Testament to refer to the core of the apostolic preaching, especially, though not exclusively, in the first proclamation of the Christian message. See, for example, 1 Corinthians 1:21; 1 Corinthians 2:4; 1 Corinthians 15:14. The corresponding verb *kerysso* (to proclaim, to preach) is found sixty-one times in the New Testament and is also used to describe Christ's preaching and that of St. John the Baptist. It designates the action of a herald, particularly of one who announces an event and summons his hearers to action.[2] The message, then, which St. Paul as the herald, *keryx,* of the eternal King is to proclaim to fallen humanity, is none other than that bedrock of Christian truths which constitutes the essential content of the Christian glad tidings. This message must bring the inner nature and worth of Christianity

[2] On the meaning of the word *kerygma* in the New Testament see A. Rétif, "Qu'est-ce que le kérygma?" *Nouvelle revue théol.* (1949), 910–922; A. Rétif, *Foi au Christ et mission d'après les Actes des Apôtres* (Paris, 1953), 11 ff.; Kr. Stendahl, "Kerygma-Kerygmatisch," *Theol. Literaturzeitung* (1952), 715–720. On the sacred and profane use of the words *keryx, kerysso, kerygma,* and *prokerysso* in connection with the New Testament, see G. Friedrich in Kittel, *Theologisches Wörterbuch zum Neuen Testament,* 3, pp. 682–717. On the significance for the catechetical apostolate see the articles of D. Grasso, S.J., "Il Kerigma e la predicazione," *Gregorianum,* 41 (1960), 424–450, and "Evangelizzazione, Catechesi, Omilia. Per una terminologia della predicazione," *Gregorianum,* 42 (1961), 242–267. On the different use of the words *kerygma* and *kerygmatic* see D. Grasso, S.J., *Proclaiming God's Message* (Notre Dame: University of Notre Dame Press, 1965), pp. 233–236.

into as clear focus as possible. It consists in the incomparable good news of the eternal love of God, Who, through His only-begotten Son, has called us to Himself and enables us to reach our true home. In brief, it is the Good News of our salvation in Christ.

It is in this sense, accordingly, that modern catechetical writing more and more generally refers to the contemporary concern for the content of religious instruction as the *kerygmatic renewal.*

From what has been said it is obvious that the scope of the kerygmatic renewal cannot validly be restricted to religious instruction given in school. It is concerned with all the various forms in which the Christian message is to be transmitted, including its preaching in church as well as catechetical instruction in schools and in homes, the dissemination of this message through the press as well as the theological formation given in seminaries and universities. But it might be well to call attention to the fact that the kerygmatic renewal involves questions pertaining to teaching even on the grade-school level, and in the chapters that follow we hope to prove this beyond doubt.

But however strongly we wish to stress the value of the kerygmatic approach, we in no way mean to imply thereby that the hard-won achievements of the first period of the catechetical movement are no longer important or to be neglected.

And the kerygmatic renewal leads not only to a better understanding of the message which we are to proclaim but also, most happily, into a more searching insight into the nature of our catechetical apostolate. Far more clearly and consciously than before, we now consider ourselves as the privileged instruments of Christ, instruments by which in our own times He continues His great catechetical apostolate as the Herald of the heavenly Father. We know ourselves to be sent by Christ; we believe that He works with us and through us. "As the Father has sent me, I also send you" (John 20:21). "Go, and make disciples . . . and behold, I am with you all days" (Matt. 28:19 ff.). These great words of Christ are spoken to us also.

Like any other movement, the modern catechetical movement, too, needed time to develop its program fully. In the first period of catechetical renewal the main interest of the great pioneers centered on developing the method of teaching religion. Then came the shift from method to content. Only in recent years have successful attempts been made to unite all important elements of modern catechetics into one complete and coherent program. These attempts were given their classical expression in the International Study Week held in July, 1960, at Eichstätt, Germany. In a special document its participants formulated the basic principles of modern catechetics. They called it "Program of the Catechetical Apostolate." This program intended to offer more than a codification of the most important principles. It had to show impressively how the whole program of modern catechetics is finally developed from one basic principle which underlies, pervades, and inspires both the theory and practice of a genuine catechetical apostolate. This basic principle has been clearly formulated in the first line of the Eichstätt Program: "Catechesis carries out the command of Christ to proclaim God's message of salvation to all men. . . . The catechist does what Christ did and commissioned the Church to do: He proclaims the Good News of Salvation. . . . All principles and methods of catechizing flow from the missionary command of Christ."[3] We are dealing here with the fundamental principle of the so-called kerygmatic approach. Whoever realizes that in his catechetical activity he is the instrument of the Divine Messenger (keryx) and acts accordingly, accepts and follows the kerygmatic approach. What modern catechetics intends is not the new word, kerygmatic, but the thoroughly Christian reality behind the word.

The most recent trends in catechetics, both for children and for adults, stress the necessity of discovering the genuine interests of the one to whom the message is to be addressed. He is to be taken "where he is and as he is" and is to be shown how Christ, His life, His work, and His message, are relevant to his own here-and-now problems.

In a sense this is a return to the first stage of the catechetical movement of this century, but with a difference. Recognition of the need to rethink and rephrase doctrinal content is a distinct advance.

Although the approach must be "anthropological," attention to content is demanded even more than before. The Christian message must be seen to be *good* news to this particular person—without itself being distorted in the process. The need for a kind of synthesis of Christian teaching—in which each different element receives the stress it deserves according to its own importance and its relevance to the whole—has not diminished but increased. The

---

[3] Selections from the text of the "Program of the Catechetical Apostolate" we present in the appendix of this book.

end of a polemical stance in theology, which directed attention almost exclusively to those elements of Christian doctrine which were under attack, should not be replaced by an overemphasis on those elements which are most attractive and appealing. Obviously, not everything need be said on every topic at once. But there should be no suppression, deliberate or indeliberate, of truths which constitute the core of what God has revealed to us in Christ.

Thus the "third stage" of modern catechetics has arrived. This stage is characterized by a harmonious synthesis of method and content, God's word understood as addressed to men. The method is seen as the handmaid of the message; the message is seen as expressed in human words for human hearts. Both method and message are interrelated and modified.[4]

This concern with man, the receiver and transmitter of God's message, is a striking quality of Vatican II. No other council tried so explicitly to speak in terms of the human needs and interests of its period. .

Just as the kerygmatic renewal found its authentic formulation in the Eichstätt Program of 1960, the anthropological approach found its pertinent expression in the Asian Catechetical Study Week of 1967 held in Manila.[5] The concern with man as the object of God's gracious invitation and saving action does not mean any opposition to the principles of the kerygmatic approach. It rather is its necessary complement. It fully brings into relief what the kerygmatic orientation virtually contained and demanded. Whoever approaches man with the same method and intention of the Word made Man cannot be satisfied by delivering an impersonal "eternal" message. He knows himself sent to a living man as he finds him here and now in his particular situation. The herald of Christ is supposed to approach him with the understanding love of his Master. In order to form true heralds of Christ, we must do more than convey an abstract acquaintance with the "heavenly" message: we must understand this message as the word of salvation for man as he is: we must have a thorough knowledge and loving concern for the man to whom we are sent.

[4] Cf. J. Hofinger, S.J., "Contemporary Catechetics: A Third Phase?" *Chicago Studies*, 2 (1963), 257–263.

[5] See the extract from the proceedings of the Asian Catechetical Study Week as presented in the appendix of this book, pages 341–343.

HERALDING WITH CHRIST

Besides the priest catechists, we have in our times millions of Sisters, Brothers, and lay teachers who help in the catechetical apostolate of the Church. Because of the canonical mission (commission given by the bishop) they participate in a special way in the teaching apostolate of Christ Himself, Who now and always until the end of the world is teaching through and in His Church. Vatican II more than any other council before has extolled the "outstanding and altogether necessary contribution [of the lay catechists] to the spread of the faith and of the Church."[6] Nor does the Council limit its attention to lay catechists on the missions. In the Declaration on Christian Education we read: "The Church is keenly aware of her very grave obligation to give zealous attention to the moral and religious education of all her children. To those large numbers of them who are being trained in schools which are not Catholic, she needs to be present with her special affection and helpfulness. This she does through the living witness of those who teach and direct such students, through the apostolic activity of their schoolmates, but most of all through the services of the priests and laymen who transmit to them the doctrine of salvation in a way suited to their age and circumstances, and who afford them spiritual assistance through programs which are appropriate under the prevailing conditions of time and setting."[7]

It is obvious that the authority of the teacher varies in the different classes of teachers used by Christ as His instruments. And this is true also of the teaching clergy. Is there not a great difference between the teaching authority of the Holy Father and that of a simple priest? Yet are not both of them instruments of Christ the Teacher? Furthermore, it would be wrong to evaluate Christ's instruments exclusively from the point of view of their authority. What is the final purpose of Christ's teaching? Is it merely to make

---

[6] Decree on the Church's Missionary Activity, n. 17. See also nn. 11, 12, 15, and 21. This and the other documents of the recent Ecumenical Council together with brief commentaries may be obtained in an inexpensive paperback: Walter M. Abbott, S.J., *The Documents of Vatican II* (New York: America Press, 1966).

[7] N. 7. See also the Decree on the Bishops' Pastoral Office in the Church, n. 30. On the laity's share in the prophetic office of Christ see the Dogmatic Constitution on the Church, n. 35, and the Decree on the Apostolate of the Laity, n. 6. On the catechetical task of Christian parents see especially the Declaration on Christian Education, n. 3, and the Pastoral Constitution on the Church in the Modern World, n. 48.

some authoritative statements in the name of His Father? Or is it not, rather, to beget and to form perfect children for His Father, who will adore Him in Spirit and in Truth (John 4:24)? Should we not, then, above all evaluate the instruments of the teaching Christ according to their formative influence?

If we are to understand our catechetical task rightly and fulfill it properly, nothing is so important as the deep conviction, born of faith, that we are sent by Christ, that we have to let Him work through us, that we have to adapt ourselves as completely as possible to Him. This basic attitude of a fully "Christian" catechist will, without further ado, give us the right attitude toward the message that we, as Christ's repesentatives, are to proclaim. It will give us the right attitude to the goal toward which we are working, and the right attitude to the students whom we are to address in Christ's name. As instruments of Christ, we desire, naturally, to teach only what He would teach these real students in these concrete circumstances; we desire to carry out our teaching with Our Lord's own deep love for and personal interest in each of these students.

This radically "Christian" view of our catechetical apostolate will also provide us with the right attitude as to catechetical methods. As soon as we desire to be nothing but instruments of Christ—but to be His perfect instruments—clearly we shall want to do our work as well as possible. And therefore we shall be eager to use every means that may help to perfect our teaching. But at the same time we shall never become the slaves of methods.[8] We shall consider it much more important to strive for a deeply religious understanding of our message than to use the "latest" achievement of methodology. Methods, then, will become for us what they should be: means to bring out our message in all its richness. And we shall therefore be more concerned with the message itself than with the methods of its proclamation.[9] We shall study particularly the basic

---

[8] Still less shall we become slaves of marks and tests. These may be necessary as part of classroom procedure, but what, finally can they test? Not the student's religious attitude, but, at best, only his knowledge of religion. And even this, in any more than a quite superficial sense, cannot be tested by the "true-false" or "objective" tests so much in use.

[9] On the other hand, the choice of the proper medium to transmit the message is most important. For those who live in an age of mass media "the medium is the message," as Marshall McLuhan points out so well in his book *Understanding Media: The Extensions of Man* (New York: McGraw-Hill, 1964). The periodical, *Living Light,* is outstanding for its articles on the use of audiovisual materials. A report on the use of radio, film, television, and other media in the missionary catechesis of Asia will be found in *Teaching All Nations,* 4 (1967), 477–503.

questions of the kerygmatic renewal: What are we to teach; what is the central core of the message we are to proclaim; what are the essential doctrines we should stress; from what viewpoint should we present this message so that it becomes truly the "gospel" of Our Lord; what would be the best arrangement of the catechetical material for the purpose of leading our pupils to understand it in a rightly religious way and to make use of it in their daily Christian lives?

These are also the questions which we shall try to answer in this book. First, in Part One we shall show how our catechetical task is, more particularly, one of progressive initiation into the mystery of Christ. Thus we not only must proclaim His message with Christ but we must proclaim *Christ*. For Christ, the great gift of the Father's love and our way to the Father is Himself the central theme of our message, just as participation in Christ's life is the proper goal of our apostolate. There also we shall answer the question of how the catechetical material must be ordered so that this central theme will shine out as clearly as possible and so that the individual doctrines will most fully contribute to the attainment of the proper goal of all catechetical activity. Then we shall be prepared more specifically to consider, in Part Two, the longest section of this book, the actual content of our message. What are, in the final analysis, the essential doctrines of Christianity; what should we stress most especially in these particular doctrines; from what viewpoint should we present them? And, obviously, in order fittingly to proclaim this divine message, we must have well-trained heralds. And so the third and final section of this book will be concerned with the important question of the appropriate formation of the catechist.

Seeing ourselves as the living instruments of Christ in bringing His message of life to His brethren, we shall never indulge in an unapostolic concern with the message in itself. We shall be aware that we are called to share in His concern for His brethren as we find them here and now. What finally counts is, not the message as such, but man to whom we bring this message and whom we win and form by this message for a life with God and for God. Thus there will develop a truly "Christian" approach in catechetics which is at the same time genuinely kerygmatic and anthropological.

CHAPTER TWO

The Central Theme
Of Our Message

Obviously, no efficient heralding of our message is possible without a proper understanding of this message we are to proclaim. Therefore we who are heralds of Christ must first of all face the question, What is, actually, the message Christ wishes to proclaim through us? In particular, what is the core, and central theme of this message, and what are the interrelations of this central theme with the other fundamentals of Christian doctrine?

OUR CENTRAL THEME: THE MYSTERY OF CHRIST

The message entrusted to us is made up of many different doctrines, but it is, by its very nature, far more than a list of truths. It is *a wonderful unity with one central idea* which we must bring out as clearly as we can.

What would you think of a guardian who handed over to his ward a beautiful palace, but instead of presenting him with the palace he gave him only the mass of stones, beams, and planks that once went to make up the building itself? Is it not a catechetical crime to transmit to our students only some incoherent fragments instead of the organic divine message?

The first heralds of Christ, the Apostles, were already aware of the catechetical problem we are now dealing with. St. Paul, the great catechist of the ancient Church, in particular was perfectly aware of the necessity of catechetical concentration on the real heart of the Christian message. His letters excel in richness of doctrine and, at the same time, they are outstanding in their luminous unity. Again and again he returns to the fact that ultimately his teaching is one all-comprehensive doctrine, a central mystery. As he sees it, his special vocation lies in the fact that to him, "the very least of all saints, there was given this grace, to announce among the Gentiles

15

the good tidings of the unfathomable riches of Christ, and to enlighten all men as to what is the dispensation of the mystery which has been hidden from eternity in God" (Eph. 3:8).

Clearly, this central mystery which is to be proclaimed to the whole world is the message of the unfathomable riches that are given to us in Christ. The same idea is brought out in similar language toward the end of his Epistle to the Romans, which more than any other epistle contains "his Gospel" (Rom. 16:25). And in the Epistle to the Colossians St. Paul again speaks of this mystery that forms the essence of his whole catechesis as, simply, "the mystery of Christ" (Col. 4:3), or, more fully and precisely, "the mystery of God [the Father], which is Christ" (Col. 2:2),[1] or "Christ in you, your hope of glory" (Col. 1:27). In other words, the Apostle's message presents Christ as the great Gift of the Father's love and proclaims how the Father reveals and gives Himself in Christ, and how He invites us to share in the life and glory of His only-begotten Son. "He [the Father] has called you, by our preaching, to gain the glory of our Lord Jesus Christ" (2 Thess. 2:14). Among many other texts see especially Ephesians 1:9 ff.; 1 Corinthians 2:7; 1 Corinthians 1:9; 1 Timothy 3:16. Thus the actual content of his apostolic message is simply Christ. He resumes his whole preaching in the classical formula: "We proclaim Jesus Christ" (2 Cor. 4:5. See also 1 Cor. 2:2; 2 Cor. 1:19; Gal. 1:16). His apostolate essentially consists in heralding the good tidings of Christ: "My own work has been to complete the preaching of Christ's gospel" (Rom. 15:19; 1 Cor. 9:12; 2 Cor. 2:12; 2 Cor. 9:13; 2 Cor. 10:14; Gal. 1:7; Phil. 1:27; 1 Thess. 3:2; Rom. 1:9).

In all of this the great catechist of the ancient Church is only expressing very clearly what is also revealed in the Gospels, which are the most magnificent documents of apostolic preaching. *The mystery of Christ is the fundamental theme and unifying principle of all Christian religious instruction.* It is the good tidings of our salvation in Christ: the divine Father reveals Himself to us in His Son; He has, in the exact sense of the word, *visited* us, given Himself to us, and taken us home to Himself, not only each of us individually but all of us together in the wonderful unity which we form through our living connection with Christ in His Mystical Body.

---

[1] An inexact translation of this important text is found in the Latin text of the Vulgate and in most English translations.

Seen in this light, our message of the mystery of Christ is truly "a message of salvation"; it is the good tidings of Jesus Christ, our Redeemer. Christ appears clearly as the blessed self-revelation and self-communication of the Father, and as our only way to the Father. This is how Our Lord Himself understood His own mission and message to mankind, and in His farewell discourse to His Apostles at the Last Supper He gave it this classic formulation: "I am the way, and the truth, and the life. No one comes to the Father but through Me" (John 14:6). Christ's message is clearly centered in the Father. Christ Himself is the most excellent gift of the Father's love to us (John 3:16; Rom. 8:32; 1 John 4:9).

It is true that Christ is the center of our message, but only because He is "the Christ," the messenger of God, the great Gift of the Father to us, and our leader in the journey home to the Father. Only in this way can we clearly see the essential aspects of our teaching, which are *theocentricity* (centered in God, that is, God the Father, the beginning and end of our salvation) and *Christocentricity* (centered in Christ, the only way to the Father). This is exactly what Christ means when He said that He and the Father are the two poles of Christian faith, and, therefore, of Christian teaching: "This is everlasting life, that they may know Thee, the only true God, and Him Whom Thou hast sent, Jesus Christ" (John 17:3).[2]

Naturally, no Catholic catechist would ever deny these basic truths of Christian teaching. But are these truths always brought out clearly and emphasized strongly in our catechetical instructions? Do we bring them out in all our teaching from the very beginning? Does the danger not sometimes exist that catechists, overly concerned with the techniques of teaching children at various age levels, do not point out these fundamental truths with sufficient clarity and emphasis? Yet it is these truths which should, at every moment, be the luminous center of religious instruction in order properly to form the religious life of Christians becoming aware of their faith. It is for this reason that we do not think it advisable, for example, to entitle a course for beginners "Jesus-Mary,"[3] since

---

[2] As for the important question how the Christian message is both Christ-centered and God-centered, but under a different aspect, see D. Grasso, S.J., "The Core of Missionary Preaching," in *Teaching All Nations* (New York: Herder and Herder, 1961), pp. 39–58, especially pp. 54–57.

[3] Alexander Schorsch, C.M., *Jesus-Maria Course of Religion* (Chicago: Archdiocese of Chicago School Board, 1955).

this cannot help giving the child the impression that Jesus and Mary are the two poles of our religion. It is wrong to think that concessions of this kind are the inevitable corollary of a method of instruction suited to the child's mentality. Should any good method of teaching alter the essential structure of doctrine? Rightly understood, methods of teaching are servants. They assist the teacher in making his teaching understood as accurately and easily as possible. But methods must never be allowed to tyrannize over the meaning of what is taught. The objection might be made that children have to be helped to learn by such means and that the necessary corrections can be made later on. But what efficient architect would allow himself to be guided by considerations of "easiness" when laying the foundations, in the hope of making essential alterations later? Obviously this would result in innumerable difficulties. As we shall show in chapter four, it is not so difficult to instruct children properly in the mystery of Christ from the very beginning. But we must first understand the supreme importance of this basic necessity. Of course, although the mystery of Christ should be from the very beginning the center of our catechetical instruction, this does not mean that we should use the term itself. It is a question, not of the *term,* but of the *matter.* The expression "mystery of Christ" does not occur once in the Gospels, and yet it is their center. We should never, then, use the term "mystery of Christ" in the lower grades.[4]

Once the catechist has understood what the mystery of Christ really means—God's redemptive plan with Christ as its center, and not simply the "life of Jesus" from Bethlehem to Calvary—then it will be relatively easy to see the other fundamental teachings of Christianity in their right order and to put them into their proper place in our teaching. And so all the doctrines of the faith can be easily and organically included.

---

[4] A good example of how the mystery of Christ may be presented to small children without using unchildlike terminology may be found in the remarkable course *On Our Way* worked out by Sister Maria de la Cruz Aymes, H.H.S., for teachers of the Confraternity of Christian Doctrine (New York: Sadlier). This course, which pioneered the kerygmatic movement in the United States, originally begun in 1957, is now being thoroughly rewritten to incorporate the theology of Vatican II and the most recent developments in catechetics.

Other remarkable examples are the new Canadian Catechism, *Come to the Father* (New York: Paulist Press) and the *Word and Worship* program by Rev. James J. Kilgallon, Gerard P. Weber, and Sister Mary Michael O'Shaughnessy, O.P. (New York: Benziger Brothers).

CENTRAL THEME AND FUNDAMENTAL DOCTRINES

For example, the place and importance in our catechetical instruction of our teaching on Mary, the mother of our Redeemer, should be entirely determined by her unique share in the mystery of Christ. And this does not mean only her share in the temporal birth of the Son of God, the fact that in her womb the "mystery that from eternity has been hidden in God" (Eph. 3:9) became man and dwelt amongst us, full of grace and truth. We have also to teach her great work in the unfolding of this mystery among men, since she is the mother of the redeemed and, at the same time, the most perfect member of the Mystical Body of Christ. Just as Our Lady's loftiest and most basic claim to our veneration is the fact of her supreme service to the mystery of Christ, so our teaching of Marian dogma and devotion must serve first of all to lead our students to a fuller understanding of the mystery of Christ and of our participation in it. In order to attain this goal of Marian catechesis, it is not, of course, enough to mention continually the beautiful principle "to Christ through Mary." The doctrine behind this principle must be explained in such a way as to indicate fully its significance. Have we as yet succeeded in doing this?

In a similar way, the important topic of *grace* can only be properly understood and taught in relation to the mystery of Christ. For this doctrine refers entirely to our unmerited share in the mystery of the incarnate Word and to the fact that only through our living relationship with Christ, only in Him and through Him, can we share in His divine life, can we obtain the gift of becoming God's children. Since grace is, in its essence, Christ's life in His members, this doctrine cannot, without serious dangers, be taught in isolation from Christ. For this aspect of the mystery of Christ St. Paul coined the classic expression "Christ in you" (Col. 1:27). Do we not sometimes endanger our students' understanding of this truth by imitating the teaching of theologians who have enlarged and complicated the tract on grace with many specialized questions, and at the same time have isolated it from its essential relation to Christ? Is the center of our catechesis of the "grace of Christ" really "Christ and His mystery"? It is certainly not enough to point out repeatedly that every grace is granted to us through the merits of Christ. Grace is not only merited for us *by* Christ; it is a living community of life *with* Christ, the new and wonderful life that comes to us and fills our being thanks to our vital connection with the

True Vine. It is, therefore, only in the light of Christ that the grace of Christ can properly be understood and explained.[5]

The same is true, of course, concerning the teaching about *the Church and her worship*. If our consideration of the Church amounts to a mere statement and description of her social and juridical structure, have we not miserably failed to teach the truth that the kingdom has become a joyful reality in our midst? The character of the Church, her final meaning, her tasks, her power, her mystery can, again, be understood only in the light of the mystery of Christ: she is His Mystical Body in which the divine life, brought to us by Him from heaven, is to be developed and perfected.

For it is through the sacraments and sacrifices of the whole People of God that we are brought into the mystery of Christ in the most living and effective way. The sacraments allow us to share in His life: the mystery of His life-giving redemption becomes effective in us. In the Eucharistic sacrifice we share in the mystery of Christ's sacrifice on Calvary; in the sacrifice of the Church the mysterious sacrifice of Calvary is completed. On Calvary Christ offered His sacrifice alone; in the Church's Eucharistic sacrifice He lets His Bride share in His sacrifice by conferring on her the honor of sacrificing with Him and allowing her to become the sacrifice with Him. Thus the sacrifice of the Head offered on Calvary is completed in the sacrifice of the whole Christ, including Head and members, on our altars.

And, finally, the new divine life which Christ gives us in the sacraments also demands of us a *new way of life according to the image of Christ:* "For we were buried with Him by means of Baptism into death, in order that, just as Christ has risen from the dead through the glory of the Father, so we also may walk in newness of life" (Rom. 6:4). Our sacramental participation in the mystery of Christ must lead to a new Christian way of life in the spirit of Christ; thus also our moral task as Christians can be understood

---

[5] Although the doctrine on the divine life communicated to us in Christ holds a very important place in Christian teaching, we should not say that "supernatural life" is the central idea. For the central idea cannot be a gift of God, but only God Himself, Who has called us in Christ to share in His life. See on this important point Joseph A. Jungmann, S.J., *Christus als Mittelpunkt religiöser Erziehung* (Freiburg: Herder, 1939). See also Franz Schreibmayr, "Ist das Reich Gottes oder Christus der Mittelpunkt des neuen Katechismus?" *Katechetische Blätter* (1953), 444–445.

and pondered only through the central idea of the mystery of Christ and our participation in it.

Obviously, then, this comprehensive view of our good tidings is of the utmost importance for the success of our catechetical instruction. Here is the heart of our Christian teaching which must be thoroughly taught and forcefully emphasized in all forms of catechetical teaching. We touch here a very decisive point in the training of catechists. If some of them do not succeed in placing Christ and His mystery in the center of all their teaching, this is usually due to insufficient training.

Catechists need not so much detailed and exhaustive explanations of doctrine—although, of course, this is necessary to some degree. Experience shows, however, that our catechetical instructors, especially the Sisters, already possess a thorough knowledge of the different dogmas. But what they need, first of all, is a magnificent, joyful, and comprehensive view of the different aspects of the mystery of Christ. We know from experience how eager and grateful they are for this insight, which is one that we really owe them.

But is it Sisters and lay catechists only who need to be given this view? It would seem to be required also in the seminaries. And, therefore, the special purpose of kerygmatically oriented theological teaching is to allow the mystery of Christ to become evident in all the theses that the students must master, so that they do not become lost or sidetracked among a collection of isolated topics by losing the vision of the whole. For true theology is, finally, a systematic effort to understand as well as possible the plan which God has made known to us in Christian revelation and which He is realizing in our salvation. And this plan consists in "gathering all creation both in heaven and on earth under one head, Christ" (Eph. 1:10).

Pre-Vatican II theological formation in seminaries was quite often defective in this regard. The Council resolutely remedied this unsatisfactory situation by prescribing a thorough and basic course on the mystery of Christ at the very beginning of ecclesiastical studies. "In the revision of ecclesiastical studies, the first object in view must be a better integration of philosophy and theology. These subjects should work together harmoniously to unfold ever increasingly to the minds of the seminarians the mystery of Christ, that mystery which affects the whole history of the human race, influences the Church continuously, and is mainly exercised by the priestly ministry."

"That this understanding may be communicated to students from the very start of their training, ecclesiastical studies should begin with an introductory course of suitable duration. In this initiation, the mystery of salvation should be presented in such a way that the students will see the meaning of ecclesiastical studies, their interrelationship, and their pastoral intent. They will be helped thereby to root their whole personal lives in faith and to permeate them with it. They will be strengthened to embrace their vocation with personal commitment and a joyful heart" (Decree on Priestly Formation, n. 14).

Nor should the fathers and mothers of families be deprived of this liberating and integrating vision of the meaning of their own Christian life. More and more they are showing signs of hunger for a deeper and richer understanding of what they had learned while still young. To satisfy this hunger is the noble task of adult religious education.[6]

---

[6] A new form of adult education is developing as the more recent series of religion texts for primary grades try to involve the parents more fully in the religious formation of their children. For a practical discussion of this see F. J. Buckley, S.J., "How Can I Teach My Child? The Role of Parents in Religious Education," *Good Tidings,* 7 (1968).

Chapter Three

The Proper Goal of Our Catechetical Apostolate

The modern catechetical movement originated chiefly as a much needed reaction against the intellectualism which, toward the end of the nineteenth century, was severely endangering the teaching of religion. While the importance of religious knowledge was overemphasized, religious formation and religious living were unintentionally neglected. Teachers all too often were content to have their students merely memorize the catechism; they sacrificed true understanding to mechanical drill. But, even where true understanding was the aim, and an aim which was achieved to a high degree, the heart and its education were still neglected. In contrast, the catechetical movement has emphasized what is the true educational function of our catechetical activity: we not only have to give our students a thorough knowledge of their faith but we must also form true Christians who truly live their Christianity. Religious knowledge in itself is not the real goal of our teaching; it is only a means. The goal of religious instruction is religious living, or, even better, full initiation into the mystery of Christ.

The catechetical movement would contradict itself if it were ever to question, or to turn away from, this, which is the only true interpretation of our catechetical task. Yet does it not seem to be doing precisely this in the most recent catechetical efforts? Are not "teaching" and "instructing" again being too strongly emphasized, the more so when scholarly expressions such as "kerygma" and "kerygmatic renewal" are being used?

Such is certainly the reaction of many people, deeply concerned with the success of catechetics, to our preoccupation with "kerygmatics." But the answer to this difficulty may be easily seen if we clarify our concern for the proper "heralding" of the Good News by reference to the central mystery of our catechetical teaching, the mystery of Christ. Like the Apostles, we too must above all *preach*

Christ. As we pointed out in the last chapter, the mystery of Christ is not only the heart of our instructions but also the theme which embraces, penetrates, and unifies all the other Christian doctrines. What, then, do we wish to achieve by teaching the mystery of Christ and how do we attain this goal?

NOT ONLY KNOWLEDGE OF, BUT PARTICIPATION IN, THE MYSTERY OF CHRIST

We must try very hard, it is true, to explain the mystery of Christ to the students entrusted to us. But, as we all know, mere knowledge of this mystery is by no means enough. Knowledge of the mystery of Christ should be, primarily, the spring of holy action, of a mysterious occurrence to which we must consent in our hearts with lively faith and in which we must share through our own action.

St. Paul saw this truth very clearly. According to him the teacher's true vocation is "in order to perfect the saints for a work of ministry, for building up the body of Christ, until we all attain to the unity of the faith and of the deep knowledge of the Son of God, to perfect manhood, to the mature measure of the fullness of Christ" (Eph. 4:11–13). This holy knowledge of God's Son must induce us to practice "the truth in love, and so grow up in all things in him who is the head, Christ" (Eph. 4:15). When he speaks of the mystery of Christ in the Epistle to the Colossians, he stresses the same truth very strongly: "Him [i.e., Christ] we preach, admonishing every man and teaching every man in all wisdom, that we may present every man perfect in Christ Jesus" (Col. 1:28). But, as St. Paul knows very well, this is not accomplished by a single effort. It is hard labor requiring much patience. And what is the goal of this educational process? "My dear children, with whom I am in labor again, *until Christ is formed in you*" (Gal. 4:19).

Christ has Himself explained His mission in the same way: "I came that they may have life and have it more abundantly" (John 10:10). All His messianic work, and especially His catechesis, is directed toward this goal. Christ does not recognize a religious knowledge sufficient in itself; each of His words is clearly concerned with a religious *life*. This is the heart of the incomparable message that He, the great Herald of the divine Father, has brought to us; the call to a new life, or, more precisely, the invitation to participate in His own life which He, the divine Vine, communicates to us, His brothers and members. Our catechetical task essentially consists in communicating this message of our divine Master to the students entrusted to us. We should actually betray our apostolate if we were ever to content ourselves with mere knowledge. As Christ's messengers, we must communicate His life, we must lead people to effective participation in His mystery.

Therefore, if we are to understand our wonderful task more perfectly and to carry it out more fruitfully, we must understand explicitly what "participation in the mystery of Christ" should mean to us. Since this is the ultimate goal of all our catechetical efforts, we cannot be vague about it.

WHAT DOES PARTICIPATION IN THE MYSTERY OF CHRIST MEAN?

We must realize clearly, first of all, that this participation is not brought about perfectly by a single event with an instantaneous effect. It is true, of course, that by baptism we receive all at once Christ's life and become His members forever. Through the unmerited grace of God we have, by baptism, been made partakers in the mystery of the life-giving death of Christ. "Do you not know that all we who have been baptized into Christ Jesus have been baptized into His death? For we were buried with Him by means of Baptism into death, in order that, just as Christ has arisen from the dead through the glory of the Father, so we also may walk in newness of life" (Rom. 6:3–4). But the life that we receive at baptism as a holy gift must be fully developed in our life as Christians; it has to mature in the organically progressive growth in Christ which St. Paul calls the goal of Christian instruction (Eph. 4:15). The question is, then, What are the main phases of this growth and how can we foster it by religious instruction and training?

Through the special kindness of God most of us were made members of the divine Vine before we came to the use of reason. When we were baptized, we could not even begin to understand what a wonderful gift God was giving us, nor could we realize that it brings with it the vocation to a life in Christ. We could not, therefore, accept this task by a free decision of our own. But God does not want to force His gift upon us; when our reasoning powers have begun to develop, we are to accept this gift with our own free will and to cooperate willingly in the development of this new life. This development is essentially God's work, but we are called upon to play our part in it.

So we see clearly the fundamental task of all catechetical teaching: we are to help the maturing Christian gradually to become aware of the magnificence of his vocation and of the greatness of his task in life as a Christian. As God's heralds, we are to present Christian doctrine to him, but not merely as something that he must "study" and "know." We are to make him aware of God's personal invitation to him, first given at baptism. From the first lesson, then, the child should realize that he is personally addressed and personally invited, not merely by the teacher, but by God. And he should also realize that God is waiting for his answer to this invitation, for his "yes" arising from his Christian *faith,* for his "yes" gratefully given to Christ and to a life to be lived in and with Christ. We do not mean, obviously, a "yes" that is given by the intellect alone; we mean the full response of Christian faith, consisting essentially in the honest will to follow unreservedly God's loving invitation to a life in Christ. Such faith is our fundamental answer to God's gift. Our Lord Himself expressed this gift in the words "God so loved the world that He gave His only-begotten Son, that those who believe in Him may not perish, but may have life everlasting" (John 3:16).

Our catechetical instruction, then, from the very beginning must be directed toward this full faith in Christ and willingness to follow Him. Our first and fundamental task is to awaken, deepen, and gradually as instruments of the Holy Spirit, to perfect this willing faith. Catholic religious instruction is, above all, instruction in *faith.* But the term "instruction" must not be understood too narrowly. Here it means not only "teaching" but from the very beginning "practical guidance," "exercise." The principle "learning by doing" is very applicable here, but it must be "doing" from the heart. And by far the most important expressions of faith are not more or less isolated "acts of faith," but rather *truly Christian prayer.* In prayer we thank the divine Father for His gift of love; in prayer we reaffirm our willingness to follow Christ faithfully; in prayer we humbly ask for God's help that our life may correspond to our faith. Do we truly try to develop our students in this kind of prayer, or are we satisfied with their mechanical repetition of prayer-forms?

Faith and its expression in prayer are, then, the first step toward growth in Christ—and even this step is possible only through grace. If this faith is sincere, then the student himself will begin to take the second step: a life growing from faith. And since all our faith is centered in Christ, this means a life in and with Christ. Such a life is our vocation: this is what we accept in making our profession of faith. We teachers, then, must show the young Christian what this "in and with Christ" means. We must first of all bring home to him the beauty of this life with Christ. Next we must not only "teach" but also guide him to good and Christlike action. For the pupil has to learn from his own experience that this life with Christ, in spite of the many sacrifices that it demands, is a wonderful and enviable life, the only life truly worth living.

In this life based on faith, reception of the sacraments and participation in the Eucharistic sacrifice play an immensely important role. It is through these means that during our pilgrimage on earth we come closest to Christ. Here we are honored by God with an objective participation in the mystery of His only-begotten Son, a participation which by ourselves, through our own religious efforts, even though these are aided by grace, we could never obtain. Undeserved by us, Christ is more and more perfectly given to us. But our own cooperation when we receive the sacraments and take part in the Mass differs greatly from our part in the reception of baptism before we had the use of reason. At that time we personally could not contribute anything. But now that we have the use of our reason and free will, we must prepare ourselves to receive the grace of the sacraments. And the more carefully we prepare ourselves, the more effective their grace will be in us. Hence, *proper guidance in receiving the sacraments is extremely important.*

In the light of these clarifications our catechetical task begins to seem more and more momentous. We need to ask, then, Can this task always be realized in each day's catechetical instruction in every class? What are the chief ways by which our catechetical goal may truly be reached, not only in the more advanced religious instruction given in high school but as early as the basic teaching given in the grades?

WAYS TO INTRODUCE
THE MYSTERY OF CHRIST

Modern catechists all agree on the areas of emphasis if anyone— child or adult—is to be properly introduced to the mystery of Christ: the Bible, the liturgy, doctrine, and the testimony of Christian living.[1]

[1] According to the "Program of the Catechetical Apostolate," worked out at the International Study Week of Eichstätt, July, 1960, "Catechesis embraces a fourfold presentation of the Faith: through liturgy, Bible, systematic teaching, and the testimony of Christian living" (Program, Basic Principles, no. 12). See the appendix of this book.

By "the Bible" we here mean the simple biblical-historical catechesis which, through the telling of the good tidings, introduces a person for the first time to the mystery of Christ. Guidance in living the sacramental life of the Church and elementary instruction about the Church's worship come under the heading of "liturgy." "Doctrine" means systematic catechesis following the order of a catechism and presenting the good tidings as a logical structure.

The "Testimony of Christian Living" means the witness of a Christian life by individuals, most especially the educators, and by the community of the faithful as the vivid expression of God's revelation faithfully received and lived by man.

This "Christian Living" is not, obviously, a course by itself. But this in no way diminishes its decisive importance in the whole process of Christian formation. In fact, it is ordinarily the way that leads the young Christian and the non-Christian to a first personal contact with Christ and the Church.[2] And the triad of Bible, liturgy, doctrine means, not three independent ways of teaching, but rather a trinitarian order forming one organic whole. In order to achieve an initiation that is progressive and effective, each one of these ways must be followed, and each one at the fitting time. Since this basic triad is of such supreme importance in religious instruction, we shall treat each of these means in a separate chapter to show their special function in a progressive initiation into the mystery of Christ, and the way in which each is to be taught so that its full fruit may be gained.

But before we deal more in detail with biblical, liturgical, and systematic catechesis, it may be good to deepen our understanding of the goal of our catechetical apostolate by a study of its missionary dimensions.

[2] See No. 10 of the Eichstätt Program in the appendix of this book. The decisive importance of the "witness sign" in bringing man into personal contact with Christ is commonly proposed by the leaders in modern catechetics. On its function and importance in both the catechesis of the faithful and in mission catechesis see for example the enlightening article of A. Nebreda, S.J., "Role of the Witness in Transmitting the Message," in *Pastoral Catechetics* (New York: Herder and Herder, 1964), pp. 67–86.

CHAPTER FOUR

The Impact of the
Missions on Catechetics

Christian catechesis started with the missionary catechesis of
Christ and His Apostles. The Lord sent them to preach the Good
News and to initiate their disciples, Jews and Gentiles, into the new
life He had brought. In fact, all other forms of the catechetical
apostolate originate from the missionary catechesis of the ancient
Church, and even now missionary catechesis remains the prototype
of an authentic Christian catechesis in which we see with special
clearness its goal and basic stages.

Missionary catechesis aims at the progressive initiation of a non-
Christian into the fullness of Christian life. Is this initiation radically different from the catechetical initiation of a Catholic student
coming from a Christian family with a Christian atmosphere
at home? Where finally is the difference? And if we admit quite a
difference, can missionary catechesis nevertheless teach us something for the religious formation of the faithful?

In times past catechetical instruction of non-Christians, to an
unduly large extent, was governed by the tacit supposition that the
non-Christian is already sufficiently disposed to receive fruitfully
the substance of the Christian message. Since it is a message for
everybody, it is by its nature understandable and adapted to everybody who listens to it. We need only get the unbeliever to listen
to this message of a new life. Even then, to be sure, he can refuse
to accept God's call. But this refusal is, at least primarily, the result
of his own free decision and not so much the consequence of lacking the necessary psychological disposition to understand and to
appreciate the Christian religion. In presenting the Christian message to non-Christians the catechist must of course, as in catechetical
instruction of believers, take into consideration the age level and
the educational standard of his audience; he also must be aware
that in the first instruction of non-Christians he cannot pre-suppose

29

any knowledge of specific Christian doctrines, but for the rest there is no basic difference in the catechetical approach to Christians and non-Christians. In both cases he may suitably start with explaining the usual catechism to believers and nonbelievers alike. And most missionaries in fact did teach this way.

It is of significance that the first strong opposition against that approach to unbelievers developed in the French school of modern catechetics with its characteristic emphasis on the psychological and human dimension of genuine catechesis. Starting from their experiences with unbelievers in France, leading authors such as P. A. Liégé, O.P., and F. Coudreau, P.S.S., began to inquire into the problem of a first presentation of Christian doctrine to unbelievers and the process of conversion. Since then these studies have been more specifically applied to mission catechesis by professors on the missiological faculty at the Gregorian University in Rome, especially by Domenico Grasso, S.J., and Alfonso Nebreda, S.J. It was only recently that the findings of the European experts were widely publicized in the missions, mainly through the Study Week on Mission Catechesis held at Bangkok in November, 1962.[1]

THREE STAGES OF PREBAPTISMAL CATECHESIS

The participants of the Bangkok Study Week distinguished three stages of prebaptismal catechesis: (1) preevangelization, (2) evangelization, and (3) catechesis proper.[2]

Preevangelization

This stage aims at establishing the first contact with the unbeliever, to arouse his religious interest and to dispose him to appreciate and accept God's message with an open heart. Preevangelization must shake off the apparent security of a life entirely "insured" by family-life surroundings, by the possession of material riches or tech-

---

[1] We closely follow in this chapter the report of A. Nebreda, S.J., "East Asian Studyweek on Mission Catechetics," *Lumen Vitae* 17 (1962), pp. 717–730, and our own presentation in *Pastoral Catechetics* (New York: Herder and Herder, 1964) pp. 144–159. On the importance of the problems discussed at the Bangkok Study Week for the catechetical apostolate in nonmission countries see the report of Father Theodore Stone in *Worship* (February, 1963), pp. 184–189.

[2] We follow here the terminology of the Bangkok Study Week. It would be more precise to call this stage the "catechumenate," as did the Decree on the Church's Missionary Activity, n. 13 and 14.

niques which transform the world. Men must experience a break within themselves if they are to be "reawakened" to the invisible and thus be ready to welcome the gift of God. Such a break may be achieved by considering the mystery of death, of suffering, of life, of human thought and love, spiritual responsibility, and similar problems.

Preevangelization therefore has a twofold function, one negative and the other positive. It must remove the obstacles for a right understanding and appreciation of the Christian message, and make the unbeliever long for the fulfillment of his highest aspirations.

The guiding principle for this first contact with the unbeliever is what the Study Week calls an "anthropocentrical" approach, by which the catechist must take the man as he is, with his thought patterns, opinions, and the influences of his environment and culture. The catechist must find out what his current interests and pressing personal problems are. In dealing with would-be catecumens the catechist must be armed with understanding, love, patience, and respect for their views.

There is no definitive subject matter for this preparatory stage. The catechist should use whatever will help best in preparing the way for the kerygma. This includes what the Study Week has labelled "positive apologetics," which proceeds from a true understanding and appreciation of whatever is good and acceptable in a man's culture. It consists in taking into due consideration the man with whom we speak and in removing the personal concrete obstacles which prevent his ready acceptance of the kerygma.

Evangelization

In the stage of evangelization the unbeliever is presented for the first time with the core of God's message—the kerygma—the joyful tidings of our salvation through Christ. Here the catechist must exert every effort to expose in a winning and convincing manner God's plan of salvation as the expression of His infinite love. In this condensed proclamation of the Christian message the compelling fact of Christ as the Lord must be put forth with striking clarity. The Bangkok Study Week formulates it in this way: "In a technical world where man feels himself lost in a lonely crowd, stressing such facts as God coming to us in Christ, Christ living among us as our friend and personally loving each of us, helps to awaken man to hope, and helps to evoke conversion."

The main goal of evangelization is conversion. "Conversion"

refers to that decisive change of mind by which man admits the basic insufficiency and error of his accustomed view of the world and of life, and willingly accepts God's message as the basis for the life he is determined to start. Conversion therefore is only another aspect of faith, provided we understand faith not merely as an intellectual assent but as personal commitment to God, Who calls us to a new life with Christ. The acknowledgment of Christ as Lord implies for the convert a decision to rearrange his whole life according to Christ's law. But at this point he will not yet possess a detailed knowledge of all the implications his acceptance of Christ as the Lord will have for his way of living. His conversion as of now is by no means complete.[3] It must make special progress during the subsequent catechumenate, but it is a process which by its very nature has to continue throughout the whole of life and lead to ever-greater transformation into the image of Christ (see Rom. 8:28 f.). Obviously not all converts have to change to the same extent when they turn to Christ. Yet the greater the alteration of his life and the faster the inner change develops, the more will the convert experience a "break" with the past.

The stages of preevangelization and evangelization constitute the so-called precatechumenate. The purpose of evangelization is to lead the unbeliever to conversion. In this stage he comes to faith and surrenders to Christ, and delivers himself to the Church to be prepared for baptism. At this point the catechumenate begins. In times past there was usually no sufficiently clear distinction between precatechumenate and catechumenate proper. The would-be convert was all too often presented with the substance of Christianity before he was sufficiently prepared for the mysteries which require in the catechumen an attitude of basic faith. That such faith is required already at the very beginning of the catechumenate proper is now clear from the teaching of Vatican II: "Those who, through the Church, have accepted from God a belief in Christ should be admitted to the catechumenate by liturgical rites."[4] In pre-Vatican II times knowledge of Christian doctrine—usually in the form of memorization of the official catechism—was in fact often more emphasized than living faith and true conversion to Christ.

---

[3] "This conversion, to be sure, must be regarded as a beginning," says the Decree on the Church's Missionary Activity, n. 13.

[4] Decree on the Church's Missionary Activity, n. 14.

Catechesis Proper

In this stage, (i.e., the catechumenate) the candidate is further acquainted with God's magnificent plan for his life, and with what a truly Christian life requires of his generosity. This more detailed exposition of Christian doctrine seeks to deepen his faith, promote his conversion, and strengthen his resolution to adhere to Christ. Evangelization and catechesis proper differ, not in their basic approach—for in both stages the Christian message must be presented as the joyful tidings "of the unfathomable riches of Christ" (Eph. 3:8)—but rather in the completeness with which they present the doctrine of salvation. Both transmit Christ's message, but evangelization aims at a reorientation of life, while catechesis brings out the implications of this reorientation and prepares the convert for his participation in the mystery of Christ through the sacraments, most especially through baptism and the Eucharist, and for a Christian life which corresponds to these holy mysteries. While still a catechumen the convert must become accustomed to the kind of life to which he is called as a member of Christ. All this is summarized by the statement of Vatican II: "The catechumenate is not a mere expounding of doctrines and precepts, but a training period for the whole Christian life. It is an apprenticeship of appropriate length, during which disciples are joined to Christ their Teacher."[5]

In recent times it has been repeatedly stressed—for example, in the catechetical study weeks of Katigondo, Uganda, (1964) and of Manila (1967)—that the stage of prebaptismal catechesis should be followed for the neophytes by special care after baptism and, if at all possible, by a course of catechetical instruction similar to the mystagogical catechesis of the ancient Church. The particular aim of such mystagogical catechesis is well expressed by the Greek word which means "initiation into the mysteries," that is, a fuller initiation of the neophytes into the sacramental life of the Church. It has to deepen and to enlighten their religious experience when they share in the mysteries of Christ and to make their sacramental life an organic unit with their Christian living. They also need help to overcome the usual difficulties met by neophytes.

Nor should formation stop after a few months or years. The whole of Christian life is a progressively deeper initiation into Christ. Christian maturity is never achieved once for all. The time

---

[5] Decree on the Church's Missionary Activity, n. 14.

immediately before and after baptism is especially important, but Christian education in the fullest sense extends until death.

In the whole process of a complete initiation into Christian religion and life a very important part falls to the Christian community in which the newcomers are to be integrated. Vatican II emphasized the social dimension of the catechumenate. "But this Christian initiation through the catechumenate should be taken care of not only by catechists or priests, but by the entire community of the faithful, especially by the sponsors. Thus, right from the outset the catechumens will feel that they belong to the People of God. Since the life of the Church is an apostolic one, the catechumens should also learn to cooperate actively, by the witness of their lives and by the profession of their faith, in the spread of the gospel and in the upbuilding of the Church."[6] This important direction of the Council also applies to the pastoral care of neophytes as well as to the integration into full Catholic life of those from other Christian churches and the restoration of fallen-away Catholics to participation in the life of the Church.

THE ANALOGUES IN THE CATECHESIS OF THE FAITHFUL

Preevangelization, evangelization, and catechesis proper (catechumenate) are the steps by which we lead non-Christians to the specific goals of conversion, faith, and finally baptism. In the catechesis of the faithful we deal with people who have supposedly already reached these goals. The stages of missionary catechesis, therefore, obviously cannot apply to the faithful in the same way. Nevertheless a little reflection will show that much can be learned from the process of missionary initiation.

The Problem

Does the mere fact of baptism received conclusively prove that the goals set for the process of missionary catechesis have been sufficiently achieved? To answer this question a distinction must be made between what may be called the ontological or sacramental level, on the one hand, and the religious-ethical level of personal commitment to God, on the other. The first means God's free gift, our ontological union with God through the grace of baptism and the other sacraments. The second refers to man's personal and

[6] Decree on the Church's Missionary Activity, n. 14.

definitive commitment to God, which is called faith. Faith here is clearly not the infused virtue of faith, but the free act and personal attitude of faith, the word being taken in its full meaning as it is used in the New Testament and in the writings of the Fathers.

The divine plan of salvation requires man's free cooperation with God's saving action. The level of faith therefore should correspond to the sacramental level. For this very reason the adult unbeliever must be prepared for baptism. Therefore, prebaptismal catechesis aims primarily at provoking and stimulating genuine faith in the catechumen, so that at the moment of baptism the level of his personal commitment may correspond to the sacramental level to which God will elevate him. Should not the catechesis of the faithful be viewed under a similar aspect? In baptism the faithful have received God's gift; they have been made children of God. From then on they must "walk in the newness of life" (Rom. 6:4); they are expected to live a life of faith. In the sacrament of confirmation they are commissioned to strive for maturity in Christian life, which supposes maturity in Christian faith. Often they receive the Eucharist, the sacrament of spiritual growth, and each holy communion opens them to an increase in their sacramental level. Who would dare to say that their growth in personal commitment to God always keeps pace with the growth made possible by the sacraments? It is the special aim of religious formation to make them realize and acknowledge the great opportunity and task awaiting them. As catechists our responsibility is to help them attain to the perfection of both levels.

The same conclusion can be arrived at if catechesis is considered in its function of guiding the catechumen to a sincere, heartfelt *conversion*. Are all the faithful we catechize truly converted? Have they in their hearts broken with Satan and the world as they solemnly promised to do before baptism? For those who have never done so, or who have unfortunately turned back to the "flesh pots of Egypt" after a first surrender to God, religious formation after baptism must of necessity possess a function similar to that of prebaptismal catechesis. It must discover and remove obstacles and prepare the way for a sincere and complete conversion.

The catechesis of *innocent, baptized children* seems at first sight to be completely different from missionary catechesis. In fact it is not. The children were baptized when they were still infants, powerless to prepare themselves for the sacrament and to acknowledge God's gift. But at the time when we teach them religion they are becoming increasingly more able to make their own personal and definitive commitment to God, which is required for the fully voluntary reception of His gifts. Our catechetical instruction therefore replaces the preparation for baptism characteristic of missionary catechesis. In both cases the aim of religious instruction is effectual guidance to a Christian life that is in full accord with their dedication to God in baptism.

If such a relationship exists between the prebaptismal catechesis and the catechetical instruction of the faithful, the three stages of missionary catechesis must have their analogues in the religious formation of the faithful. What precisely are those analogues and what are their special functions?

Preevangelization

The first task of evangelization is to awaken in the unbeliever a *religious* interest in the Christian message and life. As long as he listens merely for the sake of courtesy or for any nonreligious interest, the religious instruction of the missionary will not further him on the way to a first commitment to God by faith.

In the same way, to be fruitful, religious instruction must encounter sufficient religious interest on the part of the baptized child. Without such interest he may be able to "learn" religion and to answer well in a given examination, but the religion class will not bring him closer to God. On the contrary, religious instruction will only increase his religious disinterestedness; it will foster routine in religious matters and will finally lead to tepidity. If genuine interest is habitually lacking, religious instruction ceases to be a help: it becomes a burden and a real danger to the life of faith. This is particularly true of frequent, perhaps daily, religion classes, especially with adolescents. In times past this danger may have been negligible, when a high appreciation of religion in general rather easily paralyzed the effects of an uninteresting religion class. Religious life then was very effectively fostered by other means. The student a priori expected from the catechism class just something to "learn."

As in the case of preevangelization in missionary catechesis, the solution is not to make the catechism class merely amusing or interesting. The lesson must awaken and nourish "religious" interest. It must arouse an efficacious desire for closer union with God. Are we not in danger of overestimating the value of entertaining activities and audiovisual aids and consequently aiming at a profane or merely intellectual interest? Entertainment may help to maintain discipline, but it does not necessarily dispose the student for an encounter with God.

Preevangelization must make the unbeliever aware that something important is still lacking in his life. It must undermine his state of apparent security, self-satisfaction, and religious saturation. As it is not enough for the would-be convert to admit the beauty of the Christian religion without any personal commitment, so too in the religious formation of the faithful the message remains inefficacious unless the people realize their need for closer union with God. Self-satisfied religious saturation would render them incapable of receiving God's word with ready hearts. The best spiritual food is of no value if not received by those "who hunger and thirst after justice." In preparing a given subject for an audience on all levels of religious instruction attention must be paid to the religious dispositions of the recipients and to that special aspect under which the material ought to be presented in order to arouse genuine religious interest.[7]

The typical preevangelization themes by which the unbeliever is challenged to an initial spiritual "awakening" are not confined to this stage. If properly used and adapted to the conditions of the audience, they retain their place throughout the whole process of religious formation, especially when a reawakening of religious interest is required. Some examples of these themes are the significance of the life and death of man, of human thought and love, and of spiritual responsibility. With students of higher grades the catechist may begin with an analysis of basic human aspirations and attitudes—such as true happiness, autonomy, freedom, sincerity, and uprightness—and showing how all these lead to God and make necessary a religious orientation of our whole lives.[8]

If the task of arousing religious interest and keeping it awake is understood in this way, it is closely related to the other task of sub-

[7] A remarkable study of the characteristics and religious needs and problems of different age levels is found in Gerard Sloyan, ed., *Modern Catechetics* (New York: Herder and Herder, 1963). For the right catechetical approach to adolescents see especially the excellent books of Father P. Babin, O.M.I., as noted in the bibliography at the end of *Modern Catechetics*.

[8] A noteworthy example of how to use the theme of love and friendship is J. Lark and N. Hennessy, under the direction of P. Babin, *Friendship* (New York: Herder and Herder, 1967). The work contains a workbook for the students and a teacher's guide. It may be good to mention that the book is intended as an additional aid; it is not supposed to substitute for a religion textbook.

stantiating and protecting faith. To one who has been baptized as a child, infused faith came as his parents' most precious heritage, yet at a time when he would not realize its value. How then can he be expected to appreciate this gift adequately? A Christian family and a Christian environment beyond the narrow limits of the individual home can transmit the fundamentals of faith, but they can never supply the indispensable personal contribution of the believer himself, who must grow to the maturity of faith.[9]

The process of maturing in faith comprises a threefold element. In blind confidence the child accepted Christian faith from his parents. At the start there was no assent of faith in the theological sense of the word. As the child grows he must learn that faith comes from God and that it requires on his part a personal commitment to God, Who has called him and claims him as His very own. Here exists a close analogy with the task of the missionary in preevangelization. The catechists in the home—the parents themselves—must plant faith in the heart of the child. "I have planted" (1 Cor. 3:6) the Apostle says of this, his basic apostolate.

Since the most important requirement in the whole process of "Christianization" is here involved, the catechist in the school should never "suppose" that the parents have already sufficiently taken care of it. Without his assistance many students will remain in the embryonic stage of a "childish" faith without any personal commitment to God. The catechist, like the missionary, must bring about this basic attitude of faith before beginning a more detailed exposition of Christian doctrine. But this has to be done—again as in missionary preevangelization—in perfect accord with the psychological disposition of the pupil. He must be taken as he is, with the limitations of his age and level of education. The education to a mature faith necessarily includes a second element. The believer, according to his personal situation, should be led to realize the motives of his surrender to God in faith. The prevailing incredulity of today makes this explicit knowledge even more necessary. A starting point for guidance to such realization may be found,

---

[9] On the nature of faith and its decisive role in the whole process of religious education see A. Nebreda, S.J., "Living Faith: Major Concern of Religious Education," in *Pastoral Catechetics* (New York: Herder and Herder, 1964), pp. 121–143. Man needs to be prepared for the message of Christ by precatechesis and its analogues in the catechesis of the faithful. Father Nebreda shows impressively how this is to be done in *Kerygma in Crisis?* (Chicago: Loyola University Press, 1965).

in accord with the apologetics described above in this chapter, in the good and acceptable features of the cultural ambient. No separate course in apologetics is necessary or desirable in this case.

The third element of maturity in faith is the factual harmony of the believer's religious belief with his whole view of the world and of life. Lack of such harmony, if it does not create obstacles to faith, will at least prevent faith from penetrating the whole life of the individual and from supernaturalizing his thinking and planning. How often do we find people who cultivate certain forms of piety but whose business life and social views and attitudes openly contradict their Catholic faith. A good catechist must know that his students are greatly influenced by powerful mass media, such as radio, television, movies, newspapers, and comic books. In preparing a lesson he must always keep this fact in mind and discern how this influence may have made his audience disposed, or indisposed, for the message of a particular lesson. Quite often it may well be necessary to set aside some time to bring about a proper disposition. It must be one of the guiding principles for his teaching never to present God's message or any particular part of it before he finds his audience sufficiently prepared. Without this caution he would speak not to men, but to the walls. In a good teacher's manual a note to the teacher in each lesson reminds him of the main difficulties his students may have with this particular lesson and suggests ways of "precatechizing" the students for this particular section of the message.

In times past missionaries and other catechists all too often neglected the necessary precatechesis. In our times—by some overdone reaction against the obvious shortcomings of the past—quite a few catechists may be in danger of wasting time and of remaining in perpetual precatechesis without ever coming to a forceful and convincing presentation of the message. Precatechesis is never an end in itself; it is the servant of catechesis. Precatechesis is supposed to last as long as necessary to prepare the way for the Lord. It has to serve the Lord and not steal His precious time.

Evangelization

From the stage of missionary precatechesis we learn the right catechetical approach to those baptized who here and now are not sufficiently prepared to receive God's message or a particular part of it. Evangelization is different. The leading principles of this stage have important applications for the religious formation of all the faithful. Missionary evangelization consists in a forceful first presentation of the core of the Christian message as the joyful tidings of our salvation through Jesus Christ. In mission catechesis it precedes the more detailed explanation of Christian doctrine; it brings the unbeliever to realize for the first time the transcendence of the Christian religion. In the service of God's grace evangelization makes him turn joyfully to God Who calls. The unbeliever decides to answer this gracious call generously by a new orientation of his life. This we call "conversion."

In the catechesis of the faithful, instruction does not start with an evangelization in the form of a condensed and forceful presentation of the Christian message. But every Christian should be given the great external grace of being presented with the core of the Christian message at the crossroads of his life, in a manner similar to the evangelization of mission catechesis. This is the special way of presenting the joyful tidings in good spiritual retreats or in parish missions. In the process of religious formation this introduction to the mystery of Christ in its depth is important when one must prepare for an important decision which will give his life a definitive direction, for example, when one is about to graduate from high school or college or to enter married life. In many areas *cursillos* or their equivalent have been found valuable in giving adults an awareness of genuine Christianity.

Apart from cases in which some reorientation of life or some peculiar awareness of the Christian calling is needed, evangelization has a place in the normal process of Christian formation. Let us take a child who grows up in a good Christian family and is sent to an excellent Catholic school, where the work of the family is continued and, in collaboration with the family, gradually completed. Everything is done well; the student loves his religion and steadily progresses in the knowledge and love of God. Yet something may still be lacking, even in such circumstances. Despite his willing response the student may not yet have realized the greatness and depth of his Christian vocation. He lives his religion, but he has never experienced its full challenge; he has never been shocked.

Whoever is acquainted with the pastoral situation of today will agree that we have picked out an exceptionally favored example. In countless more "normal" cases the students know enough about their religion to pass the tests, but a more thorough analysis of their religious knowledge will show that they do not know God. They have never been initiated into the mystery. In the long years of religious instruction catechesis has in fact not achieved its primary aim, that of fostering personal faith. These students need not be taught many more details of Christian doctrine. What they need is faith: they need evangelization. With God's grace they will realize for the first time in their lives what a real Christian is, how the Christian religion is a happy destiny and at the same time an unparalleled challenge. In short, evangelization will give them a wholesome "shock."

Shock in this connection is a word widely used in contemporary mission catechetics. It refers to the profound and intense spiritual change that takes place in the convert when he awakens from unbelief and accepts Christ as the Lord. He finds himself confronted with a different view of life and of the world. Shock is obviously not used here in its medical meaning. It merely emphasizes that the first encounter with Christ by personal faith is usually experienced by the convert as a sudden agitation of mind when he realizes the undeserved gift and happiness of his Christian vocation and is led to break with the past. A similar result will take place in the catechesis of the faithful whenever anyone through evangelization awakens for the first time in his life to full consciousness of his Christian existence.

We spoke of average students. Cannot the same be said of countless adult Christians too? Obviously they need the same remedy. The consequences for priestly preaching and liturgical reform in the church are self-evident.

Catechesis Proper

Instruction, in the catechesis of the baptized, is now a preparation for the other sacraments. This sacramental catechesis should show clearly how our sacramental life is the unfolding of our baptismal life.

Because the Eucharist is the full expression of Christian life, all postbaptismal catechesis has by its nature a sacramental function, as does the instruction of the catechumenate. It aims at an ever-fuller understanding, appreciation, and acceptance of God's plan for us, "joyfully rendering thanks to the Father, Who has made us worthy to share the lot of the saints in light. He has rescued us from the power of darkness and transferred us into the kingdom of His beloved Son, in Whom we have our redemption, the remission of sins" (Col. 1:12–14).

The catechesis of the faithful who have been baptized while children is a subsequent initiation into the new life which starts with baptism, for "all who have been baptized have put on Christ" (Gal. 3:27). It therefore aims at forming Christians who are worthy of their name. Through his spokesmen Christ must reach maturity in his members. Since the faithful who are baptized while infants cannot appreciate the "unfathomable riches of Christ" (Eph. 3:8) conferred in the moment of baptism, the catechetical instruction of later years must lead them to realize the "newness of life" (Rom. 6:4) which started with baptism and is to be developed by means of the other sacraments, and which finds its most sublime expression in participation in the Mass. Thus the catechesis of the faithful has to draw from the mystagogical catechesis of the Fathers, as we find it for example in the catechetical instruction of St. Cyril of Jerusalem. It means more than just "teaching" the mystery of Christ. It means "guidance" to an evermore perfect participation in that mystery.

In mission countries the faithful who have been baptized as children quite often show less missionary spirit than the faithful who have been baptized as adults. They have never fully experienced, as have the adult neophytes, the grace of the Christian calling. By developing its immanent missionary dimensions catechetical instruction has to help such faithful—in mission countries and everywhere else—to realize more and more the gift of God they have received before they can appreciate it and to show their gratitude by handing this treasure on to others who lack it or who do not appreciate it as they should. In this way is the body of Christ built up, "until we all attain to the unity of faith and of the deep knowledge of the Son of God, to perfect manhood, to the mature measure of the fullness of Christ" (Eph. 4:12 f.).

CHAPTER FIVE

Initiation Into the Mystery of Christ
Through Biblical Catechesis

A glorious task confronts our catechetical apostolate. Not only must we give our students a sound knowledge of their religion; we must also initiate them, step by step, into the mystery of Christ. They are to enter more and more completely into a living union with Our Lord; they are to be more and more filled with Him. Beginning with the teaching given in the first school grade, we must consistently aim at this goal and gradually realize it. How is this to be carried out, first of all, in the lower grades of grammar school? Primarily through a biblical catechesis that leads to Christ through the telling of the story of salvation.[1]

WHY BEGIN WITH A BIBLICAL CATECHESIS?

The reasons seem convincing. First of all, the Apostles themselves led their catechumens, both from Judaism and paganism, to Christianity by this method. In the New Testament we find the written expression of their historical catechesis, and this leaves no doubt that the *kerygma* of the ancient Church consisted above all in the joyful proclamation of all the great things that God had realized among men through His Son. "I write of what was from the begin-

---

[1] The "Program of the Catechetical Apostolate" (see the appendix of this book) recommends that we start with "liturgy," but it means at first an elementary presentation of the story of our salvation following the main events of the liturgical year. It is merely a question of different terminology. In fact, we recommend the same for this first catechetical initiation. Its rhythm follows the rhythm of the liturgical year, and at the same time the Bible story. But it does not mean any premature study of liturgical and biblical texts. All agree that children at this age are not yet able to study the "history" of Salvation. For this kind of initiation we avoid the word "liturgy" since we often noticed that quite a few people misunderstood the word "liturgy" in this connection and thought we would recommend some study of liturgical texts or actions for the first catechesis.

43

ning, what we have heard, what we have seen with our eyes, what we have looked upon and our hands have handled: of the Word of Life. . . . What we have seen and have heard we announce to you, in order that you also may have fellowship [the Greek word *koinonia* means *participation*] with us, and that our fellowship may be with the Father, and with His Son Jesus Christ" (1 John 1–3; cf. Luke 1:1–4). In these words of his first epistle how strongly the favorite disciple of the Lord introduces his Gospel, stating that it is through the narrative of the historical life of Christ that he wishes to lead his readers to this union with the Father and the Son!

The catechesis of the primitive Church proclaimed those "wonderful works of God" (Acts 2:11) which the Apostles had already enthusiastically announced to the Jews gathered together on the first Pentecost and which St. Peter, chief of the Apostles, then summed up in condensed catechetical form (Acts 2:14–40). St. Peter proceeds in a similar manner when he is confronted for the first time with the task of preparing pagans for their reception into the Church. Here, too, he gives a historical survey of God's works among men, from the baptism preached by St. John to the glorification of God's Son (Acts 10:34–43).

St. Paul followed this same method in his systematic catechesis, as we can see for example in the draft of the catechetical speech which he gave in the synagogue in Antioch of Pisidia. He speaks of the blessings God had showered on His Chosen People, blessings which find their climax in the redemptive work of the true Messiah (Acts 13:16–41). It is interesting to see also how, in his famous speech in the Areopagus, which is not so much a catechesis as an attempt to make contact with his pagan listeners, he tries to return from his philosophical introduction to a proclamation of the historical fact of Christ, before his audience interrupts him (Acts 17:22–31).

Furthermore, we all know the principle concerning basic catechetical instruction, established by St. Augustine, the outstanding catechist of the ancient Church: "When anyone is to receive his first catechetical instruction, he shall be given the complete history (of salvation), starting from the place where it is written 'In the beginning God created heaven and earth' down to the present period of the Church" (*De catechizandis rudibus,* cap. 3 n. 5).

But such catechesis in the form of historical narration is recommended to us not only because of this most ancient and venerable tradition but also for intrinsic reasons both theological and didactic. *Theologically*—it is obvious that the method of historical catechesis is especially suited to the particular character of Christian revelation which is of its very nature above all the "story of redemption," the incomparable news of what God, the loving Father, has done for our salvation. This Good News centers around Christ, Who was sent into the world as the greatest proof of the Father's communicative love and Who is, at the same time, our only way to the Father out of a world alienated from God by sin.

From the viewpoint of *psychological method* also, modern catechists have long agreed that the historical-narrative catechesis is indeed the simplest, most adequate, and most effective method of initiation into the Christian religion.

The great precursors of the modern catechetical movement clearly realized and strongly supported the principle that primary catechetical teaching is to be presented, not as a systematically ordered catechesis, but as the narrative of our salvation.[2] The catechetical renewal in our century has from the beginning made this principle one of its basic demands, and it quickly received general agreement, at least in theory. At the first Catechetical Congress (Vienna, 1912) Wilhelm Pichler presented the first draft of a *Katholisches Religionsbüchlein* (A Booklet on the Catholic Religion), which is, in its way, a classic. It has been translated into fifty-four languages and is quite widely used in missionary countries. Numerous adaptations have followed.[3] With this masterpiece, Pichler presented, against the objections raised by his opponents, irrefutable proof that by means of the story of salvation it was possible to teach the child the substance of the Christian religion and, at the same time, to make this a spiritual experience. Catechists and spiritual advisors belonging to a long-standing school of catechetical teaching had, until then, continually objected that the stories of the Bible were doubtless beautiful and edifying, and should be valuable as additional material in catechesis, but that, in the end, the purpose of religious instruction was to impart to the child solid and accurate religious

---

[2] Archbishop Augustin Gruber, *Katechetische Vorlesungen über des heiligen Augustinus Buch: Von der Unterweisung der Unwissenden in der Religion* (Salzburg, 1830). Rev. Gustav Mey, Vollständige Katechesen, Einleitung (Freiburg, 1871).

[3] An English translation of W. Pichler's booklet has been recently prepared by Rev. Anton Rehm, S.J., *The Story of the Kingdom* (Allahabad: St. Paul Publications, 1959). A similar approach is that of Pere A. Boyer, whose catechism has been translated into English and adapted by Sister M. Elizabeth, I.H.M., and Sister M. Johnice, I.H.M., *Bible, Life and Worship Series* (Boston, Allyn and Bacon).

knowledge. This being so, a real catechism was absolutely necessary in order to bring due order and clarity into religious instruction. But now Pichler had demonstrated that this "solid and accurate" knowledge could actually be more perfectly and easily imparted by means of a properly handled historical catechesis than by the "traditional" method.

But it took several decades, unfortunately, before this theory was fully translated into catechetical practice. Even today one can still find places in which a small catechism, such as the *Catechism for First Communicants,* is used in instructing the children, and "biblical stories" are told only incidentally if time permits, more or less as a relaxation or reward for attention during the rather dry catechism instructions. In contrast to this, modern catechetics states that *it is biblical-narrative catechesis which deserves the predominance and unlimited authority in the first grades of school, together with the self-evident and absolutely essential introduction to and practice of Christian life and prayer.*

How Do We Lead to the Mystery of Christ Through Biblical Catechesis?

In order that we may really guide the student to Christ, it is necessary above all that Christ, and even more, the *mystery of Christ,* be the radiant center of our catechesis. How easy has the divine Father made this task for us by His own "catechism"! His only-begotten Son is the center of His redemptive plan, which He has accomplished in spite of all human failures. Seen from God's point of view, the classic formula of St. Paul is fully true: "Jesus Christ, yesterday—today—forever" (Heb. 13:8). From the beginning to the end everything is centered in Him. By the eternal ordinance of the Father, Christ must bring everything together in one wonderful unity (Eph. 1:10). Until His blessed coming everything is preparatory. All nations await Him (Agg. 2:8). In Him the Old Testament finds its fulfillment and perfection (see Rom. 10:4; Gal. 3–4; Matt. 5:17). With Him comes the fullness of time (Gal. 4:4; Eph. 1:10). And since the coming of Christ the history of salvation shows us in essence the growth of the kingdom of God established among us, the unfolding of the truth He has made known to us, the development of the divine life that He gave to us and that in His Church He continues to communicate to us, to nourish in us, and to bring to perfection.

The objection might be made that from the theological point of view this fact of the centrality of Christ is certainly true and that such a Christocentric view of the total history of redemption can probably be given in later years and should be seriously aimed at in the religious instructions at the high-school level and beyond. But can we really hope for any results in trying to communicate this view to children in the first grades of grammar school? Will not this theological view of the plan of redemption be even more difficult for small children to understand than is the catechism?

In answer to this we must first of all admit that in the course of his religious training the young Christian must comprehend and live the mystery of Christ more and more deeply and fully. It is the *progressive* initiation into this mystery which is important. Therefore, obviously, *we should expect understanding of and participation in this central mystery of our religion only to the degree corresponding to the child's age.* In other words, we should look for no scientific, abstractly formulated reflections, but for simple, childlike understanding and experience. And it is not difficult to achieve this by means of a childlike presentation of the story of redemption. Let us, then, now call attention to some particularly important aspects of such a presentation.

Since we do not expect the children in the lower grades to gain abstract knowledge of or to make abstract reflections on the mystery of Christ, we should *omit all abstractions from the instruction in the first grades.* Everything in its proper time. In the beginning it is quite enough to show Christ to the children in such a way that He stands radiantly before them as the Savior sent us from the divine Father out of His incomparable love. He is God the Father's own Son. He is putting in order again what men upset by their sin. He has made us all God's children. He has taught us and shown us how a good child of God must live. His strongest desire is to take us home, some day, to the Father in heaven. There is our true home. He will provide a new earth for us to be our home, incomparably more beautiful than this world.

Even first graders can easily understand these truths, especially if they are presented by means of an appealing narrative, well illustrated. Thus beginners' catechisms, according to the principles of modern catechesis, consciously omit *all abstract formulations* and should *concentrate on those basic truths* of our religion which flow of themselves from a simple and childlike proclamation of the history of redemption. But we must try our utmost to let these basic

truths shine out in their proper radiance. We should lift them from
their historical frame and take great care that the children realize
their relevance for them here and now.

And if we follow the main phases of the history of redemption,
and present them at all fittingly, Christ will naturally be shown as
the center of divine revelation, as the incomparable gift of the
Father, our leader and way to the Father. In this way we will run
no danger of giving the children that false and sentimental "Jesus
piety" which seems rather to forget the divine Father and to put the
"little Jesus" in His place. Thus while, on the one hand, we should
omit all abstract formulations in these first grades, on the other
hand, we should make every effort to present the biblical message
from the very beginning in such a way that its theocentricity and
Christocentricity stand out as impressively as possible and gradually
permeate the life and prayer of our children.

In this way we shall indirectly avoid two forms of onesidedness
which might well endanger the success of biblical instruction. First
of all, we obviously have to avoid that kind of instruction which
contents itself with a purely entertaining narration of the Bible
stories and does not take the trouble to elaborate the content of
truth contained in the holy story. Bible history, even in the very
first grades, is far more than a series of beautiful stories about Christ,
far more than the life of Christ told in a childlike way. It is the
introduction into the Christian religion by way of biblical narration. The hesitation still felt by some ecclesiastical superiors about
the use of this biblical-narrative method is usually the result of
some unfortunate experience along these lines. Just as formerly an
"explanatory" analysis of a catechism was too easily considered to
be sufficient, today it may sometimes happen that Bible stories are
told beautifully, but *the doctrine is overlooked*. It is certainly to
the interest of the catechetical renewal to be aware of this danger
and to meet it effectively by providing solid catechetical outlines
for the catechists.

And we must also guard against the opposite danger: that of
trying to develop *too much* doctrine from the Bible story. Let us
stress again that doctrine at this level should be limited to essentials.
From the point of view of method this warning might be formulated
in this way: *in the first grades the narrative presentation must predominate, not the resulting explanation*. The story must be presented in such a way that only very little special explanation of
the doctrine it contains is necessary, and the effect of the instruction

should be further deepened by such activity on the children's part as drawings and dramatizations.

Another task to be carried out by the narration is the communication of, or at least laying the groundwork for, *true religious feeling*. This task is especially important, of course, with regard to the Person Who is the center of sacred history. What a glorious task we have to carry out in our first instructions—to win our students' hearts for Christ! Even in the first grades the children should begin to gain a true, though childlike, devotedness to Christ. Love for Him must now be solidly rooted in the children's hearts and must be fed continually so that it will grow. How can we accomplish this most easily and effectively? Certainly not by means of many details of dogma which children of this age cannot understand or value, but by a proper presentation of Christ's work and person. From such a presentation the greatness and attractiveness of Christ should shine out to the children and fill them with enthusiasm for Him and for His work.

Thus, with due regard for our students' age, we must from the beginning present a picture of Christ which harmoniously unites His awe-inspiring greatness and His lovable attractiveness, His tender intimacy with each of us, and His adorable majesty. In the lowest grade, as well as everywhere else, sweet sentimentality is of absolutely no use.

In this context we might also point out the catechetical importance of the way in which Christ and also the other figures of sacred history are pictorially represented to children. These pictures should, especially in the first grade, accompany, facilitate, and deepen the effects of the biblical-narrative catechesis. Pictures should be adapted, as far as possible, to the particular instructions that they are to assist. For the first grades, therefore, we should have simple pictures, with true religious feeling, which clearly present the catechetical meaning of their subject. These pictorial representations must be of a kind which can create and bring to life the image of Christ in the children's imaginations and so in their hearts. And this can never be achieved by sentimental pictures, even in the lower grades. True childlikeness in religious representation certainly does not consist in adding as many flowers and flying angels' heads as there is room for. And the fact that in our schools can be found so many religious pictures that are the products of poor taste and poor art is certainly not a good sign of a high level of catechetical instruction. For it not only indicates a lack of that sound aesthetic feeling, which is of more than a little importance in education, but it indicates also a certain watering down and cheapening of the religious substance. But, of course, in warning against sentimentality in pictures used in catechetical work we do not wish in any way to recommend those abstruse "modern" pictures which at least in elementary school have no place in our teaching.

Finally, we should draw attention to a misunderstanding that might arise from this strong emphasis on "history" in elementary instruction. History generally means the story of the past which we contemplate from the standpoint of the present. And in Bible history also we tell of events that happened a long time ago. But we must not forget that with this particular "history" it is always a question of the present. What the loving Father has done for us from the beginning of creation to today is the basis of our present life and actions. The mystery of Christ must never be approached or presented as something past. It must include and be directed toward our present life. Beginning with the very first grade, *not* *"Christ in Judea," but "Christ in you"* (Col. 1:27) *is the actual theme of our good tidings.* In this light, religious instruction is, from the very beginning, not so much history as "mystagogy," that is, an introduction into the mystery of Christ, the holy knowledge of our vocation to a new life in and with Christ, instruction in the practice and development of this life. In this central task of religious education the proper training in Christian worship, that is, *the liturgy,* assumes an important part, which will be discussed in the following chapter.

Up to this point we have been speaking only of biblical catechesis in the lower grades. But it is obvious that in the higher levels as well biblical instruction should play an important part. But here the catechetical function, and hence the method, will be different. Space does not permit us to present a lengthy description of the instruction on the Bible in the higher grades. Let it suffice to summarize the leading principles.[4]

In the upper grades we need special Bible classes to accompany the systematic catechesis given from a catechism (see chapter six). The syllabus must provide the suitable coordination of the subject mat-

---

[4] One can find more detailed suggestions on this matter in J. Hofinger, S.J., "How to Use the Bible in the Religion Class," *The Sower,* July and October, 1961. A separate edition of these articles has been published by the East Asian Pastoral Institute, Box 1815, Manila. See the special issue of *Good Tidings* on "The Bible—God's Own Catechism" (Manila, 1962).

ter in the catechism and the Bible classes, so that they are interrelated and aid each other. The task of these Bible classes should be to help students from year to year to become better acquainted not only with sacred history and with the themes of the Bible but with the inspired text itself. The students must learn to find in the Bible the answers to their problems and the nourishment of their spiritual life. They need above all to find inspiration and nourishment for their prayer life in the use made of the word of God in the liturgy and in diligent private reading as well. Bible classes in which we read the sacred text with the students and show them its inexhaustible riches for their own lives need in a special way a thoroughly religious atmosphere. The more perfectly the teacher knows how to stand back and to let God Himself speak to the students through His inspired word, the better. And in this way the teacher will at the same time prepare the students for the right liturgical reception of God's word.

In the upper grades of elementary school the easier parts of the Bible—that is, many narratives of the Old Testament, some simple and prayable Psalms, the synoptic Gospels, the Acts of the Apostles, and some of the easiest Epistles—should be read partly in the religion class and partly by the students themselves as homework. The students must learn to use and appreciate the Bible for their own personal contact with God. Later on in high school the students should become familiar with the whole New Testament and with all the essential parts of the Old Testament. For many reasons it is not advisable to wait until the college level to give a thorough knowledge of the Bible and at that time to focus religious instruction on holy Scripture. But, of course, if a solid knowledge of the Bible has been previously neglected, it must be provided in a college course in religion.

In the Bible classes of the grade-school and high-school level one of the chief principles to be used in selecting the texts for study should certainly be their liturgical use.

It is relatively easy to provide sufficient and efficient instruction in the Bible in Catholic schools, which, especially in the United States, usually set aside a number of hours for religious instruction. The case is completely different for Catholic students attending public schools. These students must also be led to the Bible; they also have to be taught how to nourish their spiritual life and their prayer from the word of God. But classes for such students should not try to provide Bible classes running parallel with the catechism classes. The problem should rather be solved by spending a full year on the Old Testament and another on the New. And since there is so little time in these classes, it is of special importance to stimulate the students to a fruitful private study of the Bible and to show them how to develop a better understanding and more fruitful use of the biblical treasures provided by our Mother the Church in the liturgy.

In spite of the great and promising progress in recent years biblical instruction, generally speaking, is still one of the weak points in our religion teaching. Until now there are many Catholic students who are not brought into close and personal contact with the Bible, notwithstanding an intensive religious instruction for twelve or even sixteen years. After years in school many of them have not even read the whole of the New Testament. One of the main reasons for this is the insufficient biblical training in seminaries and mother-houses which the Council clearly perceived and tried to remedy. "Therefore, all the clergy must hold fast to the sacred Scriptures through diligent sacred reading and careful study, especially the priests of Christ and others, such as deacons and catechists, who are legitimately active in the ministry of the word. This is to be done so that none of them will become 'an empty preacher of the word of God outwardly, who is not a listener to it inwardly'" (Dogmatic Constitution on Divine Revelation, n. 25).[5]

Adult religious education also should make all familiar with the book of the word of God. Particularly valuable are discussion groups which try to see the relevance of God's revelation to modern life.[6]

---

[5] For a better scriptural foundation of theological studies see Decree on Priestly Formation, n. 16.

[6] Fortunately, some fine commentaries on holy Scripture are now available: the *Old Testament Reading Guide* and *New Testament Reading Guide* published by Liturgical Press, Collegeville, Minnesota, and the commentary and notes provided in *The Jerusalem Bible*.

CHAPTER SIX

Progressive Initiation Through the Liturgy

The proper goal of our catechetical apostolate is not a theoretical knowledge of Christ and His mystery, but as perfect a living union with Him as possible. Biblical catechesis, therefore, must bring the past into the present. The mystery of Christ reaches from the past into the present; it embraces all centuries, and we live and share in it as did Christ's first disciples in Palestine. The Christ to Whom the biblical narratives lead us is not merely a great figure of the past, the subject of historical narration. He is the Christ Who now continues and perfects His work in us, and Who invites and enables us to cooperate actively in His holy work. He lives and is active among us. Through our personal contact with Him here and now we receive a share in His divine life. Where and when is this especially brought about? Obviously, above all in the sacramental life of the Church, in her Eucharistic sacrifice and her sacraments—in other words, in her *liturgy*.

We can readily understand, therefore, why liturgy should play such an important part in religious instruction even in the primary grades. Leading representatives of modern catechesis have agreed upon this principle for many years and have stressed it repeatedly.[1] Yet we must admit that in this case theory is far ahead of practice. Even now after the Council's emphasis on the "educative and pastoral nature of the liturgy" (Constitution on the Sacred Liturgy, nn. 33–40) many catechists still seem not to have a clear understanding of the outstanding value of the liturgy, or at least they do

---

[1] How much modern catechetics stresses the role of liturgy in the catechetical apostolate was very clearly brought out at the International Study Week of Eichstätt. See J. Hofinger, S.J., ed., *Teaching All Nations* (New York: Herder and Herder, 1961), especially pp. 223–266. Very significant also is the passage dealing with liturgy in Eichstätt's "Program of the Catechetical Apostolate." See the appendix of this book.

not yet know how to integrate liturgy well into the whole process of religious education.

How the Liturgy Presents the Mystery of Christ

The unique catechetical value of the liturgy essentially derives from the way in which it contains and makes us familiar with the heart of the Christian religion—the mystery of Christ.

It may be true to say that in the beginning of the catechetical movement many catechists perceived the great catechetical value of the liturgy *from the point of view of methods only*. The main concern of that era was the problem of methods, and so this limited vision is quite understandable. And even from this point of view there was every reason to ask for a more intensive utilization of the liturgy in catechetics. The worship of the Church, after all, certainly offers an excellent catechetical object lesson. And this is still true even in this age of highly developed teaching techniques. Even today a real chalice that the child can observe closely is more illustrative, and more formative in a religious sense, than is a painted one. Even today a priest who, before the children's eyes, approaches the altar and begins the Mass attracts the child's attention to a higher degree than would the same scene presented in a movie or on television. The truths of our faith find an impressive, concrete, and even dramatic expression in the house of God with its liturgical objects and actions. The liturgy is an extremely versatile catechetical picture book which makes the children familiar by means of their senses with the majestic mysteries of our faith.

The didactic power of this object lesson has increased tremendously in the last years through the use of vernacular in the liturgy. Now the spoken word and the visible sign work harmoniously together in expressing clearly and strikingly the mystery of Christ in which we participate.

Moreover, the liturgy directs us to express our response to those holy mysteries again and again in prayer, and so to take a personal positive attitude toward them and to assimulate them through participation in them (learning by doing). This teaching function of the liturgy is enhanced by the rich diversity in the seasons of the Church's year, by the religious atmosphere, and by the impressive religious experience from the very beginning associated with worship.

But however much we agree upon and want to utilize fully all these values, we must realize that by themselves they do not represent the decisive catechetical value of the liturgy. The essence of this value consists in teaching us—in this concrete and educationl manner—*the substance of Christian faith and life*. The catechetical concentration on essentials, so often lacking in our religious instruction, here finds exemplary realization. Again and again Mother Church has us pray and sing the basic mysteries of our faith. And the keynote is always the mystery of all mysteries—the mystery of Christ—which we celebrate, and renew in celebrating, and which represents the central theme of the entire liturgy.

This concentration is particularly impressive in the two liturgical subjects which are of decisive importance in the lower grades, that is, the Mass and the liturgical year. In both we find the same admirable fullness of doctrine combined with an exemplary concentration on the basic theme of all Christian revelation: our salvation through Christ, or, in other words, our participation in the paschal mystery of Christ. How clearly both the Mass and the liturgical year express the theocentricity and the Christocentricity which are so essential to our religion: Christ, the great gift of the Father, Christ, our way to the Father. Anyone who participates in the liturgy with an open heart will not long be wanting in the necessary religious knowledge, and he will acquire even more quickly the basic Christian attitude which is far more important than a precise knowledge of details.

The same is true, of course, concerning a third unit of the liturgy, the sacraments. But these are not as easily understood by the children of the lower grades. By themselves they do not unfold the entire mystery of Christ in the same fullness as do the Mass and the liturgical year. And they are not experienced as a unit in actual practice—even a mature convert does not receive all the sacraments in succession during an easily surveyed period of time. While we do not deny that the liturgy of the sacraments also tells us impressively of the mystery of Christ, yet the significance of the sacraments lies more in what they give than in what they reveal.[2]

And here is the last and most decisive reason why teaching

---

[2] But valuable catechetical instruction can and should be given by means of proper explanation of the true significance of the sacramental rites, especially when such explanations accompany a demonstration of the rites. For an aid in giving such explanations see—*Bringing the Sacraments to the People—A Commentary on the Sacraments and Selected Blessings of the Church* (Collegeville, Minnesota: Liturgical Press).

through worship is superior to all other forms of Christian teaching. *The liturgy gives what it teaches.* It not only presents the mystery of Christ concretely; it also lets us immediately participate in this mystery. If there is anywhere in Christianity that a true initiation into the mystery of Christ takes place, it is here. How clearly has Christ Himself expressed this truth concerning the central sacrament, the holy Eucharist, which in its sacramental sign demonstrates most impressively our participation in the life and the mystery of Christ. "He who eats My flesh and drinks My blood, abides in Me and I in him. As the living Father has sent Me, and as I live because of the Father, so he who eats Me, he also shall live because of Me" (John 6:57–59). St. Paul uses equally forceful words to impress upon us the principle of our actual participation in the mystery of Christ by the fundamental sacrament, baptism. "Do you not know that all we who have been baptized into Christ Jesus have been baptized into His death? For we were buried with Him by means of baptism into death, in order that, just as Christ has arisen from the dead through the glory of the Father, so we also may walk in newness of life" (Rom 6:3 ff., see vv. 3–14, likewise Col. 2:12; Gal.3:27; 1 Cor. 12:13). For all the other sacraments, something similar is true, marriage being no exception (Eph. 5:32).

The Eucharistic sacrifice, above all, offers us a real participation in the mystery of Christ: the Lord includes His Bride, the Church; He includes all His mystical members in His sacrifice, sacrificing with them, and they with Him. There may be different views among theologians as to the way in which Christ's redemption is present and constantly active in the Church's worship. But Catholic theologians have always agreed that it offers a mysterious participation in the redemption through Christ, that we not only receive the sanctifying fruits of His redemption but also are enabled to participate actively in His mystery and His worship. This is true first of all and in the highest degree of the Eucharistic sacrifice. And it is also true of the sacraments and, though to a much lesser degree, of the other divine services of the Church. This participation comes about simply because, on the one hand, the mystical Christ, the Head with His members, is the actual active subject of any liturgical celebration, and, on the other hand, the actions of the mystical Christ form an indissoluble inner unity with Christ's redemptive work.

The Church's worship, accordingly, is a veritable catechetical treasure-house. Since true participation in the mystery of Christ is the final goal of all catechetical effort, the liturgy takes the first place among means of achieving that goal, and it cannot be replaced by anything else. Obviously we want to open these riches to our students as early and as fully as possible.

How to Unlock the Liturgy

As we have just seen, the liturgy has two important purposes so far as our present topic is concerned: it must effectively reveal the mystery of Christ and it must actually communicate it. As daily experience shows us, not every liturgical celebration fulfills this twofold task perfectly or even adequately. Are there not Catholics who have attended hundreds, perhaps even thousands, of Masses and yet understand very little about the actual meaning of the celebration? Their mere *attendance* does not help them greatly to understand their religion better, nor does it result in an adequate participation in the mystery of Christ. To "unlock" the liturgy means, therefore, first to conduct our liturgical services in such a way as to guide those present to a proper understanding of the mystery of Christ and, second, to train our students to take part in the holy mysteries in such a way as to grow in participation in the mystery of Christ. Whatever means truly serves one of these purposes will necessarily help to attain the other also, since they form an organic unity. They should be recognized clearly as two aspects, but they should never be separated in our intention as teachers. For this reason we shall treat them together during the rest of this chapter.

Beginning in the first grade the introductory biblical instructions are, if this is at all possible, to be given in such a way that *the course of the stories follows the course of the liturgical year.* We should prepare the children, in a way suited to their age, for the great feasts, and we should celebrate these feasts with them, especially Christmas and Easter (with Holy Week preceding it). The mysteries celebrated in these feasts should also form the high points of our biblical catechesis, and thus the effect of the biblical catechesis will be deepened by liturgical experience. Long before the child can clearly understand, his taking part in the liturgical celebrations of the mysteries of Christ enables him to experience these mysteries not merely as historical narratives but also as present religious values.

From the very beginning, then, we should try, after careful preparation, to celebrate the main feasts of the Church with the children in such a way that they are made familiar by experience with the present reality of these feasts. Of course we should begin with the historical work of the redemption, and for this reason the biblical-narrative catechesis must precede the direct preparation for a liturgical celebration. But we should not stop at the history; the mystery of the past serves to make us understand and value what Christ is now effecting in us. Both are gifts of divine love; in the mystery of the feast we celebrate and give thanks for both together. Our Christian feast days are essentially feasts of thanksgiving for the "wonderful works of God" (Acts 2:11), which in their totality form the mystery of Christ. The fact that the Eucharistic sacrifice is the climax of the celebration of these feasts clearly shows their "thanksgiving" character. Especially on feast days, then, the Holy Sacrifice is to be seen and celebrated as our communal thanksgiving to the Father, and, starting in the primary grades we must help the children to offer their thanks above all through this sacrifice.

All this must be done, of course, in the simplest and most childlike manner, but *childlike in the best sense.* In connection with Christmas, for example, certainly any average pupil in the lower grades to whom we have spoken of the state of man, of the promise of the Savior to come, of the long awaiting of mankind, and of the fulfillment of God's promise and plan, will understand that "with the Child of Bethlehem, something of heaven has fallen upon earth" (Jungmann). The Child has been given to us by the divine Father as His greatest gift; since then Christ has been our Brother, Who wants to lead us all, without exception, home to the Father in heaven. Thus the children's holy Christmas joy develops into a heartfelt thanksgiving to the divine Father. We thank Him for His Son Whom He gave to us as our Brother and Redeemer; we thank Him for the fact that He has made us children of God and called us to heaven through this Child of heaven. Over a hundred years ago a great friend of children, Christopher von Schmid, expressed this truth in a truly childlike way in the well-known carol:

> O come, little children, come all of you come,
> O come to the crib, to the stable, O come,
> And see what great joy in this night, out of love
> The Father has sent us from heaven above.

We must not think that any sentimentality is needed in order to open the mystery of Christmas to the children, but we also should not forget that in the first grades the child has a holy right not to be burdened with such theological terms as "grace," "supernatural," and so on, or with a precise theological explanation of "vicarious satisfaction." To children "Savior" should simply mean He Who has freed us from sin and reopened to us the gate of heaven. The liturgy itself gives us irrefutable proof that a simple telling of the holy mysteries is quite consistent with religious depth, with no need for theological terms and abstract expressions.

In the higher grades also we should not disregard the Church year, but rather, as far as possible, try to harmonize our subject matter with the rhythm of the liturgy, and we should try to accomplish this without artificiality. Special feasts still deserve and need preparation of the students. Help to a fuller understanding of the texts of the Propers of the Masses of these feasts should certainly be given, as well as, on the last school day of each week, a short introduction to the Mass of the following Sunday.

In addition to the elementary introduction to the Church year, we should begin in the primary grades to make the children familiar with the practice of Christian prayer, with the Church's worship, and with the sacraments which are of the most immediate significance to the children. For the first grade an explanation of baptism and the Eucharist is quite sufficient. And here again the principle holds true: let the child, whenever possible, learn by direct observation and by doing; be sparing with theoretical explanations. Offer this first introduction to the sacraments as simply as possible, but from the very beginning with the proper catechetical view: meeting Christ, participation in His life and in His devotedness to the divine Father.

Liturgy is the Church's worship, and this means, above all, prayer—the Church's prayer. To lead our students to the liturgy means, first of all, to lead them to *liturgical prayer*. One of the most common reasons why so many people, even very devout Catholics, cannot find their way to liturgical prayer, or can do so only with great difficulty, is, certainly, a faulty training in their early youth which has led them to an unliturgical spirituality that they find very hard to change in later life. But proper guidance in such prayer does not consist in using liturgical prayers for the children's own prayer life too early or too exclusively. We should always remain aware of the fact that liturgical prayer is essentially community prayer and that for the personal prayer of the individual and its formulation certain important modifications have to be made. Nor should these modifications be overlooked in the first instructions which are to awaken and to develop spontaneous Christian prayer in each child. Again, obviously, the language of liturgical prayer rarely corresponds to the child's individuality. Our aim is prayer arising truly and unartificially from the children's hearts to the Father in heaven. And certainly we should not be too narrow-minded on this point. Once we have sufficiently developed the meaning of individual prayer and its expression, it is not detrimental if prayer texts are used which the child cannot fully understand, and this is far better than giving him sentimental "children's prayers" to memorize. Children act like adults in many ways, even though their minds do not fully grasp what they are doing; and they grow in understanding by being given something above them to make their own.

In our introduction to Christian prayer we owe the child some adaptation to his own individuality. But this does not mean that we should make any concessions with regard to the basic attitude of Christian prayer. In the child's prayer, as in the adult's, the divine Father must predominate, and not, for instance, the guardian angel. As in our religious instruction we must first tell of the Father in heaven, of His power and His love, so we must begin our training in prayer with the divine Father and always refer to Him. Of course, we must also lead the praying child to Christ. But since Christ has been presented from the outset as the gift of the Father, as our leader to the Father, there will be no difficulty for the child in praying in this way also. The child finds, after all, the same situation in his prayer as in his family; he goes with his brothers to the father. And again, any good family training should stress "thank you" rather than "please," and so the child should begin with no psychological obstacles to an early training in the prayer of praise and thanksgiving.

Nor shall we in any way injure the child's personality if we begin very soon to teach him to respond in prayer to the wonderful mysteries of our faith, in other words, to pray "dogmatically" (which of course does not mean dogmatic terminology, but content, as the liturgy itself is "dogmatic"). Such a response will develop by itself if in our instructions we stress above all the religious values of what we teach and if the individual instructions generally culminate in prayer. This may be carried out by a spontaneous prayer, or by an appropriate formal prayer, or by a good hymn, or by some suggestions as to how the students can turn the subject just studied into the object of a prayer. And if the instructions really elaborate the mystery of Christ and make the children familiar with it, their prayers will certainly be directed toward this central mystery. Children so trained will easily find their own way in liturgical prayer. They will not need to readjust themselves, for they already possess the right attitude. In liturgical prayer, too, it is "the spirit that gives life" (John 6:64).

Between the Bible history in the primary grades and the systematic catechesis in the higher grades it might be advisable to give the children a kind of survey of the most significant doctrines of the faith, a survey of which the Mass and the sacraments are the center. This course would involve not merely an explanation of the liturgy of the Mass and the sacraments but also a survey of the entire mystery of Christ. But this should, in accordance with the children's age, be developed from the easily perceptible forms of worship and lead to their deep meaning. And this course should allow the relationship of this central mystery to the other basic doctrines to appear in its full light.

But in such a course we should be on our guard against the danger of going into too great liturgical detail. The understanding of the whole is what is important, and the individual ceremonies of the Mass, for instance, should always be explained with regard to their function in the whole. But what is of supreme importance here, however, is intelligent and devoted liturgical action. Here, above all, knowledge should be completely at the service of right doing. As Father Jungmann has said so well, "Not much liturgics, but much liturgy."[3] He explains this in more detail in the following words: "Much practical living of religion at home, in school, in church. . . . Needed explanations can, in most cases, be given in occasional instructions by connecting a related topic of liturgical life with the subject of the current lesson, or by using such a topic as a conclusion."

We could formulate these principles as follows: in liturgical training the leading role should be taken by *meaningful active participation in the Church's worship,* not by the religious instruction courses in school. Certainly the classes are important, but in the end they are only preparatory. The actual and decisive values of the liturgy can be acquired, not through study, but only through

---

[3] J. A. Jungmann, S.J., *Handing on the Faith* (New York: Herder and Herder, 1959), p. 102.

proper participation. And it is because we appreciate these values so highly that we should strive to attain an exterior form of worship that fully expresses them.

Formerly the choice was only between the low Mass and the sung or solemn Mass. For pedagogical reasons preference was given to the former because it allowed a combination of vernacular prayers and songs, while the latter had to be all in Latin. The postconciliar legislation has lifted the strict demarcation line between these two forms: vernacular may be used in both; not everything in a high Mass is necessarily to be sung (Introit, Gradual, Offertory, and Communion verses may be read, and instead seasonal hymns that are more understandable and adapted to the feast or season, even though not strictly liturgical, may be sung). Even the Creed may be recited in a high Mass, which perhaps corresponds better to its nature of profession of faith than the singing of it. On the other hand, parts of the Ordinary like the Kyrie, Sanctus, and Agnus Dei may be sung in a recited Mass. Flexibility has replaced previous rigidity. The rule is adapted to the community, not the community to the rule. Henceforth the basic principle is: make the celebration as attractive, meaningful, and fruitful as possible according to the resources of your community. This basic rule opens to those in charge of children's Masses a wide range of possibilities.[4]

The introduction of a three-year cycle of Scripture readings at Sunday Mass and the use of three Scriptural passages at all weekly Masses should do much to remedy the present lack of familiarity of adult Catholics with the full sweep of sacred history. Not only will they hear a wider number of texts from the Bible but the interrelations of these texts will be explained in the new missals provided for the laity. The Church has encouraged—both during the Council and after—that a homily be given at *every* Mass for a community. Not a sermon. Not a learned commentary on Scripture. But a homily which introduces the faithful into the liturgical mys-

---

[4] Some good helps for a first initiation of the little ones into the Mass are found in Grade One of the *Our Life With God Series*, Vatican II edition by Mother Marie Vénard Pfeiffer, O.S.U. (New York, Sadlier, 1965). For more details see AMEN, The Liturgical Magazine of the Faithful (Manila), No. 16, 114–119. A good form of a children's Mass is provided in J. Seffer, S.J., *First Communion Mass* (Manila, East Asian Pastoral Institute, 1966), and in *Christ's Life in Us*, Grade Two of the Vatican II edition of the *On Our Way Series* by Sister Maria de la Cruz Aymes, Francis J. Buckley, S.J., and Cyr Miller (New York, Sadlier, 1967).

tery they are at that moment celebrating, so that they may take an active part, be fully aware of what they are doing, and be enriched by the effects of their sacred action.

Vatican II has insisted that the Latin rite Mass should be reformed so that the meaning of the actions might be clear without detailed explanations. The changes already in effect are not the final steps. Much bold and prudent experimentation is still to be done, and the bishops have asked for it. The purpose of all these changes and experiments should not be forgotten: to reveal more clearly the sacred nature of the actions we perform so that they may become genuine liturgical prayer from beginning to end.

The Council has directed that the rites of all the sacraments should be revised after a careful theological, historical, and pastoral investigation. The principles underlying these revisions are plainly set forth in the Constitution on the Sacred Liturgy and should be carefully explained to the faithful. Although the changes so far carried out have met with widespread acceptance, a sizable minority of the laity have been upset, largely because the reasons for the changes had not been explained to them.

But although a properly conducted Mass is the center of liturgical training, we must carefully guard against *liturgical isolationism.* Proper participation requires preparation and explanation of the liturgy, and, what is even more important, proper participation must show its effects in daily Christian life. We must try to impress the children quite early in their training that Christian worship is not an expression of religious experience with no consequent obligations. Worship must be "religious," that is, it must bind us to God, it must stand the test of daily life, it must form our lives. We must not only celebrate Mass; we must also live the Mass. The promise of full self-surrender which we made with Christ to the Father during the Holy Sacrifice has to be realized in our lives, and so we shall truly live the mystery of Christ.

CHAPTER SEVEN

Progressive Initiation
Through Systematic Catechesis

From its beginning the modern catechetical movement has insisted that the first introduction to the Christian religion must be carried out by means of a narrative of the history of salvation. "No catechism in the early grades of school" was one of the first and most fundamental principles of the movement—a principle which has not always been easy to put into practice.

But this courageous battle against the too early use of a systematic catechism has caused some people to think that the modern catechetical movement is opposed on principle to any use of a catechism and that it only tolerates the use of a systematic catechism even in the upper grades. A few extremists who held such a view may have existed, but in general the leading experts in modern catechetics have rejected such an exaggeration.

The fact that leaders of the modern movement hold to the great importance of systematic religious instruction according to a catechism, given in the proper way and the proper place, is clearly revealed by their strenuous efforts to improve catechisms, especially in those European countries that are the most advanced catechetically. A typical example in this field is the German Catechism.[1] This catechism was commissioned by the German hierarchy, and the foremost catechetical experts in Germany worked on it from 1938 until its publication in 1955.

We do not intend here to discuss its value or to answer the question whether it is in every way a model that we should imitate. We are merely citing this German catechism as an example of how

---

[1] *Katholischer Katechismus der Bistümer Deutschlands* (Freiburg: Herder, 1955). The English translation, a work of Clifford Howell, S.J., *A Catholic Catechism*, has been published in many editions throughout the English-speaking world; for the United States by Herder and Herder, New York.

in Germany, the homeland of the modern catechetical movement, experts are agreed on the vast importance of a good catechism.[2]

The question now is, therefore, not whether we should use a catechism or not, but rather how in the higher grades of elementary school we can most effectively present in a systematic way, and so impart a more mature understanding of, the subject matter which the children already have grasped in an elementary fashion from their previous instruction, as outlined in the preceding chapters.

WHAT IS THE PARTICULAR TASK OF SYSTEMATIC CATECHESIS?

Children in the primary grades are not capable of a comprehensive view of any subject, whether it be religion or anything else. Such a mature approach has no interest for them, and in the field of religion it cannot benefit them spiritually. During these years the child's mind is capable of assimilating only concrete details. No sensible teacher would dream of presenting to first graders a "system" of geography, mathematics, or any other science. During this period those elements of knowledge should be offered to the child which will give him, from his own standpoint and according to his own way of understanding, a view of the world he lives in. These elements of knowledge should be given in a way adapted as

---

[2] Concerning the catechetical value of the German Catechism see Father Jungmann's article in *Lumen Vitae*, 10 (1955), 573–586. We must agree that this is the first catechism fully to take into consideration all the kerygmatic requirements of the modern catechetical movement. But this in no way means that the German Catechism is "the" solution for all places and for all times. Especially mission countries need textbooks which are adapted to their particular needs. See J. Hofinger, S.J., "The German Catechism and the Missions," in *Mission Bulletin* (Hongkong, 1958), 554–558, and M. Ramsauer, S.J., "A Good Mission Catechism," in *Teaching All Nations* (New York: Herder and Herder, 1961), pp. 174–191. None of the papers given at the International Study Week at Eichstätt recommended the German Catechism as "the" catechism for the missions. Recent texts like the upper grades of the *On Our Way Series* in fact seem to present a better solution than the German Catechism or the Australian Catechism. The appearance of the New Dutch Catechism has already attracted much attention and controversy. Without taking sides in the growing debate, it is safe to predict that the Dutch Catechism will have an immense impact on catechetics, particularly adult education, in the coming years. The English translation of the original New Dutch Catechism has been published in the United States by Herder and Herder (New York, 1967) under the title *A New Catechism*. Meanwhile the Dutch original is being revised.

perfectly as possible to the living conditions and concrete needs of the child. And the view of his world which he is to gain is simply a view, not an insight and never a comprehensive conspectus. It may be that when the teaching is given by means of a continuous story, a certain but still quite imperfect conspectus of the subject will be gained. But a teacher with any knowledge of child psychology would certainly avoid burdening children of this age with a continuous history even of their own country. How can we in reason expect a child's mind to follow essentially different laws when he studies religion—which deals, after all, with very lofty subjects? Or do we expect that he will here be given some miraculous grace that makes the ordinary laws of child psychology null and void?

We find that a really astonishing amount of intellectual material will be amassed by the child during the primary grades in his years of initial spiritual awakening—when the proper kind of instruction has been given. But the need to form this jumbled world of scattered details into an ordered unity develops slowly, generally much more slowly than we adults like to admit. And even when the need is felt, the goal is not all at once a complete, all-embracing, and consequently complicated order. First of all, smaller wholes are built up out of pieces of information which seem, at first glance, to belong together, and gradually these units are brought together into a more and more comprehensive and interrelated view of the world. This process closely resembles that by which a small child at home first perceives the room in which he spends most of his time as being some kind of a unit, and later he fits into one scheme the whole house, with its immediate surroundings, and still later, the whole region in which he lives. It is evident that in the instruction given in school we have to promote this spiritual process, though we must not believe that we can benefit the child in any way by a premature systematization.

The time does come, therefore, in the higher grades of grammar school when a certain systematization of the knowledge gathered during the previous years becomes psychologically possible and even necessary—in religion as in other fields of instruction. The greater degree of maturity now attained by the students enables them more perfectly to understand the doctrines of their faith. The teacher can now succeed in showing them more clearly the inter-relationships of the various doctrines and can present them with a certain conspectus of the whole.

Here, obviously, is the special task of systematic catechesis, both for children and adults. It follows the order of the catechism, which of its nature is designed to give a survey of the most important doctrines of the Christian religion. The principle of this survey is not the narration of the history of salvation—as in biblical history—but rather a logical presentation of the interrelationship of the various truths of the faith, which will show their logical unity. Its object, therefore, is to present a system of truth.

But if from the standpoint of religious pedagogy we are to evaluate rightly this systematic religious instruction and formulate it efficiently, we must not consider its didactic function in isolation. Its special didactic function is, as we have said, to give a synthesis of Christian doctrines and a better understanding of their interrelationship. But we must first ask, What is the significance of this function in the entire process of religious formation? What does it contribute to the realization of the final goal of all Christian instruction? In chapters two and three we have seen that the *mystery of Christ* is actually *the central theme* of religious instruction and that *a more and more perfect participation in the mystery of Christ* is its chief goal. This, of course, is true not only of the first years of religious instruction but of all of them, and increasingly so, for it is a question of progressive initiation into the mystery of Christ. We may, therefore, formulate the question as follows: In what way does the systematic instruction to be given in the upper grades contribute to the children's deeper understanding of the mystery of Christ and to their more perfect participation in it?

If the religious instruction in the primary grades has been given properly, then Christ and His mystery formed its center. The children will already have experienced religious instruction as being "instruction about Christ" and about what He taught and gave us. In the systematic instruction now to be given, the student must, then, be brought to understand much more clearly and practically how Christ truly is the center of Christian teaching and of Christian life. He must be enabled to see Christian teaching more and more clearly as the teaching of the mystery of Christ, and Christian life more and more as our participation in this mystery. The student has now come to the stage where he is capable of grasping the interrelationship of all Christian doctrines with this central mystery of Christian revelation. And so all his knowledge of his religion will develop more and more fully into a Christian view of the world in the full sense of the word. This view will be Christian not only because it was revealed to us by Christ but even more because it is centered in Christ: "that in all things He may have the first place. For it has pleased God the Father that in Him all His fullness should dwell, and that through Him He should reconcile to Himself all things, whether on the earth or in the heavens . . ." (Col. 1:19 f.).

If we look at it in this light, we see clearly that the systematic religious instruction to be given from the upper grades on has, in the first place, to fulfill an important intellectual task. It is to contribute to a fuller intellectual penetration of Christian doctrine. But we must not conclude from this fact that this instruction should be any the less concerned with Christian life than is the instruction given in the primary grades. "Systematic" need not and should not mean theoretic and remote from life. The "system" must never alter or obscure the central idea or the inner structure of the doctrine presented but rather elaborate it as clearly as possible. This is, obviously, the special teaching function of a system.

In systematic instruction, therefore, Christian doctrine must continue to be presented as what it essentially is: the teaching of our way to God through Christ, the teaching of the glory of the Christian life, consisting essentially in participating in the life of Christ. Thus, in the end systematic instruction should become the servant, not of religious knowledge merely, but of Christian life; it, too, should contribute to our more perfect participation in the life of Christ. We can even go so far as to say this: systematic instruction is justified to the degree to which it helps the student to perceive Christian doctrine as a compact organic unity and to understand more fully its central mystery and its value in his life.

How Can the Particular Task of Systematic Instruction Be Most Effectively Realized?

Now that we understand more clearly the special catechetical function of systematic catechism instruction, we can answer the next eminently practical question of how most effectively to carry out this task. As we have seen, this systematic instruction must give the students their first real survey of the doctrines of their faith. Let us not forget, first of all, that in the higher grades of elementary school our students are still children, only ten to fourteen years old. At this age, interest and capability for "systems" and "summaries" exist only in a rudimentary form. If the system is really to fulfill its function, the arrangement of the catechism must be as *simple, clear and impressive as possible*. This should be true both of the main divisions of the catechism and of their subdivisions. If a clear and impressive arrangement of the lessons is made possible by means of a proper organization of the basic catechetical formulas so called (the creed, the sacraments, the Our Father, the commandments), then our task will be simplified.[3]

But this clarity is not all that is necessary. Our actual task here is, as we have seen, a much more perfect catechetical concentration than was possible in the biblical and liturgical instruction of the primary grades. The basic idea of the Christian Good News and, consequently, of our Christian life is to be developed and emphasized, and individual doctrines are to be presented entirely in the light of this basic idea. And again the catechism as a whole and its individual parts must *develop the central theme of Christian revelation, the mystery of Christ, as radiantly as possible.* The very arrangement of the main sections of the catechism should reveal the centrality of this theme and so should its individual parts.

In chapter two we pointed out how all the important doctrines of the faith should be seen and presented entirely from the central viewpoint of Christian revelation. And since the goal of all catechetical instruction is Christian life, our systematic instruction must reveal not merely the intellecutal relationship of individual doctrines to the mystery of Christ but more especially their "Christian" value in life. In other words, by means of this teaching the student should grow continuously in the understanding of how all the doctrines of the catechism lead to Christ and of how they all contribute to a fuller comprehension, a deeper appreciation, and a fuller unfolding of our life in Christ.

We must admit that these necessary qualities are only imperfectly realized in the catechisms and textbooks of religion produced in the era before the advent of modern kerygmatic efforts, even though these books show improvement with regard to methods. There is a question here not only of the important problem of a better arrangement of the catechism as a whole but also of the proper presentation of the individual doctrines. The realization that small alterations and a few minor changes and additions in the text of catechisms

[3] The relationship of systematic instructions to these basic catechetical formulas is particularly important when only a limited amount of time is available for religious teaching, as is often the case with missionary catechesis, and also with the religious instruction given to students in public schools. In these instances we are, of course, concerned above all to establish firmly, by an understanding of these basic formulas, the necessary religious knowledge.

are not enough has led in all catechetically advanced countries to the *introduction of new catechisms*.[4] We do not by any means maintain that these new catechisms are entirely satisfactory in all cases. But the seriousness with which the most outstanding experts in modern catechetics are searching for a solution certainly indicates the vast importance of this problem.

It may be argued that in modern catechetics the fact is always stressed that the teacher and his *living instructions* are much more important than the lifeless textbooks or syllabus. This, of course, is true. A catechist who is well trained in the kerygmatic outlook, who truly sees the Christian message as centered in the mystery of Christ, and who brings it home to his students in this way will be able to work even with an unkerygmatic textbook. But how many of our catechists are so skillful? It is an open secret that even in countries where efforts to promote the kerygmatic approach were made very early and were reasonably successful, a good many catechists still have to be won over and trained in this new way of teaching. And to a great extent this new training can only be done by means of better texts. In Germany, for example, leading catechetical circles have never tried to conceal the fact that this is the first and most important task which the new catechism and the commentaries on it must fulfill.

But, obviously, so long as an adequate catechism does not exist, it is all the more important to offer help to catechists by means of other catechetical literature. And of perhaps even greater importance is the *proper training of future catechists* in the seminaries; in the houses of formation of teaching religious, where in many cases courses in kerygmatic theology are already being provided; and also in the training courses for lay teachers, so zealously promoted by the Confraternity of Christian Doctrine. For the catechist himself must first learn to see his message entirely in the light of Christ; otherwise even the best text will not be of much use to him unless it contains introductory remarks or good comments that will open to him the true meaning of his teaching.[5]

---

[4] "The mere revision or modifications of former textbooks or catechisms which are not drawn up according to the principles of the catechetical renewal cannot produce a work which fulfills the basic demands of catechetics." Internationl Study Week at Eichstätt, Conclusions. The same has been stressed in the "Program of the Catechetical Apostolate."

[5] Among recent texts the revised *On Our Way Series* (New York, Sadlier) excels in such introductory notes to the teacher in each lesson. So far only volumes 1–3 of the revised teacher's guide are available.

In order to help the catechist to realize that he is to act as a herald of Christ in each particular lesson, the best texts of today structure a single lesson into "message" and "response." The message stands for the steps of presentation and explanation of old, and the response, for application. What counts is not the new term as such, but the spirit which is expressed by it.

We should, perhaps, point out here explicitly that this new way of teaching catechism, which strives without artificiality to present each individual lesson in the radiant light of the whole, will also influence the *catechetical method*. For the method must be entirely at the service of the message to be communicated and of the actual goal of the instruction. A truly kerygmatic instruction will naturally emphasize "deepening," a process which modern authors of catechisms usually add after the formal step of "explanation." Obviously, in carrying out this "deepening," catechetical tact is needed in the teacher, so that he does not offer too much or too little, and everything at the proper time. In the higher grades, for example, when the subject is the resurrection of Christ, we should certainly point out its relationship to our own resurrection and also to the wonderful, but now hidden, life which we received at our resurrection in baptism. In the higher grades, again, Christ's first coming at His incarnation and birth should not be taught without instruction also concerning His second coming at the end of time.

In conclusion, when we compare the three chief ways by which we are to initiate step by step into the mystery of Christ, we must say that the *biblical-narrative catechesis is the basic way,* and that *systematic catechesis is,* from the point of view of religious understanding, *the most perfect way.* But since the final question is one, not of religious understanding, but of life in Christ, the *liturgical way always deserves the priority,* because it gives what it teaches and thus is both the way and the goal. Long after they have completed their formal religious instruction, the liturgy will remain the master teacher in leading our former students to Christ. And even our vision of God in heaven, which alone will give us final, complete, and joyful insight into the mystery of Christ, will be more like this liturgical way than any other, for in heaven also we shall know God in prayer, and in adoration participate in God's glory.

In addition to these three ways of progressive initiation into the mystery of Christ, a fourth way is frequently mentioned, that is, *the testimony of Christian living.* We learn Christian religion in a most appealing and conclusive manner from the countless manifestations of genuine Christian life we find in the history of the

Church and her saints. Already in the lower grades we often illustrate Christian doctrine by stories from the lives of saints and other great Christians. Later on, some systematic presentation of Church history can do much good if it is well adapted to the age level of the students. But even more important than the study of Christian living in the past is the daily experience of truly Christian living in the present. Each person is to be formed into a more and more perfect Christian by means of a truly Christian way of life in his family, in his school, and in church organizations. That religious training must not be restricted to religious instruction given in the classrooms is rightly one of the principles most strongly emphasized in the modern catechetical program. Only through a proper realization of what Christian life is, a realization which, in the course of the years, becomes more and more deeply understood and conscious, does the person grow to the full stature of a mature Christian. The life and action which at first were mainly the results of good habits must increasingly become the expression of personal conviction and of conscious adherence to Christ, as well as a holy living union with Him. There can be no possible doubt that in the decisive religious situation of the present day we are, more than ever before, in urgent need of such mature Christians. Can we say, then, that all our religious training is as yet consistently directed toward their formation?

Chapter Eight

The Right Ordering of Catechetical Material

In His deep love for us God has revealed many doctrines to us. He has told us how important they are for us so that we may know Him as befits His beloved children and journey home to Him safely and happily. We heralds have no right to be careless with these riches or to transmit to our charges only certain fragments of the whole message.

But the very richness of our message gives rise to a threefold kerygmatic problem. First, what is the central theme of the whole message which must stand out clearly and impressively in our proclamation? This question has already been answered. Second, how shall we select the doctrines to be presented according to the capacity and the special needs of those whom we are addressing? This question will be answered in the second part of the book. And, finally, there is the question of the right ordering of the material of our message, and it is this question which now concerns us.

This question has been, at least in the last thirty years, one of the problems most thoroughly considered. The reordering of the main sections of the catechism during these years clearly shows that to plan a new outline of the catechism by no means implies a dangerous revolution in the religion course. The danger consists rather in this: that people who are only slightly concerned with the question may consider this reordering as a mere trifle. Such people might easily think that it makes no difference whether a teacher presents the sacraments or the commandments after the doctrine on faith and that, in all probability, very few students and not many more catechists would even notice that a different order had been used. Yet the importance of a suitable ordering of subject matter is greatly stressed in modern catechetics.

WHY DO WE NEED A FITTING ARRANGEMENT?

Good teachers have always known how important it is to order their material in a way which will help the students to grasp the principal idea and the connection between the individual parts of the lessons, and not merely to retain some interesting details of it. And all students realize, from their daily experience, the didactic value of such a clear and evident ordering with regard not only to single lessons but also to the whole content of the course. They realize this value most especially if in their examinations they have not only to answer individual questions but to show how those questions are related to one another, that is, if they are required truly to understand and to penetrate the meaning of what they have been taught.

Religious instruction, more than any other, has as its goal the formation of the student and the giving to him of a clear, well-founded, and coherent view of life. Again, the importance of a suitable order is obvious as soon as we consider the question in the light of our apostolic task. As God's messengers, we are sent to proclaim not only some particular doctrines but, above all, the kerygma that we have been commissioned to proclaim. And this kerygma is, as we have already seen, the mystery of Christ. What we have been given to proclaim as one wonderful whole, one divine cosmos, we must faithfully transmit as such, as a beautiful and forceful unity. It can be said without any exaggeration that even in teaching children in the first grade we are more obliged to transmit the whole than any single part. Even with such small children, where there cannot be any question of any catechetical "system," we have, above all, to proclaim Christ. And we must select the individual doctrines to be brought out from the Bible narratives from this viewpoint: What will best help these children to grasp, in their own way, God's love as revealed to us in Christ? What will help to form them to a Christlike way of life? Thus, in this very first year of instruction we must not introduce more doctrines than will actually serve this purpose, and we must arrange our presentation of these doctrines so that it, too, will aid in achieving our true goal.

How many willing students are there in our Catholic schools, how many well-disposed faithful in our parishes, who have received any amount of religious instructions in school and in church, and yet do not really enjoy the Christian religion? The Christian religion no doubt influences their thinking and acting to some degree, yet the

Christian religion is not, in fact, the great vital force in their lives; the Christian religion does not provide them with a coherent outlook on life; it does not effectively form and unify their living; it does not make them truly happy, as the Good News should do by its very nature. One of the most important reasons for this strange and deplorable fact may be this: religious instruction is often too completely absorbed in teaching particular doctrines and recommending special religious practices, and too little concerned with the joyful message that it is meant to proclaim.

What a vast difference in the whole basic attitude underlying our presentation of religion is made by an apparently unimportant change in order. If we start from the fundamental question of the purpose of human life and present the catechetical content in the once-customary sequence of faith-commandments-means of grace, then the underlying theme will certainly be the chief duties of a Christian, through the faithful performance of which we are to obtain our last end and goal. But if we begin with the fundamental statement of God's fatherly love and interest in us, of how He has called us through Jesus Christ, then we will first show what He, in His eternal love, has done, still does, and will do for us (creed, sacraments), and how we can respond to this wonderful divine love (prayer, commandments). Immediately the incomparable values of the Christian religion occupy the center of our catechetical field of vision, and the content of religious instruction appears as the joyful tidings of God's love, to which we are to respond by a life of grateful reciprocal love.

HOW DOES A GOOD ORDER OF PRESENTATION HELP
BOTH STUDENTS AND TEACHER?

The correct ordering of the subject matter benefits the catechist himself, for it enables us to see the heritage of our faith in its true aspect, so that our proclamation of it will receive the catechetical "tone" and color given by Our Lord Himself. If the catechetical content of religion is presented, as we have said above, as being the proclamation of the eternal love of God for us and our loving response to God's love, and if the individual doctrines are presented so as to flow clearly from this central fact, then a student might not notice how his catechism was divided or he might forget its outline in later life, but he would certainly realize that the Christian religion is the religion of love, and he would find his religion class a school of Christian love, and this is what really counts. For this the catechist himself should grasp the deeper import of the main outline of the subject matter, and in the course of his instructions he should arrange single lessons in accordance with the central thought of the whole.

We may say then that it is not so important always to give each individual lesson in its exact place according to the outline. If every individual lesson is shown in its true perspective, then each part will find its place in one organic whole in the student's mind, together with the knowledge and formation already acquired. And where there is a question of the ordering of religious instruction or discussion topics to be given to adults, greater freedom in the sequence of subject matter, is, generally speaking, allowed and even recommended. In her liturgy Mother Church certainly recommends reasonable freedom in the selection of the themes, and, in any case, rigid systematizing is entirely foreign to the liturgy. The liturgical year, as we all agree, forms a magnificent unity and expresses in a sublime manner the fundamental truths of the Christian religion. And yet, obviously, strict systematization is out of the question in our preaching of the main themes of the liturgical year. What really concerns Mother Church is, clearly, not to fit all her feasts and seasons into a smooth "system," but to see to it that in the celebration of the individual feasts the fundamental ideas of the Christian religion and of all the Christian feasts shine out clearly and impressively.

In giving catechism instructions in school it is certainly advisable to teach, lesson by lesson, according to the order given in a good text unless occasionally there are special reasons for making an exception. This is the only way in which we can have the necessary certitude that the whole treasure of the Christian faith, with all its integral parts, is being treated.

THE LEADING PRINCIPLES TO BE FOLLOWED IN
RIGHTLY ORDERING THE CATECHETICAL MATERIALS

Among the characteristics of a good outline as deemed necessary by modern catechetics are three that are of special interest to us here. A perfect outline must be clear, easily understandable, and essential, that is, it must flow from the essence of the subject matter and so offer a primary means of penetrating into the true nature of the matter to be taught and studied. Clarity implies the need for only a few main topics, corresponding to one another as far as possible, which can be easily read and retained. These topics should contain the quintessence of our religion in as suggestive and absorbing a way as possible. And they should also give us a short and pertinent guide for the whole program of our lives. Mediocre students and simple people must be able to handle them easily and make use of them as a means toward leading a Christian life. The outline, then must proceed from the nature of the subject.

NATURAL DIVISION

An essential outline divides the subject in the way that best corresponds to its nature. In this factor lies the art of making an ideal outline one which will give a comprehensive view of the basic and central idea of the subject, and will present and develop it in accordance with this central point. Only in this way will the main outline provide what it is supposed to—the key to the real understanding of the matter to be presented. The essence of the subject is, therefore, of special significance. For our aim is not to display one or other fact of our religion, but to introduce the student to the spirit of true Christianity and to lead him into the innermost sanctuary of the Christian religion.

Thus, it should be clear that the ordering of the catechism—at least as to its major topics—must not be regulated by considerations of apologetics. Outlines that are apologetically oriented are busy, not with what is most essential according to the nature of Christian doctrine, but rather with the special teachings which are being attacked under the present circumstances. Such outlines place these teachings in the foreground and thus threaten the organic harmony of the whole presentation. Obviously, any vital teaching of the faith must deal with dangerous contemporary errors in an up-to-date and convincing way. But apologetic questions must never penetrate into the innermost sanctuary of our teaching of the faith. They should be dealt with in their proper place in the whole.

In avoiding an apologetic orientation one must not fall into the opposite extreme of opportunism and present only those elements of Christianity which are most appealing. Jesus did not water down His teaching to curry favor; He did not distort it to win acceptance, not even to save His life. The Apostles in their preaching did not conceal the humiliation of Christ's death or the demands of Christian life—for the call to heroism is part of the Good News and reveals to man his own dignity and what he can to with the help of God. The whole of the Christian mystery, both passion and resurrection, must be presented in its organic unity.

THEOLOGICAL RATHER THAN DIDACTIC

Another quality of a proper outline of the catechism is that it should be primarily theological rather than didactic. But what is, according to theology, the main object of Christian revelation? Not the Godhead itself, but the "God of salvation," Who has destined us in Christ to share in His glory. St. Paul calls this the *kerygma,* the message (1 Cor. 1:21; 1 Cor. 2:4; 1 Cor. 15:14), which the herald (*keryx*) of Christ (1 Tim. 2:7; 2 Tim. 1:11; Acts 20:25) is sent to announce. And this message is, simply, "the" mystery, which contains and includes all other mysteries and is designated by St. Paul himself as the "mystery of Christ" (Col. 4:3).

Theology tells us that the Christian religion is, above all, a religion of revelation, the invitation of the divine Father issued through the ages to His beloved children. Our religion is essentially the history of salvation, the glad tidings not only of the magnificent goal to which God has called us but of all that He has done and will continue to do until that blessed day when He will call us all home in glory to our Father's house in heaven. This whole divine work of salvation, from the dawn of creation to our final beatification in the kingdom of the Father, has its focal point in Christ. He is the vital center of the history of salvation: "Christ yesterday, today, and forever" (Heb. 13:8); "for there is no other name under heaven given to man, whereby we must be saved" (Acts 4:12). He is "the way, the truth and the life." No man comes to the Father but by Him (see John 14:6). Has not the Father, with Him, given His children all things ? (Rom. 8:32). For this very reason the Christian religion is, according to its innermost nature, the joyful message of the mystery of Christ, which "has been hidden for ages and generations, but now is manifested to His saints" (Col. 1:26). And since the time of the early Church this message has formed the nucleus and the guiding star of every genuinely apostolic propagation of the faith.

What Is Required?

From this sketch of the essential elements of Christian doctrine the following basic necessities for a good ordering of our catechetical elements are seen as self-evident.

1. Since our teaching essentially consists in the handing on to others of *divine revelation,* it must express as clearly as possible the distinctive character of divine revelation: the gracious invitation issued by God's love, to which our love gratefully responds by faithful obedience to His commands.

2. Since our teaching is the message, given all *through the ages,* of what God has done, is doing, and will do for our salvation, the main topics of the catechism should clearly portray the *historic character* of the Christian religion.

3. Since our teaching must definitely present the history of *salvation,* the ordering of the main topics must clearly present the subject matter as a structure of values, not as a structure of obligations. Our outline must be, therefore, not an enumeration of obligations or duties—which, in the present order, cannot help but seem to be primarily burdens—but must present the Christian religion, according to its true nature, as an unfolding of the highest values, as the proclamation of the glorious messages of joy, which together constitute these glad tidings of the mystery of Christ.

Since our teaching must show concretely how God planned and achieved our salvation through Christ, the main topics of the catechism must clearly indicate the *Christocentric* character of our message.

Toward a Better Division of the Catechism

The former arrangement of the catechism (faith—commandments —means of grace, that is, sacraments and prayer) obviously did not fulfill the demands of modern catechetics as explained above. Starting from the basic question of what man has to do to achieve his final goal, it unfolded the whole Christian message as a system of obligations, not as a proclamation of values, of "Good News." The catechism of old told us what we must believe (creed), what we must do (commandments), what we must use (means of grace). The emphasis of the whole catechism was decidedly on the action of man who has to save his soul, not on the saving act of God. The student almost necessarily got the impression that only the first part of the catechism (what we are to believe) presents God's revelation. The commandments summarized the requirements for man's admittance into heaven; they were hardly seen as man's answer in his dialogue of love with God. The sacraments stood forth as the main resources of the necessary moral strength to keep the commandments, not as the sacred mysteries by which God meets man in the saving acts of Christ and takes him into the intimacy of His own life. The historical and eschatological dimension, both so essential in Christian revelation, did not come into relief, nor did Christ shine forth as the very center of God's loving plan for us. For all these and other reasons the former division of the catechism has been emphatically denounced by all followers of the kerygmatic renewal. It is interesting to note, however, that in the search for a better solution modern catechetics relied on the guidance of tradition and made use of the insights, suggestions, and experience of past centuries.[1]

THE ROMAN CATECHISM AND ITS ARRANGEMENT

Among the catechisms already in existence there is one in particular which opens the way for a satisfactory and positive solution of our problem. It is the so-called Roman Catechism which was published by Pope Pius V, in accordance with a decree of the Council of Trent.[2] As its title expressly states, it is intended for those in charge of souls; and its purpose is to give them authoritative guidance for all the various phases of catechetical instruction. For our purpose here, we should take care to notice that the scope of its directives is by no means intended to be limited to teaching in schools. It includes the general proclamation of the Christian faith.

---

[1] A critical appraisal of the contribution of the past toward a better arrangement of the catechetical material may be found in a series of articles published, almost thirty years ago, in China: J. Hofinger, S.J., "De apta divisione materiae catecheticae," in *Collectanea Commissionis Synodalis* (Peking, 1940), pp. 583–599, 729–749, 845–859, 950–965. On account of the importance of this question for the catechetical situation of prewar Europe, Father J. Jungmann, S.J., made a German summary of the Latin articles: "Die Gliederung des Katechismus in geschichtlicher Beleuchtung," *Katechetische Blätter* (1941), 89–97. See also J. Hofinger, S.J., "Die rechte Gliederung des katechetischen Lehrgutes," *Lumen Vitae*, 2 (1947), 719–741.

[2] *Catechismus ex decreto Concilii Tridentini ad parochos Pii quinti Pont. Max. iussu editus.* Romae, 1566.

Now, how does this "most Catholic" of all Catholic catechisms arrange its material? In four books it treats the four basic catechetical formulae in the following order: the Apostles' Creed, the sacraments, the commandments of God, the Our Father. Could we, perhaps, make use of this sequence today?

This order of its four main topics has a profound meaning and can lead us into the innermost sanctuary of Christian teaching. Looking closely, we see that the first two main sections (the creed and the sacraments) might be combined under an even more basic heading, as might the last two sections (the commandments and the Our Father). St. Thomas Aquinas himself wished to have the teaching about the sacraments given in close connection with that on the creed.[3] And, surely, the sacraments and the divine life which they communicate to us constitute the greatest of the blessings which, through the mediation of the Church, are given to us in the communion of saints.[4] In this light we see that the first two sections of the Roman Catechism show us what God in His eternal love has done for us, what He is doing now, and what He will do until we attain our full participation in the glory of the First-born; in other words, these two sections give us the history of the eternal love of God for man. And the two following main sections show the right response of redeemed mankind to this eternal love: love for Love. Our grateful answering love manifests itself in the first place in prayer, which is the loving, upward look of the child to his Father, and by the keeping of His commandments from a heart filled with love.

PERFECTING THE ARRANGEMENT OF THE ROMAN CATECHISM

The doctrine on the sacraments should, whenever possible, form an organic part of the teaching given on the third section of the Creed itself. Symbol and sacraments should no longer be presented

---

[3] St. Thomas Aquinas, *De articulis fidei* (ed. Mandonnet, II, 1); *Expositio super Symbolo Apost.* (ed. Mandonnet, IV, 381).

[4] St. Thomas explains the word *sanctorum* in the Creed as being the genitive of *sancta*, that is, of *res sanctae*, the good things of salvation, among which the sacraments are supreme. So also the Roman Catechism, I, 10, 22. Concerning other catechisms see J. Hofinger, S.J., *Geschichte des Katechismus in Österreich* (Innsbruck, 1937), p. 150 ff. For the entire question see also J. Jungmann, S.J., "Die Gnadenlehre im Apostolischen Glaubensbekenntnis," *Zeitschrift f. kath. Theol.*, 50 (1926), 196–219.

as two closely linked or even interlocking basic formulae of catechetics; they should be fused into one harmonious whole, the history of the eternal love of God, the chief phases of which are already
fittingly indicated in the Apostles' Creed. "The sacraments," says
Father Jungmann, "should not be taught simply as theoretical
points of doctrine; they should rather be combined with the doctrine about the Church, its nature and growth; and we should
show at the same time that they [the sacraments] accompany the
life of the Christian, from his entrance into the Church until his
going home to God."[5]

The ordering of the second main section of the Roman Catechism (consisting of the last two topics as given above) could be
further perfected by placing the doctrine on prayer first and then
that on the commandments. Such an arrangement would be more
in line with the best psychological order. The gratitude of a
redeemed child of God expresses itself above all in true, spontaneous, childlike prayer (Rom. 8:15; Gal. 4:6). Such a presentation of
Christian prayer gives priority to the prayer of praise and gratitude,
which indeed should dominate the prayer life of true children
of God. Here would be the ideal place for teaching the Mass, our
highest act of prayer. For in the Mass, more perfectly than anywhere else, we offer to the Father in heaven our common homage
of grateful love through and with and in Christ, our head and mediator. The observance of the commandments follows from this.
What we offer and promise by taking part in the Mass—our complete surrender to the Father—must be carried out in the daily
humdrum round of a Christian life, in the faithful and loving
observance of the commandments.

Furthermore, by juxtaposing prayer and the sacraments the
nature of the sacraments as Christian prayer will emerge. The recip-
ient of the sacraments is not purely passive. He is to be actively
engaged, fully aware of what he is doing. Thus the sacraments
include both God's gift of Himself and our reponse of loving faith.
They are our encounter with the triune God.

Finally, it would be of great advantage to the whole order of presentation if the two main sections of the catechism (the love of God,
our response) were each preceded by a short introduction. As

---

[5] Joseph Jungmann, S.J., "Katechetische Fragen im deutschen Sprachgebiet,"
Lumen Vitae, 1 (1946), 66. Confer also J. Hofinger, S.J., "The Apostles' Creed Is
a Real Prayer," *Lumen Vitae,* 9 (1954), 193–208.

Father Jungmann says: "At the beginning of the catechism there should be a short chapter which, like a frontispiece, or a basic chord, contains in brief what is to follow. In this, Christ should come before the eyes of our mind, as He Whom God has sent into the world, Who calls us and invites us into the kingdom of God."[6] By this means, the contents of the catechism would, from the outset, be characterized clearly as being Christian revelation and, more directly, as being Christ's message, and thus the mind of the Christian would be from the beginning directed toward the figure of Christ.

THIS IS THE APOSTOLIC METHOD

The order of presentation given above can rightly claim to resemble the apostolic method of teaching. When the Apostles went out to proclaim the truths of the faith, their teaching was characterized by the fact that it was the values of the Christian religion that they developed most of all to their wondering hearers. On the feast of Pentecost, "drunk" with enthusiasm, filled with the Holy Spirit, they went out to announce "the wonderful works of God" (Acts 2:11). This was their general and common theme. The bare sketches given us in the Acts of the catechizing of the two princes of the Apostles show the same structure. First, the values of Christianity are unfolded, and this is done mainly by pointing out what God has done in the history of salvation. And then the duties of a Christian are explained. Particularly characteristic is the first mission sermon of the first Pope. The theme of his sermon is: Now the fullness of time has come, in Jesus Christ the Messiah, Who was crucified and lives again. Only when the listeners themselves ask, What are we to do? does He impress upon them their particular obligations (Acts 2:14–41). From such value-saturated, apostolic, doctrinal teaching came the glowing zeal of the early Church and its astonishingly vital religious energy.

SIGNIFICANCE FOR ANY FORM OF CATECHETICAL APOSTOLATE

Obviously, the ideas we have just been discussing are valid not only for religious instruction in schools but for the whole field of

---

[6] J. Jungmann, S.J., "Katechetische Fragen," p. 66; see also *Handing on the Faith* (New York: Herder and Herder, 1959), p. 140.

the catechetical apostolate, for the solid instruction of adults as well as for the Christian formation of children. In the following part of this book we shall try to present an exposition of our Christian message according to the order of presentation that we have just recommended, and, by so doing, we shall indicate how this arrangement may also be used in giving sermons to the faithful.

An important point to be considered here is how to provide the necessary variety in our religious instruction. Even the most perfect arrangement of the subject matter, if repeated too frequently, will not be effective. If a guide must show the beauties of the Swiss Alps or the sanctuaries of Rome to the same group of people again and again, would he always lead them by the same route, or would he not rather strive for variety? The same should be true of us who are guides to the beauties and treasures of the kingdom of God.

The principles to be followed here are the following:

1. From the upper grades on all the principal doctrines of Christianity should be presented in a way adapted to the age and maturity of the students.

2. We must not present the particular doctrines each time in the same sequence or from exactly the same viewpoint.

3. Nevertheless, each time we must show the particular doctrines, especially the fundamental ones, in their inner connection with the real center of the whole, that is, the mystery of Christ. Thus, for example, in teaching the commandments to adolescents we should, more fully here than in the lower classes or later on in college, discuss the problems concerning the development and formation of personality. But we should deal with these problems as being internally connected with our final task as Christians: the formation of Christ in us and how we are to serve God by cooperating in this task with filial love.

4. Whatever order of presentation we may use—and we must change this in order to provide needed variety—it must fulfill the requirement of any sound arrangement, which we explained above.

CHAPTER NINE

Catechetical Method
As Handmaid of the Message

Modern catechetics is characterized by the shift in emphasis from method to the content of the message. This shift, however, in no way minimizes the role of method in the catechetical apostolate. It leads rather to a deeper and fuller understanding of the task and special qualities of a good catechetical method. The first period of the catechetical movement brought about a remarkable increase of teaching techniques. We learned to use a concrete presentation of the subject matter, to use audiovisual aids, and to promote class activities. All these, and other techniques, spell progress in teaching the religion lesson. But this most opportune progress, in fact, quite often resulted in a one-sided concern with, and in a naive overevaluation of, the methodical aspect of catechetics. Not a few catechists expected the solution of all their problems as a result of being acquainted with the "latest" catechetical methods. A good painter must of course know the various techniques of his art. He also will appreciate being provided with the "latest" and best kinds of brushes and pencils. But even a collection of the very best tools and a perfect acquaintance with their use will not, of themselves, produce a good painter.

Thus it is quite understandable that after a short period of undue emphasis on teaching techniques the best leaders of modern catechetics cautioned the catechists against a threefold danger in this regard. There is first the danger of isolation. Method is seen no more as a means, but as an end in itself—this quite often being the case more in practice than in theory—and, therefore, method is developed independently from the message and the teacher whom it has to serve. At the very moment when method is no more seen in its proper perspective, there is also no longer a criterion for the right selection and use of the appropriate manner of teaching which is needed in a given situation. Thus method necessarily becomes stiff and mechanical.

The second danger—resulting from the first—will be an entangling multitude of techniques and methods, but none of them used in its proper way. If method is not seen anymore in the light of our catechetical task, there is finally a third danger. It is that we may appropriate techniques of teaching which are fully in accord with profane subjects, but meaningless or even harmful in religious formation.

In order to avoid these dangers, modern catechetics turned its primary interest in the field of method from the particular techniques to the basic principles which are at the root of any valuable teaching technique. They finally provide the norm for the necessary qualities of any particular technique and determine how it must be applied in a given case. These principles form what we would call the basic catechetical method.

MANY TECHNIQUES, BUT BASICALLY ONLY ONE CATECHETICAL METHOD

Just as the many particular doctrines have to be conceived and displayed as organic parts of one divine message, in the field of methods, too, the many techniques must be seen and valued as modifications and special aids of the basic catechetical method. It is in this sense that the "Program of the Catechetical Apostolate" which has been worked out at Eichstätt speaks of one catechetical method and calls it "our method." This method is not just a product of modern psychology, discovered and developed in the last fifty years. "Following God's method," it is based on "God's own way of winning men. The wonderful works of God as narrated in the Old Testament, the miracles, discourses, and events in the New Testament, lead us to an understanding of the divine message and its impact on our lives."[1] Our method is characterized by God's own gracious adaptation to our mind.

Here, too, we learn best from Christ. What method finally means appears clearly in the teaching of the greatest catechist who ever lived. We let Christ continue His special way of teaching in His faithful instrument. Even as man He has a much more sublime and

---

[1] Program of the Catechetical Apostolate. Basic Principles, no. 9. See the appendix of this book.

perfect knowledge of God's mysteries than any other messenger. And yet He was successful in conveying "the mysteries of the kingdom" (see Matt. 13:11) to the uneducated farmers and fishermen of Palestine. "No man has ever seen God; but now His only-begotten Son, Who abides in the bosom of the Father, has Himself become our interpreter" (John 1:18, Knox). Method means for us essentially this art of "interpreting" the content of our message to our actual audience.

THE PARTICULAR FUNCTION OF METHOD

In view of this outlook we immediately understand the basic principle for any good method. By its innermost nature it has a twofold relation. First it must be suited to the nature of the particular subject matter we are teaching. We do not teach religion as we would arithmetic, geography, the classics, or spelling. Method is the art of transmitting a given doctrinal content to others. As we do not present to others jewelry and ordinary food in the same kind of wrapping, neither do we transmit religion and geometry to students by the same teaching method. Religious teaching demands a method in keeping with its nature. Second, method also must be adapted to the students whom we are teaching. By adapting as perfectly as possible to their mental capacity and individual differences we want to make them capable and ready to understand and—what means so much more—to accept God's message as perfectly as possible. Like Christ, we respect in our teaching the fundamental laws which God Himself has established once and for all for the process of human learning and formation. We progress therefore from the concrete to the abstract; we ascend from the visible to the invisible; we abhor any premature use of long technical words, abstract definitions, scholastic formulations; we decline any overemphasis on systematic teaching.

From all this it is obvious that a perfect method means perfect adaptation to all those who are to be taught. In order to be perfect this adaptation must take into account the laws of human psychology which are valid for everyone who belongs to the human race. Everywhere in the world the intellect will grasp most easily that which we present in a concrete way through collaboration of the senses; everywhere it needs appealing and enduring motives to stimulate to generous and lasting actions. But besides this basic adaptation to the universally valid laws of human psychology, good teaching also requires adaptation to the special condition of the students, to their age level and standard of education, to their racial, cultural, and social differences. This is of special importance in mission catechetics, when the missionary has to address people who may be quite different from him in their way of thinking, feeling, reacting. Since we are the agents of Christ, we have to follow His unique example. Sent to us from heaven, He became a Jew with the Jews, a farmer with the farmers, a child with the children of Palestine. St. Paul followed Him in becoming "weak to the weak," in becoming "all things to all men" that at all costs He may save some (so according to the original text, 1 Cor. 9:19–22. See also Rom. 1:14). This adaptation, if taken earnestly, necessarily leads to a divestiture of the teacher. We find and admire it as most perfectly realized in Christ, Who "emptied himself taking the nature of a slave and becoming like unto man" (Phil. 2:7).

Service, indeed, seems to be the key idea which lets us understand best what a good method is and how it works: it has to serve the catechist in his apostolic service. One method is as good as any other so long as it helps the teacher to convey his subject matter to the student. It is a means; it does not work by itself, but needs a skillfull and clearheaded teacher who uses it for his own aim. The aim, of course, is to convey the Christian message to the student, and this, not just in some way, but in a most life-giving manner. It must help him not only to know but to live this message of life. Thus, catechetical method is also essentially enlisted in the service of the message. One of the finest talks at the International Study Week in Eichstätt had as its topic "The Catechetical Method as Handmaid of the Kerygma."[2]

Method must serve the teacher in transmitting his message, but the teacher must be fully aware that method must also enable him to serve his students. The catechetical apostolate is, in essence, service we render to our brethren in Christ who are committed to our loving care so that we may serve them in developing their life as children of God and brothers and sisters of Jesus Christ. He provides them spiritual food through us.

[2] J. Goldbrunner, "Catechetical Method as Handmaid of Kerygma," in *Teaching All Nations* (New York: Herder and Herder, 1961), pp. 108–121.

THE LEARNING-TEACHING PROCESS

Our service may be compared in some way with the service of the cook who provides us with the necessary and fitting food for our body. He is, of course, not supposed to eat in our place, but through his service he must help us to eat well and, by doing so, make us grow and become strong. In the same way the teacher cannot learn in the place of his students, but he must provide his students with the necessary fitting spiritual food: he has to help the student learn, he has to help him as much as possible in this process of learning, or let us better say, in the process of formation. Here already two basic principles of any good teaching are manifest. The first is the principle of activity. Since the process of learning and formation means essentially activity of the student, a good method has to render this activity possible, has to inspire it, to guide and to develop it. Second, the way of teaching has to adapt itself as perfectly as possible to the process of learning. This psychological process has its specific stages like the physiological process of nutrition. The main stages are admittedly the following three: perception (taking in the food), assimilation (digesting it), response (receiving new strength that results in action). It is the task of the teacher to follow and to help his student in all stages of his learning. Thus we arrive at a threefold activity of the teacher; to each stage of the learning process corresponds a special step in the process of teaching: presentation, explanation, application.

Perception-Presentation. The student's mind has to be provided with new material, new elements for his intellectual and moral formation. It has to be fittingly presented by the teacher in the right quantity and be well prepared so that the student likes to take the portion presented to him and is able to digest it.

Assimilation-Explanation. Any new perception, any new knowledge or experience, will help the process of formation only insofar as the new elements are well integrated with the intellectual and moral capital which the student has stored up beforehand. Just as in the process of nutrition only that food counts which is digested and assimilated into the human body, so in the process of formation only those elements are of formative value which enter an organic union with the material already acquired and stored by the learner. Explanation is the aid by which the teacher facilitates and fosters the process of assimilation.

Response-Application. We learn not for the school, but for life. What we learn in religion must bring us nearer to God, must bear fruit in our life for and with God. Through the step of application the teacher orientates the students toward this aim of religious formation.

That the three stages of learning necessarily follow one another in the sequence we have just indicated is a basic law. It is true that they are not always distinctly separated, that one sometimes turns into the other, but the direction of human learning as a whole is decidedly going on in this direction: perception, assimilation, response. Thus it is quite understandable that in the teacher's service we must find the same direction; in the process of instruction, therefore, we rightly distinguish as the corresponding three main steps presentation, explanation, application. They too are not always distinctly separated—quite often explanation and application are already sufficiently included in and given with a good presentation. But in order to show clearly the task of the teacher, we have to deal with them separately. Here, too, what we inculcate is, not mutual separation of the three steps, but their mutual collaboration and their natural sequence in the whole process of teaching.

By a simple analysis of the process of learning and teaching we came to distinguish the three main stages of learning and teaching. Since we are here concerned with method, we considered the whole process first from the viewpoint of educational psychology. But in our catechetical apostolate method and psychology are entirely in the service of our religious task of forming true Christians. We therefore rightly ask about the specific religious function of these main stages known as presentation, explanation, and application. Seen under its theological aspect, our catechetical teaching—in the classroom and in church—has a twofold basic function. As God's spokesmen we bring God's life-giving message to our audience and help them to respond to it in their life. Thus "message" and "response" are the main stages of any genuine catechesis. Like the stages of presentation, explanation, and application, message and response too do not need to be always neatly distinguished, but they must virtually present and shape our catechesis.

In teaching catechetical method it is necessary to let the future catechist consider his teaching method from a thoroughly religious viewpoint. It is for this reason that the best catechetical texts for teachers now usually structure the catechetical lesson into preparation, message, and response. The stage of message contains in fact presentation and explanation, while response is equivalent to application.

At first catechetical method had often been presented too exclusively from its psychological aspect. Now we may sometimes risk the danger of minimizing the important contribution which psychology has to give in the field of catechetics. The ideal solution consists in making full use of educational psychology, but always seen and applied in the light of the specific religious task we are to fulfill as God's spokesmen.

PRESENTATION BEGINS WITH A CONCRETE IDEA

The presentation is by far the most important part of a good lesson. We understand this easily from the comparison of our service with that of a cook. If the food is well prepared and presented in a most appealing way and in fitting quantity, digestion will not be difficult and new strength will result by itself. Three questions may help us to explain the special task of the teacher in this basic step of any teaching. *What has to be presented?* Substantial food, of course, if we want to get students who will grow strong in their religious life. What this substantial food means in our case we have already studied in a preceding chapter, and we shall deal with this important question throughout the whole second part of this book. Here it is only necessary to note that every religion lesson must offer some substantial portion of the rich treasure commissioned to us by the Lord. Something that is of real importance to the students we have before us. There is no need to provide new subject matter in each particular lesson. Sometimes we just deepen what the students have already learned by some fitting activity or by a fine recapitulation. But even then we have to come back to the essential points of Christian doctrine and present them under a new aspect.

How much material has to be presented? As to quantity of subject matter, the teacher may learn again from a good cook. The criterion for determining the quantity of food obviously is not what can be eaten, but what can be digested without overburdening the digestive organs and what is most conducive to restoring the body to its full strength. A cook is supposed to prepare food in more or less equal portions, and the teacher will do well in following his example.

How is new subject matter to be presented? Since we are here concerned with the right manner of teaching, the question of "how" to present the material is most pertinent. The comparison with nutrition of the body immediately provides the two main rules. From a good cook we expect above all that he prepare his dishes in an appetizing manner. A first glance and a first mouthful should stimulate appetites even in those of his guests who are just not hungry or suffer from some indisposition. The cook would first serve some appetizer. We teachers know from our daily experience that most of the students do not come hungry to the spiritual meal we are serving them. Here too it needs some appetizer. That is precisely the function of the first part of presentation, called *preparation* or *orientation*. It has to arouse the interest of the student. He must get the impression that there is something fine for him. It may be worthwhile to note that for the start of a good religion lesson it is not enough to awaken "some" interest. What we need is the student's interest in this very subject we are going to present; we need his "religious" interest. More than in other subjects it is in the religion lesson that the student must follow with his heart and with his personal interest. We shall try to arouse in him a fitting mood from the very start of the lesson. There is no fixed rule on how to introduce a new lesson. Sometimes we start from a recapitulation of the former lesson and develop the new lesson from the preceding one; sometimes there is no need of any preparation separate from the main topic of the lesson. In other cases we may first present a short introductory story, some current event, or some striking experience from the student's daily life. In any case a good preparation has to be interesting and short. It must win the interest of the student for the particular subject of this lesson.

Cooking means furthermore a way of making the food digestible. Even the most excellent basic foods like meat, rice, and potatoes need cooking before we can eat them. In this "dressing" we rightly see the most important task of the cook. In the process of learning we find very much the same again. Here, too, the new material must be presented in the right dressing so that the mind can spiritually digest, or assimilate, it. The cardinal rule for this spiritual digestion is this: the intellect of youngsters and of uneducated adults can only grasp what is presented to it *in a sensory way*. The intellect depends upon sense information to perceive, to operate, to produce ideas. We should never begin with an abstract notion, never with an abstract statement, never from an abstract formula or doctrinal text such as we may find in a catechism. This abstract doctrinal formulation may later on very well be the point of arrival—through the following explanation—but never the point of departure. By stressing this we simply follow Our Lord's way of teaching. He never taught by using abstract ideas but began with a concrete presentation: "Consider how the lillies of the field grow. . . ." "The kingdom of heaven is like a treasure hidden in the field. . . ." "I am the good shepherd. . . ." "I am the true vine, you are the branches." He did not begin his teaching on sin with a definition; He began with a story, the story of the prodigal son. And with this story He made crystal clear what sin really is, and how bad and disastrous it is.

Since the presentation is quite often a story, in many books of catechetical method this first step is simply called the "story." This may lead to some misunderstanding. To teach his class well the catechist must, above all, plainly understand the meaning and function of this fundamental step in a good instruction. The intellect of the student cannot grasp abstract truths if they are not first presented in a concrete way. This concrete presentation can be and very often is a fitting story. With the story of the prodigal son or with the story of Adam and Eve we teach what sin is; with the story of creation we teach God's omnipotence and love. Instead of the story, or better, in combination with it, we may present a catechetical picture. We also can appropriately start from some direct observation, from religious objects or ceremonies and actions we have first looked at or, even better, in which we have taken part; we also can analyze some common experience we thoroughly know from our daily experience. The decisive point is always this, that we present every new notion and truth first in a suitable concrete realization from which we lead gradually to the understanding of the religious truth.

Thus it is obvious that a good religion lesson is essentially more than just a nice story. The story is by its nature a means; it serves to grasp the sacred truth we want to convey to the student. Since the story is a means, it has to be fully adapted to its end; it must make an organic unit with the following explanation. We have to choose just that story, just this "dressing," which fits best the doctrine we want to explain. The "story" has to provide not only the intellectual elements we need for the understanding of the doctrine but also the affective elements needed to evaluate it rightly and to see its importance for our life.

The best source of stories for the religion class is the Bible. But there is no objection at all against using stories we may bring from the lives of the saints and also from daily life. Even those taken from daily life have to be given in the religious atmosphere which is imperative for the religion lesson. But this religious atmosphere in no way forbids cheerfulness; it rather demands it.

EXPLANATION UNFOLDS THE RELIGIOUS CONTENT OF THE LESSON

In the step of explanation we teachers are in a much better position than the cook in his service. After he has served his dishes, his work is finished, and he has no means to help further our digestion. Not so we in our service. By a follow-up explanation we can help the student in the process of assimilation. Although the "story" already contained the doctrine, a follow-up explanation can make it more explicit and it can greatly aid the student in becoming fully conscious of this doctrine; what we have presented in the form of a concrete case has now, in explanation, to be grasped in its universal validity; now we are allowed to develop abstract general notions from the concrete particular case. From the story of Adam's sin, for example, we are able to show what "sin" is, and by working out this general notion we arrive at a full understanding of what the catechism teaches about sin. Explanation must help the student to integrate the new subject matter into the whole body of his religious formation. The doctrine of sin, for instance, must be well explained in the light of God's life-giving love and His lordship. Only in this light can we grasp the ingratitude of sin and its malice. The student has to understand how by committing sin his life takes a wrong turn. We should show God's attitude toward sin by pointing to God's just punishment. The student must learn from the fact that God hates sin but is nevertheless so merciful toward the repenting sinner. The step of explanation must help join all these and other doctrines into one doctrinal organism.

From all this it is quite obvious that a good explanation must form a very close unit with the presentation. In the same way we may compare the aid we render the student by our explanation with a pill by which the physician stimulates and helps our digestion. He would not give more than necessary. We, too, should be brief to achieve a good explanation by giving just what the students need for their religious understanding of the new subject matter according to their level of age and education. The pill has as its special aim to stimulate the activity of our digestive organs. In a very similar way a good explanation should stimulate the activity of the students, help them to think, to find, to formulate, to evaluate the doctrine which is virtually already contained in the presentation. Explanation, therefore, needs discussion, needs the participation of the whole class. But the teacher guides his class toward the end he has in mind. At the end of the explanation the whole matter should become so clear that it can be *summarized in some precise sentences*. What the students have learned may now be immediately applied and deepened by an appealing class activity.

APPLICATION OF THE LESSON TO CHRISTIAN LIVING

Modern catechetics stresses strongly that the aim of catechetical work is not mere knowledge, but "lived" religion. Our students must know how to apply to their lives what they learn in the religion lesson; they must be stimulated by efficacious motives to live their religion. It is in the step of application where they receive this orientation to Christian living. The whole catechesis from its beginning needs orientation to life; throughout the whole instruction we have to show winningly the attractive beauty and the motivating importance of the doctrine we are dealing with. Thus it may happen quite often that we do not need any much-developed, separate application at the end of the lesson. A short final appeal or motivation, perhaps accompanied by a concluding story, will be sufficient. A good application must flow spontaneously from the preceding presentation and explanation. Especially with the explanation it forms a very close psychological unity. It is essentially more than some "doing" at the end of the lesson. Application means, above all, that the student seizes the importance of this religious truth for his life; it means that he is ready to live this truth in his life. Often we should discuss with our students, especially in the upper grades, what the import of a given doctrine is for our life; we should guide them toward precise and firm resolutions. We should lead them to express and to practice these resolutions by prayer. Chiefly in the lower grades we should lead them through prayer toward achieving the end of the catechism lesson. In any event, we should make it very clear that the Christian religion means life, means activity according to our faith. By stressing all this we should, however, never overlook that the task of the religion lesson is essentially the founding of the basic religious attitudes toward God: faith, filial reverence, confidence, submission, love, in one word, an ever-growing surrender of our whole self to God. Particular acts count in religious education insofar as they are the genuine and spontaneous expression of these basic religious attitudes. Modern catechetics emphasizes animated religious activity, but it hates superficial activism. Here the principle "Non multa, sed multum" is in its proper place.

VARIOUS TECHNIQUES OF TEACHING

Throughout all parts of the religion lesson the teacher has to use many techniques. They have to be understood as aids to vitalize the whole lesson and to attain as perfectly as possible the aim of the whole lessson and of its particular parts. Modern catechetics has developed a great number of such techniques and appreciates them. The International Study Week at Eichstätt in its "Program of the Catechetical Apostolate" relates a long list of techniques which the catechist should cultivate in his lessons.

"*Means to awaken interior activity*. Create an atmosphere; present a reality, bring forward its meaning, show its bearing, define it; establish comparisons with other facts or truths, a motivation, proofs; draw conclusions, present a clear summary, a repetition; drive home a point, an application, bring the lesson into contact with daily life, lead to action, arouse consent.

"*Means to stimulate exterior activity*. Narrate an event, make observations, ask questions, elucidate, show an object, cause reflection, give an explanation, start a discussion, read aloud, make others read (each one by himself, or one reading aloud, or several in turn), a recitation, learning by heart, interrogate, direct practical exercises, choral recitation, drawing either in the copybook or on the blackboard. Assign tasks and make the pupils look for facts, classify them, reflect on them, formulate them sometimes before and sometimes after the class. Assign home-work, and make them keep a note book.

"Also, hold a singing practice, recollect oneself, pray; exhort them to examine their consciences, meditate, hold a liturgical service. Celebrate a feast, stage a playlet with different actors, prepare an exhibition. Finally, use audio-visual aids, wall pictures, flannelboards, slides, tape-recordings, gramophone records."[3]

But in connection with this long list of particular techniques the same Study Week also inculcates a clearheaded use of them. "*Have recourse to pedagogical techniques* in order to give variety to the

[3] *Teaching All Nations*, pp. 403–404.

lesson and to stimulate the interior awakening and the exterior activity of the hearers. The use of techniques offers the catechist the possibility of winning not only the intellect but the whole being of the person, namely, mind, heart, imagination, creative ability and power of expression. He must always remember that these diverse means have one goal, to help the catechumen to open wide his heart to the activity of the Holy Spirit."[4]

What the statement of the International Study Week inculcates so well with regard to the techniques of teaching is most significant in considering the broader question of how modern catechetics sees and develops catechetical method. Formerly, catechetical method was, above all, considered as the special aid by which we help the student to "learn" well his religion lesson. Today we still want to transmit solid religious knowledge to the students. But we want to do much more, and we expect the catechetical method to enable us to do more. This new attitude toward catechetical method and its primary task was expressed in pertinent form by Father Goldbrunner at the Eichstätt Study Week: "Catechetical method seeks to reach the human person and to make him religious, so that his religion will not be a mere form but his very life. That is why method must do more than instruct, it must address man personally. It must have insight into man if it is to succeed in awakening his interest, so that he will become personally involved in what he is learning, will come to understand it, relate it to his life, will say Yes to it, will even change his life in accordance with it."[5]

This chapter is intentionally limited to the most basic aspects of catechetical method. There are today a good number of excellent books that present it in more detail. But no real acquaintance with these details can take place without a very clear insight into the main function and the most basic principles of catechetical methods. The catechist will be able to evaluate and to use them only insofar as he is able to understand and to apply them in the light of the leading principles which constitute basically one catechetical method, God's own pedagogy in teaching men.

[4] *Ibid.*, p. 403.
[5] J. Goldbrunner, "Catechetical Method as Handmaid of Kerygma," in *Teaching All Nations,* p. 109.

Part II

The Content of Our Message—

The Joyful Tidings of Jesus Christ

THIS IS THE MESSAGE WE PROCLAIM:

In His infinite goodness,   (Eph. 2:7)
the Father in heaven has called us   (1 Pet. 5:10)
to be united with Him in life and joy,   (John 17:21)
sharing His divine riches: (Eph. 2:7)

through Christ, His Son—   (1 Pet. 5:10)
Him He gave as a ransom for us sinners,   (1 Tim. 2:6; 1 John 4:10)
and into His likeness He desires that we be conformed,   (Rom. 8:29)

so that, born anew of water and the Holy Spirit,   (John 3:5)
and thus made partakers of the divine nature,   (2 Pet. 1:4)
we may be children of God.   (1 John 3:1)

And because we are God's children,
He has sent the Spirit of His Son into our hearts: (Gal. 4:6)

thus being the temple of God,   (1 Cor. 6:19)
we are to live the life of God's children,   (Rom. 6:4)
following the example of Christ, our first-born brother,   (Rom. 8:29)

so that we may gain the kingdom of God and His glory,
as heirs of God,   (1 Thess. 2:12)
joint heirs with Christ.   (Rom. 8:17)

INTRODUCTION

In Part One of this book we have repeatedly stated that the major concern in catechetics now is not method but content. The method must be at the service of God's message.

The Second Vatican Council reminded us of our duty to reform the Church in accordance with the Gospel and to discuss the word of God with our fellow Christians so that we may proclaim it more faithfully and effectively in the world of today.

Although to a superficial observer the reform of the liturgy, especially the changes at Mass, may seem to have affected externals, in reality these changes—and those to come—are made to make God's message stand forth more clearly in its essentials. For example, the dramatic separation of the liturgy of the word from the liturgy of the Eucharist—a separation made visible to the congregation by the double procession of the entrance rite and the offertory, by the station of the celebrant at the sedilia or pulpit instead of at the altar, by the full use of the vernacular in the liturgy of the word—shows forth the basic pattern of message-response which characterizes the relationship between man and God. In the liturgy of the word full attention is given to God's word of love. In the liturgy of the Eucharist we answer God in thanksgiving and love by giving ourselves to Him in union with Christ and by receiving from Him Christ, His living word, in the life-giving sacrament of the Eucharist.

It is simple enough to state that in catechetics we should present the essentials of Christianity. But what are these essentials? How are they to be presented in organic unity?

Part Two of this book is an attempt to answer these questions. Here we try to work out a compact presentation of Christian doctrine that incarnates the principles of kerygmatic preaching and teaching.[1]

[1] The original form of these ideas was published under the title *Nuntius Noster, seu themata principalia praedicationis christianae* (Tientsin: Seminarium

The development given here is not the only possible arrangement of materials. Some may feel that it is not even the best arrangement. They might prefer to integrate the sacraments and the commandments into the account of the history of salvation itself, so that at each step the continuity between God's actions in the past and the present and the need for a response now might be forcefully presented. For example, when teaching of creation, one could develop baptism as a new creation and explain the proper response of adoration and gratitude which we as creatures should make to our loving Creator. This response is best made in prayer, especially the Eucharistic prayer of the Mass. The sacrament of marriage could also be connected to the story of Adam and Eve; the sacrament of penance to the fall of our first parents. An imaginative regrouping of materials in this way could be very effective in demonstrating that God is ever active in history, ever summoning us to deeper union with Him.

However, we have chosen to separate creed, sacraments, prayer, and commandments in order to give a more thorough and comprehensive treatment to each element.

These elements of Christianity are arranged into some thirty-six lessons and are intended for adult Catholics. They may be particularly apt for a course for CCD teachers or a discussion group. Our aim is to offer, not fully worked out sermons or lessons, but merely outlines that will indicate the essential points of our teaching and how all together they form one message: the mystery of Christ. When we are dealing with non-Christians or even with Christians who are investigating Catholicism, some modifications of this sequence of lessons would be preferable.[2]

Regionale Kinghsiense, 1946). A Chinese edition was published in 1947, and also an edition containing both the Latin and Chinese texts. An expanded adaptation in French was published in 1955: *Notre Message, Principaux Thèmes de la Prédication Chrétienne*, Traduction adaptée par J. Seffer, S.J. (Brussels: Lumen Vitae, 1955). The material given here is an expanded English adaptation of the original notes.

[2] There is no treatment here of the first approach to be made to non-Christians (preevangelization). That does not pertain to the kerygma, but it is a preliminary stage.

For those who are "catechumens" in the broad sense (that is, without yet an act of Christian faith and conversion of heart), it would seem best to begin by bringing them to an awareness of how they are encountering God existentially through the love and concern of some Christian—the missionary, their Christian spouse, or some friend. Then this love can be traced back historically to Christ,

Our chief purpose here is to show how the kerygmatic spirit actually influences the selection and arrangement of topics, the manner and method of presentation of each doctrine, and the particular fruit to be sought from its teaching.

We hope, then, that this part of the book may assist the reader in his own meditations on the truths of the faith and enable him more clearly and fully to see each doctrine in the light of the mystery of Christ and that he may also find this material capable of being adapted in various ways according to his own particular needs.

Preliminary Instruction

THE RICHES OF OUR VOCATION—THE FATHER CALLS US THROUGH CHRIST TO HIS KINGDOM

Aim: The aim of this preliminary instruction is strictly preparatory. Like the foreword of a book, it should give an idea of the whole without going into any details. It has a function similar to that of the overture of an opera: it should win interest, bring in the leitmotiv of the whole work, create the right attitude.

Method: The same method should be used as in the subsequent instructions. We start from some concrete presentation. Here, as in the majority of the lessons, we begin with a Bible narrative that contains and presents the doctrine we wish to set forth. In our narration of the story we must keep in mind the doctrine

so that they discover Christ and His love for them, now operative in someone whom Christ has sent forth to carry on His mission of spreading the Good News and to whom He has confided His Spirit, Who enables them to love like Christ. Once their interest has been aroused by an existential experience of God, and the contact with the historical Christ explicitly clarified, the sequence of lessons given here may be used with profit. Or one might start with the mysteries of Christ's life, death, and resurrection, and then turn back to the Old Testament for a fuller understanding.

For those who are "catechumens" in the technical sense of one who has already heard of Christ and accepted Him by faith and is preparing for baptism, these lessons in a simplified and adapted form will give an adequate and balanced view of the whole of the Christian life. Vatican II distinguished between the stages of evangelization and the catechumenate in its Decree on the Church's Missionary Activity, nn. 13 and 14.

Furthermore, it is not the purpose of these condensed outlines to provide teachers with material they can use without further adaptation for the catechism class in a school.

which this narrative is to explain. The narration, therefore, must be given in such a way as to develop all the elements that will facilitate the subsequent or concomitant explanation. In this preliminary instruction the narration begins with the stirring fact that God's only-begotten Son came to teach us and bring us a great message from His heavenly Father. Through the parable of the wedding feast we shall try to give the central idea of Christ's message and of how we are to respond.

Viewpoint: The special aspect under which this lesson is to be presented is that of God's love, at once stirring us and obliging us to respond. God has called us because He loves us and wishes to enrich us with His own life and fullness, but He expects the response of our grateful love to His loving invitation. Thus we give at once the the leitmotiv of our whole message: love for Love.

DOCTRINAL SUMMARY

A. THE FATHER HAS SENT HIS SON TO TEACH US

Christianity is by its nature the doctrine of Christ; its very name reminds us of the incomprehensible fact that God has sent His only-begotten Son to teach us. "God, Who at sundry times and in diverse manners spoke in times past to the fathers by the prophets, last of all in these days has spoken to us by His Son, Whom He appointed heir of all things, by Whom also He made the world" (Heb. 1:1 ff.). It is obvious that the message which He brings us from the Father must be an extremely great and important one. If it were not of supreme importance, the Father would have sent one of His angels. But this was a message which only the Son of God could fittingly proclaim: "No one has at any time seen God. The only-begotten Son, Who is in the bosom of the Father, He has revealed Him" (John 1:18). God spoke to us through His only-begotten Son because He wished to speak to us precisely as "Father." In return for His great love, He expects us to receive His completely paternal revelation with a completely filial attitude, in faith. What, then, is His message?

B. CHRIST PROCLAIMS THE "GOOD NEWS OF THE KINGDOM OF GOD"

In the years of His public life Christ spent all His time, with complete devotion to the task given Him by His Father, in announcing His message. Christ preached many single doctrines during His public life, yet His whole teaching, finally, was concerned with one central message, "The Good News of the Kingdom of God." St. Mark summarizes Our Lord's teaching in the characteristic expression: "He was heralding the joyful tidings of God's kingdom" (Mark 1:14. This is according to the Greek text. See also Matt. 4:17–23 and 9:35). It was the same message that His disciples were to proclaim when He sent them out to preach (Luke 9:2–6). What He meant by this Good News of the kingdom He explained to His disciples and to all His faithful followers in many parables, one of the most meaningful of these being that of the wedding feast.

C. The Father Calls Us to the Great Marriage Feast

"The kingdom of heaven is like a king who made a marriage feast for his son. And he sent his servants to call in those invited to the marriage feast . . . saying 'Behold, I have prepared my dinner . . . everything is ready; come to the marriage feast.' " But they would not come. "Then he said to his servants 'go . . . therefore to the crossroads, and invite to the marriage feast whomever you shall find.' And his servants went out into the roads, and gathered all whom they found, both good and bad; and the marriage feast was filled with guests" (see Matt. 22:2–10).

This parable shows us the kingdom both in its final consummation and in its present stage of preparation. At the end of time God will manifest His power and love with perfect clarity and fullness. Then will He glorify His Son, and with Him those of us who have responded to His invitation. The kingdom of God in its final stage of completion is like a wedding feast, to the degree to which any earthly realities can in any way give us some faint notion of the incomparable delights and glories which the Father, in His love, has determined on from all eternity and made ready for His beloved children. In this heavenly wedding feast God the Father is the king, Christ is the bridegroom; we are not guests only, since the bride is redeemed mankind; the new creation made perfect will be the banquet hall. God wants to give all of us a share in this final manifestation of His divine power and love. For this reason has He sent His Son, Jesus Christ. Jesus has proclaimed the kingdom of God; He has redeemed us and made us children of God.

This kingdom is now still in its preparatory period. But through Christ it has already come to us. God now reigns as our loving

Father and gives us a share in His divine life. Christ, the divine Bridegroom, is already in our midst. In the Eucharistic banquet we already participate in the eternal wedding feast. But the full glory of God's kingdom is still veiled. *Now we must decide; now we must prepare ourselves.* God's call is transmitted to us through Christ and His heralds, and we must respond to it by *Christian faith.* This is much more than a merely intellectual assent to some religious truths revealed to us by God. Faith is, finally, the grateful readiness of our Christian hearts to receive God's word as fully and actually true, and to act accordingly, to follow the loving invitation of the Father. To His love, which we have done nothing to deserve, we respond by our grateful love. In His unfathomable goodness He has called us "into fellowship with His Son, Jesus Christ our Lord" (1 Cor. 1:9). We are to answer gratefully by our union with Christ. All our glory, all our riches, are in Him.

The Eternal Love of God
for Us

GOD THE CREATOR

From the very beginning we should strive with all our skill to give to our students (catechumens, congregations, and others) a truly magnificent idea of God. The decisive importance for any religious life, and particularly for the Christian life, of a realization of the overwhelming greatness of God can hardly be sufficiently inculcated. This is the foundation of any religion worthy of the name. For religion essentially consists in the acknowledgment of the absolute excellence of God and of our complete dependence on Him. This is the first of the two pillars of the Christian religion: the Great God is my Father in Christ! A lack of this foundation results in a lack of vigor in our entire religious life. No one wants to try to do great things for an insignificant God. We cannot rightly understand or appreciate the basic teachings of Christianity unless we first are possessed by a great idea of what God is. Without this the thought of the grace of adoption as His children does not move us, sin does not frighten us, the person of Christ does not attract us, His work does not appeal to us, heavenly life does not arouse us.

In teaching about God the Creator three principal truths must be inculcated at every opportunity:

1. *The reality and nearness of God.* God is to be thought of, not as a distant God Whom we know to exist, but as the *real* God, near each of us. He is not an abstract idea, a postulate of philosophy; He is the reality of realities. He influences our living at every moment, and we should therefore have Him always present to the eyes of our mind. "In Him we live and move and have our being" (Acts 17:28).

2. *The greatness of God* (His infinite majesty, perfection, immensity). His greatness should be shown, not by abstract reasoning, but vividly and concretely through the teaching on creation, with examples from observation and the natural sciences (astronomy,

physics, biology). Although God is so great, yet He loves me, a little creature; He created me out of pure love, He cares for me, and calls me to Himself. O wonderful mystery of love!

3. *Our absolute dependence on God.* I depend upon Him far more completely than a sunbeam on the sun, more than a newborn baby on its mother. He is our absolute master and lord: " 'You are my God.' In Your hands is my destiny" (Psalm 30). How foolish is any attempt to flee from Him—foolish since it is absolutely impossible, and even more foolish since no one loves me so much as does He.

First Instruction

THE ETERNAL GOD AND HIS CREATION

Method: Historical-explanatory. The "historical" fact of creation should be set forth in an orderly way and explained at the same time. It is important here not to separate the narration from the explanation anymore than is absolutely necessary. Although the instruction uses the beautiful narratives of the Bible, emphasis should not be given to the works of the individual "days." What God wants to teach us is not the exact sequence of His work, but the basic doctrine that everything in heaven and earth is the result of His creative power.

Viewpoint: "The heavens declare the glory of God, and the firmament proclaims His handiwork!" God's greatness and goodness are shown in the work of creation. It is the first step taken by the eternal love of God in our regard. How fitting and necessary it is that we should, in return, thank Him, love Him, serve Him!

Aim: Happy and grateful acknowledgment of the absolute dominion of God. Real acknowledgment, not mere assent. Truly You are the Lord! To serve You freely is my first duty and my special privilege. "Pay to the Lord the homage of your rejoicing, appear in His presence with glad hearts" (Psalm 99).

DOCTRINAL SUMMARY

A. THE ETERNAL GOD

Our teaching can well begin with the presentation of the eternal God, Who possesses all things, Who is perfectly happy from all eternity. What a difference between us mortals, who yesterday did not exist, and the infinite eternal God, the "immortal King of the ages"! (1 Tim. 1:17).

Why did God create anything? Not out of any need of His, but because in His inexpressible love He wanted to communicate His goodness to us and share His riches with us. From the beginning of creation He thought of each of us and prepared everything for us. Let us return love for Love!

When does God create? Creation did not just take place ten billion years ago. As an act of God it is taking place now. God exists and operates in an eternal present. At each instant my being is precarious and tends to nothingness—I depend on God for my existence, my life, my thoughts, my desires.

How does God create? Personally, in an act of knowledge and love. He chooses deliberately to create. What security and confidence I should have in His love!

B. THE CREATION OF THE WORLD

"Let there be light and there was light." What "creating" means should be carefully described and explained. Use comparisons with human making. A carpenter makes a table: What is the difference between what he does and the creative activity of God? Here a mere definition explains nothing. The students must be brought to experience the wonder of what God alone can do. How much the dominion of God over His creatures differs from any human mastery over what we have made or rule. Our return, then, should be grateful and absolute submission.

He extended the heavens in His mind (see Isaiah 40:22; Jer. 10:12; 51:15; Ps. 135:5). Behold the greatness of God! The teacher should have ready striking examples using modern statistics about the number and size and vast distances between the stars. This greater-than-imaginable space is the "small" workshop of our God. He Himself cannot be contained by the heavens (3 Kings 8:24). How small we are in the face of the greatness of God! How wonderful, how fitting, it is to serve so great a God! God planned all the marvels of creation, He "thought them out," He cares for all. All things are His.

He prepared the earth (Isaiah 45:18) for us men, His children. He made it ready for us with fatherly love, with fatherly providence.

And He saw that all things were good (Gen. 1:25). He created them well, beautifully, abundantly, wisely. We also can see that they are good. Praise the Father Who made everything so well. We praise You, O God! How can we express our gratitude and praise in deeds as well as words? By the *right use* of God's creatures, in accordance with the natures He has given them and has given us; by the *right love* of the world which is so good, by sharing God's love of what He made.

All creatures, insofar as they are objects of God's love, have an intrinsic dignity. This should influence our attitude toward the material world in science, by seeking to understand it; in technology, by seeking to bring it under ordered control; in dealing with animals, by not causing unneccesary pain; in dealing with other men, by esteeming them as persons loved by God and destined to rule over creation with Christ.

C. THE CREATION OF MAN

Let us make man (Gen. 1:26). The most solemn moment in the work of creation. The whole earth awaits its king and priest, who will be the crown of visible creation. All things are prepared for him.

Bearing Our image and likeness (Gen. 1:26). This is the true value of man, of each man. The more like God he is, the more perfect a man he is. Man is like God in knowing, in loving, in working creatively, in ruling the world.

God formed man's body and created his soul. The whole man is *from* God—therefore the whole man is *for* God. If we owe gratitude to our parents, how much more to God! I give You thanks for the life You have given me. Gladly will I live my life, and may my joy in living and all my vitality be a continual thanksgiving. Body and soul—both are good and holy to God. The body should be ruled by the soul, and the whole man ruled by God and ordered to His praise and glory. All is Yours, my God, and by rightly using my soul and my body I return them to you in grateful praise.

By work man exercises his kingship and brings the powers of the world under control. By prayer man exercises his priesthood and voices intelligently and freely the praise and adoration which all creation gives to its Maker. Nothing is so fitting to man as to pray, to acknowledge from his whole heart the goodness and dominion of God. *Worship* is the highest and noblest act of man, and, even more, the goal of human life. *Work*, too, is an indirect worship, the embracing of God's will in such a way as to share His responsibility for bringing the act of creation to completion.

NOTES ON TEACHING THIS MATERIAL

1. Our negative purpose here is to overcome religious indifferent-ism and negligence. God really *is;* we cannot escape Him; we should *want* to fit ourselves into His plan for our happiness. Reli-gious indifferentism is the worst spiritual disease of our times. So many people go to God only when they think they need His help or when they "feel" religious.

2. Today every definite idea of God as a person and every attempt to clarify our relations with Him are frequently regarded as either vain superstition or foolish irreverence toward the holy and myste-rious. In instructing adults the teacher or missionary should frankly acknowledge that God is beyond human comprehension; try as he might, man will never be able to plumb the depth of God, even in heaven. Only God fully understands Himself. Yet God in His love has revealed Himself to mankind in words and images which man can grasp. Instead of abandoning us to some vague religiosity or hesitant conclusions about the characteristics of "a higher Power," God has satisfied our longing to know Him by a progressively fuller self-revelation, which reached its climax in Christ, the Word-made-flesh.

In an age when agnosticism and atheism are raising and intensi-fying doubts, the religion teacher should be prepared to explain clearly our reasons for affirming God's existence and to answer the usual objections. At the same time he should realize that faith is not the conclusion of a syllogistic process and that the most per-suasive argument to convince a doubter is the witness-value of his own Christian life.

3. In missionary work, especially with neophytes and catechu-mens, we ought frequently to speak of the existence of the one true God and of the incomplete recognition of God outside Christianity. Special care should be taken to show the truth and value of the native religion—and how this is preserved and enriched when seen as part of the totality of what God has revealed of Himself. Where crass idolatry and superstition exist and threaten belief in God's absolute dominion, they must be corrected. But it is even more important that those who would never dream of adoring a god of wood or stone should be warned against the practical idolatry of living only for "security," "success," money, and such, and of vener-ating those who possess these things as if they were gods.

4. With regard to *evolution* explain that the purpose of God's revelation is to teach, not scientific truth, but religious truth: to tell

us about God and the relationship of man and the world to God. Man does not need a special revelation to discover the truths of natural science. The account of creation in the Bible neither affirms nor denies evolution. It describes the origin of matter, of life, and of man not to satisfy our curiosity about prehistory but to impress us with God's power and wisdom. From the very beginning God has had a plan, and history is the unfolding of that plan; its details are left for us to discover. From time to time God reveals His plans evermore clearly, but it is always some aspect of man's union with Him that God reveals, not mere physical fact.

5. With this lesson on God and His creation it is not the mind alone that must be captured but the heart also, and the whole man must be directed to the happy and constant service of God. These truths must be presented *clearly,* for our submission to God must be founded on firm and comprehensible reasons if it is to endure. And they must be presented *beautifully* in such a way as to bring our hearers to love this great and wonderful God.

Second Instruction

THE ELEVATION

The natural gifts God has given man splendidly demonstrate His love for us; His supernatural gifts show that love even more splendidly.

Method: Why did God give man all these gifts so copiously, so magnificently? Because He had decreed to adopt us as His children. A catechetical exposition of this material, unlike the scholastic one, should avoid all subtle inquiry into the nature of supernatural being. We wish to unfold above all the beauty and greatness of the heavenly gift.

Viewpoint: The inexpressible goodness and generosity of God. How wonderfully well He treated our first parents! How great was their obligation and their opportunity to thank Him unceasingly! (This forms the psychological preparation for the next lesson.)

Aim: A sense of truly filial gratitude. This attitude manifests itself in the prayer of God's children: "Abba, Father" (Rom. 8:15). From the very beginning let us teach Christians to pray in a filial way to the Father. This is the classic form of Christian prayer which ought to hold the primary place in our whole Christian life. For this essentially is the truly Christian life: continual filial prayer to the Father by words and by living and acting as His children.

DOCTRINAL SUMMARY

A. The Paradise of Our First Parents

God made man the lord of visible creation "to rule over it" (Gen. 1:28). Man is the vice-regent, the administrator of God. The first obligation of an administrator is fidelity (1 Cor. 4:2). We have to "render an account of our stewardship" (Luke 16:2). The guiding principles of our use of creatures should be given here: we are to *use* them according to the natures God has given them, *not abuse* them. We are to *use them, but not in an unlimited way.* Creatures should lead us to God, not separate us from Him by undue concern for them. Right use means to receive everything from His hand with gratitude and to use things in His service. How many great gifts He has given us in creation; with what great gratitude should we respond!

God gave the world a potential for growth and perfection. He gave man the wisdom and power to discover and develop that potential, so that the whole of creation is at the service of man—not for selfish exploitation, but to sustain the whole family of mankind on its pilgrimage to God.

God created man for happiness: a wonderful life with the companionship of God. A life worthy of man—no idleness, but free, enjoyable, and effective work. Internal and external peace. Human love and affection without shame. No fear of death such as we experience now.

But the true paradise was in man himself. The garden was only a picture and an effect of the internal paradise. All these other gifts were given to our first parents because God had adopted them as His children. This gift of adoption is the greatest gift God can give His creatures. It is the principal gift, which necessarily and in due time brings with it all other gifts. It is the gift of God's pure generosity, and it is of such a nature that no creature can demand it as a right. Compare it with natural gifts, possessions, physical and mental talents. Do not use often the terms "supernatural life" or "sanctifying grace," but thoroughly explain the reality itself.[1]

Divine adoption is essentially superior to human adoption: it gives not only a name and a right but real participation in the divine nature. It is one of the three greatest mysteries of our religion (the Trinity, the incarnation, our adoption) from the theological point of view, still greater and more fundamental than the mystery of the Eucharist. We shall never be able to understand how we creatures are truly able in a completely real sense to participate in the divine life and yet remain creatures.

B. OUR PARADISE

The garden of paradise has been lost to man, but the internal paradise, far more beautiful and wonderful than the external one, now exists in the hearts of Christians. We Christians possess the greatest gift given to our first parents—divine adoption. How rich we are! Can we help being grateful! Our adoption is the guarantee that the gifts that flowed from it in the first paradise—harmony between appetite and reason, between body and soul, between man and the rest of creation—will also be given to us in due time. And not only these joys of paradise but higher and heavenly ones. We are immensely rich now, but our riches are for the most part an internal, hidden treasure that we cannot be naturally aware of. They must at this time be believed in. Lord, I believe. *I believe in my own blessedness. I believe in Your love* (see 1 John 4:16).

NOTES ON TEACHING THIS MATERIAL

1. Here we mention for the first time the great gift of our religion: divine life, the gift of sonship. From now on we should take every opportunity of inspiring our hearers with the greatest possible appreciation of this supreme gift. This initial teaching on the divine life will be complemented especially by the teaching on baptism.

[1] As an example of how to explain the "supernatural order" without using the word "supernatural" or even "grace," see the *On Our Way Series,* by Sister Maria de la Cruz Aymes (New York, Sadlier), especially Grade One, lesson 23, and Grade Two, lesson 4. In later years we shall introduce and use the usual technical words; but even then we will have to work hard to keep the students conscious of the wonders expressed by these words.

2. In presenting the story of the creation of man make clear that the Bible does not pretend to be a scientific textbook. It is a *religious* book with a *religious* message, a message about man and his relationship to God. The author of the Genesis account, looking back over the history of his own Hebrew people, sees that God has always intended man's good and happiness; disorder and suffering are the results of man's sinful folly. God made man as the climax and crown of creation, possessing a physical solidarity with the material universe and a spiritual solidarity with God Himself, while transcending the level of all other creatures. Human sexuality is good; it underlies human interpersonal communion (Pastoral Constitution on the Church in the Modern World, nn.12, 24). Woman is an equal helper and partner to man; each brings the other to perfection.

The picture of order painted in Genesis is *true,* but it is not intended to be the *whole* truth. It is presented by way of contrast to highlight the disorder inherent in sin.

Third Instruction

THE FALL: ORIGINAL SIN

To the wonderful goodness of the Father our first parents responded by disastrous ingratitude; they destroyed their own blessedness by their sin of disobedience.

Method: Here again this should be biblical rather than scholastic.

Viewpoint: See the detestable ingratitude of our first parents. Their sin is the prototype of all mortal sin. Here we see our own image as in a mirror.

Aim: A truly religious *awareness of the malice of sin,* a real hatred of sin, the hope of forgiveness through the Redeemer, a serious will to satisfy for our sins.

DOCTRINAL SUMMARY

Our first parents were greatly blessed by God. How would we expect them to have responded? How did they?

A. THE FIRST SIN

God gave a special command to our first parents in order to test them. He wished to give them heaven, a perfect paradise, after their life in the earthly paradise, but not without a trial. They had to merit the perfect blessedness of sons of God by obedience and submission to Him. And we must do so also. The command given to our first parents was easy to obey in every way. How easily could they—and so also we—have continued to be happy. For God had given them paradise and the gift of sonship not simply for themselves, but for us also.

Our first parents were tempted by the devil, who hated them and their happiness. God wants us to be happy; the devil wants us to be miserable. God loves us and speaks the truth to us; the devil hates us and tries to deceive us. The devil contradicts what God has said. To be tempted is not to sin. But Eve played with temptation and argued with the devil.

Our first parents, deceived by the devil, sinned grievously. What did they do? *Knowingly and freely* they transgressed a serious command of God. Although they had received such great blessings, they were not content; they wished to be "like God," to be independent, a law to themselves. They deliberatedly rebelled against their most loving Father.

This is the essence of a mortal sin (in this supernatural order: the fully deliberate rebellion of a proud and ungrateful son of God against the most loving Father. Every mortal sin of its nature entails *ingratitude* (abuse of God's blessings), *pride* ("like God"), and *insolent disobedience* ("I will not serve").

B. THE DISASTER OF SIN

As soon as they sinned, our first parents *lost the paradise of the soul.* They had cast God out of their minds and hearts; He left them, and darkness came over their souls.

The all-knowing God *called them to be judged.* They wished to hide. But God sees all things. We cannot flee from God. Did they come to their senses and seek forgiveness? No, they tried to excuse themselves. They persisted in their sin. Out of harmony with God, they now experience disorder in all its forms—they feel shame; they try to shift the blame onto another or even onto God Himself; they find the material world hostile and resistant; pain and death become symbols of the moral death their sin has caused.

The dreadful consequence of their sin is that they lost once and forever the happiness of paradise for themselves and for their children. Comparisons can be made here with a father who squanders his family's inheritance or the servant of a king who wastes the treasures the king has given him for himself and his children. God wished to have us receive from our parents the treasure first given to Adam. But that treasure is gone. Such comparisons bring out fairly clearly two important points: (1) The state of original sin is the privation of the divine treasure (divine life) which, according to God's original plan, we should possess. It is the consequence in us of Adam's disobedience. It makes it easier for us to disobey in our turn, to commit our own personal sins. 2) Adam's *personal* sin had this disastrous effect on us because he was given divine life not only for himself but for all his descendants. He was somehow responsible for all mankind, as a king is responsible for his people, a father for his family. From the time of Adam human children are born, not into a well-ordered paradise, but into a world permeated with sin and suffering. So the *greatest gift* of God to man is divine adoption; the *greatest calamity* is loss of this divine life, mortal sin.

C. THE ONLY HOPE FOR MAN AFTER SIN

God in His loving mercy promises a Savior to our first parents. In the midst of disaster, when they had rejected God, God consoles them. Thus for us the only consolation and hope of the sinner is Christ, the Savior of the world!

NOTES ON TEACHING THIS MATERIAL

Once again the students should be reminded that the author of Genesis saw the creation and fall of man as a key to explaining man's sinful state as he experienced it in his day. The religious message of the story of Adam and Eve is true, but incomplete. The Old Testament, and even Genesis itself, has far more to say about man. The New Testament goes much further. As Christians we read the Old Testament in the light of the fullness of revelation given us in Christ. Because we are familiar with the whole symphony, we more readily recognize subtle variations of the theme which might otherwise escape notice. This is the function of the Holy Spirit in the Church—to call our attention to all the details of God's revelation to enable us to respond to Him with deeper love and gratitude as we better understand what He is saying to us.

Important as is the doctrine of original sin, it should not be made the central teaching about sin. Actual sin is much more central in importance throughout the whole Bible and in a Christian understanding of life. Our own choices for or against God are to be illuminated by reference to the sin of Adam.

The story of the fall of Adam and Eve should not be told to a little child. Otherwise the child receives a very distorted impression of God. He will compare the punishment of Adam and Eve with punishments he has received for eating a piece of forbidden fruit— and God's action will seem unnecessarily harsh.

Nevertheless, the child at an early age has experienced in himself the results of others' negligence or hostility. He can appreciate the connection between physical evil and sin. This should be part of his formation of conscience, particularly with regard to his own responsibility toward others.

When the story of Adam and Eve is told to children, it must be explained very clearly that this is about *adults,* that it is a fully deliberate rejection of God and His plan for them, and that, therefore, the punishment is severe.

Fourth Instruction

THE COVENANT

The basic theme of the Old Testament is the covenant made between God and His people. God wants to lead man to a life of full union with Him. God's invitation and man's response set the pattern fundamental to salvation history.

Method: Historical-narrative, based on the events of God's interventions in history.

Viewpoint: The unwearying goodness of God despite the perversity of man's sinfulness. Over and over again God rescues man from the consequences of his faithlessness. Man is grateful for awhile, and then he succumbs to pride.

Aim: A deep trust in God's abiding love and a *desire to be correspondingly faithful.* Man's attitude to God should now assume the overtones of gratitude and renewed self-dedication characteristic of a sinner who has been fully pardoned and restored to friendship.

DOCTRINAL SUMMARY

A. THE DELIVERANCE FROM EGYPT

After the fall of Adam, man sinned more and more. Genesis balances the account of mankind's progressive deterioration against God's ever-renewed mercy. No matter how evil the world becomes, God is ready to give it a new chance by raising up someone to be another Adam, another source of life and friendship with God. This is the theme of the sagas of Noah and Abraham. Through Abraham God will form a new people and make them a means of salvation to others. But the children of Abraham, too, fall into sin.

The Book of Exodus opens with a picture of utter degradation. *The people of Israel*—nomad tribes of mixed Semitic origin, related to Abraham through his son Isaac and his grandson Jacob—*have been enslaved by the Egyptians. To save them from their enemies God sends Moses, the supreme prophet* (spokesman for God, messenger of the Old Testament). By God's power Moses becomes the founder and leader of a new nation. Through him God works a series of wonders, and the Egyptians allow him to lead the Hebrews out of their country. Later the Egyptians change their minds and send troops to stop them. But the Hebrews cross the water barrier to safety, while the enemy troops are destroyed. This great act of saving power was seared indelibly on Israel's consciousness: God does love; God does hear the prayers of His people; God does break into human history to rescue his people from the consequences of sin. Christ's redemptive mission is a repetition and completion of the deliverance of man from the powers of evil. By the sacrament of baptism God continues to free His people, through water, from slavery to this world in order to bring them to His Promised Land. God's great actions are not something of the past, over and done with. As the Book of Deuteronomy reminds us, they still happen to us today. Even now God gives us freedom.

B. THE COVENANT OF SINAI

God sets man free from evil in order to bind him more closely to Himself. Once the Hebrews had escaped from Egypt, God gave them food and drink to keep them from perishing in the desert. But He did even more. He made an alliance with them by adopting them as His sons, binding Himself to protect them, and asking of them in return exclusive loyalty to Himself and obedience to His commands. The people agreed to recognize God as their protector and to observe His Ten Commandments, and sealed the alliance by a solemn sacrifice and a sacrificial meal.

From this point forward the Israelites interpreted all of God's dealings with man in terms of a covenant relationship and recast the whole of human history in this mold.

Adam is taken by God, put into a paradise, nourished by him, and given a command. Noah is rescued from the Flood and given an eternal covenant. Abraham is given circumcision as a sign of his covenant. Later on God enters into a covenant with David and promises a new covenant to be written on men's hearts, not on stone. Periodically the great covenant of Sinai was solemnly renewed—if not each year, at least at certain great turning points of Hebrew history. The annual Passover meal reminded the Hebrews of God's saving acts. In fact, every liturgical sacrifice to God symbolically reaffirmed the alliance between God and His people.

Gradually the initiative of God stood out in clearer relief as a free and unmerited loving choice. The covenant was understood to be a marriage contract by which God took Israel to be His spouse. His love calls for a return of love.

This love is given Him in Christ, the mediator of the New Covenant, to be sealed in His blood and effectively redeem all men from evil.

C. THE INFIDELITY OF ISRAEL

Despite God's mighty signs of love His people show themselves fickle. After their rescue from Egypt and before the covenant they had murmured against God and His providence. Even while Moses was receiving from God the terms of the covenant, they turned to idolize gods they fashioned for themselves. This infidelity is often repeated in their later history, and God sends other prophets who like Moses remind the people of their responsibilities toward God and call them to return to His love.

D. THE WANDERING IN THE DESERT

Before crossing the Jordan into the Promised Land, the Israelites wander about for a whole generation. Scripture describes this experience in various ways. (1) It is a period of *training, testing, purification.* (2) It is the *honeymoon stage* in God's dealings with His people, when He is especially tender and close to them. His presence is manifested by the ark, the cloud, and fire. (3) It is a *period of great temptations, apostasies, rebelliousness.* Unlike Israel, Christ conquers the temptations He faces in the desert. He sends His Spirit to write His law of love upon the hearts of His people of the New Covenant, so that we, too, may reach the Promised Land in safety and fidelity.

NOTES ON TEACHING THIS MATERIAL

1. These Old Testament events need be studied, not in isolation, but to convey a sense of the meaning of sacred history, which throughout constant variations remains always the same: God is master of the universe; He constantly acts out of love; He rescues man from evil.

2. These events must also be considered as preparing man for the coming of Christ, in Whom God's saving love stands fully revealed. We must not limit our attention only to Old Testament prophecies about a future Savior. The entire Old Testament tells us something about God and man, and this helps to a fuller understanding of the incarnation, where God and man are joined together in the unity of one Person.

3. The liturgy of baptism and the Eucharist make frequent reference to these events. Some idea of the application of sacred history to our own lives through the sacraments could be developed at this point.

Fifth Instruction

TYPES OF CHRIST

The last instruction called attention to certain events which revealed God's master plan of salvation and foreshadowed the mystery of Christ. Here several persons important to Old Testament history are seen in their relationship to Christ.

Method: Historical. First these types are presented in their own context and with their own immediate significance; then their deeper meaning as living "prophecies" of Christ is set forth. Four major categories are considered: Christ's identification as a human Son of God, his functions as priest, king, and prophet.

Viewpoint: Understanding the marvelous preparation of God's people for the incarnation should arouse admiration for God's patient adoption to the limitations of human psychology.

Aim: Appreciation of the background of Christ and His functions as regards His people.

DOCTRINAL SUMMARY

A. MAN AS SON OF GOD

Mankind's adoption by God has already been mentioned in connection with *Adam.* The theme becomes much more clearly pronounced in the biblical account of the Exodus. *Israel* became conscious that God was their Father, Who nourished and protected them. Because the *kings* somehow summed up the whole people in themselves and bore a responsibility for them, each king was called "son of God." Because of the messianic promises given to the royal line descended from David, the title "son of God" pointed not only to an adoption by God in the past but also to a future king who would be "Son of God" par excellence.

As applied to Jesus, the title "Son of God" means not simply messianic power but a unique relationship to God as Father. He is not an adopted son, but God's "only-begotten" and "well-beloved" Son, with Whom the Father shares all that He is and has and does. At the same time He is the second Adam, the new Israel, the son of David—and therefore fully human, the perfection of humanity and head of our race. Through union with Him we share in His Sonship.

B. PRIEST

Genesis has many persons who exercise the role of priesthood and therefore reveal something of the mediating function of Christ, Who gives perfect worship to the Father: *Abel, Noah, Abraham, Melchizedek.* Abel is a model of the interior dispositions of sincerity which must accompany sacrifice. Noah offers the first covenant sacrifice. Abraham is ready to give his dearest possession, his only-begotten son, Isaac, but God reveals that He does not wish death but life and assumes the responsibility of providing a suitable victim Himself. Melchizedek possesses a royal and eternal priesthood, and is superior in dignity to Abraham himself (see Hebrews 7).

Later Hebrew priests were not only liturgical mediators, presenting to God the offerings of the faithful and transmitting to them the divine blessing. They also exercised a guardianship over the Word of God, the traditional descriptions of God's mighty deeds and the clauses of the covenant of Sinai. During the liturgical celebration of the feasts they would recite to the people the history of the events of salvation and proclaim their meaning. Thus they became the interpreters of the law and exercised a judicial function.

Jesus did not call Himself a priest, for He was not of the tribe of Levi. Nevertheless, He claims that His death is a New Covenant-sacrifice in which He is both priest and victim. He comes to preserve the Law and bring it to completion by giving His own Spirit to enable us to fulfill it with love.

C. KING

To the Hebrews God Himself was king. Yet He shared his royal prerogatives and powers with certain men who were to protect God's people, conquer their enemies, and promote justice and peace. In the early history of Israel *Joseph, Moses, Joshua,* and the "judges" carried out these functions of leadership and responsibility. Later *David* and *Solomon* were true kings, though not without their serious faults. David is a model of humility and fidelity to the covenant; Solomon is praised for his prudent judgment. Since so few of the later kings lived up to the lofty ideals intended by God, the prophets criticized them severely and looked forward to a future king who would inaugurate the kingship of God over the people and usher in an age of joy, peace, and justice for all mankind. In Christ these expectations were fulfilled.

D. PROPHET

The New Testament expressly compares Jesus to several prophetic figures of the Old Testament—*Moses, Elijah, Elisha, Jonah, Jeremiah, the Servant of Yahweh.* A prophet is one who is God's messenger and spokesman. God's Spirit puts His word into the prophet's mouth; it is through the prophet that God continues His dialogue with His people by tenderly reminding them of His love or sternly calling them to repentance. The very deeds of a prophet are often more eloquent than his words—the marriage of Hosea and the sufferings of Jeremiah are a stirring and powerful message to Israel.

The prophetic mission is to be the conscience of Israel, fiercely loyal to the God Who saves, implacably opposed to all that can turn man from God. This springs from a vivid awareness of the living God, His holiness, justice, and fidelity to His promises. His intense concern with the present relationship between man and God colors the prophet's attitude toward the future. To limit prophecy to foretelling the future is to adopt too narrow a definition: prediction is only secondary in importance. Yet because the prophet is so conscious of God's holiness and man's sin in the here and now, he warns of judgment to come and looks forward to a new creation and a New Covenant, a new Lord, a new temple, a new King, a new Priest.

Jesus not only fulfills these prophetic expectations; He is a prophet Himself. His ability to read the signs of the times, His severity against hypocrisy, His purification of the temple, His demand for penance, His fidelity in preaching God's message no matter what the consequences to Himself—no wonder that the people recognize Him as a prophet sent by God. He is the very Word of God enfleshed! He inaugurates the last age of the world, yet points beyond Himself, beyond all time to the perfection of this age which is still to come.

NOTES ON TEACHING THIS MATERIAL

1. This is an ideal opportunity to urge our students to become very familiar with the Old Testament. All of it remains valuable and meaningful to us if it is rightly understood. It is a key to a deeper penetration into the mystery of Christ. If we wish to know God and Jesus Christ Whom He has sent, we must frequently ponder His word, preserved for us by the Church in holy Scripture. The few examples mentioned in this instruction should whet the appetite for this food by which man lives.

2. As an alternative, if pressed for time, you might prefer to study in depth two or three of the figures presented. Abraham, Moses, and David would be the most appropriate, for they enjoy the titles and perform the functions in a dramatic fashion.

3. Brief allusion to the appearance of these types in the liturgy, particularly the Mass and the Lenten cycle, is profitable.

THE DOCTRINE OF CHRIST THE SAVIOR

The teaching about Christ the Savior is the heart and center of our message, and to it the catechist should give his greatest care and diligence. "This is eternal life—that they may know thee, the only true God, and Jesus Christ whom thou hast sent" (John 17:3). The doctrine of Christ our Savior not only gives us the knowledge of the Son of God but also shows us the Father Himself in an entirely new light. Here especially we must lead our hearers from the knowledge they are gaining of Christ to a further knowledge of the Father.

What is the essence of the doctrine we are to teach and explain? Jesus Christ—the Son of God—the Savior. (Here we might bring in the ancient Christian symbol, the fish, showing that the Greek word *ichthus* contains the initials of the fundamental formula: *Jesus Christos—Theou Uios—Soter.*)

a. As to the *personality of Christ—Who is He?* He is at once true God and true Man: one Christ, the eternal Son of the Father, born in time of the Virgin Mary.

b. As to the *work of Christ—What does He do?* He was made the "Son of Man" to make us sons of God, ". . . who was delivered up for our sins and rose again for our justification" (Rom. 4:25). He not only destroyed sin but communicated to us in abundance the new and true divine life by opening again the gates of paradise. He instituted a new order of things: "The former things have passed away; behold they are made new!" (2 Cor. 5:17). In this new creation there is a new man, renewed in Christ, a "new creature in Christ" (2 Cor. 5:17), and a new way of living, "so that we all may walk in newness of life" (Rom. 6:4). Christ is the new and perfect Adam, the leader and head of a renewed human race. Just as all our misery comes from our physical oneness of race with the first Adam and from our personal imitation of his example, so all our salvation and happiness flow from our real spiritual oneness with Christ through baptism and from our continual and increasing daily transformation in Christ (the Christian life).

c. In our teaching the person and the work of Christ must always be shown to be intimately connected, even though at one time we stress doctrine concerning His person (the mystery of the incarnation) and, at another, doctrine concerning His work (the paschal mysteries).

Method in which all these lessons should be taught: Without any haste. This teaching, like a long-lasting and fructifying rain, should water, penetrate, and fructify the ground of the Christian heart. We should give the impression that we are always eager to speak about Christ, His most sacred person, His life, passion, and resurrection, and to remain close to Him. Our hearers should become aware that we cannot help returning at every opportunity to this, the fundamental theme of our Christian teaching and preaching.

Our teaching should use the method of concrete historical narration. By telling the life of Christ in a concrete and attractive way, we can unfold and explain the mystery of Christ. Thus we can avoid both the abstract dogmatic exposition which simple people and children cannot follow and also the *mere* historical narration which only gives the outward events of sacred history and does not rise to their inner divine meaning. By narrating historical events we lead to a deeper understanding of the mystery of Christ and its bearing on our Christian life. This does not mean however that narration—explanation-application must always be separated parts of the catechetical instruction. It is by means of this retelling of the life of Christ, above all, that we desire to draw the hearts of men to the love of God. So our narration should strive to be pleasant, fervent, clear, and filled with true and reverent affection for our Lord.

Viewpoint: "God so loved the world . . ." (John 3:16) ". . . giving us such and so great a Redeemer" (The Exultet).

Aim: To arouse deep and habitual gratitude to God the Father. To lead our hearers toward a truly "eucharistic" life. Unfailing thanksgiving for our elevation in Christ is of the very essence of the Christian life. To lead our hearers to a full and completely personal giving of themselves to God (faith, love, fidelity): "Whether we live or whether we die, we are the Lord's" (Rom. 14:8; see also 2 Cor. 5:15). Christ should be our mediator also in the psychological sphere. First we fall in love with Christ, and then He fills our hearts with love for His Father.

THE SECOND EVE

Our teaching concerning the Blessed Virgin, the second Eve, should be harmoniously interwoven with, and duly subordinated to, the teaching concerning Christ the Savior, the new Adam. We should present this teaching in a completely Christocentric way: all the perfection and beauty of the Mother comes from the Son and leads us to the Son. We want to share in Christ's own estimation of His Mother, and so we speak of her with gladness and filial affection. But we should be careful to present true Marian dogma, entirely drawn from Christology, the doctrine of the new Eve who is of such great importance because of her intimate connection with the work of our salvation. Here again we should remember the principle "not too many words, but much teaching." The perfection of preaching and teaching about Our Lady consists, not in an extended and separate treatment, but in allowing our teaching concerning her mainly to flow from that about her Son. If we properly present our instructions on the person and work of Christ, we shall at the same time instruct our hearers in the dignity and the work of the Blessed Virgin. Chapter five of the Dogmatic Constitution on the Church of Vatican II is an excellent example of how to describe Mary in relationship to Christ and the Church.

NOTE TO THE FOLLOWING LESSONS CONCERNING CHRIST

It is not difficult to set out the most important doctrines that should always be taught and preached concerning Christ the Savior. But this material can be presented in many ways. The choice of individual topics should be made by the teacher according to the circumstances of time and place under which each instruction is to be given. For example, from the beginning of Advent until the Lenten cycle begins more extended treatment could be given to Christology as it is presented in the infancy Gospels of Matthew and Luke, with stress on the divine and human natures of the Lord as they appear in these accounts which are so heavily dependent on the Old Testament prophecies and types. During the Lenten and Easter cycles we could think more of the events of the public and risen life of Christ.

Those historical catecheses on the life of Christ are to be chosen which are most suitable to the liturgical season, which are charged with dogmatic significance, and which therefore offer the best opportunity for explaining clearly and effectively the mystery of Christ. But in every kind of teaching, the *entire mystery of Christ* must be explained in the course of these instructions in its basic phases.

Here we are selecting these nine topics containing the most important phases of Christ's life and work: the incarnation and nativity, the baptism, the temptations, the miracles, the words, the training of his Apostles, the titles, the passion and death, the resurrection and ascension.

Sixth Instruction

THE INCARNATION AND BIRTH OF CHRIST

Method: Historical-explanatory.

Aim: A clear and illuminating answer to the questions: Who is Christ? Why did He come? Why did He come in such a humble way? The essence of the doctrine of the incarnation, and a religious understanding of the wonderful and supreme blessing of the incarnation, such as to be an effective incitement to Christian love.

DOCTRINAL SUMMARY

At last came the "fullness of time" (Gal. 4:6, Eph. 1:10) so long desired by the human race from the time of the fall. A brief and simple summary of the Old Testament should be given in its broad outlines: how men sinned increasingly; they founded various earthly kingdoms and cultures and failed to find God. Only a few "just" men and women even among God's Chosen People awaited every day more eagerly the promised Messiah. Now at last He comes. Here we should try to awaken our hearers to a personal desire for redemption.

A. The Announcement of the Incarnation (Luke 1:26-38)

We see a girl, most extraordinary in virtue, noble in race, herself most humble and living in a humble condition. We see the reverence of the angel. What was his message? What is happening? The will of God is being announced to the Virgin. God had chosen her as the virgin Mother of the Messiah. Each sentence of the conversation should be clearly explained, and all subordinated to the aim of this lesson, without any superfluous and extended moral applications. The humble consent of the Virgin . . . her great part in this great work of God, the work of the incarnation and the redemption. The roots of Jesus in humanity through this virgin daughter of Zion (see Zephaniah 3:14–18) and the great king David (2 Sam. 7:5–14). The initiative and power of God accomplished through the Holy Spirit.

B. The Incarnation

We should give a reverent explanation of this inexpressible mystery. Who is this Son of the Virgin? The Son of the eternal Father, the God-Man. God from all eternity, becoming a man in time; according to His divine nature having only a Father; according to His human nature, only a Mother. He is the Second Divine Person, Who at the moment of the incarnation assumed to the divine nature, which He had from all eternity, a human nature taken from the Virgin. The Word's union with our human nature is a much more intimate one than that between a man and his clothing. The human nature belongs to the Word in the intimate way in which my body is truly "mine."

C. How Christ Was Born

The description of Christ's birth should be reverent, filled with devotion and sincere love, and free of any softness, sentimentality, or exaggeration. How winning is His lovableness, how awesome His helplessness, how amazing His humility and His willingness to be humiliated, foregoing the honor due Him. Here appears the guiding principle of His life on earth: ". . . [He] emptied Himself, taking the nature of a slave . . . becoming obedient to death" (Phil. 2:7 ff.). And already the complementary aspect of this principle shines out: "Therefore God has also exalted Him" (Phil. 2:9). This is the royal road to true glory, the only road in the order of salvation. Many holy people whom Our Lord had chosen for Himself shared in this humble and hidden way of life: Mary, Joseph, the shepherds, the wise men. . . . Do you wish to follow?

D. Why Christ Came in This Way

See the work of the second Adam. The first Adam, by his pride and disobedience, brought calamity upon us and separated us from the Father. The second Adam, by His humility and obedience, leads us back to the Father again. The second Adam renounced what was due Him in order to reconcile us to the Father. The first Adam had sought himself, desiring to "be like God," in such a way as to forget God; the second Adam forgot Himself in seeking the Father's glory. The purpose of His life is "Glory to God in the highest, and on earth, peace . . ."; nothing for Himself.

"I announce to you glad tidings of great joy" (Luke 2:10). Joy and thanksgiving for such and so great a Savior, Who from the very beginning loved us so much. Love for love! Let us follow Him faithfully and devotedly. He does not seek anything we have; He seeks ourselves and our happiness.

E. The Consequences of This Mystery for Us

These should at once be explained, clearly and attractively. *Because our Savior is God,* we can hope for everything from His redemption. The eternal Son of the Father can lead us sinners back to the Father. *Because our Savior is Man,* He really is our brother, He really belongs to our family; He feels with us and for us, He can "have compassion on our infirmities" (Heb. 4:15; see also 5:2). *Because our Savior is the God-Man,* He is by His very makeup, by being what He is, the mediator between God and men. This savior is able to bridge, to close the abyss which sin opened up between God and men. Christ is thus the "Pontifex" (literally *Bridge-maker*), our High Priest, since He combines perfect divinity and humanity in His own person.

This conclusion naturally appeals to the Christian heart and awakens great joy and thanksgiving for so great a Redeemer.

NOTE ON TEACHING THIS MATERIAL

The presentation of the material given here presupposes hearers who have already been given some elementary instruction, and therefore it at once sets out and explains the mystery of the incarnation. In giving the catechesis to adults, it might be wiser to postpone these scenes from the infancy Gospels and plunge immediately into the public life of Christ, to allow His divinity to be discovered from His words and actions. For the more advanced students envisioned here the doctrines of the incarnation and redemption should be progressively developed and further deepened in the many instructions to be given on the life of Christ.

THE PUBLIC LIFE OF CHRIST

Four possible approaches could be followed here.

1. A *chronological sequence* could be chosen, along the lines of the many "Lives of Christ." This is highly artificial, however, since the Gospel writers did not intend to give a chronological account of the life of Christ.

2. The predominant features of the *kingdom* inaugurated by Christ could be studied: it involves an eschatological struggle between good and evil; it is paradoxical, for victory comes through suffering and poverty; it is incarnational and sacramental; it is institutional, being structured around the twelve disciples; it is universal, open to all and saving all; it is ruled by the law of love. All of this tells us something about Christ, but only indirectly.

3. The *special outlook toward Christ characteristic of each evangelist and Paul* could be developed. This has the advantage of a strong biblical theology, but it loses some of the momentum of salvation history.

4. The approach we have chosen combines features from each of the other possibilities, to focus attention on Jesus and maintain a forward sweep toward His passion and resurrection, while it develops the major elements of His mission as it appeared to men. If more time is available, a detailed study of one Gospel could be undertaken, together with some indications for a similar study of the other Gospels. At least the desire for such study later should be awakened and encouraged.

Seventh Instruction

THE BAPTISM OF JESUS

Method: Historical—explanatory.
Viewpoint: The redemptive incarnation of the Son of God.
Aim: To deepen our hearers' understanding of Jesus Christ, Who He is and what He does, so as to arouse them to a personal love of Christ and devoted following of Him.

DOCTRINAL SUMMARY

A. THE HUMANITY OF JESUS

Through the incarnation the Son of God becomes fully human—
like us in all things except sin (Heb. 4:15). He does everything sinners do, sin alone excepted. He drinks wine and even provides it for
a wedding feast. He chooses his friends among the scum of society—
prostitutes, rebels (Simon the Zealot), tax gatherers who collaborated
with the hated Romans against the interests of their own people,
ignorant peasants despised by the cultured city classes, men who ate
without washing their hands or observing the niceties of Jewish
law. Here at His baptism by John, at the threshold of his public
ministry, he even more dramatically associates Himself with sinners.
We cherish our reputations and try to hide our sins; we are quick
to defend ourselves when accused. But what does Jesus do? He
does not confess any sins, for He has none to confess. But to fulfill
the prophecy of Isaiah that He would be counted among the sinners,
He conceals his holiness. He quietly waits His turn, and after the
merchants and harlots and soldiers have left their sins in the water
of the Jordan, He descends into the river to take their sins upon
Himself. Sin had entered God's creation through pride; now Jesus,
the New Adam, begins his work of conquering sin through humility.
Though rich, He became poor for our sake (2 Cor. 8:9).

O Jesus, how great is your love for me that nothing I do, not even
my sins, can keep you from identifying yourself fully with me in
all my human weakness and misery.

B. THE DIVINITY OF JESUS

Jesus' baptism is crowned by the public proclamation of His
divine Sonship by the Father and the descent of the Holy Spirit.
The parallels with the transfiguration and the passion-resurrection-
Pentecost sequence should be carefully explained and developed.
He that humbles himself will be exalted. The more publicly Jesus
affirms His solidarity with mankind, the more publicly His Father
affirms His pleasures at the obedience of His Son and anoints Him
for His Messianic role by a new pouring-out of the Holy Spirit.
Later on, in our baptism, that same Spirit will be given to us, to
enable us to share in Christ's Sonship.

C. THE MISSION OF JESUS

For thirty years Jesus had been pondering God's will for Him. Now, in a vision reminiscent of those which opened the prophetic ministries of Jeremiah and Isaiah, He hears His Father's voice, proclaiming that He is the new Israel and is responsibile for the destiny of His people, with a saving mission which will entail much suffering for Himself. To strengthen Him for that mission the Holy Spirit descends upon Him in the form of a dove. Four important elements of the mission of Jesus appear in this scene:

1. Jesus is the *Messiah* (the Christ, the anointed one). As He is anointed with water by John, He is anointed with the Holy Spirit by the Father. In the Old Testament period kings, priests, and occasionally prophets were solemnly anointed as an external symbol of an interior sending of God's Spirit to enable them to perform their tasks for the people. The Jewish people at the time of Jesus were expecting a political Messiah to free them from Rome and establish a Jewish kingdom. Because of these popular misconceptions Jesus is very reserved about accepting the title "Messiah," but He publicly states that the Lord has "anointed" Him to preach the Good News to the poor (Luke 4:18).

2. Jesus is a *prophet*, anointed by the Spirit to proclaim God's message.

3. Like Jeremiah, Jesus is a prophet Who will have to suffer. God's public recognition of His Son is an allusion to the *Suffering Servant* described in Isaiah. John the Baptist calls Jesus the *Lamb of God*, another reference to the Isaian Suffering Servant and also to the paschal lamb whose blood delivers God's people from punishment. Jesus Himself recognized the somber overtones of His mission and freely accepted the sufferings of His sacrificial death, which He later called a "baptism." The sins He took upon Himself in the Jordan He will expiate upon the cross.

4. As "Son of God" Jesus is the *New Israel*. In the Old Testament God had frequently called the whole people of Israel His "Son," and the Suffering Servant spoken of by Isaiah is a kind of "corporate personality," a single individual who bears responsibility for the entire group and saves them through His own sufferings like Joseph, Moses, and Jeremiah. This identification of Jesus with Israel is strengthened by the descent of the dove, a symbol of Israel in the Song of Songs and the Psalms.

NOTES ON THE TEACHING OF THIS MATERIAL

1. Jesus and His mission cannot be comprehended apart from the Old Testament preparation. God inserted His Son into human history not abruptly but in a context where He could gradually be recognized by reflection upon centuries of experience of God's dealings with His people.

2. Since some followers of the nineteenth-century rationalists still say that faith in Jesus is superstitious belief in a foolish fable, missionaries and also teachers should from time to time set forth our reasons for professing faith in Christ. In such instructions we should show briefly:

a. That the New Testament documents are trustworthy accounts of what Christians of those days believed.

b. That their faith then was a response to the historical events of Christ's life, especially as seen in the light of His resurrection.

c. How we today, after twenty centuries, can and do encounter the same Christ in the Church and respond to Him in faith.

Eighth Instruction

THE TEMPTATIONS OF CHRIST

Method: Historical—explanatory.

Viewpoint: The redemptive mission of the Incarnate Word.

Aim: To deepen faith in Jesus as the man in Whom God accomplishes our salvation, freeing us from the slavery to which sin had reduced us.

DOCTRINAL SUMMARY

A. SATAN TEMPTS JESUS IN HIS HUMANITY

One of the consequences of being human is openness to temptation. Because Jesus has felt within Himself the pull of temptation, He can help those who are tempted (Heb. 2:17–18; 4:15; 5:7). The temptation of Jesus by Satan is not some imaginary incident; it was real. Like every man, Jesus was put to the test, probed in the depths of his personality in such a way as to reveal the freely chosen fundamental orientation and option of His personality.

1. Satan tempts him to *sensuality* by suggesting that he change stones to bread to satisfy His hunger. The devil often tries to get us to misuse our talents for our own convenience rather than for God's work. Later on in His public life the Samaritan woman asks Him to give water simply to slake bodily thirst; the crowds ask Him to provide bread all the time—and Jesus refuses. He will not be over-dependent on material things nor will He teach others to seek the bread that perishes while they neglect the bread which endures to eternal life. John tells us that many walked away from Jesus after that. He was hurt, just as we are hurt when people turn their backs on us. This was a real test.

2. Satan tempts Him to *presumption and pride,* to use His powers in a dramatic way to capture the attention of the curious. He suggests that He cast Himself down from the pinnacle of the Temple, to put God's providence to the test. Later His own relatives will urge Christ to show Himself openly; the Pharisees demand signs; Herod asks Him to work some magic tricks; on the cross Jesus hears the taunt, "If you are God's Son [the same words as Satan uses at the outset of His public life], come down from the cross. . . . Let him come down from the cross now and we will believe. . . . Let God rescue him if He wants him." And always Jesus refuses. He will not undervalue the material world as if the law of gravity were to be ignored or faith forced by external wonders.

3. Satan tempts Jesus to seek *political power,* with all the attendant compromises with evil this would entail. The Jews at that time were looking for a warrior Messiah, and political power can accomplish much good for the poor—but it was not to be purchased at the cost of serving Satan, for no man can serve two masters. The world must be served for God's sake and in relationship to Him, not in alienation from Him and His values. Over and over again during His life the crowds will try to make Jesus a king, and He refuses the wrong kind of kingship offered at the wrong time, in the wrong place, and by the wrong person. Political freedom is good. But freedom from sin is more important and more valuable for man.

B. BY THE POWER OF GOD, JESUS CONQUERS HIS ENEMIES

The temptations after Jesus' baptism telescope and epitomize a lifelong struggle between Christ and Satan. This struggle is narrated in the Gospels as they show the conflict between Jesus and the Pharisees who try to trap Him, the ignorance of His disciples, the stormy sea, the demons, sickness, sin. With the Messianic anointing of Jesus the kingdom of God has arrived in power. God's reign must be extended from Jesus throughout the whole of the cosmos by the overthrow of its present ruler, Satan. By sinning, Adam had subjected himself to Satan, and the sway of sin and disorder had spread throughout all creation, animate and inanimate. Only one stronger than Satan will be able to bind him and so free man from the tyranny of evil. Jesus is filled with the power of the Holy Spirit; at each encounter He is victorious. In St. Mark's Gospel especially the cosmic dimensions of the battle emerge: Satan opposes Jesus not only directly but also through persons or by his control over nature. Christ reduces the sea, the demons, and the Pharisees to the same discomfited silence. Why? Because, "God was in Christ, reconciling the world to Himself" (2 Cor. 5:19). In Jesus the kingship of God is at hand, is operative in the world and begins to grow and reveal itself.

C. The Temptations Reveal Christ's Mission

The circumstances in which the temptations were situated reveal even more about who and what Jesus is.

Like Israel, Jesus meets Satan in the desert and undergoes the three great temptations to which His forefathers had succumbed: they had preferred the fleshpots of Egypt to the manna given by God; they had put God to the test by demanding water; they had given idolatrous worship to the golden calf. It is no accident that in repelling the suggestions of Satan Jesus quotes Deuteronomy, the blueprint for the Messianic community of the end-time. Jesus as the *New Israel,* the beginning of a new people, succeeds where the old Israel had failed.

Jesus, the *New Adam,* undoes the work of the first Adam, who by eating the fruit of the forbidden tree had put God's threats of punishment to the test in a proud attempt to make himself like God. With good reason, then, after His Messianic anointing and His first victory over the powers of evil, Jesus can begin to proclaim the Good News: "The time is fulfilled, and the kingdom of God is at hand" (Mark 1:15)!

Ninth Instruction

THE MIRACLES OF JESUS

Method: Historical-explanatory.

Viewpoint: God acting in Jesus to meet human needs (Acts 2:22).

Aim: To foster an appreciation of God's merciful love revealed to us in the human actions of His Son, so that we may respond in love and wholehearted self-surrender to continue His work in the world.

DOCTRINAL SUMMARY

A. The Miracles as Signs of the Human Compassion of Jesus

The Gospels are full of references to Jesus' remarkable sensitivity to human needs and problems. He had compassion in the most profound sense, an ability to share the anguish of the sick or of sinners or of those torn by grief. His love for others enabled Him to enter into their crisis-situation, to make it His own, and to do something about it. His sympathy was not a passive emotion but a force leading to action. His miracles are a human response to the distress of those He loves, a sign that He cares. He not only heals the daughter of Jairus but He tells her parents to give her something to eat. He weeps for His friend Lazarus before raising him from the dead. He does not shrink from the leper but touches him and heals him— and to that social outcast the touch was an even greater sign of love than the cure.

B. The Miracles as Deeds of Divine Power

It has been truly said that the Gospels depict Jesus as "a Jew who acts like God." He acts like God because He is God. His actions reveal not only human concern but the power of God. They are signs that the kingdom of God has arrived and is rolling back Satan's rule. Through Christ God is actively intervening in the world to rescue man from evil. Sickness, suffering, death, natural calamities—all are seen to be consequences of the disorder which sin introduced into the world at the instigation of the devil. Because of this, the reign of God over men is achieved by delivering the whole man, body and soul, from the forces sin had unleashed.

Psalm 107 (106) divides God's saving acts into four categories: He rescues from hunger, darkness of prison, sickness, and storm. It is no coincidence that Jesus gives food to the hungry, sight to the blind, health to the sick, calm to the storm-tossed Apostles. The same God is acting on behalf of His people, to free them from their captivity by Satan. Miracles and exorcisms are narrated for the same purpose. Miracle stories in the Gospels are not told to entertain. They reveal who Jesus is by what He does: God is present among His people in power in order to save them. The stress is not on the upsetting of a law of nature, for the order of nature itself speaks of God's wisdom and love. Rather, miracles are striking reminders that God is always at work in our midst, that He never abandons us to our enemies. Miracles teach us to recognize God's power and help us place our trust and confidence in Him.

Christ is the incarnation of God's power, the revelation of His love for man. The deeds of Jesus do not merely confirm His teaching by showing that the Father ratifies what Jesus says. They do attest His mission, but, more important, they demonstrate in action that God is at work in Jesus and restores peace and order to a world not yet fully under man's control.

C. MIRACLES AND SACRAMENTS

Through Christ God is still acting to save His people. The struggle between good and evil, between the reign of God and the reign of Satan, is still going on. God wants us to control and conquer natural energies and sickness, not to fear them. During His life on earth Jesus did not heal *all* the sick or stop *all* the storms. He does not do so now. He will not rob us of our human dignity and responsibility by doing everything for us. But He lets us experience His power to encourage us in our task. He is still showing His love and concern through the nuclear scientists, engineers, construction workers, doctors, nurses, teachers, parents, farmers, and all others who make up His Church.

This is the *sacramental* principle, an extension of the incarnation. The Son of God took a full and complete human nature to serve as his instrument in the work of liberation. Through His hands, eyes, voice, mind, and will He brought divine life to men. Now He associates other men with Him as His instruments. We cooperate with Christ in spreading the kindom of God.

Just as the miracles Jesus worked manifested in a striking way the meaning of His work in the world, so certain actions we perform highlight the meaning of our own struggle against evil. These are the sacraments. God is still delivering His people from captivity through baptism and penance. He is still healing them in the anointing of sick, feeding them with the Eucharist, anointing new prophets and priests in confirmation and holy orders, joining them to Himself through each other in marriage.

The miracles of Christ themselves symbolized the sacramental system. The multiplication of the loaves and the changing of water into wine for a wedding feast prepared the way for the Eucharist. The opening of the eyes of the blind and the raising of the dead to life dramatized the meaning of baptism. Jesus explicitly connects the healing of the sick to the power to forgive sins.

The saving works of Jesus are not just a thing of the past. He is still at work today in His Church by advancing the kingdom of God in His sacramental actions and in every thought, word, and deed of those who share in His Sonship.

NOTE ON TEACHING THIS MATERIAL

The miracles should never be presented in a purely apologetic way. Their purpose was never simply to prove Christ's mission. In the Gospels and also today miracles cannot force faith—in the face of unbelief in Nazareth Jesus could work no miracles; and the raising of Lazarus simply provoked Jesus' enemies instead of converting them. Miracles are much more than credentials: they are the advance of God's kingdom into this world.

Tenth Instruction

THE WORDS OF JESUS

Method: Thematic. The biblical theme of "word of God" is considered in relationship to Jesus, the Word made flesh.

Aim: To present God's word in such a way as to intensify faith. Christian faith is, by its nature, our wholehearted and positive answer to God's revelation. The revelation of the Father, communicated to us through Christ, is much more than a statement of truths; it is, basically, the Father's gracious invitation, calling us to come to Him, to share His life. The *full Christian faith* that

Christ asks of us in the Father's name is essentially more than mere intellectual *assent;* it is by its nature complete *consent,* wholehearted readiness to accept and to follow His divine message. Faith includes, to be sure, the humble submission of our intellect to what we cannot fully understand, but faith is much more than this: it is the submission of our whole being to Christ's Gospel, with the firm will to follow Him. Better, it is the submission of our whole being to Christ, Who is Himself God's Word. How beautiful is the faith expressed in St. Peter's answer: "Lord, to whom shall we go? You have the words of eternal life" (John 6:68).[2]

DOCTRINAL SUMMARY

A. THE WORD OF GOD AS POWER

God's word is powerful. Through His word God communicates life. God called all things into being by His creative word. With a word Jesus heals the sick, stops the storm, raises the dead to life, pardons sins, silences His adversaries, routs demons, gives authority to His disciples, institutes the sacramental signs of the New Covenant. He is mighty in word and work. Through His words God's kingdom comes in power.

B. THE WORD OF GOD AS LIGHT

Through His word God reveals the meaning of His actions and human events. Out of love He speaks to man of Himself and of His plans for him. He lets man know that He is aware of his needs and cares for him. By His deeds and words of power Jesus embodies the creative force of God's kingdom. But He also is a prophet, and

[2] It might be useful to remind our readers that "faith" here means not only so-called "dogmatic" faith, as the term is often used in theology today, but faith in its full sense *(fides adequate sumpta)* as it is understood in Scripture and in the writings of the Fathers. Theologians may need to make further distinctions, and to consider faith in a special way, as it includes intellectual assent. But in our catechetical apostolate we must never forget that we are sent to propose and to foster faith in its fullness, that is, living faith.

Chapters one and two of the Dogmatic Constitution on Divine Revelation of Vatican II make it clear that God first and foremost reveals Himself and that faith is the response of our whole person to God.

interprets the signs of the times and explains to men the significance of His actions.

The words of Jesus as presented to us in the Gospels are almost invariably parables, figures of speech, or dialogues. There is a purpose in this. Parables and comparisons pique curiosity and demand reflection: while communicating some insight, they partially conceal the reality and preserve the transcendence of divine truth. The reactions and interruptions of dialogue provoke even fuller revelations; in their own way they have the same intent as the parable form: to teach us that God's Word demands some response from man but remains ever beyond human comprehension.

The content of Jesus' revelation is the Good News—God in Christ overthrowing the powers of evil because He loves us as His children and wants us to love Him as our Father and all men as our brothers. In the Old Testament God had adopted the people of Israel as His well-beloved, firstborn Son. But they had not given Him the response He looked for. In Jesus Christ, God's true and natural Son, mankind can now make the perfect response of sonship which Israel failed to make. Jesus unites us to Himself and teaches us to think of God as our loving Father, to speak to Him in prayer as our Father, and to share His fatherly solicitude for everyone: "Be perfect as your heavenly Father is perfect" (Matt. 5:48). In a real sense Jesus Himself is both message and response: He is God's Word to us and our word to God.

C. THE WORD OF GOD AS CHALLENGE

Jesus not only inaugurates the kingdom of God and proclaims its arrival; He not only interprets the signs God is giving; He throws up a challenge before us. Jesus summons each of us to realign ourselves in the present time of crisis. The kingdom of Satan is crumbling; the kingdom of God is advancing. All who have up to now been allied with Satan must renounce him and freely come over to God's side. We must believe His message, hope in His promises of victory, and join forces with Him in love. "The preparation time is over. The reign of God has begun. Repent and believe in the Good News" (Mark 1:15, according to the Greek).

Eleventh Instruction

CHRIST AND HIS DISCIPLES

Method: Historical-explanatory.

Viewpoint: See how Christ's mission is handed on to men, to prolong the redemptive incarnation.

Aim: Understanding the beginnings of the Church community so that our response to Christ includes the hierarchical Church as part of Himself and His task.

DOCTRINAL SUMMARY

A. CHRIST GATHERS DISCIPLES

Jesus worked, not in isolation, but in community. From the beginning of His public life He attracted followers, men who would break with the past, attach themselves to Him, listen to Him, imitate Him. Of these disciples Jesus selected a group of twelve for special intimacy with Himself. They were to be His constant companions, His friends and brothers. He gave them special training through explaining to them His parables, teaching them to preach the Good News, empowering them to work miracles in His name, instructing them in prayer. The band of Apostles was organized into three groups of four under the leadership of Peter, Philip, and James; and Peter already exercised some authority over the others by acting as spokesman for all. In this way Jesus laid the foundations of His Church, the New Israel, the completion and perfection of the People of God of the Old Testament.

B. JESUS HANDS ON HIS OWN MISSION TO THE APOSTLES

God calls in order to send: a vocation is at once personal and ecclesial—man is summoned to faith and obedience in cooperating with God's plan of salvation. So Jesus communicates His own mission and powers to the Apostles for the sake of others. "And He appointed twelve, whom also He named apostles, that they might be with Him and that He might send them forth to preach. To them He gave power . . . to cast out devils" (Mark 3:14). The Apostles are joined to Christ's person, His message, His work.

He shares all His powers with them. He is a prophet, sent by God to be the light of the world; He sends the Apostles to teach in

His name and calls them the light of the world. He is endowed with priestly power to spread God's kingdom by driving out demons, forgiving sins, communicating to others His life, offering that life in sacrifice; He trains His Apostles to do the same so that after His resurrection they will be prepared to baptize, to forgive sins, to renew His sacrifice, to feed His people with His Body. He is the master, the shepherd, the foundation of the Church; they are His ambassadors, with full jurisdiction over the twelve tribes of the New Israel, foundation stones, shepherds who so echo His voice that whoever hears them hears Him. Through the Apostles Jesus establishes the nucleus of His Church as a visible and organized society; they are to perpetuate His work until the end of time. His mission is to last until the kingdom of Satan is totally crushed. The full task of teaching, sanctifying, and directing those who believe Jesus' message and follow Him is entrusted by the risen Christ to the Apostles. Later on they will confide this mission to other trustworthy men, so that even today Christ is working in a very special way through the bishops and their head, the pope.

Here a clear and brief exposition of the structure and function of the hierarchy should be given, one following closely chapter three of the Dogmatic Constitution on the Church (*Lumen Gentium*). Remind your hearers that like any living organism the Church grows and develops and adjusts to its surroundings. We should not expect the Church of the New Testament period to have all the elaborate structure of today, but the basic lines are there: a group of Apostles with Peter as the source of unity and stability according to Christ's promise (Matt. 16:16–19; Luke 22:32; John 21:15–17) exercised then the same functions as do the college of bishops with and under the Pope now.

How can men exercise such great powers? The risen Christ is present and active in them for our sake. ". . . behold, I am with you all days, even unto the consummation of the world" (Matt. 28:20). We give our trust and obedience to Christ in them.

Twelfth Instruction

THE TITLES OF JESUS

Method: Thematic.
Viewpoint: We investigate the attitudes His disciples had toward Jesus through an analysis of the way they spoke about Him. We look at Him through their eyes and through His own.

Aim: A fuller understanding of how the closest friends of Jesus reacted to what He did and said, so that we may share their own admiration and love for Him.

DOCTRINAL SUMMARY

In this brief summary of the Christian message it is impossible to treat all the titles given to Jesus, especially the rich and varied symbols found in John's Gospel: Word, life, light, bread, vine, shepherd, and so on. Nor will we analyze the titles Christians today most frequently give to Jesus: Lord and Christ. During His public life Jesus was not called Lord in the same sense as after His resurrection; and Jesus told His Apostles not to call Him Messiah before He rose from the dead. Attention will be given here to the three titles which He freely accepted and even gave to Himself during His life on earth.

A. SON OF MAN

In the Old Testament "son of man" was a synonym for "man," stressing human weakness, particularly in the face of death. However Daniel 7 mentions a transcendant, quasi-divine figure who receives universal dominion from God; this "son of man" is a corporate personality, an individual identified with and responsible for God's people.

"... I saw one like a son of man coming, on the clouds of heaven; when he reached the Ancient One and was presented before him, he received dominion, glory, and kingship; nations and peoples of every language serve him. His dominion is an everlasting dominion that shall not be taken away, his kingship shall not be destroyed. . . . But the holy ones of the Most High shall receive the kingship, to possess it forever and ever" (Dan. 7:13–14; 18; see also 22 and 27).

"Son of man" was Jesus' favorite way to refer to Himself. Occasionally it seems to mean simply "I, myself," but, given the theological intent of the Gospel writers, it is reasonable to presume that the phrase has a deeper significance. Certainly at times He gives the expression the full force it had in Daniel—a veiled allusion to His divinity together with His human responsibility for all mankind—but He also uses it to bring out the suffering and humiliation He would undergo before His triumph.

"For the Son of Man is to come with His angels in the glory of His Father, and then He will render everyone according to his conduct. . . . and then will all tribes of the earth mourn, and they will see the Son of Man coming upon the clouds of heaven with great power and majesty. And He will send forth His angels with a trumpet and a great sound, and they will gather His elect. . . . 'you shall see the Son of Man sitting at the right hand of the Power and coming upon the clouds of heaven" (Matt. 16:27; 24:30–31; 26:64). ". . . the Son of Man has nowhere to lay His head. . . . The Son of Man is to be betrayed into the hands of men, and they will kill Him; and on the third day He will rise again" (Matt. 8:20; 17:22–23).

B. SERVANT OF GOD

The Old Testament gives this name to kings, prophets, and priests whose mission was to keep God's people faithful to the service God expected of them. That service was an honorable collaboration with God in His plan to save mankind. Special attention must be given to Isaiah 40–55, in which the people of Israel is described as a sluggish, rebellious servant. God will pardon and save Israel, His servant, and use it to bring to all nations the light of salvation. This will be done through a mysterious prophet, who also is called God's servant. As a member of God's people He will gather them and teach them; He will offer His life for Israel and by His sufferings will reunite sinners to God.

"Here is my servant whom I uphold, my chosen one with whom I am pleased, upon whom I have put my Spirit; he shall bring forth justice to the nations. . . . I, the Lord, have called you for the victory of justice, I have grasped you by the hand; I formed you; and set you as a convenant of the people, a light for the nations, to open the eyes of the blind, to bring out prisoners from confinement, and from the dungeon, those who live in darkness" (Is. 42:1, 6–7). "For now the Lord has spoken Who formed me as His servant from the womb, that Jacob may be brought back to Him and Israel gathered to Him; . . . It is too little, He says, for you to be My servant, to raise up the tribes of Jacob, and restore the survivors of Israel; I will make you a light to the nations, that My salvation may reach to the ends of the earth" (Is. 49:5–6).

"See, My servant shall prosper, he shall be raised high and greatly exalted. . . . Yet it was our infirmities that he bore, our sufferings that he endured, while we thought of him as stricken, as one smitten by God and afflicted. But he was pierced for our offenses, crushed for our sins; upon him was the chastisement that makes us whole, by his stripes we are healed. . . . Because of his affliction he shall see the light in fullness of days; through his suffering, My servant shall justify many, and their guilt he shall bear" (Is. 52:13; 53:4–5, 11).

At His baptism Jesus was identified by God as His servant, and in the temptations He showed Himself ready to suffer in order to remain faithful to His mission (Matt. 3:17; 4:1–10). He opened His ministry by saying that He was the Servant of God Isaiah had written of (Luke 4:16–22). Often He referred to His task as one of loving service, of giving His life for the redemption of sinners and bringing them the Good News of salvation. ". . . the Son of Man also has not come to be served but to serve, and to give His life as a ransom for many" (Mark 10:45); "But I am in your midst as He Who serves" (Luke 22:27; John 13:4–15). The details of the passion and death of Christ as given in the Gospels closely parallel the Old Testament descriptions of the sufferings of the Servant of God (Matt. 26:38, 63, 67; 27:14, 29–31, 38, 60). This theme was taken up and expanded in the very earliest preaching of the Church: Acts 3:13–26; 4:27–30; 8:32–35; Phil. 2:5–11; 1 Pet. 2:21–25.

C. SON OF GOD

In the Exodus and the events which followed, Israel experienced God's fatherly care and protection. All Israelites considered themselves God's children, and the whole people was called God's son, His firstborn, freely chosen by God as His own. "Thus says the Lord: Israel is My son, My first-born" (Ex. 4:22). "Return, rebellious children, says the Lord, for I am your Master. . . . And I had thought: How I should like to treat you as sons, and give you a pleasant land, a heritage most beautiful among the nations! You would call Me, 'My Father,' I thought, and never cease following Me" (Jer. 3:14, 19). "When Israel was a child I loved him, out of Egypt I called My son" (Hos. 11:1).

Because of the special choice God had made of David and his descendants, kings were called "Son of God," and this title belonged in a particular way to the Messiah, who would come from David's race. "I will preserve the offspring of your body after you and make his sovereignty secure. . . . I will be to him a father: and he shall be to Me a son" (2 Sam. 7:12, 14). "He will invoke Me, 'My father,'

. . . and I shall make him My first-born, the Most High of the kings of the earth" (Ps. 89:26–27). "I Myself have set up My king on Sion, My holy mountain. . . . You are My son; this day I have begotten you" (Ps. 2:6–7).

At Jesus' baptism God had solemnly borne witness to His Son (Matt. 3:17), and early in His public ministry Jesus was called "Son of God" by others (Matt. 4:3, 6; 14:33; Mark 3:11; 5:7. See John 1:49). He rejects the term's political-Messianic connotations, balances it by speaking of His sufferings (Matt. 16:16–21), but accepts it as expressing a unique and indissoluble bond between the Father and Himself which ensures that He always does God's will. "All things have been delivered to Me by My Father; and no one knows the Son except the Father; nor does anyone know the Father except the Son, and him to whom the Son chooses to reveal Him" (Matt. 11:27). "For whatever He [the Father] does, this the Son also does. . . . that all men may honor the Son even as they honor the Father" (John 5:19–23). "I and the Father are one" (John 10:30). "Father, the hour has come! Glorify Thy Son, that Thy Son may glorify Thee, even as Thou hast given Him power over all flesh, in order that to all Thou hast given Him He may give everlasting life. Now this is everlasting life, that they may know Thee, the only true God, and Him Whom thou hast sent, Jesus Christ. . . . glorify Me with Thyself, with the glory that I had with Thee before the world existed" John 17:1–5).

Only after Jesus' death did the Apostles understand the full significance of His sonship: God had sent His Son to love us, free us from our sins, and send us His Spirit so that we, too, could become God's children, bearing His likeness, sharing His inheritance. What He is by nature we can become by God's gracious adoption.

NOTE ON THE TEACHING OF THIS MATERIAL

1. Point out that the three chief titles of Jesus have both an individual and a collective reference, and that Jesus sums up in Himself the preparation of the Old Testament and the whole People of God of the New Testament. He is an individual, but more than an individual. His ecclesial dimension is part of the very human nature He assumed. It enables His death and resurrection to avail for the entire race of mankind.

2. Each of the titles refers both to His divinity and His humanity.

Each, as Jesus uses it, includes suffering and glorification. Each captures, therefore, something of the essence of His redemptive incarnation.

Thirteenth Instruction

THE PASSION AND DEATH OF CHRIST

Method: Historical-explanatory. The passion and death of Christ should be depicted reverently and with devotion, but also discreetly, and at the same time their meaning and import should be clearly brought out. As we present the lesson here, we suppose that there is time for no more than one instruction on this subject. When more than a single lesson can be given, one might be predominantly historical and descriptive and another more dogmatic, or several might be given on the separate main events. In some places it is customary to preach on the Way of the Cross. Such a method of preaching on the passion has some particular advantages: it connects doctrine with the pictured stations on the one hand, and with both oral and mental prayer on the other. But we should take great care to make sure that the exposition of Christ's passion and death does not consist merely in a description of what He suffered, along with pious moral applications. We should, instead, clearly set out the *dogmatic reasons* why Christ suffered all these things and how our own way to glory and true perfection consists in the constant and brave following of Christ: "To die and live together with Christ" (see Rom. 6); "I die daily" (1 Cor. 15:31). We should carefully see to it that in any explanation of the Way of the Cross (the Stations) *the fruits of Christ's passion and death* are clearly set forth. The most important station is *the final one, the fifteenth, the resurrection.*

In preaching the passion let us imitate the Church, which always organically connects the resurrection with the passion (see the Preface of the Cross and also the Easter Preface). We notice the same union in Our Lord's own way of speaking of His passion. See, for example, His predictions of His sufferings and death as given in Matthew 16:21, 17:23, 20:19. Each time He adds and emphasizes: "But on the third day He will rise again."

Viewpoint: The work of redemption is the most excellent work of the *generosity and mercy* of God. "For God so loved the world that He gave His only-begotten Son, that those who believe in

Him may not perish, but may have life everlasting" (John 3:16). "He Who has not spared even His own Son but has delivered Him for us all, how can He fail to grant us also all things with Him?" (Rom. 8.32). "In this has the love of God been shown in our case, that God has sent His only-begotten Son into the world that we may live through Him. In this is the love, not that we have loved God, but that He has first loved us, and sent His Son [to be] a propitiation for our sins" (1 John 4:9 ff.). "But God commends His charity towards us, because when as yet we were sinners, Christ died for us" (Rom. 5:8). We should notice here the important point that in all these texts the wonderful love of God the Father is most particularly emphasized.

Principal fruit of this instruction: Not a loving feeling of compassion, even though such an emotion is greatly to be desired, but the resolution to respond perfectly and fully to the love of God, to show profound and habitual gratitude to Christ and the Father, and also to have the most unshakable confidence in Them (Rom. 8:32). The cross shows us clearly both the horror of sin and the value of human life, and the wonder of God's love. The complete fruit of this lesson should be a horror of sin, true and sincere conversion, appreciation of the heavenly blessings which Christ purchased for us at so great a price, the complete giving of ourselves to the love and service of God (active participation in the sacrifice of Christ).

DOGMATIC SUMMARY

A. THE LOVE OF CHRIST

Jesus "loved me and gave Himself up for me" (Gal. 2:20). Jesus Christ is the model of love and obedience. So great is His love for the Father and for us that He is willing to undergo great pain, even death itself.

Through His loving obedience Christ overcomes sin. Sin has been seen to be a refusal to obey God and a refusal to love. God asks everyone to love as He loves and to love as Jesus does. It is not always easy to love. By refusing to love others one disobeys and offends God. This is the essence and malice of sin.

Into a world steeped in sin God sent His Son. He commanded His Son to love generously, constantly, courageously. His love aroused the opposition and hatred of sinners, yet despite their hatred Jesus did not stop loving them. Even when they made Him suffer, He continued to love and to pray for them. Nothing could shake His love; nothing could rip Him away from obedience to His Father: the light shines in the darkness, and the darkness did not overcome it. By dying on the cross out of love for us Jesus overcame evil by good.

Christ died that we may live. He is the grain of wheat that died in order to bring forth fruit (John 12:23–25). It was because of the disobedience of the first Adam that we were excluded from the family of the sons of God; it is because of the obedience of the second Adam that God receives us again and invites us once more to share in the benefits of Christ. The cross of Christ is the tree of life in the midst of the new paradise, the Church. The new order in this life must always have the quality of reparation—of Christian penance. And while our period of trial endures, we are not given all the delightful gifts of the first paradise. But the gift we do possess, here and now, the gift of divine life, far surpasses the others of the first paradise. Just as the second Adam is far superior to the first, so we who are joined to Him share more fully in God's life than Adam did. "But where the offense has abounded, grace has abounded yet more" (Rom. 5:20).

Mention can be made here of Christ as a corporate personality, a theme developed in the last instruction. It is because Christ sums up the whole of the new mankind in Himself that He can repair the damage of our sins. He does not "take our place," as if His sufferings dispense us from genuine repentance. Rather, He is one with us. He is the Head; we are His members. Joined to Him by the power of the Holy Spirit, we share His life and His love.

B. The Love of the Father

The texts given above attest God's love for us. Make it very clear also that God the Father loves Jesus. He derives no joy from seeing His beloved Son in pain. He has pointed out His Son to men, told men to listen to Him, performed wonders at His request. He wants men to love and obey His Son, not to kill Him. Yet even in the face of sin so terrible that it causes the death of Christ, His Son, God's love for men does not waver. Nor does Christ's.

What a source of strength and confidence is this measureless love of God the Father for us! What a model of obedience is the love of Christ! Jesus is what every man should be, a hero who fights back his fear of pain with a love stronger than death.

The chief stress should be laid, not on Christ's pains, but on His loyalty and fidelity to God and His generosity to us. The result should be a sorrow and sympathy for Jesus Who suffers because of His love for us, an admiration of His courage, a desire to be as faithful as He. Only that man who through grace is vitally united with Christ crucified, and who puts on the spirit of Christ, will have a share in the fruits of the cross. "But if anyone does not have the Spirit of Christ, he does not belong to Christ" (Rom. 8:9).

NOTE ON THE TEACHING OF THIS MATERIAL

In explaining vicarious satisfaction let us not dwell very long on its juridical aspects, but spend far more time in praising the *divine wisdom* which is most beautifully shown in the very manner of our redemption and which so perfectly unites the demands of *divine love and divine justice*. Let us point out the superabundance of the redemption, for "where the offense has abounded, grace has abounded yet more" (Rom. 5:20). We should bring out the fact that we must be united with Christ in order that His abundant satisfaction may be fruitful for us. A merely juridical consideration of His satisfying for our sins—the idea that the insult to God's glory given by sin was abundantly compensated for by the satisfaction offered by Christ; therefore God should be quite content, and we ourselves are free of all obligations—is false and very harmful. Only that man who through grace is vitally united with Christ crucified, and who puts on the spirit of Christ making satisfaction for sin, will have a share in the fruits of the cross. *We must make satisfaction together with Christ.* Only through our oneness with Christ making satisfaction for our sins does His satisfaction become ours.

Fourteenth Instruction

THE RESURRECTION AND ASCENSION

Method: Historical-explanatory. First, describe vividly the fact of the resurrection (narration); then show the import of this triumph (explanation and application).

Viewpoint: "Therefore God also has exalted Him and has bestowed upon Him the name that is above every name . . ." (Phil. 2:9–11).

Just as in the life of Christ, so also in the Christian life: death and sacrifice are not the final stage, but an intermediate one on the way to final triumph and joy. The Christian religion is *the religion of true life, light, and beatitude.*

Aim: "We give Thee thanks for Thy great glory . . ." (*Gloria* of the Mass). The principal attitude of those who belong to our religion of light should be one of joy and gratitude for the great glory given to us in Christ, all redounding to the glory of the Father. The victory of Christ is our victory; the glory of Christ our glory; the life of Christ our life.

Even though we thus speak primarily of the *soteriological importance* of the resurrection, we should clearly indicate its apologetical importance also.

DOCTRINAL SUMMARY

A. The Fact of the Resurrection

The resurrection should be kept closely connected to the death of Christ. Both are stages of one single movement, through death to life; Jesus did not die in a hopeless way. His love was stronger than death and burst forth into new life. By raising Jesus from the dead, God, His Father puts His seal of approval on the works and actions of His Son and shows us that Christ's love is powerful enough to overcome the death inherent in our sinful refusal to love.

Psychologically it is wise to recall the sadness of Good Friday, the grief of Christ's friends at His death. He had continued to love despite rejection and hatred, and His fidelity to His Father's command led Him to undergo suffering and death for us. Apparently evil had overcome goodness, hatred had conquered love, darkness had snuffed out light.

But Christ rose from the dead. His love had not been conquered. It had remained firm, and now it triumphed over sin and death. Christ is not dead, but alive, never again to suffer, never again to die. His victory over death is final and complete.

Full of joy, the risen Christ goes to share His happiness with His friends. They could hardly believe their eyes, that it was actually Jesus, alive again. He wanted them to be very sure that He was really the same person as ever, so He gave them many proofs of His resurrection. He spoke to them and explained Scripture just as He had done before. He let them touch Him. He ate with them, and they could recognize the very same gestures of blessing the food that He had always made. He put Himself at their service; He even cooked for them! He helped them in their jobs and guided them in their decisions.

When they finally realized that Jesus was truly alive, their hearts were full of peace. They knew that His trust of God His Father was not misplaced and that their own trust of Jesus was wise and good.

Jesus had a new job for His Apostles. Now that they shared His joy, they were to share it with others in turn. They were to go out and spread the Good News that God His Father had raised Him from the dead.

Jesus Himself would remain with them as they carried out this task. They would not be able to see Him with their eyes, but they could still recognize His voice when they heard the Scriptures read and applied to Him; they could recognize His gestures of blessing food and the sick; they could recognize His service when others showed love to them; they could recognize His guidance in their decisions.

B. The Importance of the Resurrection

1. ". . . Who [Jesus] was foreordained Son of God by an act of power . . . by resurrection from the dead . . ." (Rom. 1:4). By raising Jesus from the dead God His Father revealed Him in the fullest possible way—*He is the Lord! He is the Messiah! He is the Son of God!* And all His preaching is true. Lord, I believe. By Your resurrection You have conquered unbelief. With the once unbelieving Thomas I adore You: "My Lord and my God!" (John 20:28).

2. *"God also has exalted Him and has bestowed upon Him the name that is above every name . . ."* (Phil. 2:9). Now God the Father gives to His beloved Son that full and perfect glory which Christ Himself had renounced when He became man, emptying Himself and taking on the form of a servant. This glory of the resurrection is the fitting reward of the humiliation He freely accepted for us. Truly "we give Thee thanks for Thy great glory." Let us rejoice in the victory and glory of our Brother and Lord! Your joy is our joy, Your glory ours!

3. ". . . Christ has risen from the dead, the first fruit of those who have fallen asleep" (1 Cor. 15:20). The resurrection of Christ is *our resurrection* because the life of the Head is the life of the mem-

bers (Rom. 6; 1 Cor. 15). This unfailing life, this glorification and "divinization" of the entire man, which we contemplate with admiration in the risen Christ—this will be ours also. And it has already begun in us. Here on earth the fullness of this heavenly life is invisible. But at the resurrection from the dead it will become fully apparent. This life belongs to us only through union with Christ and is subject to the same law as His: it must be the fruit of our dying with Him. This is the life of God's children which Christ confers upon us in baptism and the other sacraments by intimate personal union, the life which He purchased by His own obedience unto death. "But if we are sons, we are heirs also: heirs indeed of God and joint heirs with Christ, provided, however, we suffer with Him that we may also be glorified with Him. For I reckon that the sufferings of the present time are not worthy to be compared with the glory to come that will be revealed in us" (Rom. 8:17–18).

How rich we Christians are! Whatever our lot in this life may be, we are rich in our union with Christ. The pattern of our life is this: to die and to rise with Him. Already here on earth we are to live the life of Christ. "Therefore, if you have risen with Christ, seek the things that are above . . . not the things that are on earth" (Col. 3:1 ff.—the Epistle of the paschal night, directed above all to the newly baptized).

THE ASCENSION OF OUR LORD

A special lesson on the ascension should be given whenever possible during the Easter season. And if in a regular course of lessons there is no time for this, then in the teaching on the resurrection we should clearly show that the ascension is the fitting and glorious conclusion of Christ's life, the crown of His victory. The human life which from its first moment was lived entirely for the Father is fittingly consummated in life with the Father at His right hand. Through the ascension of the Head the meaning of the life of Christ, and of our life also, is made wonderfully clear. "I came forth from the Father and have come into the world. Again I leave the world and go to the Father" (John 16:28). "Born of God" in baptism (John 1:13; 3:5 ff.), we must suffer many things, as did Christ, during our pilgrimage on earth, and we must follow Him toward our final perfect union with our most loving Father. There in heaven is our paradise, far more beautiful than the first earthly one, the paradise of the children of God which Christ reopened to us by His victory. There He already enjoys perfect happiness and glory, and there, with a kind of divine impatience, He awaits us, His brothers, His fellow soldiers, members of His body. "Father, I will that there where I am, they also whom Thou has given Me may be with Me . . ." (John 17:24). He is preparing a place for us with loving care (John 14:3), especially by sending the Holy Spirit to us from heaven (John 16:7).

Method: If a special lesson can be given, the method should be historical-explanatory. First the narration of the historical fact, then the explanation and application of the doctrine.

Aim: "That we also may dwell in mind among heavenly things" (from the collect of the feast). That even here and now "our conversation may be in heaven" (Phil. 3:20). That the contemplation in faith of eternal life may lift up our hearts: "For where your treasure is, there also will your heart be" (Luke 12:34).

THE DOCTRINE OF THE HOLY SPIRIT, WHO GIVES LIFE AND BRINGS TO PERFECTION

The teaching on the Holy Spirit is not completed in this instruction. Those that follow on the Church and the sacramental life begun in us in baptism belong also to the teaching on the Holy Spirit, since they help us to understand more clearly the divine life which the life-giving Spirit produces in Christ's members. It is the Spirit, too, Who writes the new law of love on our hearts. And, finally, the instructions on the Last Things show the perfection and consummation of this life, which is also the work of the Holy Spirit Who brings us to perfection. It is important that the faithful come to understand that all these instructions are part of the teaching on the Holy Spirit, so that they will daily more fully appreciate Him as being "the gift of God" par excellence Who is given to us in Christ.

Fifteenth Instruction

THE HOLY SPIRIT

Method: Historical-explanatory. Our presentation of the doctrine of the Holy Spirit will fall into two parts: promise and fulfillment. As the incarnation of the Son was prepared by centuries of

experience recounted in the Old Testament, so the definitive sending of the Spirit to the Church was foreshadowed by many events
among the people of Israel. After a brief explanation of this Old
Testament background the gift of the Holy Spirit should be presented as the crown of the paschal mystery of Christ. Christ
ascended to the right hand of the Father in order to send us His
Spirit.

To use several Bible narratives in one lesson is usually to be
avoided in the lower grades (1–4)—the "unity of intuition" is
thereby lost. But this method may be used for a good reason in
teaching adults, especially where the Bible narratives have such a
close intrinsic connection (the promise and its fulfillment).

Viewpoint: A religious knowledge of the Holy Spirit from the effects
He produces in men's hearts.

Aim: A great appreciation and ardent *desire for this most wonderful
"Gift of God."* Thanksgiving for the Holy Spirit so abundantly
communicated to us.

DOCTRINAL SUMMARY

A. THE PREPARATION FOR THE COMING OF THE HOLY SPIRIT

In the Old Testament the Holy Spirit was revealed, not yet as a
distinct divine Person, but as a transcendent force transforming
human personalities, making them capable of exceptional deeds in
order to confirm God's people in their call to holiness. He gave
judges and kings power to free and defend Israel from their enemies
and to rule in peace. He spoke through the prophets by sending
them to bear God's word to His people, to explain and interpret
God's actions, to bear courageous witness to His holiness.

Filled with the Holy Spirit from the moment of His conception,
so that His name is the "Holy One," Jesus received a new and visible
anointing with the Holy Spirit at His baptism, a consecration for
His mission as prophet and Messiah. In the Spirit Jesus confronts
the devil, frees His captives, and announces the arrival of God's
Kingdom. The Father had sent the Son to communicate truth and
life. In His turn Jesus promised to send the Holy Spirit in a special
way to His disciples to complete His own twofold mission. The
Spirit will lead them and us into an understanding of all that Jesus
had said and done and will strengthen us to bear witness to the

truth and defend it from error. Further, the Spirit will give us life, the very life of God's children, a life characterized by love. This life of love will make us one even as Jesus and His Father are one. Jesus promised to send His Spirit to us when through His resurrection and ascension He had been enthroned as Lord at the right hand of His Father. Only the risen Christ can communicate the fullness of the Spirit.

We can and must prepare ourselves for this special coming of the Holy Spirit. How? As the Apostles did: by prayer and ardent desire of His coming, themselves the work of the Spirit within us.

B. The Coming of the Holy Spirit

1. *The Pentecost event* is filled with symbolism appealing to the mind and senses. Wind symbolizes the power of the Holy Spirit. Wind and fire also symbolize holiness; both elements are mysterious and fascinating. They are active and in motion, too. Consequently they speak of life. Fire is also a symbol of love. The Spirit breathes into us the power of God's love and enables us to love as God does. Power, holiness, life, and love are given to the Apostles by the Holy Spirit. At once their love shows itself in action. Filled with strength and courage, the Apostles go out to spread the knowledge and love of Christ.

2. What He did for the Apostles, He continues to do for the whole Church and its individual members. Without the Spirit we would be like lifeless bodies. As our soul makes our body live and act, so the Spirit gives us supernatural life and vitality. The Holy Spirit is the soul of the Church, Who gives the individual members their vital union with Christ and Who forms them to the image of Christ, most especially by inflaming them with love for the Father.

The many signs of His presence—the charisms of preaching, praying, healing, bearing witness, and such—are all given to build up the Church, the Body of Christ, until all are transformed with His holiness.

We must make it very clear that here and now the Holy Spirit is communicated to men in the Church and that this is brought about especially by the sacraments, above all in baptism and confirmation. This is the reason why no special lesson on confirmation will be presented in these basic instructions, for it is treated here, at least in its fundamentals. In baptism the Spirit is given to forgive sins and to make us sons in the Son, to pour into us the life and love of the risen Christ. In confirmation the Spirit brings adult Christians to maturity and social responsibility by empowering them to bear fearless witness to Christ as they love others in a visible way, a way so striking that it is a sign to nonbelievers (John 17:20–26).[2] This prophetic consecration of the confirmed Christian endures, even though he should fall into sin. The Spirit is permanently and irrevocably given in an "objective sanctification" which calls for subjective holiness. We highly recommend, therefore, that about the time of Pentecost each year, preferably during a Pentecost vigil service, a ceremony of the renovation of confirmation be held, analogous to the renewal of baptismal promises. Such a ceremony might very well be held on the occasion of the administration of confirmation to new candidates.

3. *The Person of the Holy Spirit.* He is the Third Person of the Most Holy Trinity; He proceeds from the Father and the Son as Their Love for One Another—love so perfect that it is a Person, the Third Person in the Godhead. He is true God with the Father and the Son, "Lord and Giver of life," to be adored and glorified together with the Father and Son. He spoke through the prophets; He came down on the Church of Christ, to the Apostles and the rest of the faithful.

Sixteenth Instruction

THE MOST HOLY TRINITY

Here, after the teaching on the Holy Spirit, is the best place, catechetically speaking, to give the special lesson on the doctrine of the Trinity. Speculative theology proceeds from cause to effect, and so the tract *De Deo Trino* precedes the inquiry into the work of man's salvation. But the catechetical instruction of Christians should adopt the opposite method in following the example of divine revelation, of Christ Himself, of the primitive Church.

Method: Historical-explanatory. The doctrine of the Trinity is not meant to be something abstract that Christians "have to believe" merely to exercise their faith; it is rather the most intimate revelation of God's own "inner life" to His beloved children—of that life which the Father has called us to share in Christ.

[2] F. J. Buckley, S.J., "What Age for Confirmation?" *Theological Studies,* 27 (1966), 655–666.

Viewpoint: A clear explanation of the importance for us, the children of God, of this deepest of mysteries. This is "our" mystery. *Aim:* Not only a firm rational submission of the intellect but also, and especially, profound joy and reverent thanksgiving for our participation in this mystery.

DOCTRINAL SUMMARY

A. THE SOLEMN REVELATION OF THE MYSTERY

During the Old Testament period there was no formal revelation of the three Persons in God. The preparation of the Hebrew people took the shape of an ever-increasing insistence on the uniqueness of God, for Israel was often tempted to seek other, more congenial gods to replace or at least rival Yahweh. From the beginning this one and only God had shown Himself a Father to Israel by calling His people into being out of nothingness, providing food and drink, defending them from their enemies, teaching them righteousness, adopting them as His own.

Once monotheism had been clearly established, a tendency arose to personify the Word of God and God's Spirit. Word and Spirit are correlative but distinct: the prophet bears witness to the Word because the Spirit speaks through him; the Suffering Servant can bring salvation to the nations because the Spirit rests upon him; Israel will be able one day to observe the Word of the Law because the Spirit will write the Law in their hearts. The Word is revelation; the Spirit, transformation. Yet Word and Spirit remain personifications, not divine Persons.

In the New Testament the distinction and equality of Persons is revealed, at first in operation, then in being. After the resurrection the Apostles begin to understand the mystery of Jesus' divine Sonship. Jesus acted like God because He is God's Son; as God's Son He is Himself God and worthy of adoration. He is not God's Son by adoption, as was Israel and each Israelite; He and the Father are one in action and in dignity—no human can understand Him or His Father without a divine revelation, which He Himself makes.

Throughout the public life of Christ the Spirit acted in Jesus and with Jesus, but Jesus must return to the Father before the Spirit can be given and recognized as distinct and divine. He will be another Paraclete, to defend the disciples as Jesus had done. He will lead them into the mysterious wellsprings of Jesus' own life by giving them an understanding of Jesus' meaning and power to bear witness to Him. The Spirit is a Person Who knows, speaks, loves, guides; Who performs divine actions of forgiving sins, changing hearts, making men holy, even uniting Father and Son. He is Himself God, so that to lie to Him is to lie to God, to offend Him is to offend God. By the time of the composition of St. Matthew's Gospel the Church clearly understood and taught the distinction and equality of Persons in the Trinitarian baptismal formula, and baptized "in the name of the Father, and of the Son, and of the Holy Spirit . . ." (Matt. 28:20).

B. The Religious Exposition of the Mystery

1. This is the intimate mystery of God's inner life. Here we should proceed with great reverence for God's transcendent otherness. We can know *that* there are three Persons in one God because He has revealed it. We can know *how* there are three Persons in one God, through the Father's eternal generation of His Son, His eternal utterance of self-comprehension in His Word and through their mutual self-communication in love. We *will* know *why* there are three Persons in God, but only in heaven, and even then this will remain mysterious. The infinite God must always remain incomprehensible to finite man. We cannot put God under a microscope or subject Him to experiment. To attempt to do so would be blasphemy. God is not subject to man the way the material universe is subject to us for exploration and domination.

We must beware of making the Trinity a mathematical problem. All use of numbers implies quantity. But there is no quantity in God: the three divine Persons are not like three apples or three atoms or even like three human ideas which succeed one another in time and therefore can be numbered. When applied to God, numbers are used only analogically; relations of *quantity* are impossible in God, only relations of *origin* are possible. And even these relations are quite different on a human level. A human father can give life to a son, and in time can share his own ideas and choices with him to some extent. But he cannot give his very own life to his son or perfectly share his understanding or love. But in God exactly the same—"numerically" the same—power, wisdom, and holiness, one and the same divine perfection, belong to the Father, are communicated from all eternity by Him to the Son, and are communicated to the Holy Spirit by the Father and the Son. All three Persons are truly and properly God; not three gods, but one God, since the divine perfection is in no way multiplied.

The wonderful union of the three divine Persons. It surpasses any union conceivable between created persons. It is the divine exemplar which every created union of persons imitates from afar. A created person can never communicate his own proper existence to another, even to his most intimate friend; he can only give something of himself, of his thoughts, affection, purposes, or ideals. Such is not the case in regard to God. The Father gives the Son the perfect fullness of the absolutely unique and undivided divine perfection; Father and Son together give this perfection to the Spirit. What joy in the common possession of this one divine fullness! How different from any created sharing of possessions.

This doctrine is the most profound mystery of our religion, a mystery in the strictest sense. We can explain a little of its meaning from what revelation tells us, but we cannot understand its inner reality. We can easily see that there must be mysteries in the infinite God that far surpass the powers of our created minds—that are *above* our reason. When God reveals such mysteries to us, we believe, not because we understand, but because He has revealed them. Comparisons and explanations help us to understand more clearly what the mystery means, but they cannot make it completely intelligible. (When using comparisons, then, we should always clearly indicate wherein lies the likeness with what we are explaining and wherein the unlikeness.)

2. *This is "our" mystery,* first because it is supremely interesting to us, children of God, to know the intimate secrets that our Father has revealed to us out of His love for us. Yet as children of God we are called not only to know about this mystery but *really to participate in it.* From the moment of baptism we have a special relationship with each of the divine Persons. Father and Son send the Holy Spirit to dwell in our hearts as in a temple, to consecrate us and give us a share in God's holiness by making us the Father's adopted children, modeled to the image of Christ, Whose members we become. This is why baptism is conferred in the name of the Trinity. ". . . through Him [Christ] we both have access in one Spirit to the Father. Therefore, you are now no longer strangers and foreigners, but you are citizens with the saints and members of God's household" (Eph. 2:18 ff.). The life given us at baptism is here and now a true participation in the life of the Trinity. Our future

glory in heaven will be nothing other than the ultimate development and conscious enjoyment of this same life. How rich are we
Christians! How wonderful the redemption by which Christ has not
only wiped out our guilt but has united us to Himself and brought
us into the innermost sanctuary of God. "But when the fullness of
time came, God sent His Son, born of a woman, born under the
Law, that He might redeem those who were under the Law, that we
might receive the adoption of sons. And because you are sons, God
has sent the Spirit of His Son into our hearts, crying, 'Abba, Father.'
So that he is no longer a slave, but a son; and if a son, an heir also
through God" (Gal. 4:4–7).

NOTE ON TEACHING THIS MATERIAL

Through our vital union with Christ we participate in the life
of the Trinity. And therefore the Church, following Scripture and
apostolic tradition, does not so much pray to the three Persons
together, to the Most Holy Trinity, as she prays *to the Father,
through Christ, in the Holy Spirit*. The Church has always
defended the divinity of each of the three divine Persons and the
consequent fact that each is to be adored, as is the undivided Trinity. But by the classical form of liturgical Christian prayer she indicates that we who are redeemed in Christ look upon the mystery of
the Triune God, not from without, but, as it were, from within,
since we are taken up, in Christ, into the very current of the life of
the Triune God. And so also our teaching of this most wonderful
mystery should not dwell too lengthily on inculcating the perfect
equality of the divine Persons, but should rather, following the example of the great Greek Fathers, indicate especially the dynamic
aspect of this doctrine: the life of the Most Blessed Trinity, the
differences and the relationships of the various Persons among
themselves.

THE DOCTRINE OF THE CHURCH

The Church is the fruit and continuation of the redemption. For
that reason it is fitting that we place the teaching on the Church
immediately after the teaching on Christ the Savior and the completion of His paschal mystery in the sending of the Spirit. For
Jesus died and rose again to communicate His life to all men by

handing over to us His Holy Spirit, Who gathers scattered mankind into the unity of the Church. By this sequence we follow the order of the Apostle's Creed and preserve intact the great sweep of the history of salvation: the dynamic plan initiated by the Father, carried forward and revealed by the Incarnate Son, and prolonged and brought to completion by the Holy Spirit sent by Jesus to His Church. In our catechesis on the life of Christ we attempted to bring out His "corporate personality," His role of building up a new mankind by establishing God's reign here on earth. Thus, when we spoke of Christ, we spoke already of the Church. On the other hand, the doctrine on the Church must be linked to the doctrine on the Holy Spirit in such a manner that the role of the Holy Spirit in the life of the Church receives its due emphasis. Only by combining both aspects will we be able to present the Church as God Himself has planned and established her: the Church, instituted by Christ and born on the cross, is vivified and strengthened by the Holy Spirit, Whose action in the Church was for the first time solemnly manifested on Pentecost.

In presenting the Church in a meaningful and effective way we have the immense advantage of the Dogmatic Constitution on the Church (*Lumen Gentium*) issued by the Second Vatican Council in 1964. This document is a model of pastoral catechetics, thoroughly biblical and Christocentric, setting forth Church doctrine in language far more understandable to modern man than was scholastic terminology (necessary though that be for a scientific theological analysis). Particularly useful for our purposes here are chapters one, two, and four of the Constitution. Chapter three, which treats of the hierarchical nature of the Church, was already referred to in our discussion of Christ's choice of disciples to carry on His work.

Seventeenth Instruction

THE CHURCH IN ACTION

Method: Descriptive-explanatory.

Viewpoint: Dynamic relationship between Christ and the Church in the work of salvation.

Aim: Gratitude for what God does for us through the Church. Active cooperation to achieve the goal of the Church.

DOCTRINAL SUMMARY

A. THE CHURCH, A SACRAMENT

The Church is a sacrament, a sign and an instrument of union between God and man. Like Christ, the Church is the place where God and man come together in loving encounter. She is the visible, audible, tangible expression of God's efficacious concern for the spiritual freedom and welfare of man. In her God's saving Word abides and is proclaimed, His sanctifying Spirit is given—and to God's self-gift man responds by worship, loyal profession of faith, and love of neighbor. If this presentation sounds idealistic and unreal, it is because the human weakness of the members of the Church frequently hides the mysterious divine self-gift which is constantly being offered to man—and too often refused. The Church is not yet perfect; man does not yet perfectly respond to God. We are still in process, still on the march to our goal. When that goal is reached, the Church will cease to be a sacrament. She will remain a sign of the divine presence but will no longer be an instrument of bringing about unity between God and man, for full unity will have been achieved once and for all.

Three elements must therefore be recognized in the Church as sacrament: (1) an *outward structural tangibility* which by God's power brings about (2) an *inner* sharing in God's life through faith and love (3) which are still only *imperfectly realized*.

B. THE CHURCH AND GOD'S KINGDOM

Christ in His person, His words, and His works revealed to men God's kingdom, His saving power active in the world. After His resurrection He gave to His disciples the Spirit He had promised. Thus the Church received the mission to proclaim and to spread Christ's kingdom, and even to *be* the initial budding forth of that kingdom. Kingdom and Church are not to be simply identified, however. As under the Old Covenant Israel was God's kingdom in the sense that there His kingship was explicitly recognized, even though His rule was never limited to Israel nor even perfectly obeyed there, so the Church is the place where God's kingly power has visibly broken into history, an institution which is recognized by faith and adoration, and from which His rule will spread to the whole world until finally God is "all in all" in the definitive phase of His kingdom.

In the earthly phase of the kingdom the Church, both clergy and laity, share in Christ's royal power and work. Bishops are to govern the Church like fathers or shepherds, not lording it over their flock, but imitating the Lord Jesus, Who came not to be served but to serve. In this task of ministry they are helped by priests, deacons, and laymen. By the secular nature of their vocation and work the laity contribute to the advance of God's kingdom in a special way, by sanctifying the world from within and ordering temporal affairs —politics, economic and family life, recreation, communication, science, and so on—according to the plan of God. Not only do they conquer the reign of sin in themselves by prayer and penance but they also strive to free the material world and human cultures from disorder so that the earth may more effectively serve the needs of all men.

The Church is not a kind of superstate, a kingdom in the political sense, rivaling others. Christ steadfastly refused to identify Himself as a political Messiah or His kingdom as a competitor to Rome. Church and state are independent; civil society is autonomous, with its own legitimate concern about the temporal interests of its citizens. Yet at the same time the Church, by God's authority, continues to proclaim the rights of men set free by Christ and stands ready to condemn political actions which violate those human rights.

C. The Church is an Ever-Growing Unity

The New Testament descriptions of the Church, whether in the parables of Jesus or in statements by the Apostles, highlight two characteristics: the Church is a group united to God and to each other, and is in movement.

1. The Church is a sheepfold, a flock ruled by Christ, the Good Shepherd; a piece of land cultivated by the Lord; a vine whose branches share the life and power of Christ. She is a temple, built on the foundation of Christ and His Apostles. The Church is a bride, joined to Jesus in love. She is a family, a city, a people which is God's. The Church is the very Body of the risen Christ, the extension of His incarnation, formed by baptism, nourished by His Eucharistic Body, kept alive by His Spirit.

2. Life and growth are essential to all of these images. Even the temple is a living temple, made of living stones and growing toward

perfect unity. The bride "is preparing herself," the flock is on pilgrimage, the body is becoming mature until it reaches the fullness of God. The Church is ever in movement, agitated by the life-giving Spirit, so that the union between man and man and between mankind and God in the Church is never static and rigid, but flexible and open to new developments. This is the place to develop the doctrine of the Church as the Mystical Body of Christ.

3. It is not clearly revealed whether the Church will visibly include all men before the end of the world. Given human sinfulness, the Church may always remain a relatively "little" flock. Nevertheless, she will forever be a sign of the full union with God and cooperation in His divine plan of salvation to which all men are called. The "movement" of the Church must not be too narrowly identified with geographical or numerical expansion, for there have been periods in which the visible Church grew smaller. But never has she ceased to bear witness to the risen Lord, never has she ceased to reflect upon His message, never has she failed to respond to His invitation to divine worship and loving service of others. If we remember that the Church is the whole People of God and not just the hierarchy, we can understand that there can be genuine, though less apparent, growth even in the midst of abuses and decay. The Church is in a permanent process of purification and reform until the fullness of time is accomplished.

Eighteenth Instruction

THE CHURCH IN BEING

Method: Descriptive-explanatory.
Viewpoint: The human, communal structure of the Church as she is in the world.
Aim: Appreciation of the mystery of the Church and the dignity of those who belong to her. An understanding of my own place in the Church, my rights and duties.

DOCTRINAL SUMMARY

A. THE PEOPLE OF GOD

God does not make men holy and save them merely as individuals. He brings men together as one people. Christ came to save all men, to restore the whole human race. Those who listen, obey, and follow constitute the new People of God, the Church. This fellowship, this community, like that of a family, should, of course, be experienced before it is explained; and here we see the importance of liturgical and community life. This doctrine of our fellowship in Christ should be clearly taught even to children and should be frequently preached to the adult laity.

Even children can, in their own way, grasp the very meaning of the Church if we present her to them as the family of God's children. In later years we have to deepen this presentation. We shall explain how God even in the Old Testament already prepared the Church, how He chose a special people, how the Israel of the First Covenant was the type of the future and perfect Israel, of God's Chosen People, sanctified by God and called to the new and perfect worship of the New Covenant, when "the true worshippers will worship the Father in spirit and in truth" (John 4:23). This worship of the New Israel finds its climax here on earth in the sacrifice of the New Covenant, offered once for all by Christ in His passion and death, accepted by the Father in the resurrection, and renewed upon our altars by the community of believers as the genuine expression of a God-centered life.

1. This new, Messianic People of God has Christ for its *Head*. 2. Its *heritage* is the dignity and freedom of God's children. 3. Its *law* is the new commandment to love as Christ has loved us. 4. Its *goal* is the full establishment of God's kingdom upon earth.

B. PARTICIPATION IN THIS PEOPLE

The People of God does not yet visibly include all men, but is used by Christ as an instrument for the redemption of all: it is to be the light of the world, the salt of the earth, a seed bearing life and hope to the whole human race. All men are called to become part of the unity of this People, and in fact all are now related to it in various ways.

1. Those are *fully incorporated* in the society of the Church who possess the Spirit of Christ, accept her entire system and all the means of salvation given to her, and through union with her visible hierarchical structure are joined to Christ. The visible bands joining men to Christ in the Church are profession of faith, the sacraments, ecclesiastical government, and communion.

2. Catechumens are incorporated into the Church by desire and explicit intent.

3. Fellow Christians who do not profess the faith in its entirety or preserve unity of communion with the Pope are still linked to the Church by Scripture, faith in Christ, baptism, other sacraments, prayer, and the gifts of the Holy Spirit.

4. The Jews share with the Church faith in the God Who spoke through the Old Testament as well as the New. Not only did the Jews provide the human stock from which Jesus and His earliest disciples arose but they also remain most dear to God and remain joined to Him by the Old Covenant which, though fulfilled and surpassed by the New, has not been repudiated or cancelled by God.

5. Many elements of holiness and truth are found outside the visible structure of the Church. These elements are the work of the Holy Spirit preparing men for the Gospel; as such, they are forces impelling toward catholic unity. The same Holy Spirit compels the Church to proclaim the Gospel so that men may come to a full realization of God's work in their midst and so through charity attain full maturity in total integration in the Mystical Body of Christ.

These "seeds of the Word" planted by the Spirit in other religions enable men to be saved and to grow in holiness through a mysterious relationship to the Church. Men are saved only through union with Christ. The Holy Spirit makes men adopted children of God, "sons in the Son," even though they may be unaware that they live and love like Christ. These elements of grace in other religions and cultures can purify and enrich the visible Church, as well as they being purified and enriched by her.

C. Variety and Diversity Within the Church

1. The Church purifies, strengthens, elevates, and ennobles the abilities, resources, and customs in which the genius of each people expresses itself. Moreover, each individual receives from the Holy Spirit gifts for the good of others and the whole Church. The diversity of the Church's inner structure arises by reason of special duties of service, as among the clergy; by reason of their state of life, which manifests a special characteristic of Christ's mission, as among the religious; or by reason of charisms, distributed by the Spirit as He wishes to every Christian.

2. *Each member of the Church has part in her activity.* Both

Christ Himself (John 15:12 ff.) and St. Paul infer from our unity in Christ the fact that we have a clear obligation to collaborate with one another (e.g., 1 Cor. 12; Rom. 12:4 ff.) and to love one another in Christ.

In the Church, as in any well-developed organism, the functions of the individual members differ from one another, but there are no merely passive members. We Christians not only share in the fruits of the redemption in the Church but are actively to collaborate with Christ in the work of redeeming and sactifying the world, that is, in bringing it back to the Father. This is the active Christian aspect of the Church.

This Christian activity is of paramount importance, particulary in mission regions and in countries where Catholics are a minority. Each Christian is, according to his circumstances, to be another Christ and, therefore, an effective missionary. In all places where Catholics are a minority the danger exists of an exaggerated or pharisaical separation of Catholics from non-Catholics. To the degree that it is not possessed by the apostolic spirit Christianity is not truly Christian—for it lacks the characteristic note of "catholicity," which consists essentially in the tendency to become evermore widespread and universal. Here applies the saying "If anyone does not have the spirit of Christ, he does not belong to Christ (Rom. 8:9).

The kingdom of God cannot be established and increase as it should without the collaboration of all of us. In this great work of the children of God and members of His family, lay Catholics of course have a most important, in fact an indispensable, part. They are actively to collaborate in establishing the kingdom of God over the whole world, but first of all in and around themselves. But this means essentially much more than simply to try to "save one's own soul" with a more or less egotistic attitude. It means constant and generous efforts to imbue the world in which we live with the spirit of Christ: our family, our community, our culture. "The kingdom of heaven is like leaven, which a woman [the Church] took and buried in three measures of flour, until all of it was leavened" (Matt. 13:33). Behold the task of the Church—to renew the whole world and all human activities in the spirit of Christ! How little of this great work has yet been accomplished, even now, almost two thousand years after Christ's earthly life. And why is this so? Have we teachers of religion always stressed with sufficient earnestness the obligation of everyone to collaborate toward achieving this goal?

Have we always showed our students what they might begin to do along these lines?

3. Although all members of the Church are supposed to have an active part in the life of the Church, in her worship, and in her apostolate, *Christ has given to some members special powers* "in order to perfect the saints for a work of ministry, for building up the body of Christ" (Eph. 4:12). Through them He teaches, sanctifies, and directs all those who live on earth after His own earthly life had ended. See the "Christian" aspect of the hierarchy: "As the Father has sent me, I also send you" (John 20:21). Christ—the Apostles—bishops—priests. The most important point to be made here is the Christocentric foundation of the hierarchy. When anyone grasps this fundamental principle, he will have no great difficulties with the various dogmas that more accurately determine a hierarchical power. The good Catholic acknowledges, honors, hears, and follows Christ Himself in the hierarchy.

THE SACRAMENTS

As we mentioned above, the teaching on the sacraments constitutes part of the teaching on the life-giving Spirit. For it is in the sacraments most especially that the Holy Spirit is communicated to us; it is in the sacraments that He Himself confers His divine life upon us and day by day forms us more completely to the image of Christ.

The sacraments as sacred rites must be seen as extensions of the sacramental nature of Christ and the Church. A sacrament is a sign which symbolizes and effects union with God. Christ, the Incarnate Word, visibly unites God and man in Himself. Because of the presence of the Holy Spirit within her the Church brings about this union of man with God and enables us to participate in the nature and mission of Jesus Christ. The Catholic Church, the visible society of those whom God has called to worship Him and share His life, is a sign of what all men should be.

It is very difficult, and to some extent artificial, to separate the sacraments from the commandments. Not that the sacraments are meant as helps to fulfill the commandments. Rather both sacraments and commandments flow from the very nature of Christian life as a discovery of God in the whole of human existence and a loving worship of Him Who is at once transcendent and immanent.

All of the sacraments are an obedience to the commandment to love and adore God and to join ourselves to Him; all of them are also in a sense obedience to the command to love and serve our neighbor, for all the sacraments join us more intimately to the whole People of God, the Church. Furthermore, the commandments simply make explicit the direction of the dynamic drive to live as God's children; the sacraments, through the Holy Spirit, are the source of this life-force, and each of them qualifies and specifies this life with its own special characteristics. The forgiven sinner, the confirmed apostle, the married man, the priest, the single lay woman—all live and love in a special way.

Nevertheless, to heighten appreciation of the sacraments as gifts of God, to counterbalance the very incomplete and even misleading notion that the sacraments are "acts which Christians perform," for the sake of teaching it seemed good to devote special attention to certain sacraments here. (Confirmation is treated in the Fifteenth Instruction, holy orders in the Eleventh, matrimony in the Twenty-eighth.)

Viewpoint: The sacraments should be taught as being, above all, the great sources of the divine life, not merely means to leading a good moral life. It is true, of course, that the effects of the sacraments should show themselves in truly Christlike living. But such living should be shown to be the fruit of our cooperation with the grace of the sacraments, not an effect which can be expected without the necessary efforts on our own part. Christlike living is thus an obligation incumbent upon us from our reception of the sacraments. What they produce immediately is a new presence of the Holy Spirit and closer union with Christ, and, consequent upon it, an increase of divine life. This growth in union with Christ, then, obliges us to a more Christlike life; every reception of any sacrament includes the call to a life more fully united with Christ. To enable us to respond to this call we certainly receive abundant "helping" (actual) graces out of regard for the sacrament we receive.

These graces are given when we need them: not only at the moment of reception of a sacrament to intensify our union with Christ Who meets us but also at other moments of need, for example, when we are tempted or when we are given special opportunities to discover Christ or to follow Him generously. The measure of the graces, both sanctifying and "helping," that we in fact receive depends in great part on the disposition in which we receive the sacrament. (Example of attention paid to a teacher.)

The doctrine of the sacraments again unfolds to us the "unfathomable riches of Christ" made available to us in the Church. Therefore:

The chief effects of the lessons on the sacraments should be a deep, heartfelt, and active gratitude, which consists, not in mere emotion, but in the fervent use of these fountains of grace, a gratitude which shows itself in an increasingly Christlike life. "With joy you will draw water at the fountain of salvation, and say on that day: Give thanks to the Lord, acclaim His name; among the nations make known His deeds . . ." (Isaiah 12:3 ff.).

Within the framework of these very fundamental instructions a special instruction on the sacraments in general is hardly necessary.[3] The necessary points can easily be given in the teaching on the Church, or on the Holy Spirit, or at the beginning of the instruction on baptism. If time allows for a separate general instruction on the sacraments, the image of a fountain may well be used to explain the essential points. Christ Himself is the institutor and the source of this wonderful fountain by which He confers upon us the fruits of the redemption. "He, however, who drinks of the water that I will give him shall never thirst; but the water that I will give him shall become in him a fountain of water, springing up into life everlasting" (John 4:13 ff.). Christ gives us this fountain; we ourselves must come to the water and draw it out in abundance. Of all the sacraments baptism is the most important, the Eucharist is the most sublime. Take care, however, not to overobjectify grace as if it were something material separate from Christ. Christ Himself is both fountain and water. Grace is the effect in us of a special presence of Christ. He gives us a share in His life as Son.

---

[3] The chapter on the sacraments in general is a typical remnant of scholastic theology with its characteristic progression from the abstract to the concrete. This may be fully justified in a course of scientific theology, but elementary teaching must do just the opposite by going from the concrete to the abstract. Thus the chapter on the sacraments in general would be put after the chapter dealing with the individual sacraments. Arranged in this way, the lesson on the sacraments in general will provide a very useful recapitulation. A good example of this kind is provided by the *On Our Way Series,* Grade 5, lesson 18.

THE EFFECT OF BAPTISM

From the very nature of baptism the doctrine concerning this sacrament is of the greatest importance for firmly establishing a Christian life. In baptism the divine life is given us for the first time through a visible rite; it is then that we are "born of God" (John 1:13). Diligent care must be taken, therefore, that Christians properly esteem the grace of baptism, the source of Christian life and activity, and that they understand the obligation incurred at baptism to strive to lead the Christian life.

The most important moments of Christian life are the moment of baptism, when we first encounter Christ in a sacrament, and the moment of death, at which our final union with Christ is determined. Throughout our whole lives we should give thanks for that first moment and humbly pray and prepare ourselves for the second moment, which should be the completion of the first.

Since baptism is so important, we should eagerly seize upon every occasion to instruct our hearers thoroughly in its wonders. And we should make use of the actual administration of this sacrament, whether to adults or children, or even when supplying the ceremonies, to give an instruction of suitable length.

Method: Explanatory. The method of exposition here should consist, not in telling a narrative, but in the vivid description and explanation of the external rites. For the sacraments "confer what they signify," and the person who understands the rites of a sacrament understands the sacrament itself. Christ wished to institute the sacraments in such a way that we might easily understand His intentions and the special grace of each sacrament from the external signs, and for this same purpose the Church organized the various accompanying ceremonies.

When we are explaining the rites of baptism, we must bear in mind the fact that we are not concerned with giving a learned dissertation on liturgical science, which would tend to enumerate, describe, and minutely explain the entire rite. In addition to the essential rite only the more important additional ceremonies should be selected for explanation, ones that can be easily understood by simple people. In this instruction we should particularly explain those rites which show us the effect of baptism and, in the following instruction, those which teach us the obligations assumed in baptism.

Viewpoint: The greatness and the excellence of the grace of baptism, and the great dignity to which it raises us.

Aim: A most profound and, at the same time, most humble gratitude: "He raises up the lowly from the dust; from the dunghill he lifts up the poor, to seat them with princes, with the princes of His own people" (Psalm 112). A living consciousness of our Christian dignity.

DOCTRINAL SUMMARY

A. ENTRANCE INTO THE CHURCH

The ceremonies begin outside the church door. The catechumen is not as yet a member of the Church. In baptism we enter the Church of Christ, "built of living and chosen stones," the invisible Temple of which the church building is the image. In baptism we receive a right to the treasures of the Church, particularly to faith and to the divine life. (See the dialogue between the priest and the catechumen at the beginning of the ceremonies.) The Church leads us at once to Christ.

B. UNION WITH CHRIST

The sign of the cross, so often imposed on the candidate. Until now we have been subjects of the devil; in baptism we exchange masters: we make ourselves subject to Christ. *The baptismal character:* the sign of the cross traced externally on the candidate's forehead is a sign of the internal impression of the sign of Christ the Savior on our souls, our innermost beings; by baptism the soul is united and configured to Christ. Now Christ owns us; His mark is on us, as sheep are branded to show to whose flock they belong. The exorcisms indicate that Christ drives out the former owner who had stolen us from our Creator. But the devil does not relinquish his hold on us unless we ourselves wish it—so the climax of the negative aspect of baptism is the personal renouncement of the devil's service, immediately before the actual baptism: "I do renounce him." Thus for the remission of personal sins the necessity for sorrow is absolute, even in baptism. Through this sacrament the process of "conversion" is completed. The Church is the society of the converted, of those who, in Christ the second Adam, are turned toward the Father.

C. New Divine Life

The essential rite: the washing, which is also a rebirth. Water in holy Scripture is both destructive and creative—the flood, the exodus, and so on. So in baptism we are cleansed from sin—the power of the devil is destroyed; sin (original and personal) is destroyed and its punishment remitted. And at the same time we are reborn to the life of God, filled with light, and made beautiful in God's eyes. Thus baptism is a death, and a rebirth and resurrection. We are "plunged into" Christ's death, to die to the fallen life of sin and selfishness inherited from the first Adam; by the power of Christ risen from the dead we rise to His divine life.

Thus the heavenly Father receives us as sons united with Christ. This *divine adoption* not only gives us the rights and the title of children of God but it really makes us partakers of the divine nature (2 Pet. 1:4), so we not only are called sons of God but really are sons (1 John 3:1). A human father in adopting a child can only give him rights and possessions, but in an indescribable way the heavenly Father communicates His own life to us through the Holy Spirit, Whom He infuses into our hearts. (The Trinity, the incarnation, and the divine adoption are the three chief and closely interconnected mysteries of our religion.) All these blessings are given us because of our intimate union with Christ. The Church leads us to Christ; Christ leads us to the Father, Who receives us as sons because of our close union with His Son. An apt example would be the son of a king who finds a poor boy, loves him, takes him into his friendship, brings him home to his father, and begs him to adopt him, and shares everything with him. "But if we are sons, we are heirs also: heirs indeed of God and joint heirs with Christ" (Rom. 8:17).

D. Consecration to the Most Holy Trinity

Baptism brings us into a completely new and intimate relationship with each of the divine persons. Notice the form of baptism: "In the name [in Greek the text says "into the name. . . ."] of the Father. . . ." This signifies primarily the consecration of the candidate to the Most Blessed Trinity. This consecration essentially surpasses in reality and importance any moral consecration by which a Christian may from devotion consecrate himself to the Blessed Virgin or to a saint. The baptismal consecration is constitutive: the baptized person, through his real union with Christ, is in an entirely new manner united and given over to each of the divine Persons. He becomes an adopted son of the Father, a brother of the only-begotten Son and a member of His Body, a temple of the Spirit.[4] Thus the whole baptized person is made holy both in body and in soul. He is far more sacred than the consecrated chalice that holds the most precious blood, because his relation to God is much more intimate. Example of Leonidas who so reverently kissed his newly baptized little son, Origen.

Those of us who were baptized as little children could not even begin to understand these gifts. Let us always strive to understand them more fully, to cooperate with them, to be thankful for them.

Twentieth Instruction

THE OBLIGATION CONTRACTED AT BAPTISM

It is most important that Christians should thoroughly understand that by baptism they have been called out of the throng of "anonymous Christians" to the conscious dignity of being sons of God, to an entirely new life. How sad and shameful it would be if a baptized person were to return to a pagan life! We are children of the light, the leaven for the mass of our unbaptized fellow men. We who have been privileged to be baptized and incorporated in Christ must be the light of the world (see the candle given at baptism, the candles of the Easter Vigil lit from the paschal candle) and the salt of the earth (Matt. 5:13 f.; Phil. 2:15).

Method: Explanatory, as in the preceding lesson. An explanation of the anointing with chrism (oil and perfumes: we share in the kingship and priesthood of Christ; we are to be "the good odor of Christ" [2 Cor. 2:15] drawing others to Him), the lighted candle, the white robe of present grace and future glory, can be used

---

[4] In later years it may be good to mention that our body is rightly called a temple of the Holy Spirit (see 1 Cor. 6:19), but His indwelling must not be considered as something which belongs exclusively to the Third Person of the Holy Trinity (see 1 Cor. 3:16 f.; John 14:23). The Father and Son send the Holy Spirit. Because He is present, teaching us to love, They also come and abide with us in a special way.

instead of a narrative, together with the example of the poor boy adopted by the king.

Viewpoint: Our gratitude must manifest itself by a completely new life, one befitting a child of God.

Aim: The constant effort and eagerness to become conformed to Christ, to die to sin and to live for God.

DOCTRINAL SUMMARY

A. COMPARISON

By baptism we are taken up into the family of God's children. Let us then live the life of His sons. How will the poor boy of the example act if he has any gratitude or honor? How foolish and despicable he would be if he went away from his loving father and brother, if he offended them by his rude ways. Day by day he should try to become more like the ideal son of his new father. His exemplar will be his new brother, the born son of the king.

B. EXPLANATION AND APPLICATION

We have become "Christ-ened." The complete description of our new life is that it is "in Christ." This means far more than that we are called to follow Him by trying to imitate Him. In *vital union with Him* we are to die to sin, to live to God (Rom. 6:1 ff.).

In Christ to die to sin. We have renounced the service of Satan with all that this implies. We are no longer children of the first Adam, disobedient and proud; we are brothers and members of the second Adam (1 Pet. 1:19; 1 Cor. 5:7 ff.)—"Purge out the old leaven, that you may be a new dough. . . . For Christ, our passover, has been sacrificed"—the Easter Sunday Epistle to the newly baptized). In baptism we are intimately associated with Christ, assimilated to Him Who was obedient unto death, even the death of the cross. ". . . we have been united with Him in the likeness of His death. . . . For we know that our old self has been crucified with Him, in order that the body of sin may be destroyed [with its unregulated desires received from the first Adam], that we may no longer be slaves to sin . . ." (Rom. 6:5 ff.). "Therefore do not let sin reign in your mortal body so that you obey its lusts" (Rom. 6:12–14).

Here we should, briefly and correctly, point out the sins most often indulged in today that are particularly opposed to the Christian vocation: tepidity in the service of God, lust, avarice, deliberate hatred toward our neighbor, injustice, indifference to the needs of others, and so on—all of which are forms of "idolatry" (see Eph. 5:5; Col. 3:5).

In Christ to live to God. In baptism we are intimately united to Christ, called to an intimate fellowship with Him. "For in one Spirit we were all baptized into one body" (1 Cor. 12:3); "that the life also of Jesus may be made manifest in our mortal flesh" (2 Cor. 4:10). "For all you who have been baptized into Christ, have put on Christ" (Gal. 3:27—example of "white garment" given at baptism); we are now to be "alive to God in Christ Jesus our Lord" (Rom. 6:11).

The life of Christ is one entirely of *filial love.* The focus of His heart is His Father: see his first words (Heb. 10:5; Luke 2:49) and His last word (Luke 23:46). His whole life was dedicated to the service of His Father: "He Who sent Me is with Me; He has not left Me alone, because I do always the things that are pleasing to Him" (John 8:29). He wishes to communicate to us this spirit of filial love through the Holy Spirit Who cries out in our hearts: "Abba, Father" (Rom. 8:15). Here we should use some vivid and concrete examples adapted to the audience, perhaps from the lives of the saints, to show the ideal practice of such a life of love. Thus we transfer the life of Christ into our own circumstances.

By its very nature this spirit of filial love tends toward frequent, reverent, and affectionate conversation with the Father—Christian prayer. And it tends also to be joyful service, to the offering of pleasing sacrifices. True love asks not what it *has* to do, but what it *can* do to manifest itself. "Our citizenship is in heaven" (Phil. 3:20). Our treasure is in heaven, for our supreme treasure is the Father Whom we love with our whole heart, Whom we serve with all our heart, and with Whom we desire to be united and happy for all eternity.

It is God Himself Who has called us to this new kind of life. Through His gift we are His children and only through His continuous paternal help will it be possible for us to live according to our sublime vocation. What He expects from us, above all, is deep gratitude and a holy desire to follow His call together with the humble profession of our weakness which needs His powerful help (actual grace) so much.

NOTE ON TEACHING THIS MATERIAL

1. Since a vivid awareness of the grace and the obligations of baptism is so important, it is most strongly recommended that in every Christian community the renewal of the baptismal promises be celebrated solemnly once a year. The ideal time, of course, now established by the Church as an integral part of the liturgy, is during the great Easter Vigil. In the missions as much as possible of the Easter Vigil should be celebrated, even when no priest is present. This may be done under the direction of a properly appointed lay person or religious.

2. If the instruction on baptism is given well, a special separate lesson on sanctifying grace will not be necessary in such a course as this giving the essential teachings within the compass of thirty lessons.

THE HOLY EUCHARIST

The teaching on the other sacraments is closely connected with that on baptism. For either they increase and develop the divine life received in baptism (sacraments of the living) or they restore it (the other sacraments of the dead). But in a special way is the doctrine on the Eucharist to be closely united with that on baptism. In baptism we receive the divine life; in the Eucharist the wonderful food of this life. A consideration of the food is the best way of reaching some understanding of the life it nourishes. In the Eucharist we are given a divine and heavenly food; how divine and heavenly must be the life it feeds! Thus from the very beginning the Eucharist is to be presented as the heavenly food of the divine life given at baptism, not merely as the visit of the "good Jesus."[5]

The approach to a more complete understanding of the Eucharist is through an understanding of the Eucharistic sacrifice. In the Mass we offer the Son to the Father, we share in the Son's offering of Himself, and we offer ourselves and are offered with Him. Then in communion, the sacrificial banquet, the heavenly Father gives

---

[5] Parents are the best judge as to when a child is ready for First Communion. For a discussion of the requirements for First Communion, its relation to first confession, and the respective roles of pastor and parents, see F. J. Buckley, S.J., "Parents, Children, and First Communion," *American Ecclesiastical Review*, CLVI (1967), 393–403.

His Son to us; the principal fruit of the sacrifice is holy communion. Full participation in the sacrifice includes participation in the banquet. In the sacrifice we give; in communion we receive. Thus it follows that the best preparation for communion is the perfect offering of ourselves with Christ in the sacrifice. This is the intimate interchange of love between the Father and His children. In thanksgiving (eucharist) for all the blessings of His love, we offer Him ourselves through Christ, Who makes Himself and His sacrifice our thanksgiving to the Father. Thus to take part in the Mass is our "chief duty and supreme dignity" (*Med. Dei*). We are most alive as Christians, most fully and perfectly in act when we take part in the Mass, when by the ministry of our priest, through Christ, with Him and in Him, we offer to God the Father a pure victim, a holy victim, an unspotted victim.

Ideal instruction on the Eucharist presupposes an ideal form of participation in the sacrifice, including communion. Here again we see the importance of a liturgical renewal which has as its particular aim to make the participation of the laity more active, intelligent, and fruitful.

Twenty-First Instruction

THE INSTITUTION OF THE HOLY EUCHARIST

Method: Historical-explanatory.
Viewpoint: The greatness of Christ's love, the greatness of His gift.
Aim: True gratitude for this great gift and love—a gratitude which will manifest itself in the fervent use of this most exalted sacrament. This first lesson is also a preparation for the one that follows on the sacrifice of the Mass. This first is more affective, the following more instructive, deepening understanding and appreciation, thus leading to a more active and intelligent participation.

DOCTRINAL SUMMARY

A. PREPARATION FOR THE INSTITUTION

Christ sent His most beloved Apostles ahead to prepare for the Last Supper (Luke 22:7 ff). Our Lord's desire (Luke 22:15) and His great love (John 13:1) on the day before He suffered.

The washing of the feet: In His great love He humiliated Himself. "He emptied Himself, taking the form of a slave" (He became a servant in washing His disciples' feet; in the institution of the Eucharist He makes Himself our food). "Have this mind in you which was also in Christ Jesus" (Phil. 2:5), especially when we approach the Holy Eucharist. In preparing for holy communion we need not so much to elicit "acts" of faith and such, as to strive to be filled with the Spirit of Christ, especially with the spirit of humble love toward God and our neighbor, and so approach the sacrifice and sacrament. "I have given you an example" (John 13:15). Although we do not recommend the use of isolated acts of faith, we can never sufficiently inculcate the necessity for the attitude of faith toward this "mysterium fidei" par excellence. This is not the most fundamental mystery, but it is the most striking since it is so strikingly opposed to what the senses suggest. Here, also, faith means that we take the word of Our Lord as full living reality precisely because we have first accepted Him as Lord.

Christ Himself was much concerned with the perfect purity of His disciples' hearts. And only He can cleanse us sufficiently. "You are clean, but not all." Judas was untouched by love . . . a desperate condition . . . Christ let him go away. He respected his freedom.

B. THE INSTITUTION ITSELF

What did He say? What did He do? How? Exactly what the priest now does in the Mass.

First of all Christ produces a most amazing change. What a great miracle! In theology we call it *transubstantiation:* explain the reality itself, not the difficult word, which we should never use in the lower grades of school or in preaching to uneducated people. We should rather give the doctrine according to the Bible narrative. What did Christ take in His hands? Evidently, ordinary bread. What did He say? Are not the words perfectly clear? Could He not do what He said so clearly? What, therefore, was the result? What did He hold in His sacred hands after His consecratory words? But we should not dwell too long on this still preparatory point. We should make it clear that transubstantiation is by no means an end in itself. Christ effected this change for a twofold purpose: to provide us with a fitting gift that we could offer to the heavenly Father (sacrifice) and to provide us with the divine food for our life as children of God (sacrament). He changes the meaning, the function, the very reality of the bread and wine. The food of ordinary human life becomes the food of divine life and the sign of Christ's own gift of Himself to the Father for our sake.

Sacrifice: The bread is changed into Christ's Body "that is given up" (present tense) not only on the following day on Calvary but also here and now. The wine is changed into Christ's Blood, which "is poured out," that is, sacrificially offered here and now as "the" Blood of the New Testament (see the parallel text on the blood of the former Testament shed on Mt. Sinai, Exod. 24:4 ff.).

Sacrament: Given as food, "eat! . . . drink!" See the species of the Eucharist: the sacraments give what they signify. What kind of food is thus prepared by the Father's love for His beloved children? What kind of a life is it that they possess, that they need a food so truly divine?

Do this in commemoration of Me. What He did must be repeated by the Apostles in memory of Him. "For as often as you shall eat . . . you proclaim the death of the Lord, until He comes" (1 Cor. 11:26). The Last Supper was the anticipation of the sacrifice of the cross. Every Mass is by its nature the renewal of this sacrifice.

C. THANKSGIVING

Christ Himself gave thanks with the Apostles. This thanksgiving made together inculcates in them the greatest possible union with God the Father through Christ and in Him—but with a very practical application—the great commandment. "I am the vine, you are the branches. . . . As the Father has loved Me, I also have loved you. Abide in My love. . . . This is My commandment, that you love one another as I have loved you. . . . that all may be one, even as Thou, Father, in Me and I in Thee; that they also may be one in Us. . . I in them and Thou in Me; that they may be perfected in unity . . ." (John 15 and 17).

The principal fruit of communion: Union with Christ, but with the whole Christ, Head and members, transformation into Christ (use the analogy of ordinary food, but stress the differences. This food is not assimilated into us; it assimilates us to itself). It is no longer I that live, but Christ lives in me" (Gal. 2:20).

THE SACRIFICE OF THE MASS

Method: Explanatory. Instead of narration, use a comparison.

Viewpoint: The Mass as "the eucharist," that is, the communal thanksgiving and praise offered to the Father by those who have been redeemed. The sacrifice of the Mass as the climax and fount of Christian life.

Aim: Knowledge and a truly religious appreciation of the Mass. This instruction intends not to explain all the separate ceremonies, but rather to explain clearly the principal meaning of sacrifice and of the Eucharistic banquet. The lack of appreciation and the lack of participation shown by many Christians proceed in most cases, not from a lack of knowledge of the various ceremonies, but from want of realization and appreciation of the central action.

DOCTRINAL SUMMARY

In the Mass we do what Christ did at the Last Supper: we offer the sacrifice, we receive the sacrament. Here we desire to see what sacrifice and sacrament meant, and how they fit together.

A. THE COMPARISON

The New Year's celebration in China.[6] At the time of the new year it is the custom to have a family celebration, for which faithful children often come from far away, undertaking very difficult journeys, in order to show their filial respect and affection. The central act of the celebration is the solemn New Year's offering of filial devotion and thanks to the parents. They are seated in the place of honor, waiting for the children who come one by one, led by the oldest, and express their filial love and respect by an expressive deep bow, made by getting down on both knees and then bending over so that the forehead touches the floor—the "ko-tou." This ceremony is followed by the New Year's family meal. The meaning of this ceremony is to show gratitude to the parents, to thank them, to

---

[6] A similar comparison easily can be taken from the celebration of Mother's or Father's Day, now commonly observed in so many countries.

beg pardon for all the faults committed during the past year, and to show devotion and love. And this includes at least an implicit promise to behave well during the coming year. The parents are very pleased. How do they answer? By the family meal that follows, the symbol of family unity.

B. Application to the Sacrifice of the Mass

Through Christ we have been gathered into *the new family of the children of God,* not by any merits of our own, but only because of the marvelous generosity of the Father. How many benefits we have received from Him, and this in spite of our numberless sins, and negligences. Filial devotion urges us also often to thank our Father together, to beg pardon for our negligences, to show our love, and to promise prompt obedience in the future.

In the Mass, with Christ our Brother leading us, we offer this *community thanksgiving.* The principal celebrant is always Christ Himself; the visible ordained priest acts as His representative. We can only give the Father worthy thanks through and in Christ, not by ourselves; hence we must take our part in the sacrifice offered by the ordained priest who has received the power to act in the very person of Christ in the Mass.

The structure of the Mass is a dialogue in words and deeds between God and us. First God calls us. We come and acknowledge our faults and our need of His forgiveness. He reassures us of His love in the liturgy of the word. We proclaim our faith in Him and ask Him to bless us, the whole Church, and the world.

There follows the dialogue of deeds, the mutual exchange of gifts. We join ourselves with Christ as He offers Himself to the Father: the Father gives us Christ in holy communion to strengthen and nourish His life in us.

1. *The Liturgy of the Word*

In the first part of the Mass we prepare to offer our thanksgiving as perfectly as possible, above all by recalling the benefits we have received. The greatest of these, which includes in itself all the others, is our vocation to the life of God's children through Jesus Christ, Whom the Father sent to us to redeem us. Through the Epistle and Gospel and the sermon, God tells us of the wonders of our redemption in Christ and invites our further cooperation. Christ Himself, at the first Mass, explained the meaning of the Passover and the paschal lamb and applied it to the sacrifice of the New Testament. And so through the ages Mother Church has given us the words of God Himself in holy Scripture, explained in the sermon by the priest, to prepare us to offer our thanksgiving. Notice the special aspect under which sacred teaching is given us in the Mass: "the Gospel of our Lord Jesus Christ," that is, the good tidings about the wonderful blessings that God has given us in Christ.

2. *The Liturgy of the Eucharist: Sacrifice*

Now that we are properly disposed by recalling with happiness the benefits of the Father, we approach the act of thanksgiving itself. Would that we had a fitting gift that could adequately show our gratitude and our love for our Father in heaven. All peoples offer gifts to their gods, and we call these gifts offered to God sacrifices. The sacrificial gift stands for the giver; it takes the place of the giver; it expresses our complete surrender to God in obedient submission. Christ on the cross perfectly fulfilled the deepest meaning of all sacrifices; in His sacrifice there was both a symbol and reality; He freely offered His own life.

What, then, can we poor men offer to God? See the gifts of our lowly condition: bread and wine. We have no gift that in any way corresponds to the infinite majesty and goodness of the Father. But bread and wine, the nourishment of our physical life, represent all the gifts that He has given us, His continuing creation and providence; they also represent our lives and our work: bread is made by human labor from the seed God causes to grow, wine from the grapes. And they represent the community of the Church, all of us together: one loaf from many grains, one cup of wine from many grapes.

The bread and wine, then, stand for all that we have and are. In themselves these are in no way worthy of God's majesty. But Christ our Brother changes these merely human gifts into His own Body and Blood. Now we have a most worthy and fitting gift. Our gift is Christ Himself! As He offered Himself on the cross, so here and now, although in an unbloody manner, Christ offers Himself to the Father. *Behold our most excellent gift!* Most excellent because it contains the Body and Blood of the Lord. And truly *our gift* because it includes us, Christ's members, also. Christ offers us with Himself, and we join in offering His sacrifice through the hands of our priest. But we shall not please the Father with even this most excellent offering unless we offer it with fervent hearts, unless we truly offer ourselves in obedient love with Christ. Therefore we must strive with all our powers to offer it worthily: in the spirit of the humility, love, and gratitude of Christ. At Mass, above all, we should be one in heart and soul with our Leader. What are the principal affections that we should strive to elicit at the time of the sacrificial action, and especially during the canon? The principal affection in the sacrifice of the New Law is simply this: the gratitude of sons. Behold the "eucharist" of the redeemed, offered to the Father by our Leader, the Redeemer.

Behold the climax of our Christian life in this world! Just as the priest is most completely a priest at the moment of sacrifice, so also the laity, the holy "people" of God, are most fully themselves, most fully Christian, most fully active as Christians, when together with Christ they offer themselves to the Father and manifest their perfect love as His children.

The heavenly Father looks down on us with affection and gladly accepts this our offering, given in and with and through Christ.

3. *The Liturgy of the Eucharist: The Sacrifical Banquet*

How does the Father then respond to our thanksgiving? Greatly pleased by our gratitude, He desires to show us His goodness and His approval by giving us at once a new and wonderful gift. But even the almighty Father has no gift more excellent than His only-begotten Son. He gives Him to us in *holy communion;* and in Him and with Him He gives us also all the other gifts that are necessary and appropriate for us. Above all, with the gift of His Son He pours out abundantly into our hearts the Holy Spirit, the Spirit of the love of sons. The theological principle that "the visible mission of the Son tends toward the invisible mission of the Spirit" applies also to the mission of the Son sacramentally visible under the sacred species. Christ, the most excellent gift of the Father, is the pledge, the completion, and the crown of all other gifts (Rom. 8:32).

From this consideration of communion we can clearly see what kind of preparation and thanksgiving is the best. The *best preparation* is not to be sought in anything undertaken during the Mass aside from the action of the Mass itself. It consists, rather, in taking part as actively and perfectly as possible in the Mass, in offering the best possible thanksgiving to the Father in pure gratitude and love, in and with Christ—to wish nothing else except to praise and to please the Father with our whole hearts. The more perfect is this thanksgiving, the more abundant and excellent also will be the Father's response.

And the *best thanksgiving* after holy communion will be to strive to correspond more and more perfectly to the intentions of the Giver. This is the will of the Father, that daily we become more and more conformed to the image of His Son, in order that Christ may be the firstborn among many brethren (Rom. 8:29) and that we may daily become more transformed into Christ (Gal. 2:20).

And our gratitude also contains at least an implicit promise to finish the work to which we pledged ourselves in the oblation: to live from now on, not for ourselves, but for God. "We are no more our own," since we have given ourselves fully in Christ to the Father. The Mass must be more than a ceremony in our lives. We must live out the implications of the Mass all day long.

In order that this lesson be effective, we must also explain to our hearers in a concrete, easy, and appealing way how they should take part in the Mass in order to make it truly the "thanksgiving of sons." But a full solution of this need cannot be found without considerable reorganizing of the way in which many of the faithful still assist at Mass. The celebrant should frequently explain to the people the meaning of the sacred actions, particularly the reasons for the changes in the Mass. The laity should fulfill their proper roles of proclaiming the Old Testament reading and the Epistle. They should be encouraged to respond to the priest, who now addresses them in their own language. Above all, they should be taught to express their prayer in song.[7] The essentials are that the faithful should be able to realize by their outward actions that they come to Mass to assemble together as God's people, to pray together, to listen to God's word together, to offer themselves with Christ and to be offered with Him to the Father, and together to receive Him as the Father's gift.

[7] We recommend for this purpose (1) *People's Mass Book* (paperback) (New York: Herder and Herder, 1964), (2) *Our Parish Prays and Sings* (six editions), (Collegeville: The Liturgical Press, 1966), (3) Paul Brunner, S.J., *Our Community Mass* (Manila: East Asian Pastoral Institute, 1967).

Twenty-Third Instruction

THE INSTITUTION OF THE
SACRAMENT OF PENANCE

The teaching on the sacrament of penance is treated only briefly here, since we presume that children are prepared by special instructions to receive the sacrament of penance not only before their first confession but repeatedly during their formative years.[8] And the missionary also should take the opportunity, before hearing the confessions of a Christian community, to instruct them in some aspect of this sacrament and to help them to attain true penitence. On one occasion he might stress one commandment; on another the motives for contrition, while he varies the emphasis during the different liturgical seasons.

But whatever the best method of accomplishing our purpose under various circumstances, we should above all fight against *merely mechanical confessions*. Where there is real mortal sin (subjective as well as objective), then there is deliberate rebellion against our loving Father. This can be erased, not by any merely external ceremony, but only by a renewed and sincere conversion of heart and the grace of the sacrament. In this matter all improper indulgence on the part of a priest is really impious cruelty toward persons who, through such an attitude, may be hardened in their sins and deceived about the dangers of their condition. The priest, another Christ, is the friend and the physician of sinners. But it is no kindness to cover over real wounds; they must be effectively cured. The wonderful mercy of the Father, which goes far beyond our narrow minds, is always open to every sinner, provided he truly retracts his perverse will and really returns to the Father with a contrite heart.

Moreover the doctrine of Christian penance is Good News also and should be preached as such. And good preaching of this doctrine should bring out clearly the close connection between the sacraments of baptism and penance, which the Fathers called "another and laborious baptism."

Method: Historical-explanatory. John 20:19–23 gives the narrative.

---

[8] For a fuller discussion of how to introduce children to this sacrament see F. J. Buckley, S.J., "What Age for First Confession," *Irish Ecclesiastical Record*, (1967), 221–252.

Here the narrative is to be closely united to the explanation.
Viewpoint: This is Christ's *Easter gift:* this is the sacrament of consolation and peace.
Aim: A great appreciation of this Easter gift: active gratitude shown
by true penitence.

DOCTRINAL SUMMARY

Introduction. The connection between baptism and penance.
The calamity and the ingratitude of mortal sin committed after
baptism. Christ could most justly completely reject an unfaithful
follower who has thus broken his solemn baptismal oath, a withered
member who has deliberately cut himself off from the life stream of
the true vine. But yet Christ does not abandon the sinner. He gives
him another chance. Christ will restore him to life and health if the
sinner himself really desires it. This is a most special and wonderful
gift. And this is the reason why Christ wished to give us this gift on
the day of His glorious resurrection.

A. The Apostles After the Resurrection

They were hiding in the Upper Room behind closed doors. They
were afraid of the Jews; they were even afraid of Christ. How cow-
ardly and ungrateful they were. Truly they were unworthy to see
their risen Master. Will He not reproach them and chide them?
Such is the state of the Christian sinner.

B. Christ in the Midst of the Apostles

The doors were locked, but the glorious Christ enters. He comes,
not to chide, but to give peace and consolation: "Peace be to you"
(cf. Luke 2:14). Christ is the great peacemaker (Is. 9:6). To make
peace is His most important work as the second Adam, the Mediator
between God and men. And as the Good Shepherd He wishes to
exercise His office especially in this sacrament. He shows His Apostles His hands and His side: here is the basis of our trust when we
have sinned. The Blood of Christ can wipe out all sins, even the
worst and gravest. See the Heart of the Good Shepherd, wounded
for us! "The disciples therefore were glad when they saw the Lord."
Let us share their gladness.

C. CHRIST INSTITUTES THE SACRAMENT OF PENANCE

Again He repeats the greeting: "Peace." How He wishes to emphasize the fact that He is now dealing with the sacrament of peace and consolation! "As the Father has sent Me. . . ." The Father has sent Christ as the Good Shepherd to bring men back to God. In the sacrament we find, not a mere man, but the Good Shepherd Himself. The priest "acts in the person" of Christ, is Christ's instrument.

This sacrament, then, will produce its effects in us only if we see Christ, not a mere man. In confessing our sins we must have the sincerity and simplicity that come from realizing the presence of the all-knowing Christ, the sincerity and depth of contrition that come from realizing the presence of the Good Shepherd, Who gave His own life for our souls. The priest has Christ's power. He can forgive every sin if we confess sincerely and with a contrite heart. For Christ breathed on His Apostles; He communicated to them the Holy Spirit: "Receive the Holy Spirit. . . ." In the sacrament of penance the priest can breathe into the soul a new life, the Holy Spirit. What a great wonder! What a great blessing! "Whose sins you shall forgive, they are forgiven them; and whose sins you shall retain, they are retained."

Christ gives them a double power, but it must be used according to the mind of Christ. For this reason the priest must know the real condition of the sinner. The sinner, then, must humbly and clearly make known his condition of soul, and the priest should help him, if necessary, by some questions, above all to make sure that the penitent has the right disposition.

What is the right disposition? Genuine sorrow for having refused to respond to God's love, a readiness to make up for the damage to oneself and others caused by sin, and a firm determination to avoid sin in the future. If this disposition is lacking, no priest, not even the pope himself, has the power of forgiveness. If true contrition is wanting, if sincere conversion is lacking, then the absolution given by the priest is completely useless and, what is more, very harmful.

Heartfelt thanks for this wonderful Easter gift. This is indeed the sacrament of Christian resurrection. *Never be afraid of this sacrament of consolation and peace.* If the sacrament of penance does not bring true and profound consolation and peace of soul, we shall find that in almost every case some serious deficiency is to be found, either in preparation or in general attitude. Perhaps diligence in examining one's conscience is lacking, perhaps sincere contrition, perhaps real trust in Christ the Good Shepherd. From this last come, for example, the not-infrequent difficulties and scruples of "pious" people. If we prescind from cases in which there is some psychic disease, almost all such troubles arise from false security or the desire to find security in the wrong place. Complete security of soul is to be sought only in trust in Christ, and security founded on ourselves is to be given up.

Never abuse this sacrament. It is much better not to go than to go insincerely or even mechanically. Man goes to confession a sinner; if he goes sincerely and trustfully, he returns a new man, brought back to life, filled with strength.

Twenty-Fourth Instruction

CHRISTIAN SUFFERING AND DEATH, AND OUR SACRAMENTAL PREPARATION FOR DEFINITIVE UNION WITH CHRIST

The teaching on the sacrament of the anointing of the sick is closely connected with that on the sacrament of penance. Just as confirmation is the complement of baptism, so the sacrament of the sick is the complement of penance. The anointing heals the wounds and weaknesses resulting from sins; its healing and strengthening effects overflow to the body to restore it to physical health if God wills, or to prepare the whole Christian for the final struggle of death and definitive union with Christ. This intimate connection with the sacrament of penance should be often brought out in preaching. It strengthens the sick man against the effects of concupiscence and his attachments to sin and any evil habits he may have formed. It does this by reminding him of God's power over evil, by arousing him to trust and hope, and especially by a new infusion of the Holy Spirit, the Spirit of power, Who strengthened Christ throughout His life and death as He struggled against and defeated evil. In this way the anointing of the sick assimilates human sickness, the failing of human life, to the pattern of Christ's death and resurrection.

This sacrament has the twofold purpose of (1) *restoring us from sickness to a purified Christian life* or (2) *completing our purification for the life of heaven.* Thus it should accomplish—and in the case of the proper dispositions it actually does accomplish—all the aspects of purification which otherwise must be completed in purgatory to make us ready for definitive union with Christ. Therefore in the second part of this instruction the essential points of the doctrine of purgatory are included, and also those concerning all the sacraments for the dying. Thus the first part of this instruction deals with extreme unction as uniting us with Christ in grave sickness, and the second part deals with this and other sacraments in connection with whole preparation for final union with Christ. In this way the special sacrament of anointing of the sick—which among Oriental Catholics is given to any sick person—is clearly distinguished from the "last sacrament."

Method: Explanatory. The sacramental rites are explained.

Viewpoint: To be conformed to Christ in our sufferings and death, so as to be united with Him in His glory. Our view should be fixed on Christ, not on ourselves.

Aim: A Christocentric consideration of Christian life and death. Learning to accept unavoidable sickness and suffering in union with Christ's suffering in preparation for accepting death in union with Him. Sincere and growing desire for union with Christ in heaven. Diligent preparation, daily more fervent, like the good servants and the wise virgins in Our Lord's two parables of His coming at death.

DOCTRINAL SUMMARY

Introduction: The divine life received in the sacraments is not yet the perfect divine life of the risen Christ. The "seed of glory" given us in baptism must grow to its ultimate perfection. We are still awaiting our final change to the perfect glory of God's children (see 1 Cor. 15:51 ff.; 1 John 3:2). We Christians are to love our life on earth as being God's gift and as giving us the opportunity to take part in Christ's work of redemption for the sake of our fellowmen, but we are eagerly to look forward to the final completion of God's plan, to the day when the Mystical Body will have reached the full stature designed for it by the Father; when Christ will return in glory and will call His elect to share, body and soul, all together in His glorious life with the Father; the day when, finally, "God will be all in all." The decisive moment of baptism introduces us to the first stage: life in Christ on earth—a life that still can be lost, that must grow and develop. The second decisive moment of our death, if properly prepared for and undergone in union with Christ, will introduce us to the second stage: a permanent sharing in Christ's life and glory until the day of the resurrection. Hence all our lives on earth are a time of preparation, a time of becoming more and more conformed to Christ dying and rising again.

A. CHRISTIAN SICKNESS AND SUFFERING

1. Like death, of which they are the foreshadowing, sickness and suffering as we now experience them are effects of original sin and of all the sins of mankind (not necessarily, of course, of each individual's sins). They are, in some sense, the work of the enemy of mankind, who wishes to disintegrate and destroy God's work. God wishes us to fight against them by all legimate means—Christ Himself spent His public life healing bodies as well as souls. But God still permits us to suffer, thus to remind us of the coming of death, of the unsatisfactoriness of human life, of Himself as Master of all His gifts of life and health. Christ Himself endured great suffering as well as death and, by taking upon Himself these effects of sin, transformed them for His followers into the way to true and full life. In union with Him we cannot only be resigned to suffering but should make it a free-will offering of love to the Father in union with Christ's sacrifice. We can even experience joy in the midst of suffering by recognizing in our lives the same pattern of "glory through suffering service" which characterized Christ's life.[9]

2. But Christ's strength is needed in abundance if we are to bear sickness and suffering in fruitful union with Him. Hence, wherever possible, the priest is to visit the sick, to strengthen them, teach them, pray with them, give them the special blessing of the Church and, above all, the sacraments of penance and the Eucharist. (Preparations needed in a house for visit of sick. Catholics in hospitals should ask for a priest to visit them.)

3. When illness is so serious as to bring us in danger of death, Christ has provided a special sacrament, *the anointing of the sick,* extreme unction. Description of the sacramental sign. Oil soothes pain, heals wounds, strengthens, consecrates things and persons for the special service of God. So this sacrament soothes, heals, and

---

[9] See F. J. Buckley, S.J., "Joy in the Midst of Suffering," *The Bible Today,* (1966), 1546–1547.

strengthens the soul, and our whole psychophysical being, which results, if God wills, also in the restoration of physical health and strength. The form of the sacrament signifies the destruction of all sins committed through the instruments of the various senses, and of the wounds and weaknesses left by past sins. But even here applies the indispensable condition of aversion to sin, conversion to God. Hence it is appropriate that sacramental confession should precede the administration of this sacrament; the Confiteor reminds us of this again.

This sacrament is to restore us to a purified, more fully Christlike life on earth, or, if this is God's will, to strengthen and purify us for the life of heaven, and these effects are attributed especially to the Holy Spirit of Love. (See the three prayers after the sacramental anointing.) But as to the degree of attaining its effects, the norms noted already in the introduction to the doctrine on the sacraments apply here also. Hence great care should be taken that Christians understand the meaning of this sacrament, that they approach it with the best dispositions and collaborate faithfully with sacramental grace. And, obviously, the best time to prepare them is *ahead of time,* in sermons and instructions, not to begin when they are very ill. So, too, for the sacrament to achieve its full effects, it should be received as soon as possible after serious sickness is detected, not put off until the last moment.

B. The Sacraments of the Dying

In direct preparation for this final struggle, for the final assimilation to Christ in His death which will bring us to share in His risen glory, the Church has ready for us

1. *Final Confession.* This last confession should be, above all others, Christ's Easter gift par excellence, the sacrament of consolation and peace. But it can be this only under the same conditions as any other confession. If all our preceding confessions have been sincere, fervent, trustful, how easy this one will be; how comforting if we are accustomed in this sacrament to see Christ Himself seeking His sheep with great love. Our trust far surpasses even the greatness of our sins. But let us make ready, here and now, by seeing Christ in the priest every time we go to confession.

2. *Extreme unction.* God wishes us to leave this earthly life, our time of preparation, entirely ready for the wedding feast, for final union with Christ. This sacrament, when it is received with sorrow

for the sins of our whole lives, acceptance of our sufferings and death in union with Christ's sacrifice, and ardent desire for Christ, should complete the process of necessary purification. But if a man, sharing Christ's life, is still not perfectly purified at the moment of death, God will still cleanse him in another way. For nothing defiled can enter heaven (see Apoc. 21:27). *This is the function of purgatory,* to complete the process of purification, of transformation into Christ. Purgation in this world will enable us to avoid the far more painful purification in the next, so that we may immediately be received by Christ into the life of heaven.

3. *Holy Viaticum.* This is *the* sacrament of the dying. To receive it if this is in any way possible, to see that the dying receive it, is of *strict obligation,* imposed by the very nature of the sacrament. Hence the Church dispenses with all the precautions not absolutely essential that otherwise surround our reception of the Eucharist. A dying person may receive although he has already received on the same day; no fasting rules apply; he may even receive from a schismatic priest, or a Catholic priest may use a host consecrated by a schismatic priest. All Catholics who are in imminent danger of death may receive Viaticum, even when they are not seriously ill and so cannot receive the anointing of the sick (for example, soldiers going into battle, people in grave danger of shipwreck, criminals before execution, and such, are not subjects for extreme unction, but if possible they should receive Viaticum).

The reason for all this is the importance of this last "journey" of death, for which we need, above all, the companionship and strength of Christ as our *Viaticum,* "with-you-on-the-way." As the special formula says, Christ will "protect us from the malignant enemy," who desires especially at this decisive moment of death to snatch us away from God. And Christ will bring us through to life everlasting, the life He won for us by His own journey through death.

Thus this last communion should be the best of all the communions of our lives, as it directly prepares us for the eternal heavenly communion. But let us not forget that all our other communions also are to prepare us for the heavenly communion. Here again the same principle applies as with out last confession: the best preparation for our last communion is to receive communion frequently all during our lives.

4. The Church also has ready for the dying the Apostolic Blessing and plenary indulgence for the hour of death, and the beautiful

and most instructive Commendation for the Departing Soul. How many riches and helps for our last journey! But the best preparation for a Christian death is a *good Christian life* that looks forward to death as our meeting with Christ. The tepid Christian is in great danger of ignoring the sacraments of the dying, or if he is able to receive these sacraments, he may receive them with little or no fruit. True conversion in great illness is not an everyday grace or one that we can count on. "Behold, now is the acceptable time; behold, now is the day of salvation!" (2 Cor. 6:2).

Section II

The Response of Our Grateful Love
or
The Christian Life

HOW WE ARE TO ANSWER GOD'S LOVE
BY CHRISTIAN LIVING

The first part of Christian doctrine presents the history of divine love by proclaiming what God has done from eternity, is doing and will do out of love for us. The second part shows us how we may fittingly respond to this great love. It indicates clearly the viewpoint from which teaching on the Christian life is to be presented, namely, as·the response of our love to God's love, of our gratitude to the divine blessings.

But in making these the two main divisions of Christian doctrine we do not intend to suggest that in actual teaching and preaching, the doctrine of the Christian life must necessarily be presented as a second part, distinctly separate from the story of salvation. For example, it would cause no difficulty if these lessons on the nature and character of the Christian life were to be given immediately after the explanation of the sacrament of baptism (Twentieth Instruction), and the explanation of the various commandments distributed through the instructions on the history of divine love. In the following lessons we will give concrete suggestions as to ways of doing this. And certainly for pedagogical reasons it is highly desirable, at least in the case of a series of three or more instructions (as are often given, for example, when a missionary visits his out-stations) to include in each series one practical instruction on the Christian life to show how the dogmas presented in the other instructions are to be lived in a practical way.

Yet for the purpose of this book, in order to give a clear outline of our whole message, we are presenting the lessons on Christian living all together in a systematic way. For by so doing, it is easy for the teacher to see the viewpoint from which each particular doctrine is to be proclaimed.

199

We should continually explain the Christian life under the threefold aspect of

1. *A life lived by faith.* "My just man lives by faith" (Hab. 2:4; Rom. 1:17: Gal. 3:11; Heb. 10:38). How strongly does St. Paul emphasize this aspect of the Christian life! The Christian life is nothing other than the response of the whole man to the revelation that he receives with a sincere heart and strives to express by his whole life: divine revelation is given to us as the word of life (John 6:64-69; 20:31), as the doctrine of the divine life given us to bring us to true life in God (John 17:3). And divine revelation certainly is, of its own essential nature, the revelation of the divine love that chooses, calls, and enriches us in Christ. Therefore the Christian life must also be considered as

2. *The response of our love to divine love.* The Father's love has made us sons of God in Christ; our love makes us live as good sons "in Christ," because only in Christ are we sons of the Father. In other words, the gift of the Father's love is Christ, and the return-gift of our love is also Christ, that is, Christ formed in us, Christ expressed in the idiom of our own individuality, each of us living as "another Christ." Just as the Father gives us all His divine riches in this gift of His Son and pours them out on us, so also all our powers of giving to Him are to be drawn up into this same gift.

3. *The Christlike life.* It is obvious that these three aspects of the Christian life are interdependent; each implies and demands the other two. Would that all Catholics might come daily more and more to consider and to look upon the Christian life in this way! For this purpose an attractive and clear *separate instruction on the Christian life as such* can be of considerable assistance, and here the illustration of the beggar boy taken into the family of a king can be used even with simple people. A suitable occasion for such an explanation might follow the teaching on the obligation contracted at baptism (Twentieth Instruction) or after the teaching on prayer (Twenty-Fifth Instruction). But for the Christian formation of our hearers it is of the very greatest importance that such pondering on the implications of the Christian life becomes the daily bread which we continue always to give them, now in one form and now in another, and that whenever and however we speak of the Christian life, its Christocentric character may always be made apparent.

Ideal catechetical teaching on Christian living strives not so much to explain minutely and to inculcate diligently individual precepts, but rather to convey the interior meaning of the Christian life, the ever-continuing obligation of gratitude, the privilege, glory, and transcendence of the Christian life. Truly we have been born, or rather reborn, for great things! O that daily we may become more worthy children of God, more closely resembling our model, living more according to Christ and in Christ, more perfectly carrying out His work in the world! This is the "good tidings" of the Christian life.

And even though, when preaching the Christian life, we dwell especially on its beauty and desirability, we must also clearly teach its obligatory character. Benefits bring obligations, and the greatest benefits the greatest obligations. To live as a Christian is a wonderful privilege; it is also a duty.

Thus the ideal preaching and teaching of the Christian life will, on the one hand, call Christians to eager and delighted cooperation with the grace of their Christian vocation—the greatest things are to be sought by us and with the greatest fervor; and, on the other hand, it will duly humble them—what a great distance between this vocation and our daily lives! Thus at once we rejoice, and yet are sorrowful and consumed by a holy impatience generously to overcome the obstacles created by our own sinfulness, selfishness, and weakness. Our Christian calling, demanding a Christlike life from weak men, a divine life, far surpasses our natural powers. Thus we must come humbly to acknowledge our own insufficiency and have recourse to God with our whole hearts. Our eyes must be turned to God, from Whom comes our help. "He Who called you is faithful, and will do this" (1 Thess. 5:24). Long before we use the difficult technical word *actual grace* we lead children and catechumens to a deep appreciation of this divine reality: we could never live as children of God without His special help.

The response of Christian love, then, is twofold: first, the almost spontaneous response of the Christian heart is the *response of Christian prayer, direct worship;* and second, *love shown through action, indirect worship.* Or, for practical reasons, we might state it as being the response, first, of *loving prayer* and, second, of *loving observance of the commandments.* But we should not forget that the most fundamental precepts of the Decalogue itself deal with prayer and direct worship. And, after all, Christian living is far more than observance of the commandments, since by fully Christian living we strive to do much more than we are strictly obliged to do.

Moreover, to divide this second section according to direct and indirect worship has two special catechetical advantages: (1) It shows how the Christian message by its nature is directed to Christian worship. Christian worship in the full sense is the fruit of our catechetical apostolate; in this way, like Christ Himself, we are "heralding the joyful tidings of the kingdom of God" (Mark 1:14). Thus the close relationship of the catechetical to the liturgical apostolate becomes clear, since liturgy is the climax of Christian worship. And (2) it brings out clearly the close connection between prayer and action, liturgy and life.

CHRISTIAN LIFE MADE UP OF
PRAYER AND ACTION

True Christian living is, above all, a life of real Christian prayer. Training in the spirit of prayer is rightly considered by authorities on pastoral and catechetical theology to be the most important part of Christian education. And such training cannot be given only by means of even the most moving sermons on the excellence and necessity of prayer. Here we should learn from the Christian mother who teaches her children to pray by praying—not by theoretical discourses but by frequently repeated suggestions and motivations, by official "family prayers," and by spontaneous prayer interwoven into the fabric of daily life. So we should bring prayer into every lesson and sermon, often explicitly, always implicitly, in a few words encouraging our hearers to strive to unite themselves inwardly with God, that is, to pray.

Moreover, every doctrine should be taught in such a way as to become "prayable." Every part of our message should be so presented as to nourish the Christian mind and heart for conscious communion with the heavenly Father. Often, especially in teaching children, we should go a step further and explicitly show how each doctrine might be prayed by praying it with our hearers in a spontaneous way. But to do so, of course, requires a catechist who himself knows how to pray his message. And, like the good Christian mother, we should also frequently show our hearers by concrete examples how in each and every circumstance they may lift up their hearts to their Father in heaven, beyond any prayer formulas at all.

But good training in prayer also requires suitable prayer formulas. Concerning such formulas we must take care, above all, that they reflect the genuine spirit of Christian prayer and that, at the same time, they are formulated in a way fitted to those who are to use them. It is most helpful, if not absolutely necessary, to give children formulas that are especially fitted to their needs. But it would be completely wrong to think that adaptation to the mentality of children means sentimentality or the abandonment of the great themes of genuine Christian prayer.

The prayer of action necessarily follows the sincere prayer of the heart. Obviously any affection that does not effectively tend toward action is not truly sincere. And therefore the second aspect of our grateful response to God's love is the keeping of the commandments (Matt. 7:21; John 14:21. See John 14:15, 15:10; 1 John 5:3). But what pleases the Father is, not our works in themselves, but their prayerlike character, the disposition to spend ourselves in the Father's service and to do everything as perfectly as we can for His sake, ". . . for man seeth those things that appear; but the Lord beholdeth the heart" (1 Kings 16:7).

The only Christian law is charity (Matt. 22:37). "Love"—truly and wholeheartedly—"and do what you will" (St. Augustine). For then you will do far more than the commandments prescribe. Each and every commandment is only a special application of the commandment of love, and therefore should be explained and thought of in this light. In the last analysis they have value and power to oblige insofar as they show us how to carry out the commandment of charity.

The Christian attitude is not a pharisaical attitude toward the law: the true Christian looks primarily to the spirit and to the ultimate reason for the law, that is charity. The pharisaical attitude becomes immersed in a multitude of laws; it attributes absolute value to particular laws and thus becomes a slave to the dead letter. But because the pharisee neglects its purpose, the law for him becomes not a guide to God, but often a real hindrance. The Christian religion demands a perfect, complete self-surrender, a real holocaust. The pharisee really wants to escape from making this complete offering by making many partial gifts. His religious life is ruled, finally, not by love but by his own self-love, and so he is prepared to sacrifice everything except himself. So he wants, not to give himself to God, but to trade with God for spiritual profit.

In preaching the divine law we should strive with all our powers to keep our hearers from this pharisaical attitude or to free them from it if they are already infected with it. Therefore we must show above all the meaning and purpose of Christian law, and clearly point out how each commandment flows from the law of charity. In the explanation of each commandment its "Christian" character must always be pointed out, that is, how its observance makes us Christlike. The commandments thus help to form in us a new man, renewed in Christ in his worship of the Father, in his relationship to his brethren in Christ, to the material goods of this world, and to truth.

The explanation of each commandment should not become a sterile enumeration and description of the sins by which God can be offended. First let us explain the exact meaning of the commandment, depict the exact Christian ideal, and give its connection with the mystery of Christ; then show that the chief sins against this commandment are deplorable degradations of this ideal, and briefly but clearly indicate their "anti-Christian" nature.

The commandments also belong to the "Gospel" we are sent to proclaim. They, too, have to be presented as a joyful message, not just as a heavy and unavoidable burden. The commandments are manifestations of God's love. In the lower grades we shall convey this idea to our little ones by presenting the commandments as God's loving directions given to us for our way to heaven. The commandments are like the road signs which guide the driver safely to his destination. In the catechetical instruction of the upper grades and of adults we have to go deeper. In each commandment we must make clear how God protects some important gift for us. The commandments are not the result of arbitrary despotism, but the directions of our loving Father in Heaven.

And we should also strive to make our hearers understand that day by day they should more fully achieve the Christian attitude which no longer asks, "What am I strictly obliged to do, here and now?" but rather, "What can I do to show my love, to respond to the Father's love more and more perfectly, to become and to do what He desires?" Such stress on Christian generosity, however, must obviously not lead us to neglect making clear the distinction between commands and counsels. Nor should we omit to emphasize the chief commandments or to minimize the liberty of the children of God.

Abundant literature on the moral life already exists, and therefore we are indicating here only very summarily what is to be given in the moral instructions. We wish to make clear particularly the context in which the material is to be proposed, the chief points to be presented, and the aspect under which to present them. Therefore in the following lessons we shall emphasize especially the positive aspect of moral teaching. But, of course, something will also be said of sins against God.

In the following lessons we will introduce almost exclusively "Christian motives." Good moral training makes use of *naturally good motives as well*. But it should indicate how these natural values, such as reputation, family, country, and so on, have been sanctified and ennobled in Christ and so have been given a new meaning for Christians.

As we said above, quite often in actual preaching, and sometimes also in teaching the catechism lesson, it is advisable not to treat the individual commandments at the end of the whole course, but rather to distribute them throughout. In each of the following instructions, therefore, we indicate a suitable place, catechetically speaking, in which each might conveniently be treated.

OUR FILIAL RESPONSE BY CHRISTIAN PRAYER

DIRECT WORSHIP (THE FIRST THREE COMMANDMENTS)

Two instructions are presented under this heading, both dealing with Christian worship, but from different standpoints. The first is to give an understanding of Christian prayer, its nature, qualities, and excellence, prayer seen as the great privilege of God's children. But direct worship is not only a privilege but also a duty for God's children, and the most fundamental one. In the second lesson it is considered from this second viewpoint, and a catechetical explanation of the first three commandments is given.

Twenty-Fifth Instruction

THE EXCELLENCE OF CHRISTIAN PRAYER— CHRISTIAN PRAYER OUR GREAT PRIVILEGE

In this lesson the classic form of Christian prayer—praise and thanksgiving—is chiefly inculcated. Yet any prayer is good which proceeds from the filial spirit, and Christ Himself taught us in all our needs to seek refuge in the Father with filial trust. Psychologically, then, we may begin with impetratory prayer, but we must lead to the prayer of praise and gratitude.

The material given here is far too much for one instruction. If time allows only one instruction on this subject, the nature, properties, and principal affections of Christian prayer should above all be thoroughly explained.

Method: Explanatory, developed from a comparison with the conversation of a child in a family.

Viewpoint: From the beginning Christian prayer should be presented as childlike conversation with God. And also from the very beginning it should be shown to be the goal and culminating point of the Christian life. True Christian prayer is by its nature Christlike prayer, and, in consequence, above all the prayer of praise and thanksgiving.

An introduction should be given concerning Christian life in general: what we have explained above as to the meaning and main aspect of the Christian life should be explained here or, better, in a separate preliminary instruction. In either case, the connection of the life of prayer with the Christian life should be clearly shown, and the importance of this connection should be stressed.

A. THE NATURE OF CHRISTIAN PRAYER

Comparison with the conduct of a good child in a family. To what does the thought of his father's love and goodness urge a good child first of all? To express his love for the father, to acknowledge his goodness and benefits with a grateful heart. This nature of Christian prayer is formulated in Galatians 4:4–6: "But when the fullness of time came, God sent His Son . . . that we might receive the adoption of sons. And because you are sons, God has sent the Spirit of his Son into our hearts, crying, 'Abba, Father' " (see also Rom. 8:15). Here is the intimate relationship of Christian prayer with the mystery of Christ. It is the loving answer of Christian hearts to this mystery of divine love; it is, finally, the work of the Holy Spirit in our hearts. He communicates to us the spirit of Christ, and in this spirit Christian prayer is fully focussed on the heavenly Father.

B. THE PRINCIPAL SOURCES OF PRAYER

The principal sources from which this filial conversation is nourished are *appreciation* of the Father (knowledge of His goodness), filial *trust,* filial *love.* The chief wellsprings of Christian prayer are faith, hope, and charity. The quality of Christian prayer essentially depends upon the extent to which it contains faith, hope, and charity; in other words, the more a prayer unites us to God in faith, hope, and charity, the more perfect it is. Obviously, faith, hope, and charity are not to be made three distinct "acts" in our prayers. The simple "Father!" which the Holy Spirit allows us to pray contains in the most perfect way all these three virtues.

C. The Essential Properties of Christian Prayer

The essential properties of Christian prayer may be easily understood by a comparison of the conversation of a good son with his father. They follow immediately from the nature of Christian prayer; it should be sonlike, and therefore sincere, simple, personal, and especially Christlike, and thus follow the example of our Brother. The Christlikeness of Christian prayer consists chiefly in the fact that it is offered "in union with the same Holy Spirit" Who inspired the heart of Christ to filial prayer. Real Christian prayer is offered not only according to the example of Christ but also "through Him, with Him, and in Him," and this is true most especially when we share in Christ's sacrifice by actual participation in the Mass.

D. The Principal Affections of Christian Prayer

Again, these can be developed from the ideal of the conversation of a child with his father: gratitude, submission, admiration, and unitive love. These same affections follow from the Christlikeness of Christian prayer. Behold the chief affections of the Most Sacred Heart of Jesus, continually praying in the highest possible way.

E. The Most Excellent Formula of Christian Prayer

The *Our Father* is the classic Christian prayer. To it is due the greatest reverence, together with thoughtful, reverent, and personal use. It shows us most beautifully the spirit of the prayer of Christ. How readily and wonderfully does it illustrate the nature, sources, properties, and affections of Christian prayer. We should focus special attention on the spirit of this prayer and explain, not so much each word or phrase, but rather the spirit from which the whole prayer flows and according to which the words and phrases are to be interpreted: God in the midst of our hearts. The divine "Thou,"

Whom we embrace with reverence and love, fills our hearts and wholly occupies them. God is all in all, and all things are in God.

The *Apostles' Creed* is the second formula of ideal prayer. It is not a dry enumeration of dogmas which we "must" believe, but a joyful proclamation and acknowledgment of the benefits of eternal divine love, an admiring enumeration of the gifts of the loving God Who gives Himself. Every article of faith proclaims a new gift from God. O my God, I believe in Your eternal love; O may I believe evermore steadfastly! These are the fundamental doctrines, the foundations of the Christian life. The Creed is not only to be believed; it is also to be lived. This is the way that leads to life!

The *greatest act of prayer* is the Mass. What a magnificent exchange of love! This is the most wonderful tribute and thanksgiving possible to God's redeemed children. Christ is given and received! (See the Twenty-Second Instruction.)

Twenty-Sixth Instruction

FILIAL WORSHIP—THE MOST FUNDAMENTAL DUTY OF GOD'S CHILDREN (THE FIRST THREE COMMANDMENTS)

The first three commandments of the Decalogue are the most fundamental, since they treat of our ideal relationship with God Himself. Christian moral teaching is entirely God-centered, not man-centered. This truth should be clearly and forcibly shown to the Christians of our times, but in a positive way. The main aspect under which a true Christian looks upon the whole moral life is as our submission as children of God offered to the Father throughout this life. The second section of the Decalogue, dealing with social life, must also always be considered in this light.

Although the first three commandments are of such great importance, they can be sufficiently explained in one lesson in a series for adult Christians if the rest of our teaching is theocentric and a special instruction on prayer is given. And the chief object of these three commandments, that is, filial submission to God, may be inculcated in almost every instruction, now in one way and now in another.

In what connection: After the doctrine of the creation and elevation, and before the doctrine of the fall. The doctrine of our creation and elevation offers the dogmatic foundation; the doctrine of the fall shows the dreadful consequences of rebellion against God and thus adds effective new motives for obedience.

Method: Explanatory. Our obligations to God are easily understood from a comparison with the duties of a good son.

Viewpoint: As with all the commandments of the Decalogue, these first three are to be kept in a new spirit. This is divine worship, offered not in the spirit of slaves, in fear and trembling, but in the spirit of sons, with profound reverence and intimate filial love. Behold "the true worshippers . . . in spirit and in truth. For the Father also seeks such to worship Him" (John 4:23) and in Christ He finds them. The Christlike worship of God.

In explaining these commandments we must, of course, show what external acts are of obligation, but we must insist especially on the internal spirit of reverence and profound adoration. It is in vain to demand the performance of external duties (daily prayers, Sunday Mass, and so on) unless our hearers are first filled with the spirit of the children of God, from which these external actions and many others not prescribed will then flow spontaneously. The fact that so many Christians neglect the life of prayer is due not to external difficulties, but rather to ignorance and lack of due reverence and love for the Father.

Aim: That the Messianic age may come also for us in all its perfection; that the hour may come, and may now be at hand, "when the true worshippers will *worship the Father in spirit and in truth*" (John 4:23). The God-centered life according to the example of Christ.

DOCTRINAL SUMMARY

The foregoing lessons on our creation and elevation have shown what great benefits God has lavished on us. How rich we are! And all these blessings come from the all-good and infinitely exalted God, Whose special servants, yes, and sons also, we are privileged to be. May we be perfect children! Just as in a human family, so also in the family of the children of God, the children ought:

A. Daily To Know Their Father Better

Pagans are ignorant of Him; they adore false gods. Even we do not know our Father well enough. How blessed we are to know Him through His fatherly manifestation in Christ: "God, Who at sundry times and in divers manners spoke in times past to the fathers by the prophets, last of all in these days has spoken to us by His Son . . ." (Heb. 1:2). What a great blessing is divine revelation, to which we should respond by prompt and grateful faith (see the Preliminary Instruction and also the Tenth). We should show clearly how we truly worship God by every act of faith and hope, by acknowledging Him as our supreme Lord, as infinite Wisdom and Goodness. Faith and hope are the most fundamental acts of Christian worship.

Here we should speak about the religion classes that bring us to a more intimate knowledge of the Father and about the religious education of children in the family, which should always be urged "in season . . . and out of season." But intellectual knowledge is not enough; the acknowledgment and consent of the heart is required.

B. Daily To Love The Father More

If you truly know Him, you will also love Him. His loveableness . . . only a most ungrateful son could deny his love to such a Father. Love for the Father necessarily stimulates us to remember Him often, to recall His blessings, and frequently to converse with Him. A son who lives with his family and yet forgets all about his father, who does not answer when his father calls him, who avoids all conversation with his father, is certainly to be considered a bad and ungrateful son. What, then, is to be thought of those unhappy Christians who carelessly neglect to pray? Morning prayers, evening prayers, Sunday prayers. But a truly loving son is not content with this minimum. How happy is the life of faithful and eager love, even here on earth!

C. Daily To Honor The Father More Perfectly

We honor because we love. Who would be unwilling to honor such a Father? Even in a human family the father owes it to himself and to his children to require due respect, due reverence, as an essential aspect of his children's love for him.

Reverence toward God. Reverence in prayer. Reverence in the use of God's name. Internal and external reverence. The prayer of praise. The most excellent prayer of praise is the Mass, which is the community paean of joy and thanksgiving of the redeemed children of God, united to their Redeemer Who leads them in praise.

Sunday Mass. God our Father wants His children to gather around His table to listen to Him, to talk to Him, to love Him, and to be fed by Him. Furthermore, as members of the Church we should pray for our brothers and sisters, and with them, as a sign that God's family is one. Christ died and rose to gather God's scattered children into unity. At Mass, the renewal of Christ's Paschal mystery, we gather to join our prayer to His. The psychological and social nature of man demands that this be done frequently to keep man aware of his special new relationships. From the very first, Christians have gathered on Sunday, the day of the resurrection, to meet the risen Christ and to pray. (Matt. 28:1; Luke 24:1–49; John 20:1, 19, 26; Acts 20:7; 1 Cor. 16:2; Apoc. 1:10).

Sunday rest. The purpose of the rest: that we may have time to spend with our Father, to help others in a special way (as Jesus did so often on the Sabbath), and to acknowledge God's primacy over all other concerns in our lives. This day gives us an opportunity to intensify our awareness of God and His family, the Church, and to express this in action.

OUR FILIAL ANSWER BY CHRISTIAN WORK

INDIRECT WORSHIP (THE FOURTH TO TENTH COMMANDMENTS)

Pray and work! The prayer of the heart is to be complemented, and its sincerity proved, by the prayer of labor and work. Compare with the conduct of good children in a family, who also show their devotion to their father by diligent work. The true meaning and value of work needs to be explained attractively, especially in our times. We Christians do not by any means look upon work merely as some kind of penance imposed upon us because of original sin. We esteem work very highly, but we do not evaluate it, either exclusively or primarily, according to temporal values. Even though we clearly recognize and carefully cultivate, in their due place, these temporal values established by God, nevertheless it is the heavenly values in our work that we look to and desire above all. Therefore for us even work to which temporal success is denied can have great value. Just as it would be foolish to evaluate the work done by Christ in His hidden life according to its material value, so also the labors of God's children cannot be accurately estimated by material measures alone.

The ideal Christian life is not divided into two separate compartments: the prayer by which we obtain heavenly goods and the work by which we obtain earthly goods. As in everything else, so in our life of work, we Christians do not follow Adam before the fall or after the fall, but the second Adam, the Savior. The following lessons, then, show how we Christians are to worship and serve God *in* the different phases and activities of human life.

Twenty-Seventh Instruction

THE CHRISTIANIZATION OF THE FAMILY (THE FOURTH COMMANDMENT)

By the fourth commandment —the first to deal with the relationships of men among themselves—God solemnly recognizes and strongly safeguards the values of family life. But the Christian ideal is not a "humanism of the family" which would limit itself to human values; it is the Christianization of family life, which fully recognizes these values in their place but at the same time gives them a new meaning in Christ. The earthly family becomes a symbol of the heavenly family. Especially in the upper grades we have to explain clearly and effectively God's loving intention in giving this important commandment. What God primarily intends is not to protect parents' authority or just to make education and government "easy" for them. Rather He intends to secure the necessary conditions in both parents and children so that the children may receive completely the countless gifts which He purposes to confer upon them through their parents. Reverence, obedience, and love are the indispensable dispositions for abundantly and profitably obtaining God's gifts.

In what connection: After the instruction on the birth and infancy of Christ. The Holy Family is the exemplar for the Christian family.

Method: Historical-explanatory. The life of the Holy Family provides the narrative: the care of those holy parents for the boy Jesus; the relationship of Jesus to His parents. This description should be vivid and concrete, but not fanciful.

Viewpoint: The Christian task of the faithful family.

Aim: The Christianization of the family.

DOCTRINAL SUMMARY

Introduction: Christ wished to be born, nourished, protected, and educated in a family. By so doing He sanctified the family. The Holy Family is the exemplar of the Christian family.

A. JESUS THE EXEMPLAR OF A GOOD SON

His reverence, His love, His obedience are profound because they are entirely founded in God. See the dignity of parents in the eyes of Christ: they take the place of the Father. From his human parents the true Christian ascends "to the Father of our Lord Jesus Christ, from Whom all fatherhood in heaven and on earth receives its name" (Eph. 3:14 ff.).

Children in their own way help to make their parents holy. They respond to the kindness of their parents with gratitude, love, and trust. They stand by them as children should when hardships overtake their parents and old age brings its loneliness. Yet their affection for their parents should always be subordinated to their love for God. Jesus has given us many examples of reverence for parents (in the Temple, at Nazareth, at Cana, on Calvary—Luke 2:41–52; John 2:4; 19:25–27; see also Mark 7:11–13). He also showed us by His life and His teaching that we must be ready to leave all human ties in second place should there be any conflict between their demands and those of God (see Luke 9:59–62; 14:26; Matt. 12:46–50).

See how the Christian religion acknowledges, strengthens, and perfects parental dignity and authority.

B. THE PARENTS OF CHRIST, THE EXEMPLARS OF CHRISTIAN PARENTS

Because parents take the place of God the Father, they ought also to imitate His love, His truly paternal care, His mercy, His generosity. The religious awareness of their own dignity, authority, and responsibility should also give them reverence for their children, in whom they ought to see little brothers and sisters of Christ committed to their care. It is not a mere child of man, but a son of God, who is given to them to bring up. You are not the owners, nor the absolute masters, but the administrators of this great treasure; you are the visible guardian angels of this child. The principle "children are for the parents" is true if by it we mean the heavenly Father; it is false if applied to human parents.

But since it is a child of God who is entrusted to parents to educate and train for his lofty vocation, parents owe not only material but also mental and spiritual care to a child. To spend all their thought and energy on the acquisition of material things, even to shower them on their children, is not true Christian parental love. Parents have to strive to give themselves, the best of themselves, to their children's upbringing.

Parents should energetically acquit themselves of this duty which falls primarily on them, namely, education, and especially religious education. They are the first and foremost educators of their children. Their role is so decisive that scarcely anything can compensate for their failure in it. It is within the family that children first learn to know God, to worship Him, and to love their neighbor. It is through the family that they are introduced into civic partnership with their fellow men and into the People of God. It is there that conscience is awakened and formed. The Christian family is truly vital for the life and development of God's own people. Vatican II reiterated this in the Pastoral Constitution on the Church in the Modern World (nn. 48, 50, 52) and the Declaration on Christian Education (nn. 1–3, 6–7).

Twenty-Eighth Instruction

THE SACRAMENT OF MATRIMONY AND THE SANCTITY OF THE BODY CONSECRATED IN BAPTISM (THE SIXTH AND NINTH COMMANDMENTS)

In What connection? Many suitable places might be found for this lesson on the holiness of the body: for example, after the instruction on baptism, by which the whole man is made holy, or after that on the resurrection of the dead, which brings out the share of the body in Christ's glory. But for practical reasons it is not so advisable to give this lesson in either of these two connections, since the lesson on baptism should preferably be followed by that on the Christian life in general, and that on the resurrection by the explanation of the life of the world to come rather than life in this world. If the sacrament of marriage is treated separately, this lesson could be combined with it, or possibly with the lessson on creation. In either of these connections it will be easy to show how great is the good that God protects by the sixth commandment, namely, the physical and moral health of family life. Thus the biological and sociological importance of the commandment will be clearly apparent. In the fifth commandment God protects human life already existing; in the sixth commandment, the source of human life.

The Christian attitude to sex should be formed in relationship to marriage so that the genuine nature of sex as an expression of a total gift to another in love becomes clear.

Method: Historical-explanatory.

Viewpoint: Chastity is required of all Christians. To be chaste is an effect of, and a participation in, Christ's victory. Chaste marriage is a *holy vocation,* a call to cooperate with God the Creator, a kind of priesthood to be exercised in the "Church in miniature," which is the Christian family.

Aim: 1. That the peace of Christ may reign in our bodies also; that we may "present our bodies as a sacrifice, living, holy, pleasing to God—your spiritual service" (Rom. 12:1). 2. The re-Christianization of the modern attitude about sexual life and family life. Christian family life is endangered today by so many centrifugal forces that very special attention is necessary to make sure that the faithful understand what Christian family life can and should be. Moreover, the place of the sexual element in married life, and in life in general, is greatly distorted today. "Sex appeal" is dragged into every aspect of life, entertainment, business, and cultural activities. The re-formation of the true Christian attitude toward sex is the most essential step toward correcting the many existing abuses, and far more effective than attacking these abuses directly.

DOCTRINAL SUMMARY

A. THE ORIGINAL HOLINESS OF MARRIAGE

(Genesis, chapters 1 and 2.) 1. *"Male and female He created them. . . ."* The two sexes are of divine institution. Man, consisting of soul and body, is an admirable work of God. God gave us our various natural appetites, the appetite for food and drink for the conservation of the individual, the sexual appetite for the conservation of the human race. The sex appetite is included in God's approval of His own work: "God saw all things which He had made, and they were very good" (Gen. 1:31). And why? Whenever husband and wife carry out the marriage act and are blessed with a child, they cooperate in one holy work with God the Creator Himself, a work which, in the natural order, is the noblest that can be accomplished by man, in which they offer the cooperation of their whole selves and their love to God the Creator for the creation of a new man, who, moreover, is to become a son of God.

2. *"Be fruitful and multiply"* (Gen. 1:28). See what a holy vocation it is. God Himself, Who instituted marriage, gave it this holy purpose: "Fill the earth" . . . and we can add: Fill heaven also. Man and woman are joined in marriage for the good of their children and of the whole human race, as well as for their own advantage.

3. *"I will make him a helper fit for him"* (Gen. 2:18). Woman is not inferior to man, but a helpmate equal to him. By authentic conjugal love and the actions it inspires each is enriched by the other and brought to human fulfillment. Conjugal love involves the good of the whole person as it ennobles the expressions of body and mind. Such love leads the partners to a free and mutual gift of themselves, a gift proving itself by gentle affection and by deed. It far exceeds erotic inclinations, which, selfishly pursued, soon fade away. Genuine married love, on the contrary, grows greater and stronger by its generous activity. It is a great blessing. But this blessing can only be enjoyed if husband and wife seek one another's good and not their own (see 1 Cor. 13), if they are ready for self-denial and sacrifice.

4. *"In His own image"* (Gen. 1:27). The marriage bond is a kind of reflection of the union and love of the Blessed Trinity Itself, of the internal life and fecundity of God. God wants the human race, not to consist of single individuals thrown together, but to be organically constituted of persons intimately joined to one another in the family.

5. *"They become one flesh"* (Gen. 2:24). Marriage in paradise was monogamous: one man and one woman so that they might give to one another the total, undivided, and inseparable vigor of their love according to God's original design for marriage. This inseparable union was to endure until the end of life, as Christ Himself affirms (Matt. 19:8).

6. *"Both the man and his wife were naked, but they felt no shame"* (Gen. 2:25). The human body is not shameful, but good. The sexual appetite is not sinful. Sexual pleasure is the natural accompaniment of the expressions of married love as designed by God. God intended man to be in harmony with Him, with others, and within himself. The marriage act was to be an expression of that harmony.

B. The Effects of Sin on Marriage

Once man shattered by sin his harmony with God, he experienced disharmony with others, with the physical universe, and within himself (Gen. 3). Excessive self-love and self-indulgence, the worship of pleasure, and illicit practices against human generation have attacked the very roots of marriage, disfigured it, and often led to adultery, divorce, and other social evils.

C. The Restoration and Elevation of Marriage Through Christ

"But where the offense has abounded, grace has abounded yet more . . ." (Rom. 5:20). What the first Adam lost, the new Adam, Christ, not only restores but increases: marriage, which more than most aspects of human life had been injured by sin, now receives more abundant blessings from Christ. For He renews the original sanctity of marriage and adds new dignity to it in His kingdom.

1. Christ restored the primitive purity of marriage by restoring strict monogamy and indissolubility (Matt. 19:9) and restoring the purity of true chastity even to hidden thoughts (Matt. 5:28).

2. Christ restored woman to her rightful place as man's coequal helpmate. In the kingdom of Christ every woman is a younger sister of the Blessed Virgin.

3. Christ blessed the conception, birth, and infancy of children, and He consecrated the human family, by Himself being conceived, born, and growing up as a child in a family.

4. Christ honored human marriage at Cana of Galilee and worked His first miracle as a favor to the bride and groom. From that time on Christ is present at every Christian marriage, and He Himself joins the husband and wife who enter matrimony "in Christ."

5. Christ raised marriage to the wonderful dignity of a sacrament of the New Law in which the bride and groom are truly conse-

crated for their sacred duty of founding and directing a new "church in miniature," a human family which shall at the same time belong to the family of God. Through this sacrament the kingdom of God on earth is given the greater part of its new members, heaven is filled with saints, and the parents themselves are strengthened with ever-new graces against all the difficulties of life. This sacrament of "conjugal consecration" is administered, not by the priest, but by the spouses themselves. They are the ministers of this sacrament to one another. Bride and groom are the instruments of the grace of this sacrament to one another, as the ordained priest is in the other sacraments. Thus throughout married life not only the calling and the beginning, the purpose and the idea, the rights and powers, but also all the duties and works of husband and wife for each other and their children take on a kind of sacerdotal character.

As they render mutual help and service to each other through an intimate union of their persons and their actions, they experience the meaning of their oneness in Christ and attain to it with growing perfection. They contribute to the personal development of each other and their children and to the peace and prosperity of their family and of society as a whole. The spirit of Christ enables them to advance increasingly in holiness and thus contribute jointly to the glory of God.

6. Christ ennobled conjugal love. Since the marriage union is the image of the union between Christ and His Church, conjugal love is to be the image of the love of Christ for the Church and the Church for Christ (Eph. 5:25–27; 30–32). In the life and love of a truly Christian husband and wife all is caught up into divine love; all is made Christlike, all things are "in Christ," joys and sorrows, worries and consolations, labors and sacrifices, so long as they are in conformity with the most holy law of Christ. The love of husband and wife for each other is to be conformed year by year to true Christian charity, unmindful of self, patient and kind, chaste, prudent, holy. And by their married lives they are to learn how to die to self and live to God and so carry out their Christian vocation.

Thus the original holiness of marriage is not only restored but made more wonderful still. It is truly a "great mystery" (Eph. 5:32).

D. THE SPIRITUAL MAN RENEWED IN CHRIST

(1 Cor. 15:47–49.) An attractive and positive portrayal of the Christian law as the rule of the spirit over the flesh. Our natural

powers, given us by God, are not evil, nor is the pleasure which accompanies their due exercise. Rather, that man is evil who inverts the right order of values, who allows himself to think of created good things as his final end, and who allows or encourages the the rebellion of his lower powers against the law of God. Instead of putting sex at the service of others as an expression of his unreserved gift of self, the man who is unchaste seeks his own advantage or pleasure without accepting all the obligations imposed by love. He seeks to get rather than give. He depersonalizes sex and regards its object as things rather than human persons in all their complex relationships—physical, emotional, social, spiritual.

The spiritual man is the fully human man, perfectly subject to God, striving to subject all his desires, all his impulses, to the divine will. In carnal man the rebellion of Adam continues. Each of us must follow either Adam the rebellious or the second Adam, the Obedient. No one can serve two masters. Our bodies have become Christ's members at baptism. Now they belong, not to us, but to Christ, Who has purchased them at the cost of His precious blood and filled them with His Spirit (1 Cor. 6:15–20; 1 Pet. 1:18–19).

E. The Victory of the Cross

"And they who belong to Christ have crucified their flesh with all its passions and desires. If we live by the Spirit, let us also walk by the Spirit" (Gal. 5:24). The perfect dominion of God can be restored and preserved on this earth only by means of sacrifice, the gift of love. We ourselves must, through continual mortification, preserve what God has provided through the cross. The spiritual man dies daily during his earthly life in order to rise again with Christ. Behold our reward: participation, body and soul, in the glory of Christ!

Twenty-Ninth Instruction

FRATERNAL LOVE AND ASSISTANCE (THE FIFTH COMMANDMENT)

Christ has gathered us into the family of God's children. The principal law of this family is the law of charity, the law of love toward our Father and toward our brethren. Our love for the

Father must be shown and proved by fraternal charity. Because we love the Father with our whole heart, we acknowledge, deal with, and love all His children as our brothers. This is the mark of the true disciple of Christ. "By this will all men know that you are my disciples, if you have love for one another" (John 13:35).

God's loving purpose for this basic commandment of mutual love is obvious. As long as we are on our pilgrimage, we should experience His love especially through the love we receive from our brethren; then we should prove our love for Him by our love of our brethren. It is through our mutual holy love that we herald God's love, that we dispose ourselves and others to accept and to transmit innumerable gifts from God. By the fifth commandment, strictly speaking, God protects the precious gift of human life in a special way. He expects His children to respect this gift, use it well, and develop it gratefully in themselves and in others.

Both state and Church are intended by God to help in the development of human life. The role of the Church is developed elsewhere, especially in the Seventeenth and Eighteenth Instructions. Here the role of the state in promoting the common good should be mentioned, as well as the nature of Christian patriotism.

In what connection? There are several suitable places in which to give this lesson, but the most fitting seem to us to be after the doctrine on the miracles of Christ, on the Church, or on the Eucharist. Christ in performing His works of power gave us a striking example of coming to the aid of others and of showing love in action, particularly in service. The Church is the assembly of the children of God, and its fundamental law is the law of charity. Fraternal charity is a criterion of the true Church of Christ, already called by St. Ignatius of Antioch "the assembly of charity." Christian charity also extends to men outside the Church, because all men are called to the Church and invited into the family of God. Our charity should manifest God's invitation to them. Or, again, the lesson on the Eucharist offers a good opportunity for this lesson on fraternal charity. How strongly Christ inculcated charity at the Last Supper, when with the Apostles He gave thanks for their first communion! Every true union among brothers comes from union with Christ. Every union of branches is derived from their union with the vine.

Method: Explanatory. This is the principal law ordering the relationships of the members of Christ among themselves. Here the example of a well-ordered family may well be used.

Aim: The spirit of fraternal charity, from which the corresponding acts will flow in due course.

DOCTRINAL SUMMARY

A. THE FOUNDATION OF FRATERNAL CHARITY

The new Christian order, in which all of us are called into the one family of God's children. Christ has brought us back into an intimate unity with one another which by far surpasses the natural unity of the family (see the Seventeenth Instruction; 1 Cor. 12:12 ff.; Eph. 4:4–6; 1 Tim. 2:5). *One God and Father* of all; one Christ and Redeemer of all; one faith and hope; one common treasure, that is, the inheritance of God's children; one Spirit and Life-Giver, Who communicates to us all the Spirit of Christ. But this is the Spirit of Christ: from love of the Father to spend Himself in the service of the children of God; not to be ministered to, but to serve and sacrifice Himself for the salvation of others (Matt. 20:28; Luke 22:26 ff.; John 13:12–17).

B. THE CHARACTER OF FRATERNAL CHARITY

It is Christlike—"as I have loved you" (John 13:34). Christlike in motive, that is, for the sake of the Father, Whom we love as His children. It is Christlike in intensity, prepared for the greatest sacrifices; Christlike in universality, extending itself to strangers and even to enemies; Christlike in endurance, persevering until death in spite of injuries, annoyances, the basest ingratitude.

C. THE VIOLATION OF FRATERNAL CHARITY

We Christians are commissioned ceaselessly to manifest and to offer to the world the charity of Christ. We ought in every possible way to help men and to minister to them on the way to the Father. *See the anti-Christian nature of sins against the fifth commandment.* We ought to be, in Christ, "saviors" of the world, servants of our brethren, and authors of happiness for them. What, then, if we purposefully or neglectfully hinder or trouble their happiness, if we injure them in any way in soul or body? "Why not rather suffer wrong? . . . But you yourselves do wrong and defraud, and that to the brethren" (1 Cor. 6:7). The special obligation of the fifth commandment in the Christian order: it is concerned with saving and making pleasant the life on earth, not of slaves, but of sons of God. Since it is our special Christian vocation "in Christ" to be "saviors" of our brethren, to overcome sin in ourselves and in others, to promote the kingdom of God, and thus to "cast out the prince of this world" (John 12:31), the anti-Christian malice of scandal and of deliberately leading away from Christ is obvious. Through scandal and seducing to evil one becomes in a special way a collaborator of Satan, the enemy of Christ.

Since these sins are in such direct opposition to the Christian vocation, we can understand the astonishing severity of Christ in indicating and censuring these sins. "It is impossible that scandals should not come; but woe to him through whom they come! It were better for him if a millstone were hung about his neck and he were thrown into the sea, than that he should cause one of these little ones to sin" (Luke 17:1–2). The fifth commandment is the first example that Christ uses in the Sermon on the Mount to illustrate the essential difference between the Old Law and the New (Matt. 5:21–26). Christ demands much, but He clearly shows why. He brands the opposing way of acting as insufficient (Matt. 5:38–48). When Christ speaks of mortal sin or of hell, His typical example is almost always a violation of fraternal charity (Luke 16:19–31; Matt. 18:7, 23–35; 25:41–46).

D. The Social and Political Exercise of Fraternal Charity

Christ's command to love one another refers not only to individual relationships between persons but also to social relationships as well. Man is saved not in isolation, but as a member of God's people. He is also obliged to take an active part in the life and government of the state in order to serve the common good of all men, Christians or not. He is obliged to obey political authority as long as it is truly serving the common welfare. A generous and loyal patriotism is ennobling, but it should finally serve the welfare of the whole human family. Christ in the beatitudes praised not only those who are merciful but also those who hunger and thirst for justice and suffer for it. In our days a dedication to social justice and freedom for all men is an outstanding characteristic of Christian charity.

This love for others should inspire Christians to create peace. "Blessed are the peacemakers, for they shall be called children of

God" (Matt. 5:9). Jesus is the great Peacemaker, by His death breaking down the wall of separation to make all men one. He slew hatred in His own flesh (see Eph. 2:16; Col. 1:20–22). Earthly peace which arises from love of neighbor symbolizes and results from the peace of Christ. For this reason all Christians should plead for peace and cooperate with all men in making secure a peace based on justice and love, and particularly in setting up international agencies of peace.

In this connection the Pastoral Constitution on the Church in the Modern World, as well as the social encyclicals of recent Popes, should be highly recommended.

E. The Bond and Nourishment of Charity

The Eucharist . . . *"communion."* "Because the bread is one, we, though many, are one body, all of us who partake of the same bread" (1 Cor. 10:17).

Thirtieth Instruction

THE RIGHT ATTITUDE OF THE CHRISTIAN TO MATERIAL GOODS (THE SEVENTH AND TENTH COMMANDMENTS)

Sins against the seventh commandment spring from an inordinate desire for material goods. Avarice is the inexhaustible source of such sins. Dry up the source, and the sins will cease. To teach the seventh commandment properly, therefore, it is of decisive importance to build up in the students the right Christian attitude toward material goods. God Who has given us our body knows its needs. With divine generosity He has provided mankind with the necessary means for material life. He orders man to use initiative and diligence to bring about an increased productivity and a just distribution of these gifts—principles of Christian social doctrine!—and protects the peaceful possession and use of His visible gifts. But the protection of material goods by forbidding theft presupposes the just acquisition and just distribution of those goods. In the ancient law, too, God Himself wisely provided this distribution. Let us carefully avoid any explanation of the seventh commandment which might be misunderstood as backing laissez-faire capitalism.

In What connection? The lesson on creation is relevant, but that on death also offers a most fitting opportunity. Man must leave his riches behind. He is not the lord, only the administrator, of material things. "Render an account" (Luke 16:2).

Method: Explanatory. Proceeding from a description and analysis of the state of a dying man about to face judgment.

Viewpoint: "Blessed are the *poor in spirit,* for theirs is the kingdom of heaven!" Lift up your hearts to heaven where are true joys, where true riches will be yours forever!

Aim: A Christian evaluation of material goods and a Christian use of these goods.

DOCTRINAL SUMMARY

A. WE ARE NOT OWNERS, BUT ADMINISTRATORS

We are not the owners, but only the administrators of the goods of this world. Would that we were always faithful stewards, always administering the goods entrusted to us according to the Lord's will! We Christians are not *slave-administrators;* we are to administer our Father's goods as His children. Our conduct therefore should be regulated by our filial devotion to the Father Who has so kindly conferred these goods upon us. The meaning and purpose of material goods: the service of the whole man with all his material, intellectual, moral, and religious needs, the service of the whole of mankind of whatever race and nation. Each man has a duty to contribute according to his ability to the economic progress of his community and a right to an active share in the direction of economic development. Men are obliged to come to the relief of the poor, and to do so not merely out of their superfluous goods. Special care must be given to sharing goods in such a way that individuals and nations are not kept in dependence, but receive the means necessary to help and develop themselves.

As a matter of fact, our filial service and submission on earth consist in large part in our right use of material goods. Moreover, material things have a *special dignity* for Christians: they provide the nourishment, shelter, clothing, and such for children of God; and through them the Father manifests His paternal providence for us in many and various ways. These material things also should continuously speak to us Christians about the Father (James 1:17).

Behold the keys of heaven if you use them well (Luke 16:9). Our hearts should be filled with childlike gratitude for these good things entrusted to us (1 Cor. 10:31; Eph. 5:20; 1 Tim. 4:3).

B. These Goods Are Not Lasting

But we are *born for greater things,* and so material possessions do not merit too great affection from the Christian heart. What a desertion of Christ's service it would be for a Christian to seek avidly after such things, to try to snatch them away from others, to make his whole life consist in enjoying them. Here we should show how the principal sins against the seventh commandment—theft, fraudulent business deals, and such—flow from an anti-Christian evaluation of material goods. The necessity of restitution must be made clear. Whoever refuses to make restitution when it is morally possible clearly shows that he retains an inordinate love for the unjustly acquired goods. The disciple of Christ avoids not only actual theft but also every unjust desire for possessions and power.

Social envy! The tenth commandment. The true Christian sincerely strives to arrive at perfect peace, so profound as to be disturbed by no material cares. Christlike solicitude for the kingdom of God excludes anxiety for temporal goods. "No man can serve two masters" (Matt. 6:24). "Be not solicitous" (Matt. 6:25–34; 1 Cor. 7:30–32; Phil. 4–6). "Our citizenship is in heaven" (Phil. 3:20). ". . . seek the things that are above, where Christ is seated at the right hand of God. Mind the things that are above, not the things that are on earth" (Col. 3:1–4, used in the Mass of the Easter Vigil —the Church's reminder to the neophytes of what their new life should be).

Thirty-First Instruction

LOVE OF TRUTH AND THE PROPER ESTEEM OF GOOD REPUTATION (THE EIGHTH COMMANDMENT)

By the eighth commandment God again protects two important goods: truth and a good reputation. Only they who fully appreciate these precious goods can evaluate God's loving intention in giving the commandment.

In an age when communication has become so important, great

attention should be given to the proper use of speech, the written word, and the visual image. The various mass media—press, radio, television, movies—must be used to build up rather than tear down, to improve rather than destroy. Advertising, for example, must serve human needs, not manipulate passions for profit. The communications media have an enormous power to shape attitudes and influence others as much by what they omit as by what they say, as well as by the settings in which their message is presented.

Because of the very structure of society man has a right to information both for his own individual welfare and for the ability to contribute intelligently and actively to the common good. What he is told, whether by individuals or mass media, should always be true and as complete as charity and justice allow.

In what connection? This lesson may most profitably be inserted after the Tenth Instruction (Words of Jesus).

Method: Historical-explanatory. The life of Jesus supplies the narrative.

Viewpoint: See the Christian value of truthfulness and a good name.

Aim: Christlike love of truth and proper esteem of good reputation.

DOCTRINAL SUMMARY

A. Christ the Judge, Who Loves Truth and Restores Good Reputation

Christ, Truth itself (John 14:6), is always the greatest lover of truth: "the Truth and the Life" are the chief blessings that He brought us from heaven (John 1:14–17). The misfortunes of the human race began when our first parents believed more in the devil, the "father of lies" (John 8:44), than in the all-truthful God. When they wished to be "as gods," they lost both truth and life. The second Adam came into the world for the very purpose of conquering the prince of lies and of raising up the kingdom of truth. "This is why I was born, and why I have come into the world, to bear witness to the truth. Everyone who is of the truth hears my voice" (John 18:37). In Christ's own character His absolute truthfulness shines out splendidly. He is the Light of the world (John 8:12) that excludes all darkness. From this follows His almost vehement aversion to the pretence and lies of the Pharisees. This is the reason why in Christ's mouth the word "hypocrite" is the gravest censure, even a curse. Christ demanded of His disciples the strictest simplicity (like children and doves) and truthfulness. "But let your speech be, 'Yes, yes'; 'no, no'; and whatever is beyond these comes from the evil one" (Matt. 5:37).

At the universal judgment the King of truth will make known the complete and *conclusive victory of truth.* Then will all lies be exposed, condemned, treated with contempt by all, and severely punished. Then there will be no vain jests and delays and excuses, only a great and unbearable embarrassment and confusion, especially on the part of false disciples of Christ, lying disciples of Truth, "Pharisee-Christians." He will make them "share the lot of hypocrites. There will be the weeping, and the gnashing of teeth" (Matt. 24:51).

Then will appear the true "face" of every man. The good name of those who deserve it will be finally and definitively restored to them in the presence of the whole human race and the choirs of angels. God will most clearly reveal His judgment of each man and His reasons for so judging. Then all pretense will be at an end; all foolish esteem for transitory values will cease, together with all self-deception and all misestimation by others. God's standards of reputation will prevail, standards that judge a man according to his intrinsic worth, his Christlikeness; not the standards of men which evaluate a man by his wealth, his exterior appearance, his knowledge, success, or charm. Then "many who are first now will be last, and many who are last now will be first" (Matt. 19:30). Then "He will put down the mighty from their thrones, and will exalt the lowly" (Luke 1:52). How will you be judged? What kind of "face" will be yours?

B. CHRISTLIKE LOVE OF TRUTH

We Christians are the disciples of truth; in baptism we received the Spirit of Christ, in holy Scripture so often called "the Spirit of Truth" (John 14:17; 15:26; 1 John 4:6). Therefore we ought to seek and to love truth in all things, not only in words, but also in our actions. We should not wish to appear better than we actually are before God and men—no, not even before ourselves. *Sincerity in prayer, simplicity in conversation, truthfulness in action.* As genuine disciples of Christ we should give testimony to the truth, especially to the truth about God. That is our vocation. But men will not accept our witness unless they find us truthful and faithful in all our words and actions. Since truth is for us a good of great value, the true disciple of Christ does not refuse to make great sacrifices in order to defend and hold fast to the truth. He courageously avoids every kind of lie.

C. CHRISTLIKE ESTEEM OF GOOD NAME

We are strong only insofar as we are strong in the eyes of God. We have only as much "face" as God gives us. The esteem of men does not add to our intrinsic value. Yet the good opinion of men is of *great importance in our social life,* and especially for the sake of the friendly dealings with others that are proper to children of God. Because a good reputation is of such great importance for human life, God, by means of the eighth commandment, protects this great good against any kind of unjust injury or damage from lack of charity.

Sins against the good reputation of others (calumny, detraction, unkind words, and such) easily become mortal sins, at least objectively, because they often cause very serious damage to others. These sins proceed more directly from real hatred of our brethren than do, for example, sins against the seventh commandment, and therefore they violate charity even more gravely. Those who disturb Christian peace are to be reckoned among the worst of evildoers. They go directly contrary to the Christian vocation. They are not apostles of the Prince of Peace, but apostles of the devil. (The word "devil" comes from the Greek word *"diabolos,"* and originally meant "calumniator, disturber of peace.") How scandalous it is that Christ is so often calumniated in His members by the carelessness and, alas, often the deliberate malice of other Christians!

Because a good reputation is of such great importance in social life, the Christian has not only a right but also a real obligation to use just means in order to gain such a reputation for himself. For us Christians a good name has a special value. "For we are the fragrance of Christ for God, alike as regards those who are saved and those who are lost; to these an odor that leads to death, but to those an odor that leads to life" (2 Cor. 2:15 ff.). Pagans must be led back to the Father through our truly Christian example. "Even so let your light shine before men, in order that they may see your good works and give glory to your Father in heaven" (Matt. 5:16). But these works are not performed for the praise of men (Matt. 6:1).

Here lies the difficult art of Christian living, which is rightly carried out for the wholehearted love of God alone. This true love of God will bring it about that we sincerely seek the service of God, and not ourselves, in gaining and guarding our good name; it will effectively guard us against using less honest means to gain or preserve it, against overesteeming this transitory good. And, finally, the sincere love of God will enable the true disciple of Christ to follow his Master, when this is necessary, even to the ignominy of the cross. He will be able to be joyful even in the midst of persecutions and reproaches (Matt. 5:10–12). For he has the mind which was also in Christ Jesus (see Phil. 2:5–11) and knows that such a special and intimate likening to Christ crucified will, after a brief time, be followed by an equally special and intimate likening to Christ soon to come in His glory.

LONGING FOR PERFECT WORSHIP

Now, during the time of our pilgrimage (2 Cor. 5:2–10) our filial worship of prayer and action, even at best, can only remain a generous, but essentially imperfect, attempt. The Spirit of Christ given to us at baptism continuously stimulates us to worship the heavenly Father by prayer and action. He impels us to deep gratitude and ardent love, to strive to do much more than we are strictly obliged to do. But whatever we may do to manifest our filial submission and devotion, our actual response remains far behind the Father's love. We can never respond as He deserves. In sincere Christian humility we shall at least admit "We are unprofitable servants" (Luke 17:10) and weak sons, far too unlike our incomparable Father. This is the proper reason for the special sorrow of Christians in this world: the inadequacy of our response.

But we know that the Lord is to come and bring to perfection these poor beginnings of our love. He will lead us home to the Father, where forever, through Christ, with Him and in Him, we shall praise the mercies of God's eternal love in perfect everlasting filial worship. "And when all things are made subject to Him, then the Son Himself will also be made subject to Him Who subjected all things to Him, that God may be all in all" (1 Cor. 15:28).

Amen! Come, Lord Jesus! (Apoc. 22:20).

THE TEACHING ON WHAT IS TO COME
(THE LAST THINGS)

The teaching on the "last things" is the crown of Christian doctrine. Here we see the end of the story of divine love, its final purpose; here we learn what we hope for; here we see the full extent of the magnificent task of the Holy Spirit, the Perfector: *our definitive consummation in Christ.*

Like all of Christian doctrine, the teaching on what is to come is entirely Christocentric, and should therefore be presented in a Christocentric manner. Christ is not only the way by which we tend to the Father while we are on this earth. It is in Christ that we are to be intimately united to the Father for all eternity. The joys of heaven are nothing other than our participation in the inheritance of Christ.

The teaching on the last things is by no means intended primarily to inspire fear. It should rather put our glorious goal clearly and attractively before our eyes, and so teach us rightly to distinguish the values of this passing world from the eternal values of the kingdom of God.

Our situation at the end of life and throughout eternity will be shaped by our present response to God's loving invitation. He is even now graciously revealing Himself to mankind through the Church. Seeds of the Word are planted in every human heart, including those who never come to an explicit awareness of Jesus as the incarnate Son. As long as man follows the inspirations of the Holy Spirit as honestly and faithfully as he can, he will share in the salvation won for him by Christ. But if he refuses the call of grace, he will be held responsible.

The doctrine of the last things is thus *full of consolation* for those who are already striving toward our heavenly homeland in the right way; while, with convincing arguments and *salutary fear,* it recalls to the path of salvation those who are living evil lives. It is presented in such a way as actually to attain these two purposes: to offer deep consolation to Christians of good will and to strike great terror into the tepid.

We must also be on our guard against both false "angelicism" and false religious individualism. The eternal joy that the Father has planned for us is a fully human, though entirely supernatural, happiness. We are not to be separated souls for all eternity; our bodies are to share also in the glory of the risen Christ, in the "new heaven and earth." This will be a *fully social* life and joy—the undreamed-of realization of all men's best longings for a perfect society. And, more than this, the doctrine of the last things deals, not merely with our own individual damnation or salvation, but with the fulfillment of the Father's plan, with the consummation of the entire Mystical Body and somehow of the whole world, with the final and perfect triumph of Christ, with the eternal paschal celebration in which the enemies of God will finally be brought to eternal confusion and the friends of Christ will enter fully into His triumph.

Thirty-Second Instruction

DEATH AND THE PARTICULAR JUDGMENT

Method: Explanatory. We begin from the inescapable fact of death and give the Christian explanation of this fact.

Viewpoint: Death should be clearly proclaimed as the definitive end to the Christian's probation. The beauty, the desirability, *the "good tidings" of a Christian death:* the intimate likeness to the dying Christ. In teaching the judgment we should speak chiefly about the criterion on which we shall be judged: whether we have attained to that Christlikeness to which we are called.

Aim: To fortify us against the deceits of this world, to give us the perception and the "eyes" of Christ with which to look at, to weigh and judge this transitory life.

DOCTRINAL SUMMARY

A. DEATH TEACHES THE MEANING OF LIFE

Death shatters man's illusions of omnicompetence. As man faces death he realizes that he is a creature, utterly dependent on God at each moment. Man grows aware that he is not master of his own destiny, that this life is not enough. All the experiences, struggles, joys of this life, all the honors and pleasures, have only a passing value. They are here, but will soon be gone. And if they are the only meaning to life, then life is absurd, a mockery. Thus death is not only a door through which man passes at the end of life; even during life the existence of that door is a reminder of values which transcend the here and now.

B. Religion Teaches the Meaning of Death

It is a fact that all men die. But none of us knows exactly when or how our own death will come. In the midst of life we are in death. Even the longest life passes very swiftly. Religion teaches us the *meaning of death.* ". . . it is appointed unto men to die once and after this comes the . . . judgment" (Heb. 9:27); "wherever it [the tree] falls, there shall it lie" (Eccles. 11:3); "For what a man sows, that he will also reap" (Gal. 6:8). There is no second chance, no appeal, no more time for our plans to reform. The same Lord Who said, "No man can serve two masters," now gives to each what he deserves. For each man it is the definitive end of his probation. "Render an account of your stewardship" (Luke 16:2). For the good man it is, not the end of life, but the end of a long process of "Christian dying" and the entrance into true life. The work of "I die daily" (1 Cor. 15:31) is completely finished, and gives way to a perfect life without end. But for the evil man, who has not "died" to sin, who is not filled with Christ's life, death takes on the character of punishment strictly so-called; it is the beginning of punishment and eternal death; it is truly the end of a very brief life and the beginning of eternal death. Which kind of death do you want? You make the choice all during your life.

From considering death in this way the good Christian finds the right attitude toward death: it is not to be too greatly feared, since for us it is the gate to the life we most desire. And since we can enter into that life only through this gate, death loses its horrors; it becomes bearable and even desirable, for we are "with Christ" (Phil. 1:21 and 23). And we do not grieve too greatly at the death of even those dear to us: "They go ahead of us."

Thus there is a great difference between pagan and Christian sadness. "But we would not, brethren, have you ignorant concerning those who are asleep, lest you should grieve, even as others who have no hope" (1 Thess. 4:13). "In Christ has shone upon us the hope of a blessed resurrection, so that those who are saddened by the inevitable condition of having to die, may be consoled by the promise of immortality to come. For thy faithful, Lord, life is changed, not taken away; and though the house given us for this earthly sojourn is destroyed, an eternal dwelling-place is prepared for us in heaven" (Preface for the Dead). We Christians participate in Christ's victory over death. "Death is swallowed up in victory. O death, where is thy victory ?. . . But thanks be to God Who has given us the victory through our Lord Jesus Christ" (1 Cor. 15:55–57). Christ could have saved us by any act, but in fact He saved us by His death and resurrection. He took death on Himself as a visible expression of the sinful state of man, but also as a visible expression of His love. Death became the incarnation of Christ's loving obedience, His gift of Himself to man and to His Father. Thus His death summed up His whole life. In this way Christ changed death from the manifestation of sin to a revelation of grace and love. He moved into the emptiness of death and filled it with God's presence. The Christian, too, as he experiences himself falling into the emptiness of death believes, hopes, and loves—and this faith, hope, and love transform death. Christ has been there before us and we can find Him there. Into darkness, despair, and coldness the victory of Christ has brought light, hope, warmth.

And for this reason our grief over the death of those dear to us ought to manifest itself differently from pagan sorrow. Christian funeral and burial customs should not imitate those of "pagans," but rather show those outside the Church what our idea of Christian death really is.

Thirty-Third Instruction

THE RESURRECTION AND GENERAL JUDGMENT

Method: Historical-explanatory. In the first part of each point the future event should be described vividly, but not fantastically. In the second part the religious significance of these events should be explained.

Viewpoint: The final triumph of Christ. Union with Christ alone will bring us to final triumph and happiness.

Aim: Undaunted faith in the final victory of Christ, sheer joy with Christ in His triumph; the following of Christ through all things ("together with Him to die and to triumph over death").

DOCTRINAL SUMMARY

A. THE RESURRECTION OF THE DEAD

". . . the hour is coming in which all who are in the tombs shall hear the voice of the Son of God. And they who have done good shall come forth unto resurrection of life; but they who have done evil unto resurrection of judgment" (John 5:28). How great a manifestation of the Lord's power! How greatly it surpasses the miraculous raising of Lazarus from death, and even the glorious personal resurrection of Christ Himself! All shall rise, but differently. The good with glorious bodies that share in the glory of the risen Christ; the evil with bodies that are fitting to the state of their souls. We do not know "how" God's power will bring this about. All subtle questions about the identity of our glorious bodies with those we now have are to be carefully avoided. The general resurrection is one of the mysteries of the Christian faith.

This will be the final and perfect paschal feast: the completion of the resurrection of the whole Christ, Head and members also. The whole of human nature sinned, and the whole was restored and elevated in Christ; now the whole is to be glorified. Such glorification is due to one who is a member of Christ and a temple of the Holy Spirit, who has been so often sanctified and nourished by the Eucharist. Consider the reverence due to a Christian body, living or dead.

The superabundant restoration of the harmony of paradise. Now finally the work of restitution will be completed. The gifts of the first paradise, not yet given back to us, then will be abundantly showered on us, and much more besides. Then finally we shall see the full significance of the phrase "O happy fault" (Exsultet).

There is only one road to this perfect glory and happiness: "provided, however, we suffer with Him that we may also be glorified with Him" (Rom. 8:17; see also Rom. 6 and 7; 1 Cor. 15:42-44; John 12:23-25). Let us die now to the law of sin in our members so that the life of Christ also may be manifested in us.

B. THE SECOND COMING OF CHRIST

A vivid description of this coming, *comparing it to Christ's first coming.* Then He came in humility, now in glory; then to invite men, now to compel them; then to struggle and suffer, now to triumph completely.

Let us now in hope share the joy of Christ triumphant, have firm confidence in His final victory, whatever may happen. Let us greatly desire this victory.

Christ is He Who *perfects the Church.* ". . . from which [that is, from heaven], we eagerly await a Savior, our Lord Jesus Christ,

Who will refashion the body of our lowliness, conforming it to the body of His glory by exerting the power by which He is able also to subject all things to Himself" (Phil. 3:20). Then He will re-form to its complete perfection the Church now suffering on earth, laboring under so many imperfections. Come, Lord, come; we await you with holy impatience! May you find us watching, faithful, and ready.

C. THE GENERAL JUDGMENT

The Judge: Christ the Man, the God-Man, our Lord and most beloved Brother. He will judge with divine majesty, with knowledge that reads the heart. There is no hope of escaping this judge or of bribing Him. All will be given perfect justice, rich or poor, educated and illiterate. For those who have refused to love and serve others "it is a fearful thing to fall into the hands of the living God" (Heb. 10:31).

The nature of the judgment: The divine sentence concluding the whole history of salvation will be proclaimed to the whole world.

The object of the judgment: The history of salvation. In distinction to the particular judgment, this will be the judgment of all, and of each individual action and person with respect to the whole.

The passive subjects: All men and angels, divided into two classes according to their attitude to Christ. Not only individual men but human communities, families, peoples.

The active subjects: The members of Christ who carry out the office of judging together with Christ. Joyful acclamations: "You speak to us from the heart! Your judgment is our judgment!" Now we should by our lives already judge this world in Christ. But we should strive to be rather "saviors" than "judges."

Criterion of the judgment: Our relationship to Christ: "Whatever . . . you have done to Me." According to our works, whether external or internal; not according to our empty wishes or unproductive words. According to the end God established for us in Christ, whether we have arrived at that Christlikeness to which we were called (Rom. 8:29). What would be His judgment if I stood before His throne now?

The results of the judgment: The magnificent revelation of God. Then at last will His justice, mercy, wisdom, and especially His divine providence be splendidly shown forth to all creation. This will be the consummation of all rightful human longings for justice. It will be the conclusive restoration or loss of our "face" before God and men. Thoughts of this judgment are an effective remedy against vain human respect (Luke 9:26). This will be the conclusive consummation: "Come, blessed of My Father . . . depart from Me" (Matt. 25:34 and 41) and so be forever removed from the Father. The sentence cannot be changed. There is no hope of appeal or delay. It remains in force forever.

NOTE ON TEACHING THIS MATERIAL

The material given above should suffice for more than one instruction if time allows. Sermons on the final triumph of Christ and the eventual defeat of His enemies assist greatly in purging our souls and uniting them sincerely with Christ. If only one instruction can be given on this subject, it might be better to begin the third point with a description of the judgment itself according to holy Scripture (especially Matt. 25:31–46). Then in the explanation there should be a further development of the material on the purpose of the judgment. The remaining material may be used summarily within the preceding description.

It is needless to say that in teaching and preaching on this topic, all discussions of the time of the last judgment should be avoided.

We should take particular care here to explain clearly that this triumph is the *perfect revelation of providence*. Let us use all occasions that present themselves to remind our people about divine providence, for example, in instructions on creation (natural providence), on the elevation (supernatural providence), on the fall and the incarnation (providence for the fallen human race), on the resurrection of Christ (the most special providence concerning the Only-begotten), the law of this providence (through the cross to glory), on the Church and the sacraments, especially the Eucharist (the fatherly providence of God for His children adopted in Christ). A separate instruction on divine providence will then be less necessary if we really use such opportunities. But if circumstances, such as the special difficulties of our time or of our people, demand a special instruction, such a lesson can be very well added after the instruction on the last judgment.

DOCTRINE ON HELL AND HEAVEN

We give the doctrine on hell first so as to end the story of divine love with the achievement of the goal of that love. And, also, the teaching on hell is in a way a good psychological preparation for the teaching on heaven, since it purges the heart from earthly passions ("Blessed are the clean of heart") and so removes impediments to the contemplation of the life of heaven.

On the other hand, it cannot be denied that the religious understanding of hell presupposes an appreciation of the heavenly reward. How could one ponder the punishment of loss without pondering what the damned miss forever—heaven? From this point of view it would be better to teach the doctrine concerning heaven first. A good solution which would include both values might be this: to teach first the doctrine on heaven, then that on hell, and as a conclusion and recapitulation of the whole course of instructions, to give a summary of all that God has done for us in order to have us with Him forever in heaven.

In these instructions hell and heaven should be described, not minutely or fantastically, but rather by means of comparisons adapted to the minds of the audience. The description of hell especially should be drawn, not from one's own imagination, but entirely from holy Scripture. While teaching and preaching these things, let us strive to put on the person of Jesus Christ in a special way; the faithful require here a deep and sincere faith which will truly believe in these punishments and rewards that so far surpass our imagination and understanding.

Thirty-Fourth Instruction

HELL

Method: Explanatory. A description of hell, taken from holy Scripture, takes the place of a narrative, although to begin the lesson, some parable, as that of Dives and Lazarus (Luke 16:19 ff.), or even some picture may be used. The use of pictures in instructing the unlettered is not objectionable if the picture is really suitable for teaching and the catechist himself does not let the entire lesson consist in a description of the pain of sense only.

Viewpoint: Behold the judgment of the holy and just God on mortal sin. See the great folly of sin! How foolish to persist in self-will at the cost of being punished with such great torments. See the malice of mortal sin, which God the Just must punish thus. See the goodness of God most merciful, Who has warned us through His Son, ". . . Who has not spared even His own Son but has delivered Him for us all . . ." (Rom. 8:32) in order that we, His ungrateful and rebellious children, might be spared.

Aim: Horror of sin. "Rather die than commit sin!" This instruction is intended to bring about a radical conversion in hearers who are in the state of mortal sin, to convince them not to play with fire any longer, to remove and avoid occasions of sin at once. And this instruction is also intended to preserve the good from the calamity of sin. *Gratitude for the mercy of God,* Who has done so many and so great wonders to snatch me from this disaster ". . . thanks to the Father, Who . . . has rescued us from the power of darkness and transferred us into the kingdom of His beloved Son, in Whom we have our redemption, the remission of our sins" (Col. 1:12–14). In this way even this instruction will be made Christocentric and will bear full Christian fruit.

DOCTRINAL SUMMARY

A. WHAT OUR SAVIOR TEACHES ABOUT HELL

Christ, the Good Shepherd and most merciful Savior, Who came, not to condemn, but rather to seek that which was lost, quite often spoke clearly about hell, its fire and other torments. None of us has ever seen heaven; neither have we seen hell. But Christ had: as God He created it; as Redeemer He frees us from it; as Judge He fixes its limits; and as the Good Shepherd He warns us against it. Again and again the words of Christ distinguish a *double punishment:* of loss ("Cast him out," "Depart from Me") and of sense ("into eternal fire"). Evidently the fire is not earthly fire, but something which causes intense pain within the sinner. Just as God will reward beyond all created imagination, so also He will justly punish (see Heb. 10:31). Yet this punishment of the senses is the lesser pain, even though it makes a greater impression on us here and now. The blinded sinner who has freely rejected God and put some created object in His place is especially unable to appreciate the punishment of loss. Yet this punishment must always be pointed out and explained with fitting examples. Thus, a son who for some dreadful crime is expelled from his family. He would hardly feel this punishment while his passions are still aroused. But later on he will gradually come to feel the misery of his condition and will be tortured by a great desire for his family.

The greatness of the punishment will be increased by two circumstances nearly always mentioned by Christ: *the eternity of hell* and *the gnawing of conscience* ("worm").

In hell there is no hope, no Savior. A comparison of this saddest of moments for the damned with the sentence given after the sin in paradise. This is the state of complete and conclusive separation from God; now there can be no more "bridge and bridge-builder" (*pons et pontifex*) to reconcile the damned with God. But we still have hope because we have Christ the Redeemer. "My dear children, these things I write to you in order that you may not sin. But if anyone sins, we have an advocate with the Father, Jesus Christ the just; and He is a propitiation for our sins, not for ours only but also for those of the whole world" (1 John 2:1 ff.).

B. WHO WILL GO TO HELL?

Only those who have sinned mortally and have not sincerely repented. No one can fall into this calamity unawares and imperceptibly. Mortal sin necessarily requires *fully deliberate rebellion against God*. See the frightfulness of sin, which must be punished in such a way by the most just and holy God. Lord, from Your way of acting I realize the malice of mortal sin, "I believe" in its dreadfulness. The amazing appropriateness of this horrible punishment. Finally, and usually after long delay, many warnings and opportunities for penance, God permits the punishment of hell, which the creature chose himself by his fully deliberate rejection of God through mortal sin. In every mortal sin the sinner freely rejects God, his final and highest good, and prefers some cheap and transitory creature to Him. In his judgment on mortal sin God only ratifies the decision of the creature and gives him what he himself has impiously chosen. Hell is the prolongation of man's will to sin. Just as heaven is the flowering of the life of grace already present in man as a first installment, so hell is the flowering of the death of sin, the full revelation of selfishness. To man's deliberate turning away from God by sin corresponds the eternal separation from God (the punishment of loss); to his turning toward a creature as ultimate goal corresponds the disastrous deception and retaliation on the part of the creature (the punishment of sense). By such reasonings we do not fully solve the "mystery of hell" or the "mystery of sin"; we only intend to prepare our hearers psychologically for the ready acknowledgment of the supreme holiness and justice of

God. Ultimately these are mysteries in which we must believe; we cannot understand them fully. "You art just, O Lord, and Your ordinance is right" (Ps. 118:137).

But we should never forget that God permits hell because of His justice, and He has clearly revealed its existence to us because of His love in order to spare us that disaster. "Oh, that today you would hear His voice, 'Harden not your hearts . . .' " (Ps. 94:8). He not only warns you but He even sends His own Son, and does not spare Him in order that you may be spared. At the very moment when in His name we are presenting this terrifying doctrine, He in His merciful love again invites us all, both preacher and audience, to make use of His mercy and of the blood that His Son shed for us.

"But all things are from God, Who has reconciled us to Himself through Christ and has given to us the ministry of reconciliation. For God was truly in Christ, reconciling the world to Himself by not reckoning against men their sins and by entrusting to us the message of reconciliation. On behalf of Christ, therefore, we are acting as ambassadors, God, as it were, appealing through us. We exhort you, for Christ's sake, be reconciled to God. For our sakes He made Him to be sin Who knew nothing of sin, so that in Him we might become the justice of God" (2 Cor. 5:18–21).

NOTE ON TEACHING THIS MATERIAL

The doctrine of hell, like that of original sin, must not be given to those who are as yet incapable of mortal sin, at least not in a way that they would think that it applies to them. Otherwise serious psychological harm would result because of the distorted impression the child receives of God. Because children do not have any experience of fully deliberate rebellion against God which could affect their entire destiny, they are incapable of grasping the justice of an eternal punishment, so that God appears arbitrary and despotic. Instead of speaking of hell, speak of God's wisdom and justice in letting the sinner experience His disapproval of sin so as to correct him and lead him to repentance.

Thirty-Fifth Instruction

HEAVEN

Method: Explanatory. After Christ's own example, the doctrine of heaven is to be explained mainly by apt comparisons.

Viewpoint: Behold the full fruition of our sonship, our final sharing in the glory and riches of Christ (coheirs with Christ).

Aim: Unitive love. Intimate desire for perfect union with God. The doctrine of heaven should be presented in such a way as not to arouse hope alone (the love of concupiscence) but also to arouse charity and perfect it (the love of benevolence), together with the apostolic desire to help others attain this happiness.

DOCTRINAL SUMMARY

A. Now As in a Mirror, Darkly (1 Cor. 13:12)

Comparison with the beggar boy raised up to be an adopted child of the king. On the way to his father's palace the true son tells him about his father, about his happy life. Even though the beggar boy cannot understand more than a part of all this, since it all surpasses anything in his experience, yet he wants to hear more. He believes what he is told, and he hopes for it, yet the reality will far surpass his narrow imagination, not yet accustomed to royal dimensions. So are we with regard to heavenly happiness; we must now *"believe"* *our divine Brother.* Just as a man blind from birth cannot picture to himself the beauty of the sun and the starry skies, so the beauty and splendor of heaven entirely surpass our powers of understanding and imagination. "Eye has not seen, nor ear heard, nor has it entered into the heart of man, what things God has prepared for those who love Him" (1 Cor. 2:9). "No one has at any time seen God. The only-begotten Son Who is in the bosom of the Father, He has revealed Him" (1 John 1:18).

B. Behold, I Make All Things New—The New Paradise

The first Adam lost paradise through sin; the second Adam restores it to us. Our paradise is heaven. The heavenly life is the completely developed Christian life. These are the *riches of the second Adam.*

The new joys of paradise after the sorrows and hardships of this world. "And God will wipe away every tear from their eyes. And death shall be no more; neither shall there be mourning nor crying nor pain any more, for the former things have passed away" (Apoc. 21:4). No pain now, neither present nor to be feared in the future. How great were the joys of the first paradise—truly a "garden of delights," but how limited and worthless in comparison to heavenly joys. A vivid description of joys of paradise; application to the second paradise.

New peace of paradise after the struggles of this world. Then at last the harmony of paradise will be perfectly restored. No temptations or disturbances. Perfect peace with others also. Supreme social joy . . . as many joys as companions. Perfect imperturbable peace . . . impeccability. In the first paradise "they were able not to sin"; in the second "they cannot sin."

At the end of the world there will be "new heavens and a new earth . . . wherein justice dwells" (2 Pet. 3:13). It will be a fit abode for men and women with real bodies. There our enjoyment of natural beauty will be even more intense than our appreciation of beauty here. Now we find it hard to see God in everything; we often are distracted and forget God. But then we shall see everything in its relationship to God just as Christ did on earth: the lilies of the field, the birds of the air, human actions—all reminded Him of His Father.

Now body and soul, flesh and spirit, are often in tension and conflict. After the resurrection physical and emotional joys will flow from and reinforce spiritual happiness.

How frequently Christ described heaven in terms of a wedding feast (Matt. 8:11; 22:1–14; 25:1–13; 26:29; Mark 2:19; Luke 12:36–37; 14:15–24; 22:30; see Apoc. 2:7; 3:20; 19:7–9; 21:2; 2:14–17). Man in heaven remains social by nature. The Church endures as the People of God, the family of God, in which all of us by being joined to Christ are joined to each other. We will get to know others more intimately and personally. Men will not be afraid of rejection, but will be more ready to reveal their inner being. Repellent character traits will have been cleansed away, and each of us will be totally lovable in an almost limitless variety. Since we rise in the same body, we remain bound by ties of blood to our family. You remain the son or daughter of your mother and father just as Christ in heaven now is forever the son of Mary. So, too, our friendships remain, purified of all selfishness.

New rest of paradise (abundance). After the labors and wants of this world, full happiness, "full" joy. Then at last the human heart will be perfectly satisfied. Then we shall taste, not single drops of happiness, but perfect beatitude. Yet this rest is not a passive lassitude; it is the most intense activity possible: it is a share in the knowing and loving of God Himself, and God is Pure Act. "My Father works even until now, and I work," said the Lord (John

5:17). The Pastoral Constitution on the Church in the Modern World reminds us that in heaven we will find the values of human dignity, brotherhood, and freedom together with all the good fruits of our nature and enterprise, but freed of stain, burnished and transfigured (n. 39).

New paradisal prayer after the aridity and spiritual dullness of this world. In the first paradise, how pleasant was the familiar conversation with God. But this was only a figure of the heavenly reality. In heaven we shall at last see God face to face, not by means of an image, but in Himself, and we will love God and delight in Him. Then at last God will be "all in all" (1 Cor. 15:28). The human heart was created for love. In the eternal embrace of the Father it will at last be satisfied. The greatest delights of earthly love are as tiny droplets in comparison to the infinite ocean of heavenly delights. This new paradisal love will consist essentially in the full effusion of the Holy Spirit into our hearts, crying, "Abba, Father" (Rom. 8:15). Then finally the work of the Spirit, the Perfector, will be completed.

Happiness on earth is often found in the possession of some *thing,* but even more in the possession of a *person* whom we know and love. Now on earth this possession is necessarily limited and passing. Not even God fully satisfies us as we know and love Him in this life: we are fickle and not totally committed, and we do not know Him face-to-face as He is, but only partly, through reason and through faith. "We see now through a mirror in an obscure manner, but then face to face. Now I know in part, but then I shall know even as I have been known" (1 Cor. 13:12). ". . . now we are the children of God, and it has not yet appeared what we shall be. We know that, when He appears, we shall be like to Him, for we shall see Him as He is" (John 3:2). This will be eternal and fully satisfying.

Joy is heightened by awareness of mutual possession. A lover rejoices in the possession of the beloved, but even more in being possessed. We know by faith that God knows and loves us now, but in heaven we will be far more aware of this, for we shall share in the knowledge and love of the Trinity with full consciousness. We will not only know God as He knows us but we will also know ourselves as He knows us; we will know ourselves as totally lovable, for all that is unlovable will have been purged away.

Furthermore, our knowledge of God in heaven is going to be more intimate than our knowledge of any person here on earth. When we know others now, they remain outside us. Only our idea of them is inside us. The only one we know from the inside is ourself. Of heaven Jesus tells us, "In that day you will know that I am in My Father, and you in Me, and I in you" (John 14:20; see 17:21–26). Our union with God in heaven is compared to the indwelling of the divine Persons in each other: we will be in God and God in us as Christ is in the Father and the Father in Christ. No greater intimacy and joy is possible.

Just as the second Adam infinitely surpasses the first in dignity, merits, and glory, so also does the second paradise surpass the transitory and provisional paradise given to the first Adam. Our weak nature could not sustain such happiness; *God must strengthen, support, and help it with a very special assistance*; He gives new insight (*lumen*) and a new heart. "And He Who was sitting on the throne said, 'Behold, I make all things new!'" (Apoc. 21:5). That final, most blessed renewal will transform us perfectly into the likeness of the only-begotten Son (1 Cor. 15:47–49; Rom. 8:29 ff.).

Then at last the joys of Christ will completely be our joys: His victory, our victory; His glory, our glory: in a word, the inheritance of Christ will be our inheritance (Rom. 8:17). And so the way to such happiness is also easily understood.

C. "Provided, However, We Suffer with Him That We Also Be Glorified With Him" (Rom. 8:17)

The *only way* to participate in the glory of the risen Christ is participation in the humility of the suffering Christ. The shortest formula of Christian life: *"To die and to live with Christ!"* The more you now become like the humble Christ, the more you will become like the triumphant Christ. There is a great diversity of degrees of sharing. Let us share more and more completely in His death and His life.

We Christians do not foster any useless sorrow because of the loss of the first paradise; rather we hasten toward the Christian paradise, led by Christ, the second Adam. We desire this paradise with our whole hearts, and we sacrifice everything for it. We can lose all things in this world. On this earth we will have many afflictions. "In the world you will have affliction, but take courage, I have overcome the world" (John 16:33). "Father, I will that where I am, they also whom Thou hast given Me may be with Me . . ." (John 17:24).

This is the end of the history of
the eternal divine love.

Part III
The Heralds of Christ—
Their Personality and Formation

"Kerygmatic Spirituality" for the Heralds of Christ

Our intention here is not to promote the use of the word "keryg-matic," still less to propose a new method for cultivating the spiritual life; we already have more names and more methods than we need. But many of us are aware of the need for a deeper understanding of our apostolic vocation and for a more harmonious union of our spiritual life with our vocation as apostles. What, then, are the qualities of a true herald of Christ, the characteristics of truly kerygmatic spirituality?

A HUMBLE AND JOYFUL CONSCIOUSNESS OF OUR SUBLIME VOCATION

Anyone who has been appointed and sent to teach religion by ecclesiastical superiors is, in the last analysis, appointed and sent out by Christ Himself; he is, then, Our Lord's herald. He can say with St. Paul, "On behalf of Christ, therefore, we are acting as ambassadors; God, as it were, appealing through us" (2 Cor. 5:20).

A vital consciousness of their sublime vocation is, then, an essential element in the formation of all heralds of Christ if they are to be truly enthusiastic about their mission. They must realize that it is to be accepted as a precious and undeserved gift, a sacred responsibility. And, in fact, such humble and wholehearted acceptance of the task that God has given to them is an unfailing source of true joy for the teacher in the midst of all the difficulties, limitations, and disappointments of his work. Christ has sent him; Christ is with him; Christ is vitally interested in the work he is doing in His name. Such a holy awareness keeps Christ's herald devoted to his task, diligent without undue anxiety, cheerful without frivolity. With it he will continue to have the spirit necessary to prepare his lessons carefully and to teach them effectively.

Let us, whose duty it is to form future catechists, strive to impart to them an appreciation of the excellence of their vocation. Let us lead them to meditate on the commission which they are offering themselves to carry out, so that they may understand it and find joy in it—all in the light of Christ. Only so will they gain an adequate idea of their apostolic calling. For there exists a real danger that in the process of formation we may put too much emphasis on particular practices, devotions, rules, and recommendations, and too little on the even more important foundation—the sublime call of the future herald. A watchmaker must put together many little wheels and screws and springs and bearings. But what would we think of him if he put all these parts together and attended carefully to keeping them all clean—but never wound the watch. So these various rules and recommendations are necessary, but it is from the contemplation of his great vocation that the catechist must receive his inspiration.

Close Personal Contact With Christ

No herald will continue to carry out his task effectively unless he is closely and personally attached to the master who sent him out. Such attachment will make him careful, diligent, constant, daring. But without close personal attachment to Our Lord, the teacher will lose his zeal and his own real interest in his catechetical apostolate. He will find himself in great danger of growing more and more tired and disappointed; his teaching will be no longer a proclamation, but a tiresome "lecture." Only personal love for Christ will keep him, year after year, eloquent and inventive, zealous and practical, unwearying and obliging, patient and winning.

Yet we have still deeper reasons for close personal contact with Our Lord. Our King is not far away from His heralds; He is always with us. While we are proclaiming His message, we are instruments in His hands; He works through us and in the souls of our hearers. Thus only by close and continuous collaboration with Him can we reach our goal. Do we really believe this truth? If we do, we realize what kind of spirituality we need as heralds of Christ who can accomplish nothing unless we are united with our Master. Obviously, therefore, in the spirituality of a catechist the cultivation of an intimate union with Christ by faith and charity is absolutely fundamental.

And such a close personal union with Our Lord will result in our becoming like to Him. To proclaim His message effectively, we must be like Him, and it is with His spirit that we must proclaim His message. Just as the absolute consonance of His personality with His message shone out in His own teaching, so our personality and our way of life must be consonant with the message that we proclaim. Our hearers do not have the privilege of seeing and hearing Our Lord Himself, of being influenced by His winning personality. We can see in the Gospels how greatly His own personality aided His hearers to understand and to appreciate His teaching. One of the most glorious, but also difficult, aspects of our task, then, is that we must strive to overcome this disadvantage as completely as possible by letting Christ shine through our own Christlike personalities. We should be able to say to our hearers what St. Paul could say: "Be imitators of me, as I am of Christ" (1 Cor. 11:1; 1 Cor. 4:16; Phil. 3:17; 1 Thess. 1:6).

Of course, no one would deceive himself into entertaining the idea that he had fully realized this high ideal. We can only continue to approach it; we can never completely attain it. But we must never give up; we must always do all that we can. From the very beginning of our formation we must keep this ideal in view and tirelessly pursue it. Our Lord said: "When you have done everything that was commanded you, say, 'We are unprofitable servants; we have done what it was our duty to do'" (Luke 17:10).

DILIGENT CULTIVATION OF THE
SPECIFICALLY "KERYGMATIC" VIRTUES

As teachers of religion, we are not so much heralds *of* Christ, as heralds *with* and *in* Christ. We are the living instruments of the one great messenger sent to mankind by the Father. Christ is always the chief herald; we are His collaborators, through whom He continues His work. Thus we share in Christ's own mission: "As the Father has sent me, I also send you" (John 20:21). To fulfill this mission properly, to become fitting instruments of the divine messenger, we must cultivate the special virtues of a herald, virtues that shone forth so splendidly in Him. We might say that the chief of these are fidelity, unselfishness, winningness.

1. *Fidelity* is clearly the most important and the most characteristic virtue of a herald. As he is sent to proclaim a message to others, his fidelity causes him to proclaim his message exactly, carefully, diligently. How often the Gospels stress the absolute fidelity of Our

Lord to His heavenly Father. They show Him completely absorbed in the commission that the Father had entrusted to Him. How strongly Our Lord Himself claims that faithfulness to the message entrusted to Him is the chief characteristic of His teaching: "the things that I heard from Him [the Father], these I speak in the world. . . . of Myself I do nothing: but I preach only what the Father has taught Me. . . . He has not left Me alone, because I do always the things that are pleasing to Him" (John 8:26–29). At the end of His public teaching He states again the unswerving fidelity that was the guiding principle of all His teaching: "He who believes in Me, believes not in Me but in Him Who sent Me. . . . For I have not spoken on My own authority, but He Who sent Me, the Father, has commanded Me what I should say, and what I should declare. And I know that His commandment is everlasting life. The things, therefore, that I speak, I speak as the Father has bidden Me" (John 12:44–50). The fidelity that Our Lord speaks of here is, not the nervous faithfulness of a frightened servant, but the generous, joyful fidelity of a loving son.

Our fidelity as Christ's messengers, then, requires that our teaching convey the divine message as fully as possible. We are not the masters of our message; we are not permitted to select the material according to our own tastes and personal devotion; we are not permitted to adulterate the word of God with our own ideas. And so it is absolutely essential that we convey God's message in its own wonderful internal unity, that we bring out its real essentials, and that we focus our hearers' attention on the doctrines that form its very core.

Such fidelity to our message obviously requires a thorough and specialized study of it, and this is the purpose of so-called kerygmatic theology. This is not a new and separate branch of theology to be studied in addition to dogma, morals, and so on. It is rather a special approach to the study of all theology, with the purpose of gaining a deeper and fuller understanding of revealed truth as the message we are sent to proclaim. It stresses, therefore, the doctrines that form the substance of Christian revelation and Christian preaching, and indicates their interconnection and internal union in the central theme of Christianity, the mystery of Christ. And, further, this kerygmatic approach gives us the special aspect under which particular doctrines should be presented in order to gain a fittingly religious appreciation of them and their full fruit in Christian living. The same is now strictly demanded by Vatican II, but without using the word "kerygmatic," for the very beginning of seminar studies.[1] What counts is not the new word, but the spirit to be transmitted to the future herald of Christ.

Leading catechetical experts, therefore, declare that the more completely "kerygmatic" formation of teachers of religion is one of the most pressing needs of the catechetical apostolate today. And hence they urge a fuller use of the kerygmatic approach in the formation of future heralds of Christ in every seminary and convent, and urge that this approach be begun as early in the training as possible.

But even more important is the personal effort of every future herald to gain a truly religious understanding of his message by means of his own prayer and meditation. Hence, from the very beginning of his training the future herald should be encouraged and assisted to meditate on the message he is to proclaim. One of the greatest advantages of the kerygmatic approach is precisely that it makes Christian doctrine "prayable" and thereby inspires enthusiasm for the divine message. Heralds who make this divine message the central subject of their prayer and meditation will speak from the abundance of their hearts.

If we heralds are thus faithful to our message, faithful in this full sense of the word, then unselfishness and winningness will follow of themselves.

2. *Unselfishness* is only the negative aspect of fidelity. The perfect accomplishment of the commission entrusted to us requires that we be generous. For in proportion to the degree to which we seek ourselves and our own glory or comfort we inevitably become less capable in the service of God. But although this principle is clear to everyone, it is extremely difficult to practice. While our vocation does not call for artificial mortifications, it demands much more than these; it requires that we keep ourselves continuously silent and, as it were, dead with regard to our own interests in order to be completely free and alive for Our Lord. St. Paul's "I die daily" (1 Cor. 15:31) gives us the right perspective in which to pursue this high ideal. As heralds of Christ we are most especially to become divested of self, so that we truly are acting, not in our own name, but in the name of Christ. More than other Christians, we ought to become able to say with St. Paul, such a great herald of Christ: "It is now no longer I that live, but Christ lives in me" (Gal. 2:20).

---

[1] Decree on Priestly Formation, n. 14.

3. *Winningness.* If Christ is thus living in us, we shall win others as did Our Lord Himself. In Him "the goodness and kindness of God our Savior appeared" (Tit. 3:4) and won men's hearts. Our Lord's attractiveness did not consist only in natural charm but was also the outward manifestation of His attitude to mankind as their Savior. And this is also the only adequate attitude for the herald of Christ. We have His message to proclaim, not to stones or trees, but to living men of flesh and blood, to win them for God, to cause them to live a Christian life dedicated to God. Their response to our message is to be a new life, life in Christ. Thus as His heralds we must strive so to proclaim His message to the people of our own time that they may find it to be what it truly is, "spirit and life" (John 6:64).

So the herald of Christ should take care to allow the "goodness and kindness" of God to appear through him. But, let it be carefully noted, he should try to win his hearers' hearts never for himself, but for the Lord; he should strive to attract them, not to himself, but to Christ. In the same way, pleasing methods should be used, not to amuse our students, but to assist them to a deeper and fuller religious understanding of our message—to Christian living. And it is the consciousness of our sublime vocation that will make us eager to acquire truly Christlike attractiveness and to use attractive methods in our teaching, "for the love of Christ impels us" (2 Cor. 5:14).

Chapter Two

Lay Teachers and the
Catechetical Apostolate

This book would be quite incomplete if there was no special chapter on the laity's contribution to the catechetical apostolate. Among the most developed organizations engaged in the field of catechetics is the Confraternity of Christian Doctrine (CCD). Through this organization the laity collaborate with the hierarchy in promoting religious formation, both doctrinal and spiritual, which begins in early infancy and continues all through life. The parent-educator program shows parents how fully to exercise the most important and indispensable general form of the lay catechetical apostolate, the religious teaching and formation of their own children. Within the framework of the diocesan catechetical office, CCD members cooperate in courses for the religious formation of children and of young people, and in activities for the religious education of adults (programs during the school year, vacation schools, discussion clubs). The CCD also implements lay training courses on all levels for the purpose not only of training these teachers but also for study of the content of the Christian message, of catechetical methods, and of psychology and sociology in relation to the catechetical apostolate. And, finally, the CCD Apostolate of Good Will strives to develop in all Catholics increased love and understanding of their non-Catholic neighbors, to promote truly tactful and enlightened zeal for their conversion.

The Confraternity of Christian Doctrine is primarily a parish society. But it is the special work of the diocesan office to train, supervise, and guide catechists. This office draws up the programs for the training of teachers, lays down the conditions for the reception of applicants and the training qualifications for their official appointment as teachers. This office also has the right and the responsibility to supervise the training of teachers and their actual teaching. The syllabus and textbooks, the method and content, of all Confraternity classes in the diocese are to be determined by this office. The diocesan director is to provide all the help needed by teachers in the course of their work and to offer them opportunities for further spiritual and professional guidance. The function of the national center of the CCD is of an advisory nature, but it has a vital role in the whole organization. Its chief functions are mainly (1) to provide the best available training for leaders, (2) to inform the diocesan offices of the progress of the various forms of the CCD apostolate, (3) to prepare and make available teacher-training manuals and all the other material needed in the various forms of the apostolate.

Such a summary description of the work and the organization of the CCD cannot give any idea of the abundance of catechetical material on various levels published under its auspices, of its detailed program for the selection, training, and authorization of lay teachers, or of the number of children, young people, and adults actually reached. Suffice it to say in particular that without the cooperation of lay teachers the problem of giving an adequate religious formation to the millions of Catholic children attending public schools would be completely unsolvable, as would that of the continuing religious formation of minimally instructed adult Catholics.

The CCD itself is well aware of the many and difficult problems attending all the phases of its many-sided apostolate, and is continually studying them and finding new and improved solutions. But it definitely falls within the scope of this book to point out the special value of the lay catechist, his special needs and difficulties, and also to bring out some special aspects of the training and the help that he needs. By so doing, we may, perhaps, suggest to our priest and religious readers some further means of interesting zealous members of the laity in the catechetical apostolate, and of inspiring and assisting those already engaged in it.

THE SPECIAL VALUE OF THE LAY CATECHIST

In their daily life in the world lay catechists personally experience the irreplaceable value of religion for such a life. From their own experience they know how religion could and should penetrate, transform, and ennoble the "ordinary" life of people in the world. Thus Our Lord and His Church expect from laymen authorized to proclaim His message a special *vital quality* in their religious teaching by giving their students a formation that is close to life and fully directed to living, and that is, in consequence, especially capable of standing the test of life.

Again, the religious formation given by a lay teacher should have a special quality of *naturalness*. It should, that is, really be adapted to the concrete conditions, needs, and potentialities of the students and lead them toward Christian living informed by a spirit quite different from the secular spirit of our times and also quite different from that of any Christian "ghetto."

Needless to say, such vitality and naturalness are of special importance in teaching children who do not attend Catholic schools. Because so little of their time during the week is devoted to a study of religion, these children have a special need for a truly vital religious formation, which is at the same time truly "actual" in terms of their own needs. The very lack of any kind of religious teaching in the public schools can give the impression that religion is of no great importance in human life. Their brief "released-time" or Sunday lessons in religion, then, have at once to convince them of the supreme role of religion in their lives and to give them religious instruction. Who could be expected to carry out this most difficult twofold task more effectively for such an audience—a religious whom these children cannot help considering as coming from "another world" or a fervent layman or woman who by the very fact of his religious vitality, of his eagerness to teach the truths of the faith, shows the compatibility of religion with "real life" and the importance of religion in life? In the first years of the grade school it may not make much difference, but there can hardly be a doubt that for innumerable boys and girls in the upper grades and in high schools an intelligent, tactful, and zealous lay teacher can far more easily demonstrate the value of religion in daily living than can an equally gifted priest or sister.

Our Lord expects that His lay heralds will in a special way *form apostles,* above all, lay apostles, among their students. The fact that their teacher is a layman or woman, who in most cases is using for this teaching whatever time he or she can spare from the work of earning daily bread, of itself gives the students a practical idea of the lay apostolate.[2] This will be the more true the more the teacher

---

[2] The lay CCD teacher is, in the vast majority of cases, a voluntary, unpaid worker. But is there not also a field for qualified lay teachers working as adequately salaried, full-time "parish assistants" or catechists (such as already exist in the missions and in some European countries), who could give their full

gives his message with genuine Christian vitality, the more he shows his students again and again the important role of the lay apostle in the life of the Church today, and the more he knows how to begin to train his students as early as possible to take part in that apostolate.

He will, of course, continuously indicate and stress the special role of the ordained priesthood in Christ's Church, and point out to his students the different values of the priestly, religious, and lay life by giving each its own rank and special splendor in the harmony of the different members of the People of God. And he will also bring out continually the *necessity for genuinely Catholic respect for* and harmonious collaboration with the priestly leader in the lay catechetical apostolate. Here again a qualified lay teacher has special advantages in influencing boys and girls of junior-high-school and high-school age. And in all teaching, the layman can more gracefully and therefore more effectively emphasize the priest's authority than can the priest himself. One finds the same thing true in family life. If the older brothers in the family willingly obey and respect their father, their example will be far more effective with the younger children than will be the father's own insistence on his authority.

THE SPECIAL DIFFICULTIES AND NEEDS OF LAY CATECHISTS

The religious teaching of children attending public schools obviously presents a far more difficult catechetical situation than does the ordinary instruction given in Catholic schools. A higher quality of religious teaching is needed if these students are to be given true religious formation, and yet this teaching must be carried out under much less favorable circumstances and often under positively unfavorable ones. Let us consider these difficulties and special needs in somewhat greater detail.

Thus these Confraternity classes demand from the teacher, above all, a higher degree of catechetical concentration on the very essentials of Christian doctrine and Christian life. This concentration should never be mistaken for a mere simplification or abbreviation

---

talents, time, and energy to this work? Such lay people could also assist the priest in many material ways and thus free him for his special priestly work. One does not become less "apostolic" from the fact of receiving the means of subsistence in return for one's apostolic work, or no priest or Sister could lay claim to this title! Vatican II insists that a just wage be paid to those who devote full time to this work (Decree on the Church's Missionary Activity, n. 17).

of the material that must be taught. Simplification makes the lessons "easier" for both the teacher and the students, but only in a very short-range view. Genuine concentration is far more difficult for the teacher to achieve, but it effects true religious formation; it makes each lesson a living seed of Christian truth that can bear lifelong fruit in Christian learning and living.

Again, there is so little time available for these classes—in some places hardly a full hour each week of the school year, with vacations, holidays, and such taking away even from this minimum. For this reason, again, the teacher must be able to center his whole teaching on the essentials of Christian doctrine and to build up a genuine Christian life on these essentials. To be lost in accidentals detracts from any kind of Christian formation, but in these classes it would be disastrous.

Furthermore, these classes need to be made more attractive, more interesting to the students than do the classes in religion given in Catholic schools. If children in Catholic schools find some of their religion classes dull, they will still not usually be allowed to leave school, and one can hope that the Catholic environment of the school and the whole atmosphere of the education given in it may compensate for a low quality of religious instruction. But in the classes for public school children—will the children continue to come, and come regularly, if they find the teaching dull? And if they do come, how will they benefit from a class that gives them no religious inspiration? But how difficult it is to make classes truly interesting for such children! Many of them come from families with no religious background. The hour appointed for the class is often, if not generally, not very convenient for them; the place is frequently not too suitable; the teacher does not have at hand the technical helps available to a teacher in a regular school class. In such classes, therefore, more than almost anywhere else, the teaching must bring out as clearly and attractively as possible the values of Christian doctrine and of true Christian living. The children must come to feel that we are *leading them to a real treasury;* our message must truly be experienced as the Good News. Everyone connected with this work, of course, realizes this necessity; the difficulty is to carry out the required kind of teaching in actual practice.

Since the apostolate of lay catechists is so important and, at the same time, so difficult, the catechetical movement must strive in every way to prepare these teachers as well as possible and to facilitate their arduous task.

SOME SUGGESTIONS

The apostolic spirit of the Catholic laity makes it relatively easy to secure the required numbers of volunteer catchists: in some places, it seems, more people apply for the preparatory training than are actually needed. Where this is true, it will be possible to choose among those who apply. The more we appreciate the great intrinsic difficulties of the apostolate to children in public schools, the more we see the need for a clear-sighted selection of candidates even for the preparatory course, and still more for the actual appointment of teachers. Obviously, not every fervent Catholic possessing sufficient knowledge of Christian doctrine also possesses the capacity to be trained for this particular kind of teaching or can successfully conduct such classes. The best training course cannot work miracles, and this kind of teaching, it is needless to say, requires the moral qualities not only of a good Catholic but also of a good catechist and educator.

Again, training for this kind of teaching needs, obviously, to provide the candidates with the necessary knowledge both of Christian doctrine and of catechetical method. In most cases, therefore, two courses are given, one on doctrine and one on method. As we mentioned above, the classes given to children attending public schools call in a very special way for concentration on essentials, for vitality, and for effective direction in Christian living; they call for a presentation of Christianity which will show the beauty of Christian doctrine and the values of Christian life. In other words, might we not say that the lay catechist needs, above all, to acquire a thoroughly "kerygmatic" mentality and to know how to incarnate the kerygmatic approach in each and all of his lessons? He needs to come to see clearly, for himself, how the fundamentals of Christian doctrine form a wonderful unity, the mystery of Christ. He himself must come to be enthusiastic about Christian doctrine as being completely centered in Christ; "Christ in you; the hope of glory" (Col. 1:27). Teachers of future lay catechists should not in any way take it for granted that people who have a fairly adequate material knowledge of Christian doctrine, that is, of the individual doctrines in themselves, necessarily also possess this kerygmatic insight into Christian doctrine as a living and life-giving whole. How could they, when in the past the religious training given in Catholic schools has seldom been given this orientation? The courses in doctrine given to lay catechists, then, need to be clearly and inspiringly "kerygmatic" in order to enable them—perhaps for the first time—to see Christian doctrine and Christian life in its true light. And, obviously, this vision will give them most valuable and efficacious assistance in their own spiritual life. Before they are allowed to proclaim the Christian message to others, they should themselves experience the transforming power of the Christian message, rightly proposed. This is precisely what St. Paul meant when he emphasized the "power" (*virtus*) of his preaching: "And my speech and my preaching [the Greek original has *kerygma,* message] were not in the persuasive words of [sophistical] wisdom, but in the demonstration of the Spirit and of power" (1 Cor. 2:4).

In this connection might we also suggest that the regular retreats recommended for all lay teachers be thoroughly "kerygmatic." In particular, a retreat given at the end of the training course would have great value. Such retreats would show these future teachers in a living way how the fundamentals of Christian doctrine actually are the pillars of Christian spiritual life, how they are to strive to live the message that they are undertaking to proclaim to others.

The course on method given to future lay catechists should make the students acquainted with a very simple but efficient method of religious formation. Here we intentionally use the singular—"method" rather than "methods." For the danger in proposing many methods is that future teachers will not learn to handle even one, and when they go out to teach, after some futile attempts of various kinds, they will return to the obsolete and fruitless, but easy, method of explaining the text of the catechism word by word, and then asking the students to memorize this "beautiful" doctrine. Would we not do well to follow the example of Father Jungmann; in his *Handing on the Faith,* which is written for professional teachers of religion in the very homeland of the catechetical movement, he introduces only one method, "the" catechetic method which is the fruit of the recent efforts in the field of religious didactics, and then he shows how this one method applies to different kinds of religious instruction by allowing for and even requiring appropriate modifications.[3] When we do so, we can be much more hopeful that the

---

[3] Joseph A. Jungmann, S.J., *Handing on the Faith* (New York: Herder and Herder, 1959), p. 174. For the training of lay catechists there are now several good books available, such as Mother Jean Fletscher, *Bearing Witness to Christ* (London: Chapman, 1966); Sister Romain, *Tell My People* (London: Chapman, 1965); Sister Margaret, *Heralding Christ* (London: Chapman, 1966); and Rev. A. McBride, *Catechetics* (Milwaukee: Bruce, 1966). Some may also find useful *ABC's of Modern Catechetics,* which is in fact a summary of earlier editions of this book, prepared in collaboration with William Reedy (New York: Sadlier, 1962).

students are really understanding the method we are teaching them and that they are becoming thoroughly acquainted with it by the necessary catechetical exercises. This course on method must also give the future teachers the fundamentals of religious education, for in the classes they are to teach they must not only impart knowledge but truly educate their students.

Everyone connected with the work of training lay catechists realizes, of course, that without a thorough spiritual formation they cannot adequately fulfill their apostolic task. If such formation is necessary for priestly and religious teachers, obviously it is needed for laymen also. And this formation must, for them too, be of such a kind as to teach them how to carry it on for themselves, how continually to deepen and grow in their personal participation in the mystery of Christ all through their lives. Otherwise, there is obviously far greater danger than with those who are living the priestly or religious life that these lay teachers may lose their living interest in the message they are proclaiming and that their catechetical efforts will therefore bear little or no fruit.

May we suggest, therefore, that every lay teacher needs most especially to be brought into close and personal contact with *sacred Scripture* and with the *liturgy,* and this both for his own sake and for the special kind of teaching he is to do.[4] For his own spiritual vitality he needs continually to be more completely formed to the image of Christ by the word of God in sacred Scripture and by the very life of Christ given us in the Mass and the sacraments. These are the living sources of Christian vitality, the great means Christ gives us in the Church for growth in His life and union with Him.

And, in addition, the CCD teaching is concerned above all with providing an elementary initiation into the Christian religion and making this elementary initiation the fruitful seed of the students' future religious development. Sacred Scripture and the liturgy are, precisely, at once the most fruitful means of elementary initiation, as we saw earlier in this book, and the perennial sources of growth in Christ. The teacher, then, needs both to lead his students to these sources and, at least in some degree, to show them how to find here the unfailing means to ever-fuller participation in the mystery of Christ. And how can the teacher do so if he has not experienced this for himself?

---

[4] This need was specifically discussed in the Workshop in the Lay Apostolate at the CCD National meeting at Buffalo, N. Y. 1956.

But also with regard to the liturgy we should never forget that children in the CCD classes need, even more than others, a full development of the catechetical power of the Mass and the sacraments. Since their formal religious education is often limited to less than one hour a week, how important it is that every Sunday Mass should become an efficacious means of religious formation. Although a lay teacher can explain the Mass and prepare his students for better participation in the Mass, the proper celebration of the Mass which makes such participation possible, easy, and fruitful is not in his power. Only the priest can do this. How greatly they can benefit from a well-performed dialogue Mass with fitting hymns at the right places and with readings and responses so arranged that the real meaning of the Mass and its structure shine out as clearly as possible! We priests can certainly not require an intensive initiation into the liturgy from our lay teachers unless we ourselves are ready to provide a celebration of Mass that is catechetically developed. The bishops have called for experimental Masses for children. Once these have been prepared, tested, and evaluated, several forms of Eucharistic celebrations adapted to children of various age levels and cultural backgrounds should deepen their understanding of the Mass, awaken a fuller response, and lead to a better participation in the parochial Mass on Sunday.

The basic training given to lay catechists before their appointment as teachers needs to be continued by careful guidance, both spiritual and professional, during their entire time of teaching. And, in addition, they need the aid of printed material to help them in their difficult work by giving the hints necessary for the preparation of each class. Until recently there has been a lack of catechetical material completely adapted to the special needs of such teachers. We are happy to say, in this connection, that a group of Sisters, priests, and laity headed by Sister Maria de la Cruz, H.H.S., has worked out a course that excels from the viewpoint both of content and of method.[5] Although it is constructed for children attending public schools, this course also deserves the attention of religion teachers in Catholic schools, since it follows the principles

---

[5] *On Our Way Series,* by Sister Maria de la Cruz Aymes, H.H.S. (Sadlier, New York). For the CCD classes in the high school we suggest The Confraternity High School Religion series published by Sadlier. An inexpensive mission edition of this series is available through the East Asian Pastoral Institute, P.O. Box 1815, Manila.

of modern catechetics, especially with regard to content, consistently and without any compromise.

And one more important aid to the work of lay catechists is a catechetical review edited to suit their particular needs. Such a review can do much not only to present helpful new material for teaching and to illustrate by concrete articles the various adaptations of the modern catechetical method but also to continue and further the educational, kerygmatic, and spiritual formation of the catechists themselves.[6]

The great work of the CCD is entrusted to the laity. But it obviously needs, and is receiving, the active collaboration of the clergy and of religious teachers. Some further suggestions as to the special help that the parish priest can give to his lay assistants in the catechetical apostolate may be found in the chapter on the priest as the herald of Christ (pp. 290 ff.). Religious teachers not only assist in the training of CCD teachers and guide them but are themselves actively engaged in the CCD apostolate. In many places religious who work hard in Catholic schools during the school year give special courses for public school children on Sundays and in the summer. And religious who engage in this work affirm that it gives them valuable insights and inspirations for their regular school teaching. Above all, such religious become eager to use every opportunity to open the eyes of their students in school to the wonderful and urgent apostolate awaiting them in the work of the CCD. And here, may we say, is the most valuable form of assistance that Catholic schools can give to this work: to provide their own students with excellent religious formation and with the apostolic spirit. More and more lay teachers are needed and will be needed in the future if the millions of Catholic children in the public schools are to receive any kind of religious training. And the graduates of Catholic schools and colleges should be the first to be ready and willing to answer this urgent call.

In this chapter we have stressed the work of the lay teacher through the CCD, since this is the special field assigned to them by the Church. But, conditions being what they are, more and more lay teachers of religion will be needed also in Catholic schools themselves. The situation of such teachers is substantially the same as

---

[6] Such reviews have now appeared: *Good Tidings, The Catechist, Religion Teacher Journal,* and *Today's Catholic Teacher.* On a deeper level we recommend: *Living Light, Lumen Vitae,* and *Teaching All Nations.*

that of religious teachers, and they need, therefore, a similar catechetical training (see the following chapters).

A most important development of the catechetical apostolate of
the laity was the foundation of the Institute of Lay Theology at
the University of San Francisco in 1960. Father Eugene R. Zimmers,
S.J., established a professional program to train laymen to integrate
theology with psychology, sociology, communications arts, and man-
agement skills so that they could operate parochial and diocesan
programs of religious education and ecumenical relations. One of
the major goals of these lay theologians is to turn the parish and
diocese outward to face the broader problems of the Church and
the modern world, to renew the Christian life of the entire community so that it may bear more effective witness to Christ, and
thus to reach out to all the people of the area. Graduates of the
Institute of Lay Theology already work in twenty-nine dioceses of
the United States, Canada, and Mexico and are actively involved
in international organizations of the lay apostolate, even at the
executive level.

Obviously there are many other ways in which apostolic-minded
lay people can spread Christ's message according to their special
talents and circumstances. But we are not mentioning them in this
book, since it is concerned with the catechetical apostolate properly
speaking. But it should always be remembered that the first field
for the catechetical apostolate of the married laity is in their own
families. The religious teaching and training of their children is
the inalienable right and duty of Catholic parents. They are the
first messengers of Our Lord to their children before they attend
any school, and no school can make up for the lack of a thoroughly
Christian education in the family, an education which the school
should need only to complement.

CHAPTER THREE

Religious and the
Catechetical Apostolate

Throughout the whole Catholic world teaching in Catholic schools is done, for a large part, by religious. Their help is most needed in countries where private schools are not subsidized by the government. It was only because the religious teachers were content to work for a token salary that a powerful system of Catholic education could be established and maintained. No judicious Catholic, however, would evaluate the contribution of the religious to Cathoic education only from the economic aspect of their work. It is the quality of their educational activity which secures for them the esteem and confidence of Catholics, most especially in the field of religious education. The inner connection between their religious vocation and the fundamental requirements of religious education is obvious. His holy vocation obliges the religious to use his freedom from engagements in the world for the direct and wholehearted service of God in the Church.[1] Everybody expects from him a fully developed appreciation of religious values. What enables him to lead others to God is not so much a deeper knowledge of God, but his proper esteem of God and whatever belongs to God.

It is not only yesterday that the Catholic Church knew of these educational potentialities of the religious vocation. Since the Middle Ages she availed herself of them. In the last centuries she called increasingly for the collaboration of nuns in the task of religious education. Modern catechetics, however, has brought out very clearly the particular reasons why the religious is so well fitted for the catechetical apostolate. To learn the catechism by heart requires only an exacting teacher who is sufficiently acquainted with the techniques of memorization. In order to understand the catechism lesson we need teachers who are well trained in Christian doctrine.

---

[1] See the Council's Dogmatic Constitution on the Church, n. 44.

Modern catechetics, however, requires essentially more. The religion lesson has to win and to form the hearts of the students. God must become the central value of their life. They must learn to strive for evermore intimate union with God, and faithful service of God has to be acknowledged and practiced as the chief aim of all their actions. Who will ever deny that the religious teacher is, by his own holy vocation, in a most privileged position to help others to find God and to grow in their personal union with Him? It is not, however, his juridical status as a religious that qualifies the religious teacher for teaching religion. As the saying goes, "It is not the habit that makes the monk." Only by the generous use of their special helps for personal union with God will the religious find God and become able to guide others to a similar union with God.

This does not mean, though, that the religious is supposed to educate his students as little monks by burdening them with forms of piety which are not intended for them. The religious teacher must never forget that the vast majority of students is called by God to a Christian life in the midst of the world. From early years therefore they should be educated for this calling. In our times not a few Catholics embrace the opinion that the religious teacher is, generally, less qualified for this important task than the lay teacher. There is some truth in this opinion. The religion teacher who lives in the world knows from his daily experience the kind of life for which the students must be trained. He is less in danger of practicing forms of piety which are better fitted for a religious community than for a Christian family. One should simply admit that from this particular aspect the lay teacher is in a better position than the religious teacher. But the religious teacher who is really conscious of his task and keeps up the necessary apostolic contact with the environment of the students can also quite easily find out what is fitting for the students. Nor is the right selection of the exterior manifestations of piety the most important point in educating fine lay Catholics. They have to live in the midst of the world, and are continuously exposed to the influence of a dechristianized world with its materialistic principles. Secularism in all its forms is today by far the greatest danger for our Christian brethren in the world. Whoever realizes this danger in its fullest measure will be able to evaluate the contribution we expect from the religious educator. If he is above all a religious, he will first develop in his own personal life that radical dedication to God in the world which is most necessary for all teachers of religion especially in this age of rapid secularization. Here, too, we have to apply the principle that the habit as such does not make the monk. More than in the Middle Ages the Church today needs many religious teachers who fulfill their educational apostolate as exemplary "religious." Are we not sometimes in danger of overrating the undeniable advantages of the powerful educational organizations we find in the well-developed religious congregations, while not evaluating enough the importance of the religious life of the individual teacher?

In its Decree on the Appropriate Renewal of the Religious Life (n. 2) the Council distinguishes clearly two main aspects of this renewal: (1) the renewal of religious life by a continuous return to the sources of all Christian life and to the original inspiration behind a given community and (2) an adjustment of the community to the changed conditions of the times. The latter is necessary in order to educate the youth for a truly Christian life in the Church of today, while the former is imperative in order to secure the true religious vigor of the educators. Both are necessary, but the Council leaves no room for doubt that the religious renewal is even more fundamental.

"Since the religious life is intended above all else to lead those who embrace it to an imitation of Christ and to union with God through the profession of the evangelical counsels, the fact must be honestly faced that even the most desirable changes made on behalf of contemporary needs will fail of their purpose unless a renewal of spirit gives life to them. Indeed such an interior renewal must always be accorded the leading role even in the promotion of exterior works" (n. 2e). Is there not at present an acute danger that the concern for the necessary adaptation is sometimes taken as a pretext for neglecting the even more pressing need of deepening the genuine religious spirit?

SISTERS' PART IN THE CATECHETICAL APOSTOLATE

In the Middle Ages the possibilities for direct apostolate for nuns were quite limited. But now more than nine-tenths of the religious teachers who are not priests are Sisters. In continents like North America and Australia, Catholic elementary education is for the most part in the hands of Sisters. They are the decisive factor in Catholic high-school and college education for girls. This great part that Sisters play in our times in the catechetical apostolate of the

Church certainly justifies a more detailed study of their special catechetical call and contribution.

The Church alone of course is the bride of Christ. The role of women religious in the Church is to symbolize and make evident the selfless devotion of the Church to Christ, her bridegroom. That is why the Fathers of the Church and the liturgy make such extensive use of bridal imagery when speaking of those women who have dedicated their lives to following the path of the evangelical counsels. To be used properly in our days such terminology must be purified of sentimentality and filled with deep reverence. It must be used with full awareness of its ecclesial dimensions.

In this sense a Sister is a "woman of the Church" par excellence. The Lord sends this woman to the children, and all her work for them must be done in awareness of her vocation to make the Church visible. This fundamental call modifies, inspires, and sometimes also limits the Sister's apostolic activity. Her catechetical apostolate receives its special appeal, value, and efficacy from the very fact that it is done by a woman called to be a sign of the Church.

Our Lord's Vocation

For a deeper understanding of the Sister's status as herald of Christ we may look to the divine vocation of Our Lord Himself. The Father sent Him to us to proclaim His Father's message. He is the divine herald par excellence. Our Lord Himself emphasized again and again that in all His teaching He is acting as the faithful herald of His Father. At the same time as He stresses His mission as herald, He also stresses His divine sonship, since His mission as the divine messenger cannot be understood except in the light of His dignity as Son of God. By proclaiming the message the Father has entrusted to Him, He shows His filial attachment to the Father. His whole teaching receives its special significance, its dignity and value, its unparalleled vigor, from the fact that He is the only-begotten Son of the Father Who sent Him. First of all, He is from all eternity the Son of God the Father; whatever He does by the command of His Father, He does with the spirit and ardor of a fully devoted Son.

The Sister's Vocation

When a Sister considers that Christ in His love gives her a share in His own work, then her Martha activity actually becomes a function of the contemplative Mary at the Lord's feet; her cate-chetical apostolate becomes a manifestation of loving response, a means of uniting her heart with the Lord. Then not only the per-sonal spiritual life of the religious teacher but also the catechetical apostolate is furthered.

We do not need to dwell on the fact that apostolic zeal is the unfailing result of Christian love. And genuine zeal is also the soul of catechetical activity. Without this zeal the teaching of religion becomes a lifeless routine for the teacher and a worthless mechanism for the pupils. Only religious zeal coming from a loving heart will bring religion to the hearts of the students. Religion is essentially more than a system of reasoning; by its nature it is life, a life of love.

Only a deep personal love of Our Lord will keep the Sister's heart young and willing to endure the burden of the classroom while she practices an intensive religious life—not only for a few years but for a whole lifetime, even after she has reached the period of life when many others seek and obtain an easier schedule.

The Special Catechetical Contribution of Sisters

Might we, then, say that the Sisters' vocation as women of the Church should not only inspire their catechetical apostolate but should also, to a remarkable extent, give a special tonality to their message itself? At first glance this seems inadmissible. Is not the mes-sage we proclaim as heralds of Christ always the same revelation? Even the Holy Father may not change this divine message in any way; he must proclaim exactly the same message as that which was proclaimed by Our Lord in His Father's name and announced by the Apostles sent by Our Lord. How could a Sister ever be permitted to change this eternal message? Of course there is no question of real change; we are not masters of the message we are to proclaim, but heralds commanded to transmit it faithfully. Yet, we must be willing instruments in the hands of the only herald of the Father, that is, of Jesus Christ.

Let us show by a simple comparison how modification can be made without any real change. Cannot a musician play one and the same melody on different instruments? The instruments do not change the melody, but each instrument renders the melody in its own special tonality. Does this not fully accord with the intention of the musician himself? He knows why he prefers here and now this particular instrument more than that. This is also true of our divine musician and herald. Whatever the instrument He uses, He wishes to play the same divine melody, to proclaim the same message in different tonalities. When He desires to make one point in His message certain and clear for everyone, He uses His big trumpet of Rome; hence this instrument must excel, and does excel, all others in authority, exact formulation, and reliable guidance. But this is not His only instrument. If He wishes, especially in our times, to proclaim His message also by melodious violins, who should dare to rebuke Him? But we may ask, What might be His divine intention in using the gentle tone of His violins—what may be their special function in the whole symphony? And we may also ask here, What can Sisters as women confer upon the catechetical apostolate and what should be the characteristic feature of their catechetical work?

A SPECIAL UNDERSTANDING

First of all, Our Lord expects from these women a special understanding of His message. This does not mean special scholastic training. Such training may be useful for Sisters who are to teach religion to upper classes in high school or in college, but Christ does not expect from all Sisters charged with catechetical work the scientific analysis and profound speculation of a theologian. He expects rather a genuine religious understanding—the fruit of unselfish love and diligent meditation. He expects a well-developed understanding and deep appreciation of His principal ideas and religious ideals. Their spirituality must be founded solidly on His fundamental doctrines and nourished continuously by diligent reading and meditation of the Bible, especially of the Gospels. The time seems to have gone by when the spiritual life of Sisters was frequently overloaded with many isolated devotions and was too little formed by the substance of Christian dogma. For the religious, more than for anyone else, His fundamental doctrines should be, in the full sense of the word, the very light of life.

In recent years many Sisters have received special theological training as a better formation of the catechetical apostolate. Would that every Sister who is to teach religion could have special theological training! But such training must be adapted to their particular needs. It would be a mistake to have this training imitate the theological studies of future priests in a mechanical way, and a still greater mistake if emphasis were put on a misunderstood scholasticism too concerned with the cultivation of abstract reasonings and too little concerned with a deeper religious understanding and appreciation of Christian dogmas.

How would Our Lord teach and form these Sisters if He were directing these courses? When He taught His disciples, the result was not only a clear conceptual understanding but deep and solid religious enthusiasm. "Was not our heart burning within us while He was speaking on the road and explaining to us the Scriptures?" (Luke 24:32). If anywhere, certainly in theological courses for Sisters we must use the kerygmatic approach, that is, we must emphasize the religious value of Christian dogma and its relation to Christian life. "The words that I have spoken to you are spirit and life" (John 6:64–65). However, such kerygmatic teaching by no means excludes sound scholastic theology in its rightful place.

FAITHFUL AND ARDENT PROCLAMATION

Love renders the Christian pliant to the ideas of Christ. In the catechetical fields this means that the Sister will introduce her own ideas as little as possible and as much as possible the favored doctrines of her Lord. Her catechetical fidelity will let the Lord speak; she will be His willing instrument. She will not dilute the magnificent message of her Lord with her own attempts at embellishment. But at the same time she can give a remarkable emphasis to the affective element of the divine message. This is genuine Sister catechesis; it is the tonality of the Lord's violins. No doubt He attracts and forms many souls more effectively by the soft melodies of His violins than by the somewhat louder sound of His trumpets. This does not mean, of course, that unbecoming sentimentality should ever be allowed to spoil the magnificent melodies of Our Lord. A Sister who in her own spiritual life is not able to distinguish deep, tender, but noble religious emotion from inferior sentimentality will never be able to do so when teaching religion. Here, especially, any deficiency in solid spiritual formation inevitably has unfortunate consequences in educational activity.

PROCLAIM THE GLAD TIDINGS

Since the apostolic work of the Sister-teacher is inspired and directed by her love of Our Lord, the Lord is the center of her message, just as He is the center of the message entrusted to His lay catechists and to priests. How greatly, therefore, can Sisters profit from the recent catechetical tendency stressing the mystery of Christ as the central theme of Christian doctrine, and participation in the life of Christ as the chief goal of the catechetical apostolate. What a pity it is that some teachers do not yet seem to have an adequate idea of the mystery of Christ! This mystery which we must proclaim is: Christ sent to us by the heavenly Father as our Leader to bring us back to the Father. It is not Christ detached from the Father, but Christ as the gift of the heavenly Father and as our only way to the Father.

In proclaiming this mystery of divine love religious women should certainly possess the right understanding of their message and present it as the joyful tidings of God's eternal love. Hence, Sisters will especially appreciate the kerygmatic tendency of modern catechetics that emphasizes that our message is, by its nature, a real *evangelium,* that is, the Good News of God's eternal love manifested to us in Christ, and of how we must respond in Christ by giving love for Love. Sisters by their particular vocation are in a special way called and disposed to understand, to appreciate, and to proclaim this sublime message of divine love.

"The Spirit Gives Life"

Although religious women are privileged messengers of divine love, it does not follow that in their instructions they should use the word "love" as often as possible. They are worthy messengers of the New Covenant, the covenant of love, yet "not of the letter but of the spirit; for the letter kills but the spirit gives life" (2 Cor. 3:6). We proclaim God's love not by tiresome repetition of any word, but by showing what God has done for us sinners; how "God, Who is rich in mercy, by reason of His very great love wherewith He has loved us even when we were dead by reason of our sins, brought us to life together with Christ . . . and seated us together in heaven in Christ Jesus . . ." (Eph. 2:4–7). This is, in fact, the climax of God's unfathomable love and the core of our message: that the eternal Father "gave his only-begotten Son" (John 3:16) in order to give us rebellious servants forgiveness in Christ and a share in His life, glory, and happiness.

And what is the right answer to this stirring love that we are sent to proclaim? What could it be except that which Our Lord Himself emphasized as the central point of Christian law and Christian life: " 'Thou shalt love the Lord thy God with thy whole heart, and with thy whole soul, and with thy whole mind.' This is the greatest and the first commandment" (Matt. 22:37–38). Here again we meet with a very fine point in the catechetical apostolate of the Sister. The deeper she understands the greatness of Our Lord's love for us, which we do not deserve, the deeper and more painfully she feels her own incapacity to answer by a similar love—our heart is too narrow. Yet Sisters have the wonderful possibility of compensating in some way for the insufficiency of their own love by the sincere and deep love they are promoting in their pupils. Evidently what our students may give can never dispense us from giving the whole of what we have, but even giving the whole, we know, is too unequal an answer. We wish to give more and more, and we are happy to do so through our students. The love Christ asks of us and of our students consists, not in sweet words and feelings, but in progressive union with Him in life and in progressive transformation into Him.

Thus the Sisters' catechetical apostolate will reach its proper goal: progressive participation in the life of Christ, formation of Christ in souls. How blessed are those Sisters who can prove the sincerity and fecundity of their sublime love by feeling and working as did Our Lord's great Apostle: "my dear children, with whom I am in labor again, until Christ is formed in you!" (Gal. 4:19).

THE CATECHETICAL CONTRIBUTION OF THE BROTHERS

The hundreds of thousands of Sisters who are engaged in the catechetical apostolate of the Church do a very marvelous work. But their contribution, like any human work, has its limitations; it needs complementation by others. Sisters are supposed to present Christian doctrine as the message of love. This is their special call and chance in the catechetical apostolate. It has to be done without any sentimentality, but Sisters will of course do it in their own motherly way. This is excellent, but there is also need for a thoroughly virile presentation of the same Christian message by other catechists. Here we see the particular task of Brothers in the catechetical apostolate. This is the case especially in countries like the United States or Australia, where the Sisters have so decisive a part in teaching religion, whereas the parish priests are overburdened with other work and have, in fact, a minor role in the catechetical apostolate. So the Brothers must try to develop more perfectly the manly aspect of Christian doctrine in their religion classes. For more than one reason the number of Brothers will always be less than the number of Sisters. The numerical majority of Sister and woman catechists will not have any disadvantages if their excellent work is well complemented by the catechetical instructions given by Brothers and priests. Brothers must have a very prominent place not only in the religious education of boys but also in developing excellent catechetical literature.

CHAPTER FOUR

Training Sisters for the Catechetical Apostolate[1]

In order to do their work well the Sisters, like everybody else, need a solid professional training. The Sisters themselves realize this need. Almost everywhere in the Catholic world we find nowadays the generous efforts of the Sisters compensating for the somewhat short training of former times and providing the younger generation with a thorough formation for their fine apostolate. Many congregations of Sisters include courses in theology even in the novitiate, which continue through all the years of professional training. Quite often Sisters indicate an even greater interest in theology and in further theological formation than do many priests. It is amazing to observe how, summer after summer, thousands of Sisters, after an exhausting school year, are eager to attend theological courses, and how hard they work to garner the full fruit of such courses. The catechetical formation of Sisters is indeed a popular movement—but still there may remain, here and there, difficulties in establishing a program of formation which fully answers the special needs of Sisters assigned to the catechetical apostolate. Hence we are presuming to summarize some guiding principles for an adequate catechetical training of teaching Sisters.

THE NECESSARY ASCETICAL TRAINING

Catechetical training requires essentially more than an additional course in theology. Theological courses to provide Sisters with the necessary religious knowledge are obviously to be welcomed. A Sister who is to teach religion in a high school obviously needs a

---

[1] What we are saying in this and the next chapter about the training of Sisters also applies very much to the catechetical training of Brothers and, within the limits of their special condition, even to the formation of lay catechists.

different and more complete training in religion than does a Sister who is to have charge of the kitchen. Yet it would be erroneous to suppose that additional courses in theology will, of themselves, solve the whole problem of training catechists, or to suppose that such courses are the most important factor in forming good teachers. Mere theoretical instruction is not sufficient.

If a Sister who did not know how to drive had to be required to drive the convent car, you would give her a course in driving. That, together with sufficient practice, would make her competent. To acquire this skill it would not be necessary for her to have assimilated the whole ascetic formation of the religious life.

If, however, you are training a Sister for service in a hospital, you can teach her the necessary medical knowledge and techniques of nursing in special additional courses—just as you would teach the skills of driving a car—but is that all she needs for her apostolate of charity? No, from the very beginning of their religious vocation Sister nurses must be trained in a special way for the humble tasks of self-forgetting charity, for the patience and sympathy they will need so much in the service of their patients. They must be formed in the right interior attitude, in the virtues proper to their future apostolate—these principles of Christian spirituality must penetrate the whole formation of religious nurses.

Is this circumstance not more true in the case of Sisters who are being formed for the catechetical apostolate? Religious education, which is the forming of Christian personality, demands in a special way that the educator—the catechist—have a personality fully formed and developed according to the message that she must proclaim and the goal for which she must strive. Therefore, *catechetical training must penetrate and color the entire ascetical formation of the religious catechist.*

DEVELOPMENT OF KERYGMATIC SPIRITUALITY

The ascetical training of Sister catechists must from the beginning be focused on a truly kerygmatic attitude and spirituality for the future messengers of Christ. What we mean by this was explained in the first chapter of this section. This fundamental attitude is not the fruit of some additional catechetical courses given to young Sisters; it must permeate the whole process of spiritual training. This fundamental attitude will bring with it a rightful understanding of, and eagerness for, the special "kerygmatic" virtues: fidelity, unselfishness, winning manners. A good catechetical formation cannot insist too soon upon the cultivation of these virtues.

Modern catechetics rightly emphasize three points inseparable from our task: (1) catechetical concentration on the very essentials of Christian doctrine, (2) a presentation of our message in keeping with its nature as the joyful tidings of our salvation in Christ, and, finally, (3) that the catechist consistently expresses the doctrine she teaches in her own personality. What do these principles imply in the training of future catechists?

Why, for example, does the teaching even of willing and pious catechists so often show a deplorable lack of the necessary concentration? Why is the teaching even of Sisters sometimes too much absorbed in accidentals? The first reason for this rather common defect is a defective ascetical formation. Lack of ascetical concentration necessarily involves lack of catechetical concentration. Give the novices a spiritual formation plainly centered on the essentials of the Christian religion, and you can be sure that afterwards in their apostolate they will focus their teaching upon these same essentials. If the herald of Christ is sent to proclaim a message which is essentially the Good News, her training cannot begin too early to transform her into a "fellow-worker in joy," to use the fine expression of St. Paul (see 2 Cor. 1:24).[2]

In her future catechetical apostolate the Sister who now is being formed and trained will be the herald of Christ. The mystery of Christ will be the central theme of her teaching; the mystery of Christ is the proper goal of all her catechetical activity. Hence the mystery of Christ, and not some sentimental "Jesus-piety," must from the beginning be the center of her conscious spiritual life. To "live Christ" must be the core and the summary of all her spiritual endeavors—generously, constantly, with all its applications to daily life.

A genuine kerygmatic spirituality, thoroughly based on the mystery of Christ, means, above all, a Father-centered spirituality—"the mystery of God [the Father] which is Christ" (Col. 2:2, Greek text), in other words, how the heavenly Father, moved by "His exceeding charity wherewith He loved us" (Eph. 2:4), has called us, and has revealed and given Himself to us in His only-begotten Son. In a spirituality based on the mystery of Christ as presented in the Bible and the liturgy Christ is always seen as the great gift of the Father's

---

[2] On this important aspect of the catechetical apostolate see J. Hofinger, S.J., "Fellow-Workers in Joy," *Catholic School Journal*, March, 1957.

love and as our mediator and way to the Father. "I am the way. . . .
No one comes to the Father but through Me" (John 14:6). Christ
is the way; the Father is the goal.

Sources of Catechetical Spirituality

It should not be difficult to communicate this kerygmatic spirituality to novices and even to postulants. We need only lead them to
the essential "sources of all Christian life,"[3] and they will be filled
with a truly Christian spirit. *The principal sources of catechetical
spirituality are the Bible, the liturgy, and Christian doctrine.*

The Bible

The Bible, especially the New Testament, holds first place among
these principal sources; and in relation to our message it is by far
the most important document. Its principal author is God Himself.
Through the inspired writers He has composed and transmitted to
us these writings as His message, as the bread of our souls. Here we
see in the most striking way how under His special influence the
first great messengers, above all His only-begotten Son, understood
and formulated the divine message entrusted to them. All historians
of our times, even the rationalists among them, admit the undeniable fact that the writings of the New Testament are the classical
documents of the spirituality of the primitive Church and of apostolic preaching. No master or mistress of novices in the whole Catholic world would ever deny these facts, but do all draw from them
the conclusions necessary for a sound spiritual formation of the
future heralds of Christ? In every religious community we are rightly
eager to lead our novices to the best writings that contain, in their
primitive purity, the ideals and spirituality of our own religious
group. Is it not even more important to lead them to the first sources
of genuine Christian spirituality, composed, ultimately, not by man
but by God Himself? Is there not a real danger that in the formation
of our young religious we are too much concerned with our "specialties" and too little concerned with the fundamentals of all genuine Christian spirituality? But the novices we train will, after all,

---

[3] Decree on the Appropriate Renewal of the Religious Life, n. 2. See also the
Constitution on the Sacred Liturgy, n. 14.

be sent by Christ, through His Church, to spread His Gospel and to communicate His spirit.

In theory and in practice the Bible must be our most esteemed and most used source of spiritual formation. Compared with the Bible, even the writings of our founders are only supplementary reading. The young religious must have sufficient time to read and to meditate upon the Bible, and also they must receive the right guidance to truly Catholic reading of the Bible. Scientific exegetical lectures and studies are not sufficient for this purpose. In order that the Bible may really serve to nourish genuine kerygmatic spirituality, it needs to be more lived than discussed, more experienced than analyzed, more prayed than studied. It is our duty to help the young religious to acquire the true taste of the Bible—not always easy in our times —to find the principal ideas of the Bible and to build up their spiritual life on them, to find the answer to their personal spiritual problems in the Bible. Our own conferences with our young religious must be nourished from the Bible—and this does not mean that we should interlard them with countless quotations: the Bible was given to us by God, not to be a literary adornment for our own compositions, but to guide us, to communicate God's own ideas to us. The spirituality we present must conform to the Bible not only in its individual elements but as a whole, so that it emphasizes the same fundamentals, presents them from the same dominant viewpoint, stresses the same fundamental attitudes. Thus the young religious will take with them for their whole religious life a deep practical love of the Bible. Is it asking too much, at least of professional messengers of Christ, that once a year they should carefully read the New Testament, the principal document of the Christian message and Christian spirituality?

THE LITURGY

Just as the Bible ranks first among spiritual books, so the liturgy holds first place in the practice of prayer. Here also first place means, not merely a theoretical evaluation, but something eminently practical—first place in our daily prayer life; first place with regard to careful instruction, guidance, and performance.

Novices who are continuously nourished with the word of God as we have it in the Bible will, it is true, very easily find the right Catholic attitude to the liturgy—yet they need help, the more so because perfect participation in the liturgy requires the necessary arrangement on the part of superiors. We cannot deal here with details of how young Sisters are to be trained in the liturgy, but at least two points call for stress. Participation in the liturgy according to the genuine Catholic spirit—nowadays so much emphasized by the Church—means not only interior participation but also active exterior participation. The idea to be found, strangely enough, in religious communities that participation in the liturgy is the more sublime the more it is merely spiritual, that is, interior and silent, is scarcely Catholic; it destroys the Catholic conception of sacramental life and the incarnation: that divine being and life are communicated to us in visible forms, signs, and actions. Would it not be deplorable and simply wrong if a Catholic girl who in secular life became accustomed to intensive participation in the liturgy found less active participation in the convent? Why did Christ institute the Mass if not to draw His beloved bride the Church into His own sacrifice? Who, therefore, in the Church should be most eager for active participation in Christ's sacrifice? One would think that it should be the religious who by their vocation represent, in the most striking way, the Church as Our Lord's bride.

Those who are at all familiar with the modern trend in catechetics know what emphasis is placed on the catechetical value of the liturgy. The reason is evident. Liturgy teaches and reenacts in an unparalleled way the mystery of Christ. The Mass provides the most perfect participation in the mystery of Christ that we can receive on this earth. The mystery of Christ is the central theme which we heralds of Christ are commissioned to teach. Participation in the mystery of Christ is the proper goal of all our catechetical activity.

CHRISTIAN DOCTRINE

The third principal source of catechetical formation is Christian doctrine. Obviously a training based on Bible and liturgy will of itself lead to a vital understanding of the fundamental Christian doctrines. Yet the fruit the young Sisters should receive from the diligent study and use of the Bible and participation in the liturgy can be essentially deepened by a special course in Christian doctrine. This should give them an impressive survey of the subject, which is at the same time fully directed to life: it should show them how our own spiritual life must be based on the message we are sent to proclaim. The doctrines to be included in this survey are, of course, the ones we meet continuously in the Bible and the liturgy, but here they are proposed in a more systematic form, which facilitates a still deeper penetration and concentration. Thus both our message and our spiritual life will be even more consciously seen and experienced as a wonderful unity; the various doctrines will more and more be seen to unite, to form one overwhelming message, "the mystery which hath been hidden from eternity in God" now realized "in Christ Jesus Our Lord" (see Eph. 3:9–11). And in the same way the various duties, aids, and practices will unite to form one central duty and activity, that is, to bring Christ to life in us (see Col. 2:2). Is not this unity what catechists need most, both for their own spiritual life and for their apostolate?

To accomplish its purpose fully, such a doctrinal survey should fulfill the following conditions. First, it should be solid, but not more scientific than is necessary to achieve the thoroughly ascetical goal of this training—not knowledge making arrogant, but love building up character (see 1 Cor. 8:1). Second, it should be a survey of the whole of Christian doctrine and not merely of some theological treatises; the whole as a whole, but with a special stress on the points that are of greater importance for our spiritual life and the omission of less important points and theological controversies. Finally, it should be closely related to the Bible and the liturgy, even in the formulations that are used; it should help to find and to meditate upon the same doctrines in the Bible and the liturgy, where they are found in a less systematic form. Since this doctrinal survey must serve and nourish the spiritual life, the only efficient approach to be used is the "kerygmatic."

CHAPTER FIVE

Theological Training for
Sisters and Brothers[1]

The ascetical training discussed in the previous chapter should be completed by courses theological in the literal sense of the word. But the formative value of such courses depends to a great extent upon the way in which they are arranged and given. As is so often the case when a new form of training is proposed, some people are too skeptical and try at once to prove the uselessness of the innovation by the classical argument that it was not used in the good old times; others, on the contrary, expect the new method to produce a magic effect and to be the solution of all difficulties. The appeal to the "good old times" in this case certainly proves that we need a more complete catechetical formation of teaching Sisters and Brothers than was usually given in the past. But courses in theology will provide this formation only if they are fully adapted to the special requirements of the students.

For what Sisters and Brothers need is not "theology" as such, but a solid doctrinal training for their own spiritual life and for their teaching apostolate, which training should include many elements of theology. Not every form of theology, however, is adapted to their special conditions. Since these courses are required by their apostolate, the right ordering can be worked out, not a priori from the notion of "scientific" theology, but only from the viewpoint of the future catechetical activity. This seems so evident that one is

---

[1] Some of the ideas proposed in this chapter were examined by Rev. R. J. Henle, S.J., in his article, "Father Hofinger's Theological Courses for Sisters," Catholic School Journal (1957), 257 f. My answer to Father Henle's objections can be found in *Catholic School Journal*, March, 1958. We do not think that we have to change anything in this chapter, but it may be useful to note that the chapter is concerned, not with the whole question of Sister formation, but only with their theological training. That Sisters who teach in schools need a liberal arts education concluding with an A.B. is beyond question.

ashamed to mention it, but if we consider the way in which theological courses are occasionally arranged, it seems useful to state this explicitly. Theological courses, then, are wrongly ordered from the outset if they follow in a more or less slavish manner the arrangement used in seminaries with regard to the material to be taught, or the method to be used, or the sequence of the various subjects, or the goal pursued.

WHAT IS THE PRECISE AIM OF A THEOLOGICAL COURSE FOR SISTERS?[2]

To answer this decisive question let us start from the "good old times." As long as there have been nuns in the Catholic Church, there have been among their number many outstanding personalities possessing extensive religious knowledge and deep understanding of the Christian mysteries. Nevertheless, as a rule there was no special religious instruction given to the nuns in addition to instructions for their spiritual life. Nuns who were capable of a deeper religious formation obtained it from their own diligent spiritual reading and study. The libraries of ancient monasteries show how much the nuns of past ages made use of this opportunity, as do also the written works of great nuns like St. Gertrude, St. Mechtild, or, especially, St. Teresa —works which indicate the remarkable theological formation of their authors.

The need for a special doctrinal training for all nuns first became evident when religious who had formerly led a purely contemplative life began to participate in the educational apostolate of the Church. Even in the Middle Ages, true enough, nuns undertook some educational work. But the educational activity of that time can in no way be compared with the intensive educational work of today. Only a few members of the community, usually one or two, had anything to do with education, and they did not need any special theological formation for the very simple kind of instruction which they had to give—if, indeed, any separate catechetical instruction was given. And in the hypothetical case that they needed such special training the quiet rhythm of those good old days left them time enough to attain the necessary formation by themselves from the learned books in the library.

But nowadays the situation of teaching Sisters is quite different. Very often the strength of the whole community is absorbed by edu-

---

[2] What we say here about Sisters can be easily applied to Brothers.

cational activities. Even Sisters who teach in an elementary school need a deepening of their religious knowledge. They need it first of all for their teaching as such. To give today a good course in religion in the upper grades requires on the part of the teacher herself a very solid foundation. If she is to do her work well, in religion as well as in other subjects, she must know more than she teaches. No one denies that a fully trained teacher in an elementary school needs more than an ordinary high-school training. The school systems of all countries that are at all advanced in modern education require, or at least request, of their teachers considerably more academic formation, often beyond a college degree. Why should teachers of religion be the only exception to the rule?

Furthermore, for their own spiritual life, teaching Sisters today need a much more solid doctrinal training than in former times. Modern teachers receive an intensive preparation in secular subjects before they are permitted to teach, and for teachers of religion, especially religious, it is of great importance that their religious formation be kept on the same high plane as their secular formation. A notable inferiority in their religious formation would have unfortunate consequences both for the Sisters' own spiritual life and for their educational apostolate. A Sister whose religious education is not on a level with her general intellectual culture is in danger either of minimizing religion or of embracing irrationalism and sentimentality in the field of religion.

These new conditions, then, point not only to the general necessity of "theology for Sisters" but also to a fairly exact formulation of what teaching Sisters of our times need for their religious formation. At the beginning of their novitiate they usually have no more religious education than that provided in an ordinary Catholic high school. They must, therefore, be given additional training in Christian doctrine which will give them the developed religious knowledge necessary for their educational apostolate and for the harmonious development of their religious personality. And in working out the details of the syllabus we should continuously ask, Is this what the Sisters need for a well-developed, cultivated, spiritual life, or for the thorough Christianizing of their secular teaching, or for their catechetical apostolate proper? Anything that does not contribute to this threefold goal may have a place in a theological seminary for priests, but for Sisters it will be not a help but a burden.

In this connection it is well to know that even in training for the priesthood the very best authorities recognize the danger of overburdening the student with superfluous material. Some years ago Father Karl Rahner, S.J., declared in a famous study of this problem: "A large part of the material with which a seminarian nowadays has to concern himself is, in fact, a dead weight from which he ought to be freed." Nor would anyone who is acquainted with Father Rahner's[3] works charge him with advocating a superficial simplification of theological studies.

FOR WHOM ARE THESE THEOLOGICAL COURSES?

There should be no controversy on this point. The courses given to the whole group of young Sisters and Brothers are intended for those who will teach religion in an elementary or high school; their goal is not to provide philosophical or theological specialization for the cream of the community. If some students need a theological formation for a special purpose, this specialization must be given separately. The ordinary course must give the ordinary student what he needs and can acquire with ordinary diligence. Especially in the courses we are discussing, any teaching that is over the heads of the students would prevent the course from benefiting the spiritual life of the religious and their apostolate. Such teaching would lead to a fictitious education from which even the gifted students would not obtain the specialization they need, but which might mislead them into spiritual pride. We are concerned, then, only with a course intended for the whole group.

THE BASIC COURSE IN CHRISTIAN DOCTRINE

Obviously a course intended to form more perfect messengers of Christian doctrine will definitely stress those subjects which directly contain the Christian message—dogma, morals, and ascetics. In seminaries these subjects are treated separately for practical reasons. In former times, as is shown by the great theological summas of the Middle Ages, especially the *Summa Theologica* of St. Thomas, dogmatic, moral, and ascetic theology were taught as one theological

---

[3] Karl Rahner, S.J., "Gedanken zur Ausbildung der Theologen—Gründe, die eine Änderung in der theologischen Ausbildung nahelegen," *Orientierung* (Zurich) (1954), 149–152, 165–168. Auxiliary Bishop Dr. Joseph Maria Reuss stresses the same need in his article: "Priesterliche Erziehung heute," *Wort und Wahrheit* (Vienna) (1954), 85–105.

discipline. Such "systematic theology" presented and treated the whole of Christian doctrine as one complete system, in which the more theoretical fundamentals and the more practical doctrines concerned with Christian life formed one whole—the doctrine of the one entire Christian revelation. In a course for Sisters and Brothers there is no reason why "what God has joined together" should be artificially separated. On the contrary, they are very much in need of an insight into the essential unity of Christian doctrine. Is not lack of unity a deplorable fault in nearly all forms of teaching religion—from classes in the elementary school to theological studies in the university? Do not take it for granted that religious have, when they enter the novitiate, a clear view of the internal unity of the message they are preparing to proclaim. Their teachers must stress this internal unity constantly and explain it lucidly. Whenever we begin a new section of Christian doctrine we should, by a brief, clear introduction, show the place of this individual section in the whole Christian message. This is necessary in connection with every important doctrine that we teach.

Keeping our goal in mind, we must put special stress on a thorough exposition of the revealed doctrine. Together with a clear explanation of the *exact meaning,* we must carefully and impressively show the *religious value* of each particular doctrine and its importance for Christian life—the spiritual life of the teachers and the Christian formation of their future students.

Every religious should finish the course with an indelible impression of the wonderful unity of Christian doctrine and an insight into the joyful message of Christ Our Lord. He should also have a well-developed discernment between essentials and accidentals, since even revealed doctrines are not all of the same importance. According to St. Paul the *kerygma* is precisely that essential part of Christian revelation with we are to stress in our catechesis. Therefore a solid kerygmatic formation necessarily implies an efficient training in distinguishing essentials from accidentals. If we focus attention on the essentials of Christian revelation, we shall not find much time for those theological deductions from Christian dogma which are of secondary importance, and we shall find much less time for theological controversies which do not contribute to the goal of our basic course.

Moreover we must take the time for giving the *necessary suggestions concerning a good catechetical presentation* of the doctrines we are expounding. Thus, for example, in dealing with the doctrine of the most holy Trinity we must show not only the meaning of this fundamental mystery of Christian faith and its importance in Christian life but we must also indicate how it should be presented on different levels of catechetical instruction—lower grades, upper grades, and high school. We should also suggest what might be the best comparisons to use to clarify the meaning of this mystery and how to use the comparisons. Failing to give such practical help to the future teacher, our course may be excellent in aiding contemplative nuns in their own spiritual life but of little use in training efficient messengers of Our Lord. In order to answer the real needs of our teachers, the basic course must be given in such a way that it makes the Christian message understandable to them, and also admirable, prayable, teachable, realizable.

It may be somewhat difficult to find a fitting textbook for such a basic course fully adapted to the special needs of Sisters. The ordinary scholastic textbooks of seminaries cannot be recommended, even if written in English, and still less the *Summa Theologica* of St. Thomas Aquinas. St. Thomas would be the first to acknowledge that his grandiose *Summa* was written for a quite different purpose.[4]

ADDITIONAL COURSES

While it should be clear to teacher and students that the basic course is of supreme importance, other courses are useful and even necessary.

Study of the Bible

Since the religious education of teachers of religion should certainly not be inferior to the religious education of college students in Catholic universities, future teachers should be thoroughly trained in sacred Scripture. The basic program should include introductory courses in both the Old and New Testament in which the Bible is studied for its religious content, not for a cultural history of the Hebrew people or some other subordinate purpose. The students must be stimulated to diligent Bible reading, and their study enriched by good commentaries. The lectures should be specifically adapted to their needs and interests, and not be repetitions of lectures to seminarians.

---

[4] It is evident that the catechetical hints given in the suggested short survey of Christian doctrine (Part Two of this book) are only a small part of the suggestions which teaching Sisters need for a complete catechetical training.

Religious Education

A good course on religious education, including catechetical methods, is absolutely necessary. It should be substantial and practical, and stress the guiding principles which underlie any useful method rather than be a confusing exposition and evaluation of many methods. It should make clear to the students that a method is an aid to teaching and should not be permitted to overshadow the truth that is being taught. For even the best methods, whether used in teaching or in our own religious self-education, become in reality a hindrance rather than a help as soon as they are used mechanically and slavishly.

Church History

We presuppose that at some time in their formation Sisters are given a course in Church history. This course should not be overburdened with historical facts, but should relate impressively the actual life and growth of God's People. It will point out how we, in our own day, can learn from the mistakes as well as from the outstanding efforts and successes of the past. Church history, taught rightly, has definite catechetical value, and, when presented to Sisters and Brothers, should include methods of teaching in the upper grades and in high school.

The Place of Liturgy

In a well-planned novitiate the religious will be familiar with the liturgy from the beginning of their religious life. Their basic course in theology will offer many opportunities to broaden their understanding and enhance their appreciation of the official prayer life of the Church, and their course in religious education will show them how to use the liturgy on the various levels of religious education. To use these opportunities of correlating the liturgy with the other phases of spiritual and professional formation together with an intensive liturgical life of the community is even more important than a *special course in the liturgy*. But such a course is to be given to show the place of liturgy in the Christian religion, to explain the various parts and aspects of the liturgy, how to celebrate it best under the given circumstances and how to give it the right place in Christian education. Very special emphasis is to be laid on the religious meaning and importance of the changes brought about by Vatican II. We have to learn from the Council, especially in connection with the necessary liturgical training in seminaries and houses of formation, wherein it stresses so much the spirit of the liturgy (see Constitution on the Sacred Liturgy, nn. 14–17).

Social Doctrine

Although as a general principle we do not favor the multiplication of courses, special attention should be given to the social teaching of the Church. This social concern is one of the major themes of Vatican II, yet it was woefully lacking in the previous training of religious. Not knowing the full social import of the Church's teaching, religious often failed to transmit to their own students a sense of urgency for social reform. The result is generations of Catholic school students left largely untouched by Christian social doctrine, highly resistant to statements of the Church in the area of race relations or international cooperation. Catholic education should broaden the horizons of the students beyond that of their own class and subculture. In order to do this properly, the teachers should be very well informed and socially alert.

PRESENT NEED OF FORMATION

A modernized formation of teaching Sisters and Brothers is of great importance to themselves and to their future apostolate. As all concerned with this problem are well aware, such a vital matter must not be left to chance; it must be planned carefully and carried out resolutely. Priests who take part in the training must work according to the syllabus and follow the program. The best program will fail without qualified teachers, and therefore no sacrifice and expense should be spared to obtain them.

However, even the best training course is *only a good initiation.* The teachers must have facilities to continue their own formation. To do so efficiently they need three things above all: first, sufficient time for their own development through private reading; second, the right material for this reading, consequently, a well-selected library; third, occasional courses in the content and methods of religious education for teachers already working in the catechetical apostolate to acquaint them with current problems and their solutions. Those who during the time of their formation never had an opportunity to participate in a course giving a kerygmatic survey of the whole of Christian doctrine should be permitted to attend such a course at least in later years.

This whole chapter dealt with the general training which is to be given to all religious who are supposed to teach religion. It is another question whether, in addition to the basic training, there should be an *opportunity for a more thorough theological training of a real élite*. We answer, definitely, yes. But even this "theology" ought to avoid any slavish imitation of the academic courses for priestly theologians. Even such advanced training for Sisters has a final apostolic goal, and, consequently, it must be given with the kerygmatic approach.

CHAPTER SIX

The Priest and the Catechetical Apostolate

The efficient assistance given to pastors by religious and lay apostles makes it less necessary for the pastor himself to give religious instruction than is the case in countries where the priest has to teach unaided or where he cannot hope for so many or such well-trained collaborators. But it would be wrong to assume that even the best teaching religious or lay teachers could ever render superfluous the catechetical function of the priest himself. To some extent, certainly, their help makes it possible for the priest to teach for fewer hours every week, but it can never dispense him from his obligation to teach religion skillfully and fervently. In a country with a relatively small number of fully trained physicians the government would be well advised to take all possible measures to increase the number of nurses and to train them fully. And it would also be most reasonable, in such a situation, not to burden the few doctors with administrative work which could be done by people without any special medical knowledge. By these means the doctors themselves would be fully able to concentrate on the medical activity proper to them as doctors. But it would surely be strange if in such a situation the doctors were to reduce their strictly medical activity and devote themselves mainly to administration, and give as their reason for so doing the large number of well-trained nurses now available. So in the field of priestly teaching. The happy fact that he has many well-trained helpers should not mean that the priest reduces the scope and extent of his proper work as a priest to confine his activity to ecclesiastical administration. Rather, it should induce him to devote his time more exclusively to the activities which are proper to him as priest and which can therefore not be carried out by anyone else with this special quality of priestliness.

With regard to religious instruction the effect of having efficient help should be, first, that we priests devote ourselves to those kinds of religious instruction which can properly be carried out only by a priest, and that we develop these forms of our priestly catechetical apostolate to the greatest possible perfection. And, second, that in our whole catechetical apostolate we priests cultivate as highly as possible the specifically priestly qualities of religious instruction.

WHAT, THEN, ARE THE MOST IMPORTANT FORMS OF "PRIESTLY" RELIGIOUS INSTRUCTION?

The first place in priestly teaching belongs, obviously, to the homily to be given to the assembled Christian community *at Mass.* Its special worth and pastoral importance is shown historically by the fact that in the ancient Church this instruction was given mainly by the bishop himself—the writings of the Fathers of the Church are, for the great part, the homilies which they preached to their people during Mass. This is indeed priestly teaching *par excellence,* since it forms, together with the Scripture readings, an integral and significant part of the liturgy of the Mass. Its pastoral importance is obvious: here the pastor addresses the flock entrusted to him by Our Lord to lead them in the Christian way of life, to provide the spiritual food so necessary for their souls in this secularized world, and so to form real Christians. What a great mistake it would be to think that our catechetical task—to initiate the faithful more and more fully into the mystery of Christ—ends with the religious instruction given in our schools! This progressive initiation must be continued in our pastoral care for the adults of our flock. And we do so primarily by the priestly instruction given at Sunday Mass, which is followed by the people's active participation in our offering of the Eucharistic sacrifice.

The extensive help we receive from Sisters and lay apostles may excuse us from giving a great deal of religious instruction in our schools. But our generous helpers and our flock have a right to expect that, for our part, we concentrate all the more on improving the quality of the specifically priestly instruction given during Mass. The magnificent efforts that are being made to extend and improve the quality of the religious instruction given in schools will not achieve their full effect unless this instruction is developed and completed by sermons of the same high quality.

After the homily the next most important catechetical task of the priest would seem to be *the guidance and continued formation* of the catechists who teach in his schools and Confraternity classes.

This guidance and formation, obviously, should include much more than the work of administration. The teaching given by our catechists—including Brothers and Sisters—would be vastly more effective if they could work under priestly leadership, properly understood. They need real spiritual guidance for the continual deepening of their religious life, since religion can only be properly taught by a deeply religious person, by a teacher who lives his message. And both religious and lay catechists also need help with the problems of method and content involved in their religious teaching.

Obviously, this catechetical task of the priest means that he must continually see to the deepening and enrichment of his own spiritual life, for only in this way will he be able to deepen and enrich the spiritual life of his messengers. And it means also that the priest must be familiar with both the theory and actual practice of modern catechetics, for only so can he guide and further the work of his catechists. How discouraged they would be if their pastor did not understand their efforts, or, even worse, if his catechetical formation were inferior to theirs and, being unwilling to recognize this fact, he were to try to force them to use ways of teaching which they knew to be ineffective! And, on the other hand, how encouraged are teachers of religion who find in their pastor a sympathetic and enlightened guide! But pastors can hardly be capable of giving such guidance without a continuous study of modern catechetics or without actual practice in teaching. If only for this reason, the priest, then, should never completely dispense himself from conducting classes in religion, and this exercise of the art of teaching will also help him to improve the instruction he gives by means of his Sunday sermons.

And, finally, it is his special priestly privilege and duty to *complete the religious instruction given by his assistants.* In order to do so he needs frequently to visit the various classes conducted by his helpers. And he should do so, not so much to examine the students in order to find out how successful his assistants have been, but to deepen and complete their religious formation by his specifically priestly influence. Surely every visit of the pastor to a classroom should leave behind it a priestly impression, should bear some special fruit of priestly action. Or would anyone say that it suffices to make some witty remarks to the children and to make sure that they are learning the catechism by heart?

And, obviously, besides his homilies in church and his teaching in his schools the *instruction of converts* is a most important part of the priest's catechetical apostolate, a typically pastoral form of religious teaching.

But in all these forms of teaching the priest must not only present sound Christian doctrine—we take this for granted—but proclaim his message in a specifically priestly way. Thus we come to the question:

WHAT ARE THE SPECIFICALLY "PRIESTLY" QUALITIES OF RELIGIOUS INSTRUCTION?

The majority of the faithful believe that the priest possesses a special teaching authority simply by virtue of his ordination. But this is, strictly speaking, not true, at least not in the direct way envisioned by many people. The only teaching authorities in the Church are the Holy Father and the bishops. The bishop can give other people a share in his task of teaching his flock by giving what we call a canonical mission to preach. But the bishop does not have to give this mission to every priest, and he may give it to people who are not priests, even to laymen. The ordination of a deacon, it is true, especially disposes a man for "the ministry of the word"; and this may be even more fully the case with the ordination of a priest. Nevertheless, even a priest does not get any direct teaching *authority* with his ordination. This authority does not seem to be the most specific priestly quality of our teaching—speaking, that is, of the religious instruction given by priests and not by bishops.

But what is more characteristic of specifically priestly instruction is that it is given by a man who, because of his priesthood, has a special likeness to Christ Who is at once priest and teacher. The high priesthood of Christ and His supreme authority to guide and to teach form together in Him one wonderful and organic unity, and make up the threefold office of His redemptive mission. But of these three, the fundamental office is certainly His priesthood. It is as the eternal high priest that He works our redemption, by offering for us and with us the most holy and pleasing victim to the heavenly Father and bringing us divine life. His priestly mission animated, penetrated, and directed His whole teaching, for the final goal of this teaching is to communicate to us a living knowledge and loving appreciation of the divine life which, as priest, He communicates to us, and to form us to take part in the perfect worship of the New Covenant in order that the eternal Father may be adored in spirit and in truth (John 4:24).

Anyone who participates in any way in Christ's mission to mankind as "the" messenger of the heavenly Father must strive faithfully to transmit this priestly message of Christ. He must strive, in other words, to initiate his hearers into the mystery of Christ. But it is evident that the ordained priest is expected to emphasize most especially this priestly aspect of Christ's message. Thus the great themes of the religious instruction that we give as priests should be the divine life that we receive from Christ through the sacraments, and the filial worship that we offer through Christ, in Him, and with Him. Christian doctrine is by its nature directed to divine worship, but the priestly teacher has a special call to bring out this "liturgical" character of the Christian message. Might the fact not be that some of the obvious deficiencies of the catechetical apostolate flow from our having forgotten to stress this essentially priestly and, therefore, liturgical character of the Christian message?

As soon as a priest really grasps this priestly aspect of his office as pastor and teacher, he becomes at once a friend and promoter of the liturgical movement. For he sees that its aim is the same as his own: to form his people for a more perfect participation in Christ's own worship.

And such a priest will also realize that it is his special task and privilege to attract his people to divine worship, not only by teaching the liturgy but by the right performance of the liturgy. Religious and lay teachers can instruct people in the liturgy, but only we priests can provide our flocks with a celebration of liturgical services which makes them understandable, attractive, and truly formative. Here we priests in a very special way "teach by doing." One of our most urgent tasks, then, even from the purely catechetical point of view, is to provide the faithful with a celebration of the liturgy so arranged and carried out as to make possible and encourage their full and active participation. And such a celebration of the liturgy will also offer the greatest possibilities for catechetical development.

And, finally, our catechetical apostolate as priests is necessarily influenced by our *special theological training*. Both the bishops who send us out and the faithful who come to hear us rightly expect from us *doctrinal clarity and exactitude*. It is in order to fulfill this expectation that we received such a lengthy and solid scholastic formation in the seminary, and it is obvious that we have need of such careful training in order to carry out our catechetical apostolate in the Church. Mother Church herself has so frequently stressed this point that nobody should be in danger of minimizing it in any way.

But we must never forget the fact that doctrinal solidity is not the only quality to be expected in a priest's religious instructions. With equal, and even greater reason, the Church and the faithful expect a priest to give teaching that is truly the "word of life." He is expected to present the faith not only correctly and clearly but vitally and inspiringly, so as to display "'the unfathomable riches of Christ," and by this to win the faithful for a new life in Christ.

But such a combination of doctrinal clarity and religious vitality needs to be systematically developed in the course of the formation given in the seminary to a future priest. Who would be so rash as to say that scholastic training alone can bring about this desired result? What is needed here above all, in the theological formation of our students, is the harmonious combination of the scholastic method and the kerygmatic approach. Some years ago, during the International Study Week on Religious Education held at Leopold-ville in the Belgian Congo, I had the opportunity of speaking with the rector of a mission seminary in Africa. The conversation turned upon the proper priestly education of future missionaries and, in particular, upon the best way of imbuing them with the Christian doctrine which they are later to proclaim. The rector became quite vehement: "Father," he said, "I know from my experience in our seminary that a merely rational [that is, the wrong kind of scholastic] approach is not 'formation,' but 'de-formation.'" Is this judgment of an experienced educator valid only for Africa, or does it hold good for other countries as well?

A solid theological training should also give the priestly messenger of Christ the priceless advantage of becoming acquainted with *the first and principal sources of Christian doctrine:* the Bible, the liturgy, the Fathers. But one sometimes receives the impression that priestly teaching as a whole is not much influenced by these primary sources of the Christian message. The quotations from the Bible found in sermons give one the feeling that they have been added for the sake of adornment, and we hear practically nothing of liturgy or the Fathers. What can the reason be for this not uncommon, but yet somewhat strange, state of affairs? May it not be traced to the incomplete way in which these primary sources were treated in theological courses given in seminaries?

For it is obvious that a seminarian who becomes accustomed to consider holy Scripture, the liturgy, and the Fathers too exclusively as means to prove his scholastic theses can hardly have been given the proper and full appreciation of these inexhaustible sources. He sees enough of them during his tiresome preparation for his examinations; when these are passed, he is happy to bid farewell to them as to his other "textbooks." He has never learned how to nourish his own spiritual life from these wellsprings: he has never become acquainted with them from the point of view of his own future proclamation of Christ, although they are the fundamental documents of the Christian *kerygma*. But the fact is that by careful study of these fundamental sources the future priestly messenger would be prepared in the best possible way for his priestly teaching. And he would learn how to find in them the continual inspiration and deepening of his own priestly life, so that he can most effectively inspire and deepen the priestly life of his catechetical assistants. The final solution of this question, then, comes back once more to the need for planning how best to use the kerygmatic approach in theological studies and how to combine it most harmoniously and organically with the scholastic method in the seminary curriculum in order to form the candidates for their future priestly apostolate. A major achievement of Vatican II is its insistence upon a decidedly pastoral orientation of seminary studies. ". . . the whole training of students ought to provide for the development of true shepherds of souls after the model of our Lord Jesus Christ, who was Teacher, Priest, and Shepherd."[1]

---

[1] Decree on Priestly Formation, n. 4. A thoroughly pastoral orientation is especially significant in the chapter on "The Revision of Ecclesiastical Studies" (nn. 13–18). It is followed by an additional chapter on "The Promotion of Strictly Pastoral Training" (nn. 19–21).

On the kind of training the seminarians need for their future catechetical apostolate see J. Hofinger, S.J., "The Catechetical Training of Missionary Priest," in *Teaching All Nations,* pp. 305–316. That this training involves a well-planned rearrangement of the seminary training was stressed by Archbishop D. Hurley, O.M.I., in his address to the bishops at the International Study Week of Eichstätt, "The Bishop's Role in the Catechetical Renewal," *ibid.,* pp. 341–356. Very valuable contributions toward a more pastoral orientation of the whole seminary training have been made by the Christopher Study Weeks in recent years. About this see especially James Keller, M.M., ed., *Apostolic Renewal in the Seminary in the Light of Vatican Council II* (New York: The Christophers, 1965). A remarkable "study in the theology of preaching" (subtitle) is presented by Domenico Grasso, S.J., *Proclaiming God's Message* (Notre Dame: University of Notre Dame Press, 1965).

CHAPTER SEVEN

Kerygmatic Theology: Its Nature and Its Roll in Priestly Formation

By his ordination the Catholic priest is called to take part in a special way in the teaching work of Christ. And when his bishop gives him the canonical mission to preach, he thereby receives an exalted and important share in Christ's own mission to be the herald of the heavenly Father. "As the Father has sent Me, I also send you" is said to the priest in a far fuller sense than to other fellow workers with Christ in the teaching apostolate.

Since a future priest is thus to be an especially qualified herald of Christ, he must receive a special training; the Church strictly prescribes a lengthy formation of at least six years in a major seminary. The thorough doctrinal training given him during these six years is, as everyone admits, concerned above all with his formation as a priestly teacher. He needs these long and solid studies in order to become a fully equipped priestly herald of Christ. For him, then, this theological training is not an end in itself, but the means to make him a fully trained herald, able to proclaim Christ's message (*kerygma*) to his brothers: "Go, therefore, and make disciples . . . teaching them to observe all that I have commanded you . . ." (Matt. 28:19 ff.).

Seeing a priestly vocation in this light, Vatican II gives the following basic direction: "Therefore, every program of instruction, whether spiritual, intellectual, or disciplinary, should be joined with practical implementation and directed toward the aforementioned pastoral goal."[1] Learning from the discouraging experiences of the past and fearing the resistance of some superiors even after Vatican II, the Council intentionally added: "In loyal obedience to the authority of the bishop, let all directors and teachers ener-

---

[1] Decree on Priestly Formation, n. 4.

getically and harmoniously bend their efforts to the pursuit of this objective."[2]

THE QUESTION OF KERYGMATICALLY ORIENTED THEOLOGY

In the light of absolutely clear and strict ecclesiastical legislation and the countless utterances of ecclesiastical authorities, there is no question with regard to three points of priestly formation: first, that the priestly herald needs a lengthy and solid theological formation; second, that the training in the seminary is not an end in itself, but is for the purpose of training the seminarian for his future work as a priest. The primary object of the seminary is to train, not professors of theology, but capable pastors. This doctrinal training is, then, in a special way directed to the teaching function of the future priest. Third, for his teaching function the priest needs a solid rational foundation in Christian doctrine. From his training in theology the priestly herald should know clearly what the Church teaches, what the individual doctrines of the Church mean, and how they differ from opposing or nearly related errors in order to help him form the People of God.

The only question is, then, whether this rational aspect of Christian doctrine is all that the future herald of Christ needs for his complete formation. Or, in the message he will have to proclaim is there also another, more dynamic aspect which should be taken into consideration, studied, and developed together with the rational aspect?

There is no question in this regard either of minimizing the rational aspect of the Christian message or of replacing this aspect by more affective elements. The question is simply one of eventually complementing this rational aspect by also bringing out the equally important and essential *dynamic* aspect of the Christian message.

The phrase "kerygmatic theology" has recently come to be used, especially in Europe, for a study of theology which explicitly emphasizes this aspect. But, of course, the reality is nothing new. There are, and there always have been, those who teach scholastic theology so as to bring out both the rational and the dynamic aspects of Christian revelation. What we wish to show here is the need and the possibility of making this second aspect an explicitly recognized and formulated part of the theological formation of future priests.

[2] *Ibid.*

We shall briefly survey, then, the beginnings of the kerygmatic renewal. Then we shall deal with the essentials of its program, thus to clarify the relationship between the kerygmatic and the traditional scholastic approach to theology; and, finally, we shall point out what results are to be expected from the right use of the kerygmatic approach in the formation of priests.

A Brief Survey of the Modern Kerygmatic Renewal

A far-reaching *revival of scholastic theology* began about the middle of the nineteenth century, with which such famous names are connected as those of Matteo Liberatore, J. S. Gaetano Sanseverino, Joseph Kleutgen, S.J., the Cardinals Tomaso Zigliara, O.P., and Johannes Franzelin, S.J., together with many others. In 1879, Leo XIII published the great encyclical *Aeterni Patris,* by which this revival was promoted as being one of the great concerns of the Church. From the very beginning this revival produced excellent results in the preaching of Christian doctrine. In opposition to the influence of the preceding period of the "Enlightenment" the scholastic revival gave a new emphasis to the correct and clear formulation of Christian doctrine; it pleaded for the predominance of the strictly religious, over the moral, aspects of religion; and it insisted strongly on the supernatural character of Christian doctrine.

The classic example of this influence is the catechism by Joseph Deharbe, S.J. (1847). But this same catechism is also a typical example of the less happy effects of neo-scholasticism on the catechetical apostolate. The too exclusively rationalistic approach of scholastic theology thus affected even catechism classes and their texts, to produce that very clear, but also very dry, textbook of religion, the Deharbe catechism, which soon gained worldwide prominence and appeared in countless adaptations, one of which was the Baltimore Catechism.

Characteristic of this famous catechism is its undeniable clarity and absolute orthodoxy. But characteristic of it also is its lack of clear presentation of the central theme and the core of the Christian message. How did it happen, then, that for more than fifty years, during which scholastic theology was flourishing in all Catholic universities and seminaries, no scholastic theologian pointed out the obvious logical weakness of this classic "scholastic" catechism? Was this due to a lack of understanding of Christian doctrine as being a "message"? Or was if from lack of interest in the catechetical apostolate? In any case, it would seem to indicate that the scholastic formation of the time did not train priests adequately for the catechetical apostolate. For an analysis of the scholastic textbooks of the time would show the same characteristics as Deharbe's catechism, and there can be no reasonable doubt that the teaching of the professors was largely influenced by these textbooks. And so we can easily understand why it was that many religious and apostolic-minded students complained that they received very little inspiration for their religious life and future apostolate from theology as taught in the seminary.

But scholastic theology need not suffer from such deficiencies, and this was proved in the early years of the scholastic renewal by Matthias Joseph Scheeben, now commonly considered the greatest theologian of the nineteenth century. His works are outstanding both in theological speculation and in the exact exposition of Catholic teaching, and are founded in a solid study of its sources. He demonstrated, in classic form, the organic relationship of the Christian mysteries to one another and the preeminence of religious values (*Mysteries of Christianity, Glories of Divine Grace*). His writings enrich the reader also from the strictly religious viewpoint: his theology leads to prayer. This dynamic quality of Scheeben's work is due, in great part, to his thorough study and extensive use of the Greek Fathers.

Thus Scheeben's work had shown, early in the course of the scholastic revival, what valuable inspirations Christian contemplation and preaching could receive from scholastic theology, though in his own time very few theologians appreciated his work. But the twentieth century has brought, step by step, a turning away from the exclusively rational approach. This process has been quite slow, but it has been unmistakable. Since World War I there has been an increasing tendency to provide a more complete dogmatic basis for, and formation in, the spiritual life. A classic author of this movement is Abbot Columba Marmion, O.S.B. (*Christ the Life of the Soul, Christ in His Mysteries*). At the same time there was in France and Germany an increasing tendency to stress the connection between Christian dogma and Christian living (for example, A. Tanquerey, *Dogma and Devotion;* A. Rademacher, *Religion und Leben,* 1921–1926; P. Lippert, *Credo,* 1916–1923).

Along the same line are the various presentations of theology for educated laymen, widely used by priests as well, which appeared from this time on, in Germany to begin with, but also, and in increasing numbers and variety, in France, England, and the United States. Such books not only offered a useful "popularization" of scholarly theology but were also superior to most of the scholastic textbooks in their theological concentration and their orientation to life. More than one priest found that he began to realize the true richness of Christian doctrine only when he happened to read such a popularization.

But the decisive impulse to the kerygmatic renewal was given by *modern catechetics,* as we saw in the first chapter of this book. It began to be seen, some twenty-five years ago, that our catechetical task involves more than good teaching methods only. We need, above all, a deep understanding of our message itself. And this deeper and fuller understanding presupposes a more kerygmatically oriented training of the messenger. In other words, it requires a more fully kerygmatic orientation of theological training in seminaries.

Both the pressing need for, and the program of, this kerygmatic renewal were given a historical basis and clearly set out for the first time in the classic book by Father Joseph Andreas Jungmann, S.J., *Die Frohbotschaft und Unsere Glaubensverkündigung (The Good News and its Proclamation,* 1936).[3] Father Jungmann's basic ideas might be summed up as follows: a change in methods alone can never solve the catechetical problem. To give to the teaching of religion in church and in school the vital force it should have, all those concerned with such teaching must first explicitly realize what is the essence and specific character of the Christian message. Present-day defects in preaching and teaching are traceable, in part at least, to the fact that textbook theology has not been greatly concerned with this message, this *kerygma,* as such. Indeed textbook theology has its own nonkerygmatic method, which could not help exercising a far-reaching and unhappy influence on the teaching of Christian doctrine. For scholastic theology and catechetics, although obviously related to one another, differ greatly in both their material and formal object. The proclaiming of the truths of Christianity, even to well-educated people, is definitely different from the strictly scholastic method used in professional theological training. A great effort needs to be made, therefore—far greater than has been done in the past—to supplement scholastic speculation with a thorough

---

[3] A synopsis-translation of this important book has been prepared by W. A. Huesmann, S.J.: *The Good News . . . Yesterday and Today* (New York: Sadlier, 1961).

study of holy Scripture and the Fathers in order to bring out the meaning, nature, and character of the Christian message.

In this sense Father Jungmann, although more implicitly, asked for a theology oriented to preaching and teaching (*Verkündigungstheologie*), and other professors then at the University of Innsbruck made the same point explicit in various writings. Hugo Rahner, S.J., in *A Theology of Preaching*, and F. Dander, S.J., in *Christ All in All*, presented a kerygmatically oriented survey of Christian dogma. J. B. Lotz, S.J., in *Scholarship and Preaching*, tried to present the philosophical basis of Jungmann's ideas, and F. Lakner, S.J., in *The Central Object of Theology*, tried to present the theological basis. Both these last men overstressed the need for, and the possibility of, a special kerygmatic theology within the framework of seminary training by contrasting such a theology with an "absolute" theology conducted in the traditional scholastic way for those pursuing higher ecclesiastical studies. On this point they were rightly opposed by H. Weisweiler, S.J., and M. Schmaus, in particular.

After World War II, Father Jungmann's ideas were further worked out in a positive way by G. B. Guzetti, who incorporated Jungmann's ideas into the pattern of scholastic theology, which, after all, permits of different emphases.

In the meantime the belief has been gaining ground that a more pronounced kerygmatic orientation is needed in professional theology if we are to have a kerygmatic renewal in the field of catechetics. And it is a fact that in countries in which the necessity for a kerygmatic renewal in the education of priests has not yet made itself felt, there is, generally speaking, little interest in a more kergymatic approach to catechetics.

But great uncertainty exists everywhere as to the best way in which to carry out this pressing need for a more kerygmatic orientation in the theology courses given in seminaries and in universities. A textbook by Maurus Heinrichs, O.F.M., written during World War II for use in mission seminaries in China, incorporates remarkable suggestions for the organic combination of the scholastic and kerygmatic approach. This work is a notable first attempt, but it is not a final solution of the problem[4]. And, furthermore, the combining of the scholastic and the kerygmatic approach needs to be

---

[4] On this question and this particular textbook see Johannes Hofinger, S.J., "Das Problem des Textbuches in Seminarien der Missionländer," in *Neue Zeitschrift für Missionswissenschaft* (1956), pp. 46–63.

done quite differently at the different levels of theological formation. It is important from this point of view that leading professors of scholastic theology at the Gregorian University in Rome, such as J. Alfaro, S.J., J. Alszeghy, S.J., G. Flick, S.J., J. Fuchs, S.J., D. Grasso, S.J., have been striving to give to their theological lectures the needed kerygmatic orientation. In the field of moral theology it was above all B. Häring, C.Ss.R., who brought about the long-needed kerygmatic renewal. Of great value is also the contribution of some French Dominicans like P. Liégé, O.P., and A. Henry, O.P. Their review *Mission et Parole* is outstanding in the field of preaching. Father Karl Rahner, S.J., expresses well the new attitude we find among almost all outstanding theologians of today by saying that any theology which takes its task seriously will necessarily have a kerygmatic outlook.[5]

In mission countries especially two famous theological faculties of India excel in the same line, namely, the Pontifical Seminary in Poona with J. Neuner, S.J., and the theologate of the Jesuits in Kurseong with J. Putz, S.J.

WHAT KERGYMATIC THEOLOGY REALLY IS

From this brief historical survey we can see what is now asked for in the training of future priests is a study of theology more definitely oriented to the preaching and teaching of the Christian message, what is called, for purposes of convenience, *kerygmatic theology*. Such a name is, obviously, of no assistance in making popular what it stands for, and it would be most helpful if a good English designation could be found. But at least the Greek origin of "kerygmatic" fits in with the similar origin of the word "theology," and it indicates clearly what it stands for: that kind of theological teaching which truly fulfills its task in relation to the proclaiming of the *kerygma,* the Christian message.

For genuine theology has as its first purpose *a thoroughly religious understanding and appreciation of divine revelation . . .* not any kind of understanding of Christian dogmas, but a religious one, which causes us to understand more deeply God's perfection

---

[5] "In fact the strictest theology, that most passionately devoted to reality alone and ever on the alert for new questions, the most scientific theology, is itself in the long run the most kerygmatic." *Theological Investigations,* Vol. I (Baltimore: Helicon Press, 1961), p. 7.

and our relation to Him. And since the object of theology is by its very nature of the highest value—this value being an absolutely essential element of it—any true theology must bring out this value and lead to the religious appreciation of the divine doctrine revealed. Christian revelation is, by its nature, *evangelium,* Good News, a message concerned with religious values. And any theology which does not present this essential aspect of Christian revelation rightly and impressively is ipso facto deficient.

Everyone admits that a good biography of George Washington, for example, must bring out the historical importance of his personality and his work for the United States. All the relevant historical facts must be considered and evaluated in this light. Any history of his life which lost itself in historical details without showing his great personality and his historical importance would, certainly, be a poor one. And would not everyone also admit that a treatise on the Blessed Sacrament, for instance, should, above all, show clearly and impressively the unfathomable divine love shown in this divine gift and the place of this doctrine in our whole "evangelium." And that, consequently, a treatise which is primarily a cosmological analysis of the meaning and consequences of transubstantiation gives a rather poor "theology" of the Eucharist?

Nor does this mean to belittle the importance of precise theological analysis aided by sound philosophy—any more than a true work of history can do without thorough historical research. But the focus of historical science and of the presentation of history are not the detailed research that go into them; the focus of theology is not scholastic analysis.

True theology has as its *second purpose: efficient help for the correct, and at the same time, efficacious proclamation* of Christian revelation. This is especially true with regard to theological courses given in seminaries, and the Church has emphasized this more "practical" view in countless documents on seminary education. Or is it only in theology that we must say: "Non vitae, sed scholae discimus"? The scholastic rational approach admittedly is of great assistance in the correct teaching of Christian doctrine, and therefore the Church wisely demands a sound use of this approach in theological training. But correctness is not the only aspect of genuinely Christian preaching. Christ's heralds must proclaim a message which is, finally, not for the mind alone, but for the whole man, for life and action.

As we saw in the first part of this book, the final goal of all our catechetical activity is participation in the mystery of Christ. Since our message thus calls for action, for men to follow Christ's gracious invitation, we have to show them the motives for so acting. And this means that we must present the values of Christianity, for values alone have motivating power. Theological training must, therefore, bring out these values and develop them, so that the future priest may himself be fully aware of them and able to proclaim them clearly and inspiringly.

Moreover, the future herald of Christ needs to find in his theological formation another aid to his future work. He needs to be shown what are the essentials of his message and what is its interior structure and coherence. Good theological formation in seminaries, then, must bring out the essential points, the right order, and the interconnection of Christian doctrines. Are our seminarians not at least occasionally in danger of overlooking the substance of Christian doctrine among the many single theses they have to study, not being able to see the woods for the trees? They can answer individual theses very accurately, and yet they are unable to bring together these various single stones to build up one glorious doctrinal structure. And from this, surely, results the lack of unity and of catechetical concentration in preaching the faith which have so frequently been criticized.

Obviously, every form of theology does not have to serve the work of teaching and preaching in the same way or to the same degree. A great difference necessarily exists between detailed theological studies and a summary presentation of the whole of Christian doctrine. And an even greater difference exists between theology courses for training professional theologians and courses for lay catechists which are exclusively and directly for the purpose of training for teaching. But the more specialized theological courses also need to be seen and given in the light and vivified by an awareness of the holy service which theology must render to revelation, to faith, and to the proclaiming of God's word. Even research needs to be undertaken in the same light and with the same awareness. And this awareness is shown above all by the choice of themes and by the way in which the problems are posed and treated.

Thus we can see that the objections which are still raised from some sides against the idea of kerygmatically oriented theology have their source either in an erroneous concept of the proper task of theology in general or, more frequently, in mistaken ideas about the nature and goal of "kerygmatic theology."[6]

ERRONEOUS IDEAS ABOUT "KERYGMATIC THEOLOGY"

1. Kerygmatic theology is not a *new branch of theology* which is proposed as an addition to the already numerous subjects in the seminary curriculum. What is desired is, rather, the functional orientation of theology, especially dogmatic theology, moral theology, and exegesis, toward the living appreciation and, as a consequence, to the vital and effective teaching and preaching of the faith. Thus, to exclude misunderstandings, it would be preferable to speak of the the "kerygmatic approach to theology" rather than "kerygmatic theology."

2. Although the kerygmatic approach is different from the scholastic approach, the *kerygmatic approach is not antischolastic.* In the same way positive theology is, not opposed, but rather complementary, to scholastic theology. What St. Ignatius said, in his rules for having the true spirit of the Church, of the relationship between positive and scholastic theology can also be applied here: "The eleventh rule is to praise both positive and scholastic theology; for, as it belongs to the positive teachers, such as St. Jerome, St. Augustine, and St. Gregory, to stir up our affections to love and serve God in all things, so it belongs rather to the scholastic doctors, such as St. Thomas, St. Bonaventure, and the Master of the *Sentences,* to define and explain for our times what is necessary for salvation . . ." (*Spiritual Exercises*). It might be opportune to notice that St. Ignatius considers that scholastic theology of its nature should be kerygmatically oriented: as a message "for our times" it presents "what is necessary for salvation."

3. Thus it is clear that "kerygmatic theology" does not mean a simple, practical kind of theological course for seminarians who are unable to follow deep theological teaching of high academic value.

---

[6] An example of the latter is *S. Thomas et Theologia "Kerygmatica"* by Rev. J. Kunicic, O.P. (Angelicum, 1955), pp. 35–51. The "kerygmatic theology" here described does not correspond to that advocated by modern catechetics, and is one against which both St. Thomas and we ourselves would object as greatly as does Father Kunicic. Unfortunately the author does not quote any actual authorities on kerygmatics. *Die Verkündigungstheologie* by E. Kappler (Freiburg, 1949) does not present the kerygmatic question correctly, but the author does give, in the first part of the book, a detailed report of great value on kerygmatic literature.

On the contrary, the kerygmatic approach strives in a special manner to grasp in the deepest way possible both the religious beauty and the inner relationship of the Christian mysteries, precisely because it wishes to bring out the religious values of Christian doctrine.

Again, this kerygmatic orientation does not consist in making numerous practical applications of the matter studied to the spiritual life or to use in sermons and so on. It consists rather in a kerygmatic outlook on the whole presentation and organization of material, although its connection with Christian life and preaching should also, at the proper times, be brought out and discussed.

4. And, lastly, "kerygmatic theology" *is not lay theology* as contrasted with the traditional scholastic theology used in seminaries and in faculties of theology in universities. The kerygmatic approach obviously should play a very important part in religious instruction given in high schools and colleges and in the training of lay catechists, but the theological training in seminaries itself can and needs to be given the kerygmatic orientation.

In order to give the kerygmatic approach its due place in the theological training of future priests, we need to see both the differences between these two approaches and how they may be harmoniously combined.

Most Characteristic Differences Between the Kerygmatic and Scholastic Approaches

Different goals. Scholastic theology aims primarily at an intellectual elaboration of Christian doctrine. It calls, therefore, for formulations that are as precise as possible, for solid argumentation with a manifest preference for syllogistic form and deduction aiming at a speculative penetration and development of the revealed truths. But "kerygmatic" theology aims at the religious appreciation and the missionary proclamation of the revealed truth. Its principal question is, then, What, out of the abundance of revealed truth, is the essential matter to be meditated and proclaimed; under what aspect is our message to be presented? Christian preaching must proclaim doctrine as "glad tidings"; it must call and direct men to a life altogether new. "Kerygmatic" theology, then, strives to understand Christian doctrine in relation to Christian living, to bring out its religious values.

Different objects. Since their goals are different, both the material and formal objects of these two approaches to theology must be different also. Scholastic theology is, in principle, concerned with the whole of revealed truth (see *Summa Theologica*), although its preference is for those parts of revealed doctrine that offer the richest material for its special formal object, that is, for a rational elaboration of the revealed truths that draws heavily on philosophy. But the kerygmatic approach limits its interest more to those aspects of revealed truth which are in a special way meant to be lived and proclaimed. Its formal object is, precisely, the nature of Christian doctrine as God's message to mankind.

The *different values* of the two approaches can now be clearly seen. Scholastic theology offers us a precise formulation of Christian doctrine; it assures orthodoxy; it develops the gift of a clearer discernment between truth and error in doctrinal matters. The kerygmatic approach, on the other hand, develops especially the sense of the substance, the relations, and the religious values of Christian doctrine. It gives us the ability to pray, to meditate, to appreciate, to live Christian doctrine. The difference between these two approaches might be compared with those existing between microscopic and artistic photography, which also have different purposes, different objects, different values—and fundamental compatibility.

The very differences between the scholastic and the kerygmatic approaches indicate the possiblity and the necessity of completing and complementing the one approach to theology by the other. This is obviously supposed by Vatican II. When the Decree on Priestly Formation comes to speak of the theological studies of the seminary, the very first thing it demands is precisely a harmonious combination of the scholastic and kerygmatic approaches: "Under the light of faith and with the guidance of the Church's teaching authority, theology should be taught in such a way that students will accurately draw Catholic doctrine from divine revelation, understand that doctrine profoundly, nourish their own spiritual lives with it, and be able to proclaim it, unfold it, and defend it in their priestly ministry."[7] The truly kerygmatic character of such theological formation becomes especially clear from the beautiful text the Council quotes in this connection from the *Itinerarium mentis in Deum* of St. Bonaventure: "Let no one believe that it is enough to read without unction, to speculate without devotion, to investigate without wonder, to observe without joy, to act without godly zeal, to know without love, to understand without humility,

---

[7] Decree on Priestly Formation, n. 16.

to study without divine grace, or to reflect as a mirror without divinely inspired wisdom."[8] Bishop Alexander Carter, in his commentary to this passage of the decree, is right when he says: "If intelligently interpreted and applied, the directives on theological studies will completely renew the theological course."[9]

How May These Approaches Be Combined?

A harmonious combination does not mean either that the two approaches be given separately or that they be mechanically combined. We do not want a course in "kerygmatics" that would be a kind of expanded catechetics in addition to the regular scholastic course in dogma. And neither do we want the dogma course to be presented entirely according to the rational, scholastic approach with some kerygmatic considerations added at the end of each thesis. No. The kerygmatic orientation must pervade the whole.

Reasons are advanced to keep the usual sequence of treatises. These reasons are not altogether convincing. Even students of theology may follow the psychological patterns of learning by proceeding from what is more obvious to them and advancing to what is less obvious. Only after they have learned the material should they rearrange it according to a strictly scientific pattern of synthesis. This may be done at the end of their priestly training or be left to graduate studies.

However, should the present sequence of treatises be kept, the students must be reminded that this scientific order is not that of catechetical exposition, and be given the reasons for the difference between the two methods. And the same principle should be applied to the selection of material to be taught.

Thus in a kerygmatically oriented course it is possible to begin, as is customary, with the treatise on God the One and Triune. But we would show the students why scientific theology demands this ordering and why the catechetical presentation in grade schools requires a different one. By so doing, obviously, we shall not only aid the seminarians in their future apostolate but we shall at the same time deepen their theological understanding. So, again, to use the kerygmatic approach in no way means that we should omit the

---

[8] *Ibid.*, ftnt. 47.

[9] Walter M. Abbott, S.J., ed., *The Documents of Vatican II* (New York: Guild Press, 1966), p. 451.

section on the divine relations in God because we do not use this material in ordinary teaching and preaching. True, we do not, but this study is nonetheless necessary for a solid and scientific understanding of the doctrine of the Trinity, and it is strictly necessary for answering various objections against this doctrine. And, besides, it can be very useful in giving us a deeper understanding of our own participation by grace in the life of the Blessed Trinity. But the seminarian should be enabled to understand why he should study this rather abstract section of theology, and we should not spend more time on it than is really necessary.

Again, a kerygmatic approach to the presentation of individual doctrines would not mean that the scholastic thesis form should be abandoned. But everything need not be presented in this form, and the structure of the thesis itself might be modified somewhat.

To begin with, it would be highly desirable that *only dogmas of great importance* be proposed in thesis form. The other theological material could be better presented in the form of *asserta,* or of *scholia* and *corollaria.* By these means the seminarians would learn what the essentials of doctrine are and how to concentrate their attention on them while not neglecting the other material as ordered around these main points. Furthermore, these key doctrines should not be treated only in thesis form. They deserve a thorough investigation from many different human standpoints. The thesis form may conveniently be used to summarize and highlight this investigation.

But for the sake of this proper concentration and ordering, the kerygmatic renewal pleads for a thorough examination of the matter to be taught and for the courageous elimination of everything that is not truly useful for the solid training of the future priest. By "useful" we mean, of course, what serves the formation of a well-rounded, deeply spiritual, and solidly trained priest. Such a priest must have what we might call a solid professional education, although he does not need the specialized training of a future professor of theology or research scholar.

This solid education of future pastors and preachers is not served by, for example, the detailed study of all the theological controversies of former times. Even the more important controversies could be presented in a fairly short and substantial way, so that the truth would shine out and the Catholic answers to objections made clear. But in many of our "traditional" textbooks do we not find rather that the controversies themselves come to seem more important than the truth revealed by Christ? What importance would Our Lord Himself give to these controversies if He were personally to train His messengers today?

Thus the individual theses should be proposed, first of all, in clear relation to the whole of Christian doctrine. Before beginning on an individual thesis, we should first indicate the main problem which this thesis is to answer. And we should never introduce a new section of theology, much less a new treatise, without giving a brief and vivid introduction which will show the connection of this particular section with the whole, and the special importance of what we are about to study in relation to theology itself and to Christian preaching.

Then the exposition of the thesis itself should be ordered toward an intelligent and well-founded, but also a truly religious, understanding and appreciation of the doctrine proposed. And for this purpose no more scholastic terms, distinctions, divisions, and so on should be used than are really necessary.

The customary paragraph(s) on the opponents of this particular doctrine should, of course, be retained. But it should plainly serve the purpose of clarifying the Catholic position and helping us to understand the opponents of our own times. Let us do away with all defunct adversaries whose objections are of no significance today. But if an opponent is considered of real importance, then let us, not simply name him and his works and the dates of his birth and death, but rather give the essentials of his teaching, of how he came to hold his erroneous doctrine, the forms in which this error is still to be met within the world today, and how best to lead people from this error to the fullness of Catholic truth. It is true that sometimes we have to deal with errors which are no longer of great importance but which formerly had a great influence on the development of Christian doctrine. Thus, for example, in a solid theological course we must deal with the great Christological controversies of the ancient Church and show how these controversies helped to clarify Christian teaching on Christ.

Furthermore, in a genuine ecumenical spirit the truth contained in the adversary's position should be clearly and honestly set forth, and a sincere attempt made to integrate that truth with that presented in the thesis by indicating what is certain, probable, and so on.

It would also seem most advisable to set in the very heart of every thesis a brief but substantial theological and religious consideration of the place and value of this particular doctrine in the whole structure of Christian doctrine and life.[10]

Again, holy Scripture and tradition should not be used only as means for "proving" each thesis. Their teaching should be given in such a way as to enable the student to begin to grasp the richness and depth of God's own revelation. In the thesis on divine providence, for example, we should not only introduce some classic texts that prove the "tenor" of our thesis. We should give the students some idea of how rich are both Scripture and tradition with regard to this doctrine and of how they teach much more than we can express in the tenor of a single thesis.

Again, a kerygmatic orientation would have nothing to do with *merely formalistic objections*. The syllogistic form ought to aid in showing what the real problem is, not to hide it. Here or, perhaps better, in the explanation of the thesis itself, we should ask, How does this particular doctrine *meet with the problems of our times?* One of the weak points in our formation of priests frequently is that their theological training has not equipped them to deal with the special needs and problems of our times, and particularly with those of the actual people to whom, and the culture in which, they are to proclaim Christ's message. A kerygmatic formation should, then, not only consider divine revelation in itself but also take into consideration its special relevance to the mentality of the people who are to receive it today. If we cannot show that our message answers the problems that weigh on people today, how can we be surprised at the fact that they take no interest in it?

And, lastly, at the end of the thesis, at least occasionally, it would be well to add some suggestions as to practical ways of teaching and preaching this particular doctrine. If the whole matter has been presented with the proper kerygmatic orientation, then such practical notes at the end can be made very brief and yet most useful.

These, then, are the general lines along which a soundly scholastic, and yet vitally kerygmatic, seminary course in theology might be constructed. This would mean no turning away from the true spirit of scholastic theology, for, as it would not be difficult to show, the greatest scholastic teachers ever since the Middle Ages

---

[10] The textbook by M. Heinrichs, O.F.M., *Theses dogmaticae*, mentioned earlier in this chapter, illustrates how such theological considerations could be presented. We would prefer to have these *momenta thesium* in a more systematic form. In China also we publish a series of such *momenta thesium* in the *Collectanea Commissionis Synodalis* (Peking, 1944).

have perennially felt the need for such kerygmatic orientation and have tried to fill that need in one way or another for their own times.[11]

Thus, while no textbooks constructed according to these principles are as yet in general circulation,[12] an experienced seminary professor who is convinced of the need and the value of this orientation would find no insuperable difficulty in giving his courses along these lines, even though he used an exclusively scholastic text. Here it is certainly true that it is the spirit that gives life, and the most ideal text would be of little use without it. For the seminary professor is, obviously, the key figure in this whole question. If he begins to teach along more kerygmatic lines, then the spirit of the kerygmatic renewal will spread out rapidly from the seminary in ever-widening circles for the renewal of Catholic life and the vastly increased effectiveness of missionary work of all kinds.

CATECHETICAL AND MISSIONARY VALUE OF KERYGMATIC THEOLOGY

For the spiritual life of the priest himself. He would be trained to see the Christian message not only as true but as good, beautiful, and livable, as something to be so highly loved and appreciated that he cannot help wanting to share it with others. He would be trained to find the nourishment for his spiritual life in its unfailing and God-given sources, holy Scripture, the liturgy, and the Church's greatest commentators on these, the Fathers. Thus he would have the means himself to continue to grow intellectually and spiritually, even in the busiest of lives, and so the means continually to enrich others.

The great *catechetical value* of kerygmatic theology flows from its very nature. Kerygmatic theology is catechetical theology in the true sense of the word, and, in practice, it merges with catechetics insofar as content is concerned. And it is precisely the content that needs to be developed and perfected more than techniques of presentation. Kerygmatic theology answers *ex professo* exactly those ques-

---

[11] When, many years ago, I began in China to seek a more kerygmatic orientation of seminary training, and published some material to aid in making this orientation, Father Heinrichs, O.F.M., wrote me: "Father, I suppose you realize how much your aims are in line with those of our great Franciscan theologians."

[12] On the problem of a textbook, which is especially urgent in relation to mission seminaries, see the article mentioned above, *Das Problem des Textbuches in den Seminarien der Missionländer.*

tions which are the focus of catechetical interest: the right selection of material, the organization of the catechetical material, the special relation to the whole in which the individual parts of the material are to be presented. We should note here the particular importance of the kerygmatic approach to bring about the much-desired deepening of the religious instruction in Catholic schools, and also of the instruction given to Catholic students attending public schools. And the importance of the kerygmatic renaissance is also evident for the mission of the Church within the United States, for the regeneration and deepening of Christian life and for the attraction and instruction of converts.

The specific *missionary value* of kerygmatic theology follows clearly from the specific character of the missionary proclamation. This is essentially:

A proclamation to others, necessitating a special consideration for, and adaptation to, the intellectual attitude to which the missionary is addressing himself. Kerygmatic theology of its nature should effect the cultivation of this consideration and adaptability in the future messenger.

A fundamental proclamation which must lay the solid foundations of a future indigenous Church where now no Church exists. Kerygmatic theology, being a theology of catechetical concentration, should provide the future missionary with the ideal training for making such a proclamation.

A living and forceful proclamation which will give to new Christians the special impetus needed to overcome successfully the innumerable difficulties of their surroundings and the latent or open persecution they may have to face, and which will enable them to become in turn effective apostles of the Christian faith. As the theology of Christian values, kerygmatic theology should show the missionary how best to give such a proclamation of the Christian message and inspire him to do so fervently and effectively.

In our times even countries in which the Catholic population is numerically strong have been more and more closely approximating missionary conditions with regard to the preaching of the faith. Our priests today not only have to minister to a docile flock; they must also strive to bring into Christ's fold the many people in their parish who at present are not interested in His message. Only a truly dynamic preaching of this message will attract their attention and effectively bring them to Christ.

In the early days of the kerygmatic renewal, when Father G.

Delcuve, S.J., was beginning his catechetical apostolate in Belgium, he was once told by Father Emil Mersch, S.J., the famous theologian of the *Corpus Christi Mysticum:* "Father, the better teaching of religion that you are trying to bring about in grade and high schools is very important. But don't forget that there is little hope of a far-reaching renewal of teaching in Catholic schools so long as we have not renewed the theological training of our priests." Is this true only for Belgium?

Appendix

Extracts From the International
Catechetical Study Weeks

International Study Week on Mission Apologetics, Eichstatt, Germany, July, 1960

GENERAL CONCLUSIONS

I. CATECHETICAL REVIVAL

At the present time we are faced in our mission apostolate with an extremely urgent and responsible task. Complete success in this task will never be achieved by any mere increase in catechetical activity. What we need is something more: a reform that takes into account of the findings of modern psychology and the conclusions reached by the recent kerygmatic renewal.

The chief aim of this kerygmatic renewal is to present the truth of our faith as an organic whole. Its core is the Good News of our redemption in Christ. Its fruit should be the grateful response of our love.

It is in the light of this central message of Christian catechesis that all other truths of the faith must be viewed, presented, and made fruitful for Christian life.

II. NEED FOR A CLEARLY OUTLINED PROGRAMME

We need a general but clearly outlined programme for the catechetical apostolate. Such a programme should meet the special catechetical needs in the mission lands today, but in no way neglect such needs in every country.

III. LITURGY

There is latent in the liturgy a colossal wealth of meaning and a tremendous instructive power. These lie in its prayers, songs, and readings; in the actions of the priest and people; the frequency of its celebration; and the assembly for it of all the faithful. Therefore, the liturgy should be celebrated in a manner which will bring out to the full its catechetical content and which will enable the people to take an active part in it devoutly and intelligently. Hence, in order that the liturgy may produce its due catechetical effect, it should display its intrinsic excellences by means of its intelligibility, beauty, and clarity. Only thus can its full catechetical value be exploited. But this cannot be done unless certain reforms are introduced.

IV. BIBLE

The Bible must be given a very prominent place in catechetical teaching because it is the inspired word of God and the most important of all the Church's didactic books. It sets forth the divine actions whereby God has revealed Himself; its method of presentation is so vivid and lively that it is suited to man's capacities, and it is explicitly ordered toward man's salvation.

Hence catechetics must be solidly built on a biblical foundation; every age group should be taught biblical texts and made familiar with events in biblical history.

V. TEXTBOOKS

Good textbooks are an absolute necessity for catechetical work. The suggestions which are most important for their compilation have been set forth in a special section.

Those who teach religion in the missions need a teacher's aid book even more than do those similarly engaged in countries where Christianity has already been established. These aidbooks should not only provide the necessary material but also give guidance for its use.

The mere revision or modification of former textbooks or catechisms which are not drawn up according to the principles of the catechetical renewal cannot produce a work which fulfills the basic demands of catechetics.

Good new textbooks can be composed only by authors who are thoroughly acquainted with the findings of modern catechetics.

VI. POSTULATA ON THE CATECHETICAL CENTERS

To ensure the practical cooperation of all in the catechetical apostolate, the participants in this Study Week wish:

1. To see a catechetical office functioning in each diocese, according to the decree *Provido sane concilio*. Besides the appointment of a diocesan commission, this implies the formation of a catechetical center from which teachers of religion can get both advice and catechetical material.

2. The director of this diocesan center must be prepared for his task by special studies and be given time and opportunity to promote the catechetical renewal in an efficient manner.

3. In each country a national center shall serve as a link between the various diocesan centers and the catechetical movement abroad. Such a center may organize efforts toward a better adapted catechesis by means of enquiries, study sessions, publication of books and magazines, and the like.

4. Wherever necessary the national centers should work in close cooperation with regional centers fulfilling the same task on a linguistic basis.

5. The various national centers, especially those in the mission countries, should help one another by pooling their documentation and the fruits of their experiments in the catechetical apostolate.

6. In particular, the help already given by several institutes for the formation of specialists in catechetics should be still increased, so that all future directors of religious instruction in the missions would be really able to obtain the special preparation they need.

VII. CATECHISTS (LAY TEACHERS)

All catechists should have at least one year of solid training. This must impart to them above all a complete grasp of the fundamentals of Christian doctrine concerning man's salvation together with an adequate competence in catechetical methods.

At the same time great stress must be laid on the spiritual training and character formation given to catechists as well as on their social behaviour so that they may become not only good teachers but also "witnesses to Christ."

In their religious training the Bible and the liturgy must be given the prominent place due to them in the catechetical apostolate later on.

VIII. CATECHETICAL TRAINING IN SEMINARIES

The catechetical renewal has not as yet brought forth its due fruit in the missions. The chief reason for this is the inadequate training in catechetics of the future missionaries. This applies not merely to indigenous priests but also to those from the home countries.

It is absolutely essential that future missionaries be given a training in catechetics suited to the needs of our own day. This would involve a series of lectures and also sufficient training in practice; the course would have to familiarize the future missionary with the aims, viewpoint and technique of the modern catechetical movement, would be designed expressly in the light of the missionary apostolate, and would impart to him a certain degree of competence in teaching catechism.

It is just as important that the major subjects of theology (dogma, moral, exegesis) should be presented to the future missionary from the same angle so that he may grasp vividly and clearly the organic unity of the Christian message of salvation, the religious content of each doctrine, and its application to Christian life.

IX. COOPERATION

Catechetical cooperation of Christian countries with mission countries will assume various forms, notably the developing of inter-communication among catechetical centers and experts in missionary countries, and with those of other countries; the helping of one another in the catechetical and pastoral training of seminarians and priests, in the study of the psychology of the peoples to be evangelized, and, in addition to this, in the studies of missiology and ethnology, in the progress of catechetical institutions, in the foundation of catechetical centers, and in the improvement of books and periodicals.

SPECIAL CONCLUSIONS ON CATECHESIS AND LITURGY

I. As it is noted in the general conclusions of this Study Week, it seemed necessary to the Congress that some reformation of the liturgy be undertaken to bring its catechetical value to light.

That this reform be prudently elaborated, this Congress first requests that the whole matter be properly examined by the forthcoming Ecumenical Council.

II. Regarding questions of a particular nature, the Study Week proposes the following conclusions of its deliberations.

1. The Study Week adopts as its own the conclusions of the First International Study Week on Mission and Liturgy held in the past year at Nijmegen. The conclusions are

   a. that it be permissible for all chants belonging to the people and choir to be sung in the vernacular;

   b. that the readings be given directly in the vernacular by the appropriate minister or celebrating priest;

   c. that the pericopes of readings should be enlarged and spread over several years by means of an appropriate cycle;

   d. that the Prayer of the Faithful be restored in a proper form;

   e. that all duplications be avoided so that the celebrating priest need not recite in a low voice those parts which are duly carried out by others.

2. The greater part of the Study Week desires a further reform of the liturgy of the word, or Mass of the Catechumens, which is especially destined for the catechetical instruction of those present. The catechetical efficacy of this part of the Mass might well be augmented if, in every Mass celebrated in the presence of the people, be it a low or a high Mass,

   a. the vernacular be employed in the entire Mass of the Catechumens;

   b. since the Mass of the Catechumens is the liturgy of the word, it could be celebrated not at the altar but at a sedile and lectern as is now the case in the restored Easter Vigil.

3. It seemed to not a few of the participants that attention should be given by experts to the question of whether the entire Mass could be reduced to some simpler form in order to bring out its catechetical efficacy and cause its structure to stand out more clearly.

4. Finally, it was generally agreed that permission be sought to adapt certain ceremonies of the Mass originating in Western usage to the prevalent and meaningful customs of mission countries.

   It was also noted that many things which answer the needs of the missions may even now be introduced by the local ordinaries themselves, on their own authority, as *Pia exercitia.*

III. Comments

1. These proposals do not intend that Latin, which is acknowledged as a symbol of the unity of the Church, should be excluded from the liturgy, but rather that permission would be given to employ the vernacular along with Latin in those places where, in the judgment of the ordinary, the mother tongue appears useful or necessary.

2. For places where a variety of tongues or other reasons hinder the use of the vernacular in the liturgy no change should be imposed.

3. To avoid too much variety in a particular territory, it is likewise agreed that the ordinaries of the region should proceed according to their common consensus.

PROGRAMME OF THE CATECHETICAL APOSTOLATE

A. BASIC PRINCIPLES OF MODERN CATECHETICS

OUR AIM

1. *Catechesis carries out the command of Christ to proclaim God's message of salvation to all men.*

Christ carried out the will of His Father by giving His Church the commission "to preach the gospel to every creature," "to make disciples" for Him, and to provide Him with "witnesses throughout the world" (Mark 16:15; Matt. 28:19; Acts 1:8). The catechist does what Christ did and commissioned the Church to do: he proclaims the Good News of salvation; he helps men to accept it and to become disciples who will give witness to it. Catechesis then does more than teach the doctrines of the Church; it wins men (children, adolescents, adults) for Christ, and after baptism unites them further to Him. All principles and methods of catechizing flow from the missionary command of Christ.

OUR MESSAGE

2. *Catechesis proclaims the merciful love of the Father for us and the Good News of God's kingdom.*

Carrying out the commission of Christ, the Church brings a message from God which surpasses by far what the heart of men can conceive or hope for (1 Cor. 2:10; Eph. 3:20).

The Church proclaims to all people that the eternal and grace-giving kingdom of God is at hand, a kingdom prefigured in the Old Testament, begun by Christ in the New, and growing toward the fullness of glory at the end of time (Mark 1:15; Matt. 24:14, 25:34). All men are invited to the wedding feast prepared by the King of Kings from all eternity (Matt. 22:2ff.).

This message proclaims that God is not merely an idea or a remote and silent being, but a living personal God, the almighty Creator and the eternal Father. It tells of a world not drifting into chaos but being transformed into "a new heaven and a new earth" (Apoc. 21:1). It speaks not of the dissolution of all things but of a "new creature" and of an eternal and living union with our Father in heaven.

3. *Catechesis is Christ-centered, reflecting the fulfilment in and through Christ of the Father's loving design.*

God the Father carried out His plan through Christ, His Son, born of the Virgin Mary, our Saviour and Lord. Salvation is found only in Him (Acts 4:12). Through Christ we know about the Father and receive the Good News of the Father's kingdom. By His death, resurrection, and ascension Christ saves us from our sins. He works in us through the Holy Spirit and leads us toward that day when He will judge all men and bring the world to its perfection. He is the Word (John 1:1), and the Mediator (1 Tim. 2:5), the way and the Life (John 14:16).

Catechesis gives due importance to the historical treatment of God's design: how God prepared for Christ's coming in the Old Testament, how His coming brought about our salvation, and how Christ continues to communicate Himself through the Holy Spirit till He returns as the Lord of glory.

4. *Catechesis proclaims that Christ continues to live and work in His Church through the Holy Spirit and the ministry of His shepherds.*

By the action of the Holy Spirit in the Church and particularly in the hierarchy Christ gathers men together through His word, sanctifies and gives them life through the mystery of His passion, resurrection, and ascension communicated in the sacraments, and gives them power to be witnesses before the world.

The Church is truly Christ's Body. He unites the members to Himself, the Head, and to one another, and assigns to each member a specific function. The Church is the chosen race, a people God means to have for Himself, a holy people called to priestly service in the world (1 Pet. 2:9). The Church is the city built on the mountain top, illuminated by Christ's light and shining brightly for all nations to see (Matt. 5:14; Is. 2). It is the family of God on earth, the home which the Father offers to all wanderers, the community of men advancing to its eternal destiny.

5. *Catechesis emphasizes that worship is the heart of Christian community life.*

Whenever the Church celebrates liturgy, she assembles as a holy people. Christ is in her midst and she is vivified by the Holy Spirit. In the service of the word (Mass of the Catechumens) Christ nourishes His Church by the word of life and carries her prayer up to the Father. In the celebration of the Eucharist (Mass of the Faithful) Christ engulfs her in the sacrifice of the redemption and saturates her anew with His life. By the one Eucharistic Bread the many are made one body (1 Cor. 10:17). By the good tidings, prayer, and sacramental celebration the people are filled with inner strength, spiritual knowledge and understanding, enabling them to proclaim the word of God without fear (Acts 4:31).

Worship is primarily directed to the praise of God. At the same time it is the supreme expression of catechesis. Catechesis leads to worship and draws its life from worship. Worship is the inexhaustible source of faith, grace, and the apostolate.

Our Response

6. *Catechesis teaches us to respond to God's call by an inner change of heart manifested in a life of faith and hope and of loving obedience to His commands.*

Man's first response to the message of salvation is that inner change of heart described in the Gospel as absolutely necessary to enter the kingdom. Turning to God, man begins to realize all that God has done, is doing, and will do for him. In this acceptance of Christ, which must be made by catechumen and Christian alike, man recognizes the God of Love Who will save him from his sins. Repenting of his sins and filled with joy at the recognition of his Savior, he is moved to obey the commandment of love. "He who has My commandments and keeps them, he it is who loves Me" (John 14:21).

7. *Catechesis makes the Christian aware of his responsibility for the world and the betterment of its condition.*

The Christian sees the world as the work and possession of the Father in heaven, and feels responsible for it as "son and heir." What is called the "profane" or "natural" order is no less from the hand of God. The Christian must value it in itself if he is to contribute to its sanctification in Christ. This is particularly true of the social order. If the Christian does not endeavor to restore it to its proper condition in regard to family, professional, economic, civic, and cultural life, he is betraying the trust of his heavenly Father.

8. *Catechesis leads the Christian to share the faith with others.*

Catechesis makes the Christian keenly aware that the growth and welfare of God's kingdom depend on him. It stimulates the missionary spirit so that the followers of Christ strive for sanctity not only for the sake of their own salvation and greater happiness but also that their fellowmen may see their good example and praise the Father Who is in heaven (Matt. 5:16). It is the Holy Spirit Who makes them witnesses of His word and life, and enables each one, according to the measure of his faith and the gifts he has received from God, to communicate the message of salvation with its spiritual values to all with whom he comes in contact. Sanctity of life, the praise, the joy of Christians, their contentment and assurance, their willingness and ability to share the message and especially their love, which embraces even enemies, are the signs by which others are led to experience the realities and values of God's kingdom.

OUR METHOD

9. *Catechesis, following God's method, proclaims "the wonderful works of God," which show forth the truth and especially the love contained in them, moving the heart and inspiring the whole of life.*

Catechesis follows God's method of proclaiming the glad tidings of salvation. The wonderful works of God as narrated in the Old Testament, the miracles, discourses, and events in the New Testament, lead us to an understanding of the divine message and of its impact in our lives (Heb. 1:1). In these events God has come close to us, has revealed and united Himself to us, and has shown us the way to live through Him and in Him. Catechesis is at the service of this divine revelation and adapts itself to God's own way of winning men.

10. *Catechesis embraces a fourfold presentation of the faith: through liturgy, Bible, systematic teaching, and the testimony of Christian living.*

Each of these forms of presentation has its own specific function in the winning of the non-Christian and the development of the Christian. Catechesis strives to combine liturgy, Bible, doctrine, and the testimony of Christian living, so that the organic unity of the Christian message is more clearly presented.

The *liturgy* does more than communicate the Christian mystery to the mind of the participant. It uses sound pedagogical principles, namely, the intuitive process, activity, teaching by experience the imparting values. It appeals to the entire person, the sensibilities, the intellect, and the will. It is the means of impregnating the whole life with the Spirit of Christ. For in the liturgy the mystery of redemption is not only proclaimed through the words of holy scripture but is also expressed in prayers and hymns, presented in sacred signs, and rendered sacramentally present and efficacious.

Catechesis is as inseparable from the *Bible,* the inspired word of God, as a plant from its roots. The Bible is the basis of the Church's proclamation and thus also of her catechesis. We use the Bible to follow the history of salvation in the way God Himself made it known. These sacred books take us from the creation of the world to its end and show us how Christ is the fulfillment of all.

The *systematic presentation* of the faith has its roots in the creeds and preaching of the early Christian proclamation, and has derived its organic development from the authoritative teaching of the Church throughout the ages. The catechism gives the learner spiritual insight into the relationship between the faith and Christian life and enables him to cope with the questions of the day as an articulate Christian, and to express his faith to those who enquire about it.

The Christian message and teaching is borne out through the *witness of a Christian life.* The life of the Church and her saints show us repeatedly that Christ lives and works in the Church. The witness of a Christian life by individuals and by the community of the faithful not only nourishes the faith of Catholics but is the way that ordinarily leads the non-Christian to Christ and to the Church.

11. *Catechesis adapts itself to the life and thought of peoples, shows due appreciation of their laudable views and customs, and integrates them harmoniously into a Christian way of life.*

The message of the living God should contact the living man, move his innermost heart, and convert him from within. Before the catechist begins his task God has already worked in the individuals and nations of His creation through His truth and grace, and moves them to seek and attain their salvation in Christ (Acts 17:26–27). In the love of the Good Shepherd the catechist seeks to recognize the special character, manner of thought, outlook, customs, and culture of his catechumens. Beginning at the point where they can follow him, he seeks to instruct them according to the psychology of age group, sex, and special circumstances. Guided by the Holy Spirit, he enters into their hidden problems and leads them to adopt Christ's way of thinking as the best solution. He seeks in patience to correct whatever is false and erroneous, but humbly endeavours to mould into the Christian way of life "whatever things are true, whatever honorable, whatever just, whatever holy, whatever lovable, whatever of good repute, if there be any virtue, if anything worthy of praise . . ." (Phil. 4:8).

12. *Catechesis introduces the catechumen into a living community and helps him to strike root in it.*

The life of faith is a life in the community of believers. The Apostles received their formation in the community which Christ gathered around Himself as the family of God (Matt. 12:19). Those who were converted at the sermon of St. Peter were taken into the community of the faithful, which was inspired by the Holy Spirit (Acts 2:41 ff.). They found a home in the communal life of the primitive Church. Likewise, believers today should welcome and embrace the newly baptized. Special groups may be needed, apart from the family and the parish, to sustain and stimulate the new Catholic in his faith. For only in a community can a Christian recognize the full meaning of the Lord's message and experience the bonds of charity which unite all men in Christ.

B. THE PRACTICE OF CATECHETICS

I. THE DISPOSITIONS OF A CATECHIST

The sense of prayer. The catechist speaks in the name of God, and it is God alone Who will give him the words of truth and open the hearts of his hearers.

Purity of intention. The actions of the catechist must radiate the love of Christ in his own life, so that his hearers will recognize the message of our Lord in his words.

Fidelity to the Church. The catechist has the right to preach or teach only because it has been given to him by the bishop in the name of the Church. He preaches not his own ideas, but the doctrine of the Church.

The desire to communicate a living faith to others. The goal of the catechist is to win not only the intelligence but, even more, the heart of his hearers and to lead them to live by Christ in His Church. A mere acquaintance with the faith which does not show itself in action is not a living faith.

II. THE PERIOD OF PRECATECHESIS

Precatechesis. For the instruction of those who are not yet believers it is necessary to have a period of precatechesis, more or less long, before the complete formulation of the doctrine is given to them. During this period the catechist should endeavor, with the help of grace, to awaken in the catechumen a desire for God, to stir up his unquenched spiritual longings, and to show how these longings find their fulfillment in the divine truth. He must help them to realize whatever is disorderly in their lives, as well as their attachment to earthly values. He should arouse in them a longing for forgiveness and a desire to give themselves to God. In this way he will prepare the soil for the sowing of the word of God. Unless these spiritual powers are awakened in them, the catechumens will remain incapable of understanding the meaning of the Christian message.

III. THE MAIN POINTS IN A LESSON

Awaken interest. This cannot be done in a superficial manner. In the beginning the catechist must reach the secret aspirations and problems of his hearers to awaken in them a spiritual interest. It is important that his opening words be not commonplace or depressing, but the answer to an interior need. This is especially important when the catechumen is still far from the faith.

Present a living reality. Take an event, a passage from the Bible, a liturgical action, an incident from Church history, the life of a saint, or daily life. Expose it in a simple, calm manner, direct enough to touch the heart.

When giving a biblical catechesis, the teacher may start by reading the text aloud, slowly and impressively, and then bring out its deep significance.

Bring out sense of what has been told, always in such a manner that it will reach the mind and heart. That is why the catechist must avoid making a purely intellectual exposition. The best effect comes from a simple and lively discussion in which the listeners have full freedom to participate. Such a dialogue enables each one to seek with the catechist and to express in his own words the truth discovered. The catechist directs and develops these findings until the truth is clear and alive. He tries to have all the points understood and then ends by a clear summary of the different steps.

Stimulate a personal response to the call of God. It does not suffice that the catechumens have understood the truth, but they must be led by the catechist to answer it. He must show them how to pray, either spontaneously, or by using a prepared formula, or by a short liturgical ceremony. He must invite them to review their lives, to see more clearly the duties which await them, and to make the resolutions they need.

Some memorization is demanded (especially for children) of certain biblical passages and texts essential to the lesson, not only that they be rooted in the memory but that they may penetrate the thinking and life of the person. The memory must always be at the service of the faith. That is why the catechist should never cause passages to be memorized which have not been explained in the lesson or clearly understood by the hearers. A mechanical memorization of formulas is not sufficient to grasp the vitality of Christian doctrine.

Avoid rigidity in the use of the above steps. The catechist should employ the above method with a certain suppleness and freedom according to the matter to be explained and the age or mentality of the catechumens.

IV. SOME CONCRETE POINTS ON
PEDAGOGICAL TECHNIQUES AND METHOD

Have recourse to pedagogical techniques in order to give variety to the lesson and to stimulate the interior awakening and the exterior activity of the hearers. The use of techniques offers the catechist the possibility of winning not only the intellect but the whole being of the person, namely, mind, heart, imagination, creative ability, and power of expression.

He must always remember that these diverse means have one goal, to help the catechumen to open wide his heart to the activity of the Holy Spirit.

Means to awaken interior activity. Create an atmosphere; present a reality, bring forward its meaning, show its bearing, define it; establish comparisons with other facts or truths, a motivation, proofs; draw conclusions, present a clear summary, a repetition; drive home a point, an application, bring the lesson into contact with daily life, lead to action, arouse consent.

Means to stimulate exterior activity. Narrate an event, make observations, ask questions, elucidate, show an object, cause reflection, give an explanation, start a discussion, read aloud, make others read (each one by himself, or one reading aloud, or several in turn), a recitation, learning by heart, interrogate, direct practical exercises, choral recitation, drawing either in the copybook or on the blackboard. Assign tasks and make the pupils look for facts, classify them, reflect on them, formulate them sometimes before and sometimes after the class. Assign homework, and make them keep a note book.

Also, hold a singing practice, recollect oneself, pray; exhort them to examine their conscience, meditate, hold a liturgical service. Celebrate a feast, stage a playlet with different actors, prepare an exhibition. Finally, use audio-visual aids, wall pictures, flannelboards, slides, tape-recordings, gramophone records.

V. Prayer, Action, Community-Consciousness

Religious formation is not only instruction but education; therefore it must be directed towards prayer, action, and community consciousness.

The catechist will cultivate a taste for *prayer* in his hearers if he encourages them to pray in their own words and to use formulas which they understand. To this end he will offer them a certain number of prayers which they can slowly make their own. Naturally, the common prayers of a Christian, the daily prayers, the psalms, and texts from the Missal, should be the foundation of this collection, which should reflect the faith and prayer of the Church. It should be, at the same time, an expression of personal piety.

There is no genuine religious formation without education to *action* and, above all, formation of conscience. The catechist must continually and persistently inculcate this in his hearers. He must likewise endeavor to lead them to personal maturity, to self-reliance, and to the sense of responsibility.

Moreover, because Christian life unfolds itself day-by-day in the Church, the catechist must avoid forming in his hearers an individualistic personality. To this end he must bring them into contact with the parish *community* and, above all, with its liturgical life. He must make them realize the duties they will have to perform for the community, and he will encourage them to take part in the groups or associations proper to youth or adults. In this way he will introduce them into a concrete and realistic charity, and he will give them a sense of apostolate among Christians and non-Christians.

Catechesis does not stop with the reception of the sacraments nor with the end of the years at school. Catechesis must constantly grow and deepen throughout the whole life of a person, as a child, an adolescent, and during the years of adulthood. The catechist must lead his catechumens or Christians to a more intimate union with God and to a more personal conviction of the Christian truths. This will bring them gradually to, become adults in the faith in order that through their lives and actions they may share in the fullness of Christ (Eph. 4:13).

It is by study, reflection, written notes, and prayer that the catechist should prepare his lessons. He must be constantly thinking in terms of those to whom he will speak. Before addressing his hearers, the catechist should recall three questions. What am I going to teach (content)? Where should I be leading my hearers (pedagogy of the living faith)? How shall I arrange my lesson?

A lesson of catechesis is a work of art which is acceptable only if it is well prepared. Without constant effort it is impossible to be a good catechist.

From the Bangkok Study Week*
October 31-November 3, 1962

I. The Main Characteristics of Modern Catechetics

1. *Basic idea*. Modern catechetics considers the catechetical apostolate as a mission imparted by the Church to participate in Christ's proclamation of the Good News of salvation. The whole of catechetics is to be inspired and regulated by this basic idea.

2. *Aim*. The aim of the catechetical apostolate is, not knowledge as such, but living faith—a faith which responds to God's call (message).

3. *Message*. The emphasis is on content more than on method. With regards to content, modern catechetics emphasizes concentration on the central theme of God's love accomplished in Jesus Christ (dead, risen, and living in His Church), presented as a Gospel (Good News), oriented to life.

4. *Method*. The main lines of method are to follow the dynamics of faith: to present the religious facts, to unfold their religious meaning, to stimulate a personal response to this call of God in Christian living.

As such, method is a handmaid, but an indispensable one. In all its phases it needs thorough adaptation to those who are catechized.

5. *Fourfold presentation of the Faith*. Genuine catechetics requires the sound equilibrium of a fourfold presentation of the Faith: through liturgy, Bible, systematic teaching, and the testimony of Christian living. Systematic teaching is not to be begun before the age of ten or twelve, and even then needs to be completed by, and thoroughly informed with, biblical and liturgical catechesis.

6. *Catechist*. Because the teacher of religion is Christ's spokesman and witness, the teacher is more important than the textbook. He must first assimilate the message personally. He must build up his religious life from the message in harmony with professional training.

7. *Textbooks*. Textbooks are in the service of the teacher and the pupils. Good texts, which take into account the development of present-day theology, are required. Outdated texts cannot be modernized by mere modifications and revisions.

* See *Lumen Vitae*, 17 (1962), 721, 723–725.

II. THE THREE STAGES[1] OF THE KERYGMATIC APPROACH FOR THE MISSIONS

	A. *Preevangelization*[2]	B. *Evangelization*[6]	C. *Catechesis Proper*
1. Addresses:	unbelievers	prepared unbelievers	catechumens
2. Aim:[3]	arouse interest, prepare the ground, the dialogue, bridge the gap for the kerygma . . . arousing his hope and awakening his sense of God	challenge, win, convert	form, instruct, initiate into Christian life, Christian personality . . . building up the Faith
3. Guiding principle:	anthropocentric[4]—take the man as he is and where he is	theocentrical-Christocentrical —what God revealed, the way God revealed	theocentrical-Christocentrical —what God revealed, the way God revealed . . . ecclesial emphasis
4. Virtue of catechist:	patience, love, understanding, respect	faithfulness to God and His message	faithfulness to God and His message
5. Content:	dialogue: anything is all right, e.g., positive apologetics,[5] motives of credibility	a dynamic heralding of the core of God's message	a detailed development of the message, always orientated to the core
6. Procedure:	personal contact, witness	challenge, shock[7]	personal, active, adaptive, use of godparents
7. Result:	a spiritual readiness to accept God's message	conversion	formed Christian

EXPLANATION OF NOTES

1. *The three stages.* Although these three stages are the normal chronological procedure, yet according to the persons and the circumstances, the evangelization may precede or go along with the preevangelization. Some authors even hold that a certain form of evangelization comes normally first, to shake the subject from the world, where he is enclosed and open him to the religious problem; but, even then, a minimum preparation should have preceded, if the evangelization itself is to be understood.

2. *Preevangelization.* In this stage we consider persons as individuals, and not the community. It is obvious, however, that we should take into account the influence of the environment on the individual. The apostle has not only to work on the individual but on the structure and on the mentality of the milieu which influences him.

3. *The aim of preevangelization.* A more complete explanation of the aim of preevangelization is as follows:

a. To shake off the apparent security of a life entirely "insured" by the familiar life-surroundings, by the possession of material riches or of techniques which transform the world. Men must experience a "break" within themselves if they are to be "reawakened" to the invisible and thus be ready to welcome the gift of God.

The preevangelization prepares such a "break" by making men consider the mystery of death, of life, of human thought and love, spiritual responsibility, and so on.

b. To show how the various ways in which man expresses and confronts himself with the realities of this world need to be integrated into a higher Unity (these "various ways" include practical judgments, technical activity, science, social and economical development, spiritual aspirations). ("A higher Unity" refers to the one brought by the redemptive love of God.) This unity cannot be reached through the various non-Christian practices, magic or ritual.

c. To purify the "sense of the Sacred." Preevangelization must lead to the sense of God, the personal Creator Who is both transcendent and immanent to man. If this is not secured, the whole catechesis runs the risk of being ambiguous, even if its exposition is exact and complete. Preevangelization, on this point, must influence the spontaneous and subconscious representations of the Godhead, as well as bring out clear ideas about it.

4. *Anthropocentrical.* The guiding principle of preevangeliza-

tion is anthropocentrical because we must start with the man as he is. The way must be prepared in order that a person be able to understand the message, not as a mere presentation of words which make sense to us, but as a challenge by words which make sense to him. This follows from the very essence of message, which demands that we speak to and not at a man (see Alfonso Nebreda, S.J., *Distinguishing the Different Stages in Missionary Preaching* [Rome, 1962], pp. 23–26).

5. *Positive apologetics.* Positive apologetics proceeds from a true understanding and appreciation of whatever is good and acceptable in a man's culture. It consists in taking due consideration of the man with whom we speak and in removing the personal concrete obstacles which prevent his ready acceptance of the kerygma.

6. *Evangelization.* Once the unbeliever has acquired a sense of God and appears spiritually ready to accept God's message, a short résumé of salvation history is to be presented in such a way that the compelling fact of Christ as the Lord comes out with striking clarity. In a technical world where man feels himself lost "in a lonely crowd," stressing such facts as God coming to us in Christ, Christ living among us as our friend and personally loving each of us, helps to awaken man to hope and helps to evoke conversion.

7. *Shock.* Shock is the internal spiritual change in a man whereby he accepts Christ as the Lord. The catechist, by close observation, can recognize this conversion by such signs as repentance, prayer, a new eagerness to meet Christ, a living according to the Christian pattern, etc.

From the Katigondo Study Week*
Katigondo, Uganda, August, 1964

The Christian Message and African Culture

In proclaiming the Christian faith in Africa we must seek out whatever is of value in African traditional belief and endeavor to give it a Christian fulfillment. Thus, starting from the traditional view of God we must make known how God intervenes personally in human history, speaks, calls, establishes an eternal Covenant in Jesus Christ, and seeks a free and personal response from man as He introduces him into a new community.

To bring about His encounter with man God chooses to use as signs things that pertain to man's life. In imitation of Our Lord's teaching by parable, catechesis must absorb the realities of African life and use them as signs, developing their potentialities by way of biblical symbolism.

In this connection, since catechesis has its great basic sign in the ecclesial community, it must recognize and make the most of the African community sense and direct it toward membership in the People of God. Similarly, to make known the Covenant that God establishes by his Word, ratifies by the Supper and the cross, and offers for participation in the Eucharistic sacrifice, catechesis can utilize the African appreciation of the spoken word as a source of communion and life, and the African familiarity with the blood pact and with the ritual meal as a sign of fraternal communion.

Many elements of African life seem to be providential signs that catechesis can place at the disposal of the great signs common to all the people of God—Bible, liturgy, and living Church.

* Taken from the official report in *Teaching All Nations,* 1 (1964).

338

The Formation of Adult Catechumens

In the formation of adult catechumens of non-Christian origin it would be well to recognize the following stages based on an analysis of initiation into the Catholic community:

Preparation. God draws the candidate through the community (God's chosen sign) and its representatives. This is the stage of contact, dialogue, and influence which destroys the candidate's contentment with his previous religious attitude.

The first call of the Good News. To the well-disposed candidate the Church presents the message of salvation. Once again the sign is the community, made manifest now in its warm and loving welcome. The content of the message is Christ, crucified and risen, head of the community and glorious Lord of all, Who one day will come again. Christ is presented in a brief outline of salvation history that also deals with the mystery of sin. The culmination of the announcement is commitment or conversion, which includes total adherence to Christ and a renunciation of false cults. This stage of evangelization is called in Africa the precatechumenate, and its conclusion can be usefully marked by a liturgical celebration by which the candidate formally becomes a catechumen.

The catechumenate proper. During this stage the person converted to Christ receives detailed initiation in the faith and life of the community. Wherever possible this should culminate in baptism during the Easter Vigil.

Final stage of initiation (mystagogy). In this stage the initiation of the neophyte is completed when he joins fully in the liturgy and life of the community. As far as possible, this should occur between Easter and Pentecost.

The Formation of Adult Christians

The formation of adult Christians is a task which has become necessary in Africa today if we are to have Christians who can remain true to their faith in a society which is rapidly changing. Such formation will have two purposes: to build up real communities of faith, living to the full their Sunday celebration; and to raise up and educate very thoroughly a Christian elite of mature faith, capable of discharging its responsibilities in society. Very special attention must be given to the training within the family in order to make parents aware of their responsibility for initiating their children into the Christian religion.

The formation of adult Christians will have to be adapted to new conditions and to a new mentality. Individuals are now becoming self-reliant and are not so easily influenced by the public opinion of social groups or even of the Christian community. Catechesis must therefore lay stress on a sense of responsibility and on the grasp of Christian values by each individual; it will stress also the need for dedication to Catholic action and other forms of the apostolate. In accordance with these purposes, full meaning and vigor must be restored to the institution of sponsorship (godparents).

Such pastoral concern for the faith of adults will find a way to integrate all that is good and constant in the African mentality with the circumstances of modern life. To this end all the ways of diffusing knowledge, the mass-media of press, radio, cinema, and television, must be utilized. Moreover the intellectual elite must be given particular care, not only during their university studies but also afterwards, when engaged in their professions. In this connection those who study abroad must not be neglected because their situation presents special difficulties to their faith.

From the Asian Catechetical Study Week
On Recent Developments in Catechetics*
Manila, April, 1967

I. Notion of Anthropology

It must be noted that anthropology as understood in the continental sense and as used in the catechetical movement is concerned with man whole and entire, with human experience and human values. It implies attentiveness to man, reflection on him and on his varied situations in life. Its practical meaning in catechesis or in the stages of first approaches to unbelievers or non-Christians consists first of all in evoking, describing, and analyzing major human situations; secondly, in interpreting their significance for man; and thirdly, in discovering their fuller significance and fulfillment in revelation when assumed by Jesus Christ.

This anthropology is a traditional and yet new concern in its interpretation. Of course we know that the plan of God has to develop in history in and through human events. We have to analyze these events in order to give relevance to Christian life, but we have also to recognize that this Christian experience involves many human realities that can exist and in fact do exist independently of Christian faith.

II. The Christian and Non-Christian Situation

1. We will take first the non-Christian situation: anthropology gives a common ground, a crossroad at which non-Christians and Christians can meet. The missionary dialogue involves a sharing in the human experience, a deepening of it, and a search for its significant meaning up to the point where no further human meaning and fulfillment are to be found. Now arises the question of faith,

---

* Taken from the official report in *Teaching All Nations,* 4 (1967), 377–379.

the possibility of giving a Christian meaning which can be fully accepted or refused by the non-Christian.

2. With our Christians we find often that they are unaware of human realities, inadequate in their concept of God. We have to look for the elements of human experience involved in the Christian life in order to renew faith and to deepen conversion.

III. CONDITIONS FOR THE ANTHROPOLOGICAL APPROACH

1. The necessity of concentration on the receiver of God's word so that the message may be expressed in terms suitable to the person.

2. Unconditioned acceptance of man where he is and as he is.

3. It is not a matter of examples or exterior comparisons but a mutual sharing and discovery of fundamental human aspirations.

4. A need to develop sensitivity to the whole human background: family, neighborhood, education, economic status, society, traditional culture and mass culture, religious heritage and values, and so on. This concern is not a compromise with human weakness or a manipulation of man but a development of our understanding of the way in which the word of God grows among men.

IV. CONCLUSIONS OF THE DISCUSSION REGARDING THE ANTHROPOLOGICAL APPROACH

1. *Ideas concerning catechetical anthropology cannot yet be considered as definitive.*

The very nature of the discussions showed that there is a general searching for meaning and understanding. Considerable time was spent on the notion, and it was found necessary to illustrate the approach by concrete examples. One such example was the search of man for freedom within the family environment as a reflection of one of the fundamental aspirations of man. Certain members of the group found difficulty in finding how this approach could apply to certain categories.

2. *Anthropology belongs to all levels of catechesis as an attitude or approach, rather than a technique or a mere pedagogical device.*

It was agreed that distinctions must be made in the manner of application for different groups. Obviously, it is with the adult, be he Christian or non-Christian, that this approach comes into its own. There are some aspects of life, especially crisis situations, in which it is easier to discover the meaning of one's experiences. However, reflection on all aspects of life, positive or negative, can serve as a starting point for the journey toward God. This is true for the adolescent with his problems, for man in face of the challenges of today, for the non-Christian searching for a more satisfying meaning of life, and for the catechumen preparing for baptism. Obviously with non-Christians this approach will spread over a greater span of time.

3. *This approach demands great concentration on the preparation of catechists and especially of those who will train them.*

Discussion was held on the transformation of attitude required by persons in the missionary apostolate. Techniques will develop once the correct attitude is formed. The general view was expressed that missionaries in general are far too remote from the people they serve. They are over busy with sacramental administration and social work, but their people are not known as persons and this lack is felt by the people themselves. The training of seminarians and Sisters was criticized, but details of renewal in this area were left to other groups.

4. *Development of openness to others will be the deep and personal responsibility of all concerned in the missionary apostolate of the Church.*

This is merely a reflection of the spirit of Vatican II.

5. *The anthropological approach is not a mere reformulation of a technique long used—certainly it has its roots in the past and in the Gospels—but as emphasized today it is the approach par excellence demanded by the civilization of modern times.*

In the past it has been the tendency to present the Christian message under the same biblical, dogmatic form to all peoples. Now we realize that this has to be interpreted in and through the culture of an area as well as through the personalities of those giving and receiving the message. Two elements are present: on the one hand, the anthropological signs which investigate the fundamental human aspirations and situations; on the other hand, there is the wide range of descriptive surveys showing us the varied ways in which through song and saga, novel and folk experience, man expresses his fundamental aspirations in different societies. These factors, together with the live experience of the missionaries, form the material of an approach.

Bibliography

Aymes, Sr. Maria de la Cruz, S.H. *On Our Way Series.* New York: Sadlier, 1957.

Aymes, Sr. Maria de la Cruz, S.H.; Bordes, Sr. M. Laetitia, S.H.; Buckley, Francis J., S.J.; and Miller, Cyr. *New On Our Way Series.* New York: Sadlier, 1966.

Babin, P. *Crisis of the Faith.* New York: Herder and Herder, 1963.

Babin, P. *Faith and the Adolescent.* New York: Herder and Herder, 1965.

Babin, P. *Options—Approaches for the Religious Education of Adolescents.* New York: Herder and Herder, 1967.

Babin, P. *Teaching Religion to Adolescents.* New York: Sadlier, 1967.

Becker, Antoinette. *Children Ask About God and Everything.* New York: Herder and Herder, 1966.

Buckley, Francis J., S.J. "How Can I Teach My Child? The Role of Parents in Religious Education." *Good Tidings,* 6 (1968).

Buckley, Francis J., S.J. "Parents, Children, and First Communion," *American Ecclesiastical Review,* 156 (1967), 393–403.

Buckley, Francis J., S.J. "The Christian Criterion." *Teaching All Nations,* 5 (1968).

Buckley, Francis J., S.J. "What Age for Confirmation?" *Theological Studies,* 27 (1966), 655–666.

Buckley, Francis J., S.J. "What Age for First Confession?" *Irish Ecclesiastical Record,* 107 (1967), 221–252.

Carter, Bishop Emmet. *The Modern Challenge to Religious Education.* New York: Sadlier, 1961.

Collins, J. *CCD Methods in Modern Catechetics.* Milwaukee: Bruce, 1966.

Cooke, Bernard J., S.J. *Formation of Faith.* Chicago: Loyola University.

Coudreau, Francois, SS. *The Child and the Problem of Faith.* Glen Rock, N.J.: Paulist Press, Deus Books, 1966.

Doctrinal Pamphlet Series. Glen Rock, N.J., Paulist Press.

Drinkwater, F. M. *Telling the Good News.* London: Macmillan, 1960.

Fargues, M. *Our Children and the Lord.* Notre Dame, Ind.: Fides, 1965.

Flanagan, Neil. *Salvation History.* New York: Sheed & Ward, 1964.

Godin, A., S.J., ed. *Child and Adult Before God.* Brussels: Lumen Vitae Press, 1961.

Godin, A., S.J., ed. *From Religious Experience to a Religious Attitude.* Brussels: Lumen Vitae Press, 1964.

Godin, A., S.J., ed. *Research In Religious Psychology.* Brussels: Lumen Vitae, 1959.

Goldbrunner, Josef. *Realization: The Anthropology of Pastoral Care.* Notre Dame, Ind.: University of Notre Dame Press, 1966.

Goldbrunner, Josef, ed. *New Catechetical Methods.* Notre Dame, Ind.: University of Notre Dame Press, 1965.

Grasso, D., S.J. *Proclaiming God's Message: A Study in the Theology of Preaching.* Notre Dame, Ind.: University of Notre Dame Press, 1965.

Hofinger, Johannes and Reedy, Wm. J. *The ABC's of Modern Catechetics.* New York, Sadlier, 1962.

Hofinger, Johannes, S.J. *The Art of Teaching Christian Doctrine.* Notre Dame, Ind.: University of Notre Dame Press, 1962.

Hofinger, Johannes, S.J., and Stone, Theodore C. *Pastoral Catechetics.* New York: Herder and Herder, 1964.

Hofinger, Johannes, S.J., ed. *Teaching All Nations. A Symposium on Modern Catechetics.* New York: Herder and Herder, 1961.

Jungmann, Josef, S.J. *Handing on the Faith.* New York: Herder and Herder, 1958.

Jungmann, Josef, S.J. *The Good News Yesterday and Today.* New York: Sadlier, 1962.

Lance, Derek. *Teaching the History of Salvation.* Glen Rock, N.J.: Paulist Press, 1964.

Lefebvre, Xavier, S.J., and Perin, Louis, S.J. *Bringing Your Child to God.* New York: Kenedy, 1963.

Lefebvre, Xavier, S.J., and Perin, Louis, S.J. *Going to God. Preparation for Confession, Confirmation and Holy Communion.* London: Chapman, 1964.

Let's Be Catechists. An outline of courses for training catechism teachers. Paris: National Center for Religious Education, 1962.

Lewis, Eve. *Children and Their Religion.* New York: Sheed & Ward, 1962.

Link, Mark J., S.J., ed. *Faith and Commitment.* Loyola Pastoral Studies. Chicago: Loyola University Press, 1964.

Link, Mark J., S.J., ed. *Teaching the Sacraments and Morality.* Chicago: Loyola University Press, 1965.

Margaret, Sr., D.H. Sp. *Heralding Christ. The Spirit of Modern Catechesis.* London: Chapman, 1966.

Moran, Gabriel, FSC. *Catechesis of Revelation.* New York: Herder and Herder, 1966.

Moran, Gabriel, FSC. *Theology of Revelation.* New York: Herder and Herder, 1966.

Mission Catechetics Series. Manila, P.I.: East Asia Pastoral Institute.

Mussner, Franz. *The Use of Parables In Catechetics.* Notre Dame, Ind.: University of Notre Dame Press, 1965.

McBride, Alfred O. *Catechetics—A Theology of Proclamation.* Milwaukee: Bruce, 1966.

Nebreda, Alfonso M., S.J. *Kerygma In Crisis?* Chicago: Loyola University Press, 1965.

Newland, Mary Reed. *We and Our Children.* New York: Kenedy, 1959.

Nutting, W. *The Catechetical Crisis.* Notre Dame, Ind.: Ave Maria Press, 1966.

O'Shaughnessy, Sister Mary Michael, OP; Kilgallon, James; and Weber, Gerard P. *The Child and the Christian Mystery.* New York: Benziger, 1965.

Parents as Teachers Series (nine pamphlets). Notre Dame, Ind.: Ave Maria Press, 1965.

Romain, Sister, HHS. *Tell My People.* Notre Dame, Ind.: Fides, 1965.

Sheed, F. J. *Are We Really Teaching Religion?* New York: Sheed & Ward, 1953.

Sloyan, Gerard S., ed. *Modern Catechetics.* New York: Macmillan, 1962.

Sloyan, Gerard S., ed. *Shaping the Christian Message.* New York: Macmillan, 1958.

Trese, Rev. Leo J. *The Faith Explained.* Notre Dame, Ind.: Fides, 1965.

Van Caster, Marcel, S.J., and others. *Ecumenism and Religious Education.* Chicago: Loyola University Press, 1965.

Van Caster, Marcel, S.J. *God's Word Today.* New York: Benziger, 1966.

Van Caster, Marcel, S.J. *The Structure of Catechetics.* New York: Herder and Herder, 1965.

Van Caster, Marcel, S.J. *Themes of Catechesis.* New York: Herder and Herder, 1965.

Index

Abbott, Walter M., S.J., 12, 309
Abraham, 121, 122
Acts and apostolic method of catechesis, 83
adoption,
  as God's children by baptism, 177
  as greatest of God's gifts, 115–116
adult religious education, 22
Aeterni Patris, 299
Alfaro, J., S.J., 303
Alszeghy, J., S.J., 303
anointing of the sick, the sacrament of, 193–198
  connection with the sacrament of penance, 196
  prepares us for definitive union with Christ, 196–198
  purposes of, 193–194
Apostles,
  communication of Christ's power to the, 166–167
  as heralds of Christ, 15
apostolic method of preaching, 83
Augustine, St., and biblical-historical method of catechesis, 44

Baltimore Catechism, the, 299
Bangkok, Study Week on Mission Catechesis, 30–31, 334–337
baptism, sacrament of, 175–181
  connection with sacrament of penance, 191
  demands new way of life, 20
  effects of, 175–178
  explanation of rites of, 175–177
  gives us new divine life, 177
  life received in, 19
  obligations contracted at, 178–181
  unites us with Christ, 176–177
baptismal character, explanation of, 176

Bible, the holy,
  importance in training of lay catechists, 260
  in kerygmatically oriented theology, 312
  means of introduction into mystery of Christ, 27–28, 43–52
  as religious rather than scientific, 117
  source of kerygmatic spirituality, 277–278
Bible, Life and Worship Series, 45
Bible narratives, 74
Bible study,
  need for improvement in, 52
  in training of Sisters and Brothers, 286
  on various educational levels, 50–51
biblical-historical catechesis, 43–52
  and doctrine, 48
  and life in Christ, 49–51
  means of introduction into the mystery of Christ, 43–52
  method suited to nature of Christian revelation, 44
  method used by Apostles, 43–44
  psychological advantages of, 45
  and true religious feeling, 48–49
bishops, successors of the Apostles, 167
Book of Exodus, 121
Bringing the Sacraments to the People, 55
Brothers, catechetical apostolate of, 272–273
Brunner, Rev. Paul, S.J., 189
Buckley, Francis, S.J., 160, 181, 195

Canadian catechism, 18
canonical mission to teach, 9, 12
catechesis of the faithful, 34–42
  analogous to missionary catechesis, 34–42
  catechesis, 41–42

347

evangelization, 39–41
preevangelization, 36–39
catechetical formulas, the basic, 68
catechetical methods, 85–97
    applications, 95–96
    educational psychology applied to,
        90–91
    explanation, 94–95
    function of, 87–88
    learning-teaching process, 89–91
    need for new, 3–5
    presentation, 93
    right view of, 13
    teaching technique, 96–97
catechetical renewal,
    first period of, 3–6, 9
    as reaction against overintellectual-
        ism, 23
    second period of, 6–10
    third period of ("anthropological ap-
        proach") 10–11
    and true function of religious educa-
        tion, 23
Catechism for First Communicants, 46
catechists,
    heralds with Christ, 11, 12, 13, 26
    as living instruments of Christ, 10,
        12, 14
catechumenate, 32
    social dimension of, 34
Central Object of Theology, The, 302
charity, fraternal, 219–223
children of God, duties of, 208–211
Christ,
    the ascension of, 156–157
    baptism of, 133–136
    the birth of, 130–133
    the great gift of the Father, 19
    the great Peacemaker, 223
    herald of the Father, 9
    and His disciples, 144–145
    His life of filial love, 180
    miracles of, 139–141
    mission of, 135, 138
    Mystical Body of, 168
    passion and death of, 150–153
    public life of, 133–157
    purpose of His teaching, 10
    resurrection of, 153–156

the Second Adam, 131–132
second coming of, 71
teaching the doctrine of, 127–130
temptations of, 136–138
titles of, 145–150
vocation of, 267
words of, 141–143
Christ All in All, 302
Christ in His Mysteries, 300
Christ the Life of the Soul, 300
Christian doctrine,
    basic course in, for Sister catechists
        and Brothers, 284–286
    as a source of kerygmatic spirituality
        for Sisters, 279–280
Christian life, the, 199–229
    made up of prayer and action, 202–
        205
Christian living,
    means of introduction into the mys-
        tery of Christ, 69
    our response to God's love, 199–205
    testimony of, 71–72
Christian prayer,
    chief formulas of, 207–208
    essential properties of, 207
    excellence of, 205–208
    expression of faith, 26
    nature of, 206
    our filial response to God's love, 112,
        114–115, 205–211
    our privilege, 205–208
    principal affections of, 207
    source of, 206–207
Christian work, our filial response to
    God's love, 112, 211–212
Christocentricity of Christian teaching,
    17, 55, 79
*Christus als Mittelpunkt religioser
    Erziehung*, 20
Church, the,
    in action, 165–168
    in being, 168–172
    doctrine of, in relation to Christ, 19–
        20
    as family of God's children, 168–172
    teaching the doctrine of, 164–172
    our union in, 168–172
    variety and diversity within, 170–172

Church history, course in, 287
Come to the Father, 18
commandments,
the first three, 208–211
place of, in arrangement of catechism, 57, 59
communication, proper use of, 226
communion, holy,
preparation for, 181, 182, 188–189
as return-gift of the Father, 188
thanksgiving after, 189
see also Eucharist, the, *and* sacrifice
of the Mass, the
confession,
necessity for instructions in, 190
necessity for true contrition, 192
our last, 196
trust in Christ in, 193
see also penance
confirmation
effects of, 159–160
instructions in, 159
Confraternity of Christian Doctrine,
253–254, 260, 261, 262
conversion, 31, 35
Coudreau, F., P.S.S., 30
Covenant, the, 120–123
Covenant of Sinai, 121
creation,
explanation of, 109–114
reason for, 111
creatures,
intrinsic dignity of, 112
use of, 112
Credo, 300
Creed, the Apostles',
as ideal formula of Christian prayer,
208
place of, in arrangement of the catechism, 75, 81, 82

Dander, F., S.J., 302
*Das Problem des Textbuchs in Semina-
rien der Missionländer,* 302
death, 231–233
Deharbe, Josef, S.J., and his catechisms,
299
Delcuve, G., S.J., 315
deliverance from Egypt, 121

development of human life, role of
state in, 220
*Die Frohbotschaft und unsere Glau-
bensverkündigung,* 6, 301
Die Verkündigungstheologie, 306
doctrine, systematic catechesis in, as
introduction into mystery of
Christ, 27–28, 64–72
The Documents of Vatican II, 12, 309
Dutch Catechism, the New, 65
dying,
after baptism most important action
of life, 195
sacramental preparations for, 196–
198

Eichstätt, Germany, International
Study Week, 10, 27, 53, 97,
319–333
general conclusions of, 319–322
Programme of the Catechetical Apostolate, 324–333
special conclusions of, 322–324
eighth commandment, the, 225–229
elementary grades, teaching religion in,
43–50
Eucharist, the Holy,
as the food of our divine life, 181
institution of, 182–184
teaching the doctrine of, 181–182
see also communion, holy, *and* sacrifice of the Mass
evolution, 113–114
extreme unction. *See* anointing of the
sick

faith, basis of Christian living, 25–26
Fall, the, 117–120
family, Christianization of the, 212–214
fidelity, as kerygmatic virtue, 249–250
fifth commandment, the, 219–223
filial gratitude, characteristic of God's
children, 114–115
Flick, G., S.J., 303
*Foi au Christ et mission d'après les
Actes des Apôtres,* 8
fourth commandment, the, 212–214
Franzelin, Card. Johannes, S.J., 299
Friedrich, G., 8
Friendship, 37

general judgment, the, 235–236
German Catechism, the New, 64–65
Glories of Divine Grace, 300
God,
    the greatness of, 109–110
    the importance of a magnificent idea
        of, 109
    nearness of, 109
    our dependence on, 110
    reality of, 109
Goldbrunner, J., 88, 97
*Good News Yesterday and Today, With
    Essays in Appraisal of Its Contri-
    bution,* 6, 301
good repute, Christian attitude to,
    225–229
grace, relation to mystery of Christ, 19–
    20
Grasso, Domenico, S.J., 8, 17, 30, 296
Gruber, Archbishop Augustin, 45
Guzetti, G. B., 302

Handing on the Faith, 61, 259
heaven,
    description of, 242
    the new paradise, 241–244
    the only way to, 244
    teaching the doctrine of, 241–244
Heinrichs, Maurus, O.F.M., 302, 312,
    313
hell,
    teaching of Christ on, 238–239
    teaching the doctrine of, 237–240
    who will go to, 239–240
Henle, R. J., S.J., 281
Henry, A., O.P., 303
heralds of Christ, sublime vocation of,
    247–248
historical catechesis, 43–52
Hofinger, Johannes, S.J., 11, 53, 65, 80,
    81, 276, 296, 302
Holy Family, as exemplar for Christian
    family, 212
Holy Spirit,
    the coming of, 159–160
    as gift of God, 158
    teaching the doctrine of, 157–160
Howell, Clifford, S.J., 64

Huesmann, W. A., S.J., 6, 301

incarnation, the, instruction on, 130–
    133

The Jerusalem Bible, 52
Jesus-Maria Course of Religion, 17
Jungmann, Joseph Andreas, S.J., 6, 7,
    8, 20, 58, 61, 65, 80, 81, 82, 83, 259,
    301, 302

Kappler, E., 306
Katechetischen Blätter, 20
Katholisches Religionsbüchlein, 45
Katigondo, Uganda, Study Week, 33,
    338–340
kerygma, 8, 31, 43, 78, 104, 296, 297, 303
Kerygma in Crisis?, 38
"Kerygma-Kerygmatisch," 8
kerygmatic and scholastic approaches,
    combining of, 309–313
    differences between, 307–309
kerygmatic orientation, need in semi-
    naries for, 21
kerygmatic renewal,
    scope of, 9
    survey of, 299–303
kerygmatic spirituality,
    characteristics of, 247–252
    sources of, 277–280
kerygmatic theology, 250, 297–315
    catechetical value of, 313–315
    erroneous ideas about, 306-309
    missionary value of, 313–315
    nature of, 303–306
    not antischolastic, 308
    not "lay" theology, 307
    value of, in spiritual life of priest,
        313
    value of, in training of priests, 309–
        313
kerygmatic virtues, 249–252
kerysso, 8
keryx, 8, 10, 78
Kleuten, Joseph, S.J., 299
Kunicic, J., O.P., 306

Lakner, F., S.J., 302

last things, the, teaching the doctrine of, 230–231

lay catechists,
apostolate of, 253–263
collaboration of priests and religious with, 262
guidance of, 261
retreats for, 259
selection of, 258
special difficulties and needs of, 256–257
special value of apostolate of, 254–256
training of, 258–263

Leo XIII, Pope, 299

Liberatore, Matteo, 299

Liégé, P., O.P., 30, 303

life in Christ, our vocation, 25

Lippert, P., 300

liturgical prayer, instruction and practice in, 57–61

liturgical renewal, post-Vatican II, 62–63, 103

liturgical year, the, 76
and biblical catechesis, 57–59

liturgy,
catechetical value of, 53–54
course for Sisters and Brothers in, 287–288
how to "unlock" its riches, 57-63
importance of proper conduct of, 57, 60
instruction in participation in, 53–62
means of introduction into mystery of Christ, 27–28, 53–63
source of kerygmatic spirituality, 278–279
and survey course of doctrine in middle grades, 61
and "systematization," 76
in training of lay catechists, 260–261
use of vernacular in, 54

Living Light, 13

Lotz, J.B., S.J., 302

love for love, *leitmotif* of our message, 106

Lumen Gentium. See Dogmatic Constitution on the Church

Lumen Vitae, 30

McLuhan, Marshall, 13

man,
creation of, 112–114
elevation of, 114–117

Manila, Asian Catchetical Study Week, 11, 33, 341–343

Maria de la Cruz, Sister, H.H.S., 18, 62, 116, 261

Marmion, Abbot Columba, O.S.B., 300

marriage, 214–219
loss of holiness of, 217
original holiness of, 215–217
restoration and elevation by Christ, 217–218

marriage feast, parable of, 107

Mary, Mother of the Redeemer,
place and importance of, in catechetical instruction, 19
presentation of doctrine on, 128–129

material goods, Christian attitude toward, 224–225

material to be used in instruction,
how much, 91
what, 91

matrimony, sacrament of, 214–219

means of grace, place of, in arrangement of catechism, 75

Mersch, Emil, S.J., 315

Mey, Rev. Gustav, 45

miracles and sacraments, 140–141

missionary catechesis, 29–34

Moses, 121, 125

mystagogical catechesis, 33, 42

Mysteries of Christianity, 300

mystery of Christ, 78, 84
center of true biblical-historical catechesis, 46–50
central theme of our message, 15–22
influence on catechetical method, 67
means of introduction into, 27–28, 43–52
participation in, goal of catechetical apostolate, 23–28
progressive initiation into, 53–72
as unfolded by historical narrative method, 127–130

Nebreda, Alfonso, S.J., 28, 30, 38
Neoscholasticism. *See* scholastic theology, renewal of
Neuner, J., S.J., 303
New Testament Reading Guide, 52
ninth commandment, 214–219
Noah, 121, 122, 124
non-Christians, catechetical instruction of, 29
Notre Message, 104
Nuntius Noster, 103

Old Testament history, presentation of, 117, 119–120
Old Testment Reading Guide, 52
Old Testament "types," instruction in, 123–126
On Our Way Series, 18, 62, 65, 116, 174, 261
order or presentation of doctrines, necessity for variety in, 91–94
Our Community Mass, 189
Our Father, classic form of Christian prayer, 207–208
Our Life With God Series, 62
outline of catechetical material, qualities of, 85–97

paradise, 115–116
parents, duty as educators, 214
Parish Mass Book, 189
particular judgment, the, 231–233
St. Paul, 19, 24, 44, 46, 56, 88
and the central object of revelation, 78
herald of Christ, 8
vocation to announce the mystery of Christ, 15–16
penance, sacrament of,
Christ's Easter gift, 191
as "Good News," 190
institution of, 190–193
teaching the doctrine of, 190–193
People of God, the, 169–170
Pichler, Msgr. Wilhelm, 45
pictures, use of, in religious instruction, 49–50
"positive apologetics," 31
prayer. *See* Christian prayer

prebaptismal catechesis,
catechesis proper, 33–34
evangelization, 31
preevangelization, 30–31, 104
stages of, 30–34
precatechumenate, 32
priestly religious instruction,
forms of, 291–293
special qualities of, 293–296
priests,
catechetical apostolate of, 12, 290–296
formation of, 297
principles to be followed in ordering catechetical material, 73–84
Proclaiming God's Message, 8, 296
providence, divine, teaching the doctrine of, 236
public school children,
importance of dialogue Mass for, 261
special difficulties of teaching religion to, 255–257
purgatory, function of, 197
Putz, J., S.J., 303

Qu'est-ce que le kerygme?, 8

Rademacher, A., 300
Rahner, Hugo, S.J., 302
Rahner, Karl, S.J., 284, 303
redemption, the, 127–128, 150–152
Rehm, Rev. Anton, S.J., 45
Religion und Leben, 300
religious,
catechetical apostolate of, 264–273
importance of apostolate of, 264–266
religious education, course in, 287
religious instruction, need for variety in, 96
religious living, goal of religious instruction, 23
resurrection, the,
as our resurrection, 155–156
historical fact of, 154
resurrection, the general, 235–236
Retif, A., 8
revelation, central object of, 78
right ordering of catechetical material, 73–84

aid to students and teachers, 75–76
and character of Christianity as revelation, 78
and Christocentric character of Christian message, 79
essential, not apologetical, 77–78
importance of, stressed in modern catechetics, 73
reasons for need of, 74-75
significance of, for all forms of catechetical apostolate, 83–84
theological rather than didactic, 78
Roman Catechism, the, 80–83
arrangement of, 80–81
perfecting the arrangement of, 81–83

sacraments, the,
as participation in the mystery of Christ, 27
place of, in arrangement of catechism, 75, 80, 81, 82
teaching the doctrine of, 172–174
sacrifice of the Mass,
active participation in, 181–184, 186–189
as community thanksgiving, 184, 189
as a dialogue, 186
explanation of, 185–189
as participation in mystery of Christ, 27, 54–57
St. Thomas, and order of presentation, 81
St. Thomas et Theologie "Kerygmatica," 306
sanctity of Christian body, the 214–219
Sanseverino, J. S. Gaetano, 299
Scheeben, Matthias Joseph, 300
Schmaus, M., 302
Scholarship and Preaching, 302
scholastic approach to theology, 307–309
scholastic theology, revival of, 299
Schorsch, Alexander, O.S.B., 17
Schreibmayr, Franz, 20
Scripture, holy. *See* Bible, holy
Seffer, J., S.J., 104
seventh commandment, the, 223–225
sickness, Christian attitude toward, 195–196

sin,
actual, 120
disaster of, 118–119
mortal, 191
original, 117–120
punishment of unrepented, 237–240
Sister-catechetists,
ascetical training of, 274–275
development of kerygmatic spirituality of, 275–277
special apostolate of, 266–267
special qualities of teaching of, 268–270
training of, 274–280
vocation of, 267–268
sixth commandment, the, 214–219
Sloyan, Rev. Gerard, 37
Stendahl, Kr, 8
Stone, Rev. Theodore, 30
The Story of the Kingdom, 45
suffering, Christian attitude toward, 193–196
Summa Theologica, 284, 286
systematic catechesis, 65–72
and Christian life, 67
in higher grades, 68
how it can achieve its aim, 68–70
importance of, 64–65
particular task of, 65–68
when to begin, 65

Tanquerey, A., 300
teachers of religion, as heralds of Christ, 9
Teaching All Nations, 13, 17, 53, 96, 262, 296
tenth commandment, the, 223–225
theocentricity of Christian teaching, 17, 55
theological training for Sisters and Brothers, 281–289
aim of, 282–284
theological training in seminaries,
importance of renewal of, 297, 314–315
need for kerygmatic orientation in, 21
Theologisches Wörterbuch zum Neuen Testament, 8

theology, purposes of, 303–304

Theology of Preaching, A, 302

tradition, in kerygmatically oriented theology, 312

training of future catechists, importance of, 72

Trinity, the Most Holy, 160–164
  baptismal consecration to, 177–178
  as "our" mystery, 161, 163–164
  religious exposition of mystery, 162–164
  revelation of mystery, 161–162

truth, love of, 225–229

"types" of Christ,
  king, 125
  man as Son of God, 124
  priest, 124–125
  prophet, 125–126

Understanding Media: The Extensions of Man, 13

unselfishness, as kerygmatic virtue, 251

Vatican II, 11, 12, 32, 296
  Constitution on the Sacred Liturgy, 53, 63, 288
  Declaration on Christian Education, 12, 214
  Decree on Priestly Formation, 21–22, 52, 296, 297, 298, 308–309
  Decree on the Apostolate of the Laity, 12

Decree on the Appropriate Renewal of the Religious Life, 266, 277

Decree on the Bishops' Pastoral Office in the Church, 12

Decree on the Church's Missionary Activity, 12, 30, 32, 33, 34, 105, 256

Dogmatic Constitution on Divine Revelation, 142

Dogmatic Constitution on the Church, 12, 145, 165, 264

Pastoral Constitution on the Church in the Modern World, 12, 117, 214, 223, 243

Viaticum, Holy, 197

Vollständige Katechesen, 45

Way of the Cross, explanation of, 150

Weisweiler, H., S.J., 302

winningness, as kerygmatic virtue, 252

Word and Worship, 18

work. *See* Christian work

worship, as fundamental duty of God's children, 208–211

worship, direct. *See* Christian prayer

worship, indirect. *See* Christian work

worship, perfect, 229

worship of Church, in relation to mystery of Christ, 20

Zigliara, Card. Tomaso, 299